7   REQUEST *(Element #4)* (continued)
Another Level in the Word — Promises versus Conventional   170
Promise Keeper   171
To God be the Glory   171
A Spiritual Shift in Prayer   173
Saving Knowledge of God   174
Overflow Blessings and God's Glory   175
Notice: 178
In the Name of Jesus — In the Spirit of Jesus   178
Faith to Believe   180
Having Need for the Lord   182
Keep His Commandments and Improve the Possibilities   184
Living in Sin Negates Prayers   185
Motives and Pretenses Effect Belief and Affect Prayer   187
Conviction Through Thoughts of Being Chastened   189
What's Good and What's Convenient   193

8   DISCERNMENT *(Element #5)* **199**
What to do with It   204
Seek the Instructions   205
Submission is the Way   208
Limited Sight   209
Waiting   210
Prepared but Spiritually Disconnected   211
Preparation through Growth   212
Action Packed Prayers and Living   214
Faith to Discern   215
Eliminate Foolishness   216
A Biblical Illustration of Discernment   219

9   SIGN *(Element #6)* **223**
Remove Flesh and be Clothed in Spirit   227
Directions, not Doubt   228
Word, Signs and Mysteries are not Always so Literal   230
What is our Motivation: Reverence or Proof?   231
A Sensitized spirit   232
Directed and Guided   234
Commitment is a Must   236
Listening to the Wrong Things   236
Our Way of Living Affects our Hearing   237
Dialogue   239
One of the Greatest Signs Given   240
Truthful Claims of Scriptures vs Cliche Artist   240
Staying the Course   242
To What Are You Listening?   243
God's Directions   245
Make or Break   250
A Biblical Illustration of Sign   254

10   PRE-PRAISE THANKSGIVING (Element #7) **259**
Honour and Glory are God's 262
Higher Level of Faith 264
Sold-out 264
Spectacular, Providence, Mercy or Miracle 266
Seeing Pass the Pain 267
Praise Him Through What He has Done 268
Praise Him for Who He is 269
Praise Him for His Promises Made 270
Unleash the Power 271
The Larger the Issue the Larger the Thanks 273
A Change is Going to Come 274
Growth and Change or Name It and Claim It? 275
Emphasis 278
Where Did All the Thanks Go? 278
Misdirected Thanks 279
The Holy Spirit's Activation 281
Our Humility, His Credit 281
A Story of Pre-Praise 283

11   MEDITATION (Element #8) **287**
Spirited Energy 291
Denied Access 292
Meditation is the Fullness of Monologue 294
Overflow and Meditation 295
Don't Block Your Blessing! 297
Becoming More of a Listener 297
In Agreement Through Submission and Dialogue 298
Solitude vs Noise 299
Hearing from God is the Essence of Prayer 302
Defiance Negates Trust 304
Better Listeners 304
You Talk Too Much 304
The Need to Receive 305
He Already Knows, so We Might as Well Listen 306
Training to Listen 307
Relationships and Listening 307
Having a Thirst 309
Not Just Hear, But Answer 311
Our Hearts Desires 313
Be Careful for What You Pray 315
Sounding Board? 317
Do Not be Afraid of Success 318
Convinced in Advance 319
Importance: Cry or Listen 320
A Change 321
Not a Substitute for Prayer 321

POWERFUL Prayer PROGRESSION for Prayer Warriors™

The 8 Elements of Prayer Progression™

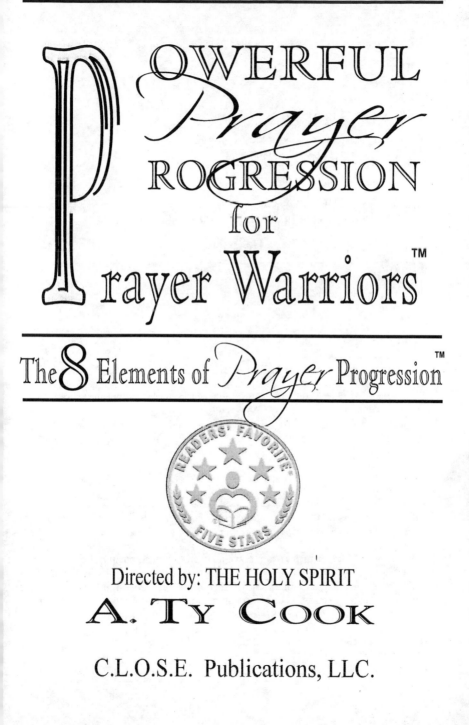

Directed by: THE HOLY SPIRIT

A. TY COOK

C.L.O.S.E. Publications, LLC.

Published by C.L.O.S.E. Publications, LLC.

Powerful Prayer Progression for Prayer Warriors
The 8 Elements of Prayer Progression
Copyright 2011 by C.L.O.S.E. Publications, LLC.
ISBN-13: 978-0-9849357-0-3

Request for information should be addressed to:
C.L.O.S.E. Publications, LLC., P.O. Box 22484, Baltimore, MD 21203

Cook, Reverend A. Ty —
   Powerful Prayer Progression for Prayer Warriors / Reverend A. Ty Cook
   (The 8 Elements of Prayer Progression)

Interior production by C.L.O.S.E. Publications, LLC.
Printed in the United States of America

To God our Father, the gracious Lord Jesus Christ and the blessed Holy Spirit. The day has come and is that You have chosen this Your servant to write such a document to empower and prepare Your children. Bless Your holy name for giving me a spirit of obedience and faithfulness unto Your voice and directions. You alone are glorious and great.
And so it has begun and is.

To Mom, Joy
who has gone on to see the King.
Bless you and thank you for teaching me how
to knot a basic and classic tie. You taught me cores of life.

To a group of devoted friends and study partners
who have taught me precepts of dedication:
Dwight, Tiffany, Ralph, Curtisha

To a pair of friends and college mates of old:
Willie and Shelly
Thank you for the push and the motivational support
through these many years of writing.

To all who have been a backbone of support and blessedness.
Your spirited support and loving kindness has been a blessing.
Erica, Delores and Ed, Brenda, Cory, Maudnell,
Word4TheDay, and the countless others
who have stood secure in my corner.

To you who sings my song:
I've learned to stand the rain — a song to sing for a lifetime
through a water covered rose in a glass!

CONTENTS

1   HIS WILL BE DONE   10

2   INTRODUCTION   11

3   FORWARD MESSAGE ABOUT PRAYER   17
    Prayer — Power   18
    Direct Communication   19
    An Inherent Responsibility   20
    Intimacy with God   21
    Honesty in Prayer   25
    Dishonesty and Disrespect   26
    Binding Force Rightly Applied   27
    Pray for Yourself   28
    A Soul's Connection   29
    The Order of Worship and Progression   29
    Overall Increase   30
    Not of Science, but of Spirit   32
    Transformation Through Submission   34
    Humble Beginnings   35
    Submission: His Grace and His Mercy   36
    Finding a Community's Transformation   37
    Spirit Led Success   38
    The Holy Spirit: The Charger for Our Change   39
    Hope Makes All the Difference   42
    The Hope to Have Vision   44
    100,000 Making Effectual Changes   45
    Dependence and Subjection   46
    Excitement to Walk with the Lord   47
    The Approach of an Introduction   48
    Having Excitement for Prayer   49
    The Pain of Not Calling on the Lord   50
    Comfort: The First Order of Business   51
    Empowering   52
    More Time Spent on the Mainline   53
    There are No Excuses for Any of Us   59
    What do Others See?   62
    Put in the Work   64
    How We Request (Time, Blessings, Directions)   68
    No Faking It Till You Make It!   70
    What can be Expected   70

4   ACKNOWLEDGMENT — RECOGNITION *(Element #1)*.............   77
    Who is God to You?   80
    The Spirit to Pray Always   80

[handwritten inscription:] 7/1/15 To Pastor E.P. Wilson May the Lord continue to bless your spirit & your ministry greatly. We do serve an awesome God. Grace & Peace. Matthew 6:33

4   ACKNOWLEDGMENT — RECOGNITION *(Element #1)* (continued)
A Renewal from Weariness in Prayer 81
Why Acknowledge the Lord's Deity at all? 86
Acceptance and Appreciation 88
Driven by Faith 89
Surface Value Acknowledgment 91
Heart is Fixed 91
Acknowledgment vs Thanksgiving 93
A Story of Acknowledgment 94
Names of God 96

5   ADORATION - PRAISE *(Element #2)* 101*
His Deity 105
I Know Him for Myself 106
Getting God's Attention — a bi-product 107
How Easy is it? 110
Something about Praise 111
The Example of David 112
Knowledge of God and Devotional Praise 113
A Spirit Connection of Praise to Prayer 113
A True Blessing 114
The spirit's Condition 114
Fixed and Set 115
A Biblical Illustration of Praise to that of Progression 116

6   THANKSGIVING *(Element #3)* 121*
Appreciation is in Order 124
What has He Done for You, Not for Your Neighbor? 125
Unfruitful Entitlement 129
Who Owes What to Whom? 131
Self-Centered? It is Not about You 133
In His Presence 138
Submission is Strength 140
Maturing Appreciation 142
Appreciation Through His Word 144
Appreciation Through Communion 145
Eager to Get Into His Presence 146

7   REQUEST *(Element #4)* 151*
What are You Asking: Need or Desire? 155
List of Patterns 157
The Will of God and Our Request 157
Handling Disappointments in Request 165
Stating His Promises to Make the Appeal 167
List of Promises 168
Praying in Accord with His Promises and Word 169
Praying His Promises Encourages Us 170

12 ATTRIBUTES, CHARACTER AND NATURE OF GOD **327**
Pray to Whom You Know 329
Unjustifiable Claims 330
Beyond Doing the Right Thing 330
Beyond Good Intentions 331
Guidelines 331
Attributes Begin to Manifest 332
Oh, The Change! 333
The Attributes of God and Our Prayers 336
    Love 336
    Jealous 338
    Inscrutable 340
    Self-Existent 341
    Omnipotent 342
    Omniscient 342
    Omnipresent 343
    Immutable 345
    Faithful 346
        Faithful Parameters 347
    Righteous and Just 349
    Forgiving 351
    Merciful 354
    Good 358
    Gracious 360
    Truth 361
    Self-Sufficient 364
    Sovereign 366
    Infinite 368
    Incomprehensible 371
    Attributes Over All 378

13 CONCLUSION **383**

14 KEYS **385**

15 LIST OF BIBLICAL PRAYERS **389**

16 SELECTED BIBLIOGRAPHY **391**

HIS WILL BE DONE!

I thought twice and thrice about submitting this document to you even after all writing was complete. A feeling arose in me that some who are not of the Spirit may attempt to use these principles with ill intentions, since I see so many people trying to fake it till they make it. Help us God! Therefore I prayed that God reveal unto me whether He truly wanted these *Elements,* principles, keys and mysteries revealed. The Lord pricked my spirit with two things. First, this document will serve as a strong vehicle for believers and non-believers, alike, to get closer to Him. Second, the Lord sent me to I Corinthians 2:6-14 *(esp. vv7,14).*

6   *Howbeit we speak wisdom among them that are perfect: yet not the wisdom of this world, nor of the princes of this world, that come to nought:*

7   *But we speak the wisdom of God in a mystery, even the hidden wisdom, which God ordained before the world unto our glory:*

8   *Which none of the princes of this world knew: for had they known it, they would not have crucified the Lord of glory.*

9   *But as it is written, Eye hath not seen, nor ear heard, neither have entered into the heart of man, the things which God hath prepared for them that love him.*

10 *But God hath revealed them unto us by his Spirit: for the Spirit searcheth all things, yea, the deep things of God.*

11 *For what man knoweth the things of a man, save the spirit of man which is in him? even so the things of God knoweth no man, but the Spirit of God.*

12 *Now we have received, not the spirit of the world, but the spirit which is of God; that we might know the things that are freely given to us of God.*

13 *Which things also we speak, not in the words which man's wisdom teacheth, but which the Holy Ghost teacheth; comparing spiritual things with spiritual.*

14 *But the natural man receiveth not the things of the Spirit of God: for they are foolishness unto him: neither can he know them, because they are spiritually discerned.*

Thus, with a joyful teary eye I do present this document unto all who will receive of His Spirit's voice. It is because of His love for us that we may now receive the great gift of communion He ordained from the beginning of time. Receive of these pages and give glory to Him who ordained the words and the authority. *(See also: Proverbs 24:7; Matthew 13:11).*

INTRODUCTION

Much joy unto you for having an eagerness to grow in prayer. Now pray unto the Father to open your heart, mind, spirit and soul to receive of the increase from this document's *8 Elements of Prayer Progression.*™ The term *Progression* is not a matter of structure, but of a spiritual heightening. The ultimate goal of the *Progression* is to prepare us for making a request unto God, and sensitizing our spirits to hear an answer from Him.

Another goal of this document is to show fruit of 100,000 true prayer warriors, prepared for the present day and armed for the soon coming days. Each generation has gotten a little more challenging than the last, but it is no secret that we are now living in overtly perilous times. In these tough times we are in need of prayer that changes things.

This document is rooted in prayer, yet it will be a blessing unto our living, as well. It shall be illustrated, amongst other things, how a quality prayer life can effect change in our living, relationships, communities and faith walks. It will be explained how our living is then manifested in our prayer lives, as well.

You will find this document is not so much about defining prayer as it is in defining us within prayer. Most books on prayer have a pre-occupation about defining that which we are to do, rather than empowering us for what it is we are to do to succeed in prayer. This document is an empowering tool! Fact is, all of us should come into a truthful realization of what it is to be a prayer warrior after reading this document. This will occur not so much from definitions as it will be manifested by the Spirit.

One of the glorious blessings of these *8 Elements* is that each *Element* naturally and spiritually leads into the next *Element*. There is a spiritual flow which occurs as one *Element* prepares us for the next; leading up to making a *request* then onto receiving an answer or directions. These *Elements* are not as a mere sequence of a list, but a spiritual movement who's end is the overflow of the Lord our God. It is a goal of this *Progression* to enter us into the presence of the Lord where our victories are made manifest and change is made evident.

Progression from one *Element* to the next is made fluid and evident by our being truthful within each *Element*. Our honesty and truthfulness not only makes *Progression* through Prayer a natural experience, but it gives us three benefits for our living, as well: helps to further develop a closer relationship with the Lord; increases our sensitivity unto the Lord's voice and directions; and elevates our submissiveness unto the Lord. Each of these benefits is quite necessary for the sustaining of a fruitful communion with the Lord.

After this Introduction follows a Chapter aptly titled *"Forward Message About Prayer."* This message is full of meat which can be paralleled only by the subsequent Chapters of the *8 Elements of the Progression of Pray-er.*™ Do not forsake this section which includes additional principles for prayer and living, and is intended to prepare our spirits to receive of the *Progression of Prayer Elements* with added power.

There are sections in the beginning of each chapter which illustrate the who, what, why, when, where and how of each *Element* of prayer along with supportive scriptures. This is a teaching tool which strengthens the learning of each prayer *Element.* Teaching has historically come from the position of definitions and component's coordination, whereas, it is of great benefit and increased awareness when the "5-w's" and "1-h" have been instituted into the instructions. Biblical illustrations of the who, what, etc. increase the readers awareness of personal ownership and application. Most books and lessons on prayer omit the true importance of application. Biblical and Seminary students, alike, should be familiar with the necessity of application and true context of messages, and all Christians should ask the question when receiving word, "So what does that mean to me?"

In this section lies the power of the who should pray, why we should pray, where we should pray, when we should pray, how we should pray and what we should pray; along with parallels in each *Element* and Chapter. It doesn't get much simpler nor more powerful than these applications. This section will make scripture personal to each of us and give us greater enthusiasm to pray in a progressive manner. It is great to merely be excited over word, but today's issues and persecutions beg for us to receive strong application in order that we may truly fight against the wiles of the devil. Do not forsake studying these sections, for this entire document is quite interconnected and earnestly appeals that we read and digest all sections and chapters in order to realize the power of prayer.

Element #1, Acknowledgment, is where we set the tone for prayer as we recognize God for who He truly is to us individually. It is important that we are truthful in acknowledging the Lord since there is nothing worse than beginning a fellowship on the wrong note. The balance of our prayers relies on our recalling who and what the Lord truly is to us. Moving to the second *Element of Praise and Adoration* is otherwise false and superficial if we exclaim cliche's that the Lord knows to be false in our individual cases. The fact is, giving the Lord praise will come naturally and with greater spirit when we truthfully recall and proclaim all He has actually done for us or all that He actually means to us individually.

Our truthful worship and praise in *Element #2* grants us the spiritual access needed to begin to move more fully into the Lord's presence. It is our spirits' connections and conditions which begin to sensitize our hearts unto submission. It only makes sense to understand we cannot truly give the Lord *Thanksgiving* in *Element #3* if we do not have fruitful adoration for Him. Our thanksgiving comes by way of the why we adore and praise Him.

The *Thanksgiving Element #3* is when appreciation is given unto God for who He is and for the past and present things He has done for us. This is the first of two thanksgivings given unto the Lord within the *Progression of Prayer,* and it resides heavily in our submission and dependence unto God. Persons with spirits that are not submissive unto the Lord nor dependent on His power and provisions will think of themselves as the reason for all they enjoy in life. Our thanksgiving must display our acceptance of God as our sole provider, who is worthy of all our thanks. We will have the strong faith necessary to move into the next *Element of Request #4* after we truthfully accept and thank God as our sole provider.

It is by strong faith built upon our submission and dependence upon God which gives us great confidence and assurance to believe Matthew 21:22, "And all things, whatsoever ye shall ask in prayer, believing, ye shall receive," and John 14:14, "If ye shall ask anything in my name, I will do it." *Progression* through *Elements #1, #2* and *#3* heightens our spirits connection with God's Spirit, character and will, to a level where we are better prepared to make a request in *Element #4.* The fruit of this is that by the time we reach the *Request Element #4* our will and our spirits become more concerned with God's will and desires; thus we grow to a spiritual level where we no longer make frivolous, selfish and fleshly request. This is one of the greatest fruits, amongst many, which will be made manifest from this *Progression of Prayer.* Teachers, students and all the congregation, alike, should spend large amounts of time and effort to ensure this *key* has been received. A major point to understand is that this is when we have a great opportunity to ensure victory in our prayers. In other words, we are assured success with what we have requested because the request made is reflective of what God placed upon our spirits through our truthful and spirited acknowledgment, adoration and praise, and thanksgiving.

Most of us have always thought prayer ends after the request is made. Sad to say this mind-set has caused us not only to destroy many of the blessings we have received, but caused us to tarnish the relationships we have had with the Lord, as well. It is so very important that our requests are followed by our seeking discernment as illustrated *in Element #5.*

Receiving discernment serves several purposes: first, we gain wisdom on how to handle the blessings we receive; second, our hearts become supple to understand whether we must wait on the blessing, move into the blessing or accept the Lord's answer of no; third, our heightened spiritual awareness strengthens us to become more submissive unto any answer the Lord gives for our prayers (which helps greatly with our success record in prayer).

A prayer warrior with a discerning spirit will automatically seek a *Sign* from the Lord *(Element #6).* Many Biblical characters sought signs from the Lord because they knew how important it was to get their directions from Him, and they refused to lean unto their own understanding. In other words, they knew how important it was to get it right. As a prayer warrior it is imperative to follow the Lord's directions; eliminating doubts and eliminating most of the errors caused by fleshly decisions. It may take more time for some of us to receive directions from God through our prayers, depending on our current spiritual conditions, but it is made increasingly possible as our spiritual sensitivity is heightened by this *Progression of Prayer.*

At this point in prayer we can give God faithful *Pre-Praise Thanksgiving (Element #7)*; as we are highly assured in our spirits that our request are in line with His desires and His character. In the past, most of us have immaturely shouted thanks to the Lord in advance of our receiving from Him, all the while lacking truthful assurance in our hearts. It is almost mandatory that our request stand in line with God's desires in order for us to have the audacity to claim victory before it happens. It's all about being truthful. Giving the Lord praise and thanks in advance is a statement of faith in His power to do the impossible, even. Much of prayer is about our faith in God's ability and willingness to answer our prayers favorably.

At the end of our high praise communion with God, it is then time to listen more fully for His voice's directions. Our spirits are to be sensitizedenough to hear from the Lord at any point within prayer, yet the *8th Element of Meditation* is solely our time to listen and to be ushered into God's overflow. Through it all, this is what prayer is all about: hearing from Heaven. The significance of this _Element_ sheds light on why solitude and our thirst to hear from God are important _keys_ for the success of our prayers. Our prayer experiences boil down to this moment when God will speak to us if we have been honest in acknowledging Him, spirited in praising Him, truthful to thank Him for all He has done for us, connected to His Spirit in our requesting, earnest in our seeking instruction and discernment, sensitized to receive a sign, believe enough to give Him pre-praise thanksgiving and listening sharply enough in meditation.

Also included throughout this document are keys to draw added attention to certain precept and principles, which are not to be overlooked. These keys are not the only points of learning, yet greater emphasis should be given them. I reiterate, it is not wise to study the keys only, since this document is to be received in its entirety in order to exact change and power in prayer and living. Each chapter concludes with _General and Advanced Questions_ to challenge students and congregants, alike, in their development as prayer warriors. _Instructional and Personal Exercises_ are listed for each chapter to aid in this development. Find pleasure in the process while these exercises stretch our abilities to apply those things read and learned.

For added increase, acquire the _Workbook_ to accompany this document. It is truly an added blessing as it shall provide and provoke additional spiritual learnedness with instructional guidance. Also, teachers are urged and encouraged to acquire, follow and expound upon the _Instructor's Workbook_, so to broaden the classroom experience and to strengthen the student's prayer foundation and faith.

The power is ours and it will be unleashed by the Spirit's working through this document's _8 Elements of Prayer Progression._™ Let us open our tent doors and receive what saith the Lord of host. Turn the page and let us begin our fruitful trek into power and blessings; for it is a blessing to be able to pray truthfully. After reading this document we shall be able to declare as had Micah, "But truly I am full of power by the spirit of the Lord ..." _(Micah 3:8)._

FORWARD MESSAGE ABOUT PRAYER

This chapter is not a foreword, but a forward message as in progressive words to powerfully usher you into the spirit of this document. Prayer simply defined is a spiritual dialogue and communal experience based in faith, having the objective of receiving directions, blessings and power from God. There have been many definitions of prayer throughout the centuries and they served their purposes for each extent, I'm sure. Here, we will mention a few terms defined of prayer in the Hebrew and Greek, then swiftly move forward into prayer's power and application. This is in no way a full list of all the word's terms, but the few to be mentioned will prick our spirits of the path upon which we are to embark.

- <u>Chanan (Khaw-nan) O.T.</u> – refers to a bending, stooping and supplication, which is similar to Tsel-aw' *(II Chronicles 6:37)*.
- <u>Deomai (Deh'-om-ahee) N.T.</u> – is to beg, petition or make request *(Luke 22:32; Acts 8:24)*.
- <u>Euchomai (Yoo'-khom-ahee) N.T.</u> – is to will, wish or pray *(James 5:16; II Corinthians 13:7)*.
- <u>T phillah (Tef-il-law) O.T.</u> – is intercession or supplication *(Psalm 6:9,61:1)*.
- <u>Siyach (See'-akh) O.T.</u> – is to ponder, converse, commune, meditation or pray *(Psalm 64:1)*.
- <u>Lachash (Lakh-ash)</u> – more of a whisper or private prayer *(Isaiah 26:16)*.

No matter the case of definition, it is not the aim nor duty of this document to impress readers with words of expansive nor profound definitions, yet this has been sent of the Lord to impress a great amount of spiritual power upon the reader.

A prayer warrior is not just someone who likes to pray. So many people love to talk and hear their own voices, yet are not heard of by God. Being a prayer warrior is not just seeking to speak to God, but it is more about having the strong ability to be heard of by God. Not only that and just as important is the fact that prayer warriors have the ability to hear back from God. This is the major essence of having a dialogue with the Lord. Question is, "What difference does it make to pray to God if we never hear from Him?" From this day forward we will no longer think of prayer warriors as believers who merely accost Biblical words that impress the flesh but are of no true eternal help to the spirit. What is the cause of our prayers if we never hear His response? How much stronger can our prayers become when we are filled with the assurance that we will undoubtedly hear back from the Lord? This is the place unto where this document will attempt to graduate us. Having confidence and faith in hearing from God can be the make or break in our prayers. The balance of this document shall be as an additional expression of what it is to be a prayer warrior.

Let this be as meat and strength unto our spirits — being a warrior of prayer is not just about having an ability to pray tough things into fruitful blessings, as much as it is about being able to resolve the conflicts that disallow our abilities to be moved by God. The actual war we must seek to have victory is the war which satan, and even ourselves at times, pose against our abilities to commune with the Lord with sensitivity of spirit and with submission in heart. A prayer warrior knows the battle is not so much about getting a prayer through to God, as it is about being of God's Spirit and being able to be used of Him. Prayer is life and our source for connecting with God in spirit. Without this source our living is often for naught and is as useless as dust in the wind, swirling about in a desolate western town having no true intent.

The larger and most prominent war is not about our having means to pray the removal of evil spirits, as much as it is about the means in which we commune with the Lord in our living and our prayers. Some may say of other people that those are the evil spirits. Nevertheless, the question arises, "Are we of the Spirit and are we seeking the Lord?" That withstanding, a warrior of prayer is more concerned with time spent in the Lord's presence and Spirit than they are concerned of how much they can say to the Lord. Fact is, the greatest blessings and some of God's greatest glory is being grown within us by His Spirit while we commune with Him.

Prayer — Power

Prayer is power. Simply put, if we do not pray we do not have power. Here are a few ways we have power in prayer:

1) Power of the filling of the Holy Spirit.
2) Power of moving in the will of God (our hearing then being directed).
3) Power by being submissive unto God (He can then use us).
   - He then works through us and in us.
4) Power to make correct decisions (in relation to numbers 1, 2 and 3).
   - He can direct us when we are filled.
   - The winning formula is our desiring to do His will; not vice-versa.
   - Our submission unto Him gives us the sensitivity to hear from Him, be moved by Him and be blessed by Him. We abide in Him as He abides in us by the extent of our submissiveness and faith; both of which are needed to keep His commandments.

This indwelling and filling of power is reason satan tries to keep us from praying. He surely knows if we do not hear from God we resort to other things, including: the devil's evil, our neighbor's fleshly thoughts and our own wicked desires. Resorting to those things renders us powerless, since there is no power where God and prayer are not present. We must connect to the vine in order to receive power and divine blessings.

"I am the true vine, and my Father is the husbandman. Every branch in me that beareth not fruit he taketh away: and every branch that beareth fruit, he purgeth it, that it may bring forth more fruit. Now ye are clean through the word which I have spoken unto you. Abide in me, and I in you. As the branch cannot bear fruit of itself, except it abide in the vine; no more can ye, except ye abide in me. I am the vine, ye are the branches: He that abideth in me, and I in him, the same bringeth forth much fruit; for without me ye can do nothing. If a man abide not in me, he is cast forth as a branch, and is withered; and men gather them, and cast them into the fire, and they are burned. If ye abide in me, and my words abide in you, ye shall ask what ye will, and it shall be done unto you. Herein is my Father glorified, that ye bear much fruit; so shall ye be my disciples. As the Father hath loved me, so have I loved you: continue ye in my love. If ye keep my commandments, ye shall abide in my love; even as I have kept my Father's commandments, and abide in his love. These things have I spoken unto you, that my joy might remain in you, and that your joy might be full" (John 15:1-11).

How then might we become connected if we do not speak to the Lord in prayer? No prayer, no power. Many devil's would rather we remain fooled into thinking that all we need to do is attend Sunday service in order to constitute our having fellowship with God. Others may even be convinced that all it takes is to make a sacrificial effort by attending Bible study during the week and Sunday school on the weekend. They are sadly mistaken. They are mistaken to think essential power can be acquired without a dialogue with the Lord. If a married couple never communicates with one another, how can they know each others needs, wants and directions? So, how much more are we married to God as His children, standing in tremendous need to commune with Him in prayer?

Direct Communication

Prayer is our direct communication with God. Jesus tore the veil in half on the day of His crucifixion so that we may have unhindered access to the Father. Jesus still intercedes on our behalf, yet it is no longer a requirement that we need an earthly priest to intercede for us in order to have communion with the Father. "Who is he that condemneth? It is Christ that died, yea rather, that is risen again, who is even at the right hand of God, who also maketh intercession for us" (Romans 8:34). The

Holy Spirit also makes intercession for us as the Comforter and Sealer. "Likewise the Spirit also helpeth our infirmities: for we know not what we should pray for as we ought: but the Spirit itself maketh intercession for us with groanings which cannot be uttered. And he that searcheth the hearts knoweth what is the mind of the Spirit, because he maketh intercession for the saints according to the will of God" *(Romans 8:26-27).*

There became a great blessing of our having the opportunity to go directly to God by the tearing of the veil. What a blessing it is to be able to talk with the One who died for us so that we may have life and have it more abundantly. Oh, how truly a blessing it is that our spirits can be joined with His Spirit. A joining that strengthens our spirits all the more. Oh, what a blessing it is to be able to talk directly to the One who has our fate in His hands. Oh, what a blessing it is to receive an answer directly from the Provider, even as we pose our request.

An Inherent Responsibility

Along with the blessings comes a tremendous responsibility; hence this document. Do not be taken aback, for the truth is our entire faith walk is a matter of responsibility. A responsibility that many of us take lightly; therefore we end up missing out on the blessings as well as the power. We all should know there is great power in having a strong relationship with the Lord through prayer. There are not many practices that can strengthen our relationship with God like that of having a strong and non-ceasing prayer life.

Now that the shock of responsibility has been smoothed over, let me get close to some people by mentioning the shared portion of the blessing created by the tearing of the veil. The shared element is our responsibility to not only go to the Lord in prayer, but to hone our prayer skills, also. There is nothing more sad than for a Christian to not have a strong prayer life. What may be just as sorrowful is for that same Christian to take prayer lightly and to babble in prayer; hence this document! This responsibility includes seeking a meditative experience that goes beyond simple isolated meditation and normal devotionals. Prayer is a time to experience the fullness of God's joy through strong communion. We should not only get excited to pray to God, but we should be overjoyed and bursting at the seams to actually commune with Him as we pray.

Learning how to pray is one of the most essential exercises for a Christian. Speaking to the Lord is as essential to a Christian as the branch needs the vine. Much of a Christian's sustenance is provided through prayer: sustenance for living; sustenance for direction;

sustenance for spirituality. We must keep at the foremost of our minds the fact that a strong spiritual life begins and is regulated through prayer. That is to say, an open and regular prayer life can provide the sustaining power needed to walk and/or run from grace to grace. "Let us therefore come boldly unto the throne of grace, that we may obtain mercy, and find grace to help in time of need" *(Hebrews 4:16)*.

Falling and failing in life are normal activities of all who lack in prayer. "Where to turn?" is the customary question of those who do not have a strong communal relationship with the Lord. If ever there is a desire to feel inadequate in life, try not hearing from the Lord. It is justifiably assumed that most people want power, success and strength in their lives; hence this document and hence the responsibility.

This document of *Progression of Prayer Elements* has been provided to us through the Spirit of God in order to give unto us strength and power. Within these pages is a releasing power needed to make it through the coming days. Make it a priority to digest and put into action these very *Progression of Prayer Elements,* and assume the responsibility. Find power in these pages and live life more fully in the joy of His presence.

Intimacy With God

Prayer involves a level of intimacy regulated by, both, our willingness to submit unto the Lord and by our having a strong desire to hear from Him. For many of us, our intimacy stops at the point of our one-sided conversation with the Father, wherein we are drone like in our asking Him for what it is we think we want or need. True intimacy cannot exist without both parties contributing and melding; as this holds constant for any type of fruitful relationship. As we should imagine, intimacy is even more essential when it comes to our communing with God.

It is no secret that many of us have concerns or debatable issues with being intimate. It could be due to so many different events in our lives, or it could be that we never spent the quality time with God needed to teach us how to be truthfully and faithfully intimate. We must have intimacy with the Father in order to find fruit within our prayer lives. Not having intimacy with the Father will equate to having little or no fruit in life. Religion has little to do with feelings, for feelings do come and go, but surely prayer is a matter of closeness of heart and spirit in faith unto the Father. Our hearts must truly desire to be intimate in prayer; for heart felt prayer is prayer which invigorates the spirit to hear a word from Heaven. We must have hearts which desire to speak to and hear from the Lord. "Oh to hear from Heaven," should be the motto for us all.

Our hearts drive our spirits to desire to hear from the Lord, while the level of our heart's drive is built upon our individual expectations of intimacy. Yes, we all have needs and wants, but the crux of our desire to pray must be built upon a foundation of wanting to first and foremost be intimate with the Lord. Our desire to get on our knees should not be foremost based upon a need or desire of anything other than to be in His presence. Let me make it a little more plain, for this is a *key*. When we are in trouble our desire should be, of course, to get out of trouble ultimately, but our initial reaction to the trouble should be to get into the presence of the Lord. We can have freedom and fullness of joy in the Lord while in trouble, shackled or in pain; provided for by the blessing of intimacy we have with God. This was the heart of Jesus as He would always slip away from the crowd to get into the presence of the Father; especially when trials were upon Him.

It is only natural to want to be delivered when our bodies, minds or living are wrecked with suffering, but we must realize much of the pains can be rectified by our having the intimacy of the presence of the Lord. In His presence is healing. In His presence is joy. In His presence is deliverance. Not that the affliction or the suffering is removed immediately, but the Lord has a mysterious way of blessing our hearts when we are in His presence. I do not know about you, but I feel a lot better about life when I'm in His presence. I feel the weight of the world lift off me when I'm in communion with Him; such that my joy becomes full, my heart is elevated, and my spirit gets lifted.

If that is not enough, a miraculous thing happens when in spirited and heartfelt communion with the Lord. He gets busy working things out in our situations as we consume ourselves with His presence. It is a blessing to be in His presence with greatness of joy, but it is icing on the proverbial prayer cake to have our prayers answered through the intimacy of communion.

Make no mistake about it, receiving the breakthrough or blessing is great, yet the ultimate blessing is to be in God's presence. Just to be in His presence! "Glory and honour are in His presence; strength and gladness are in His place" *(1 Chronicles 16:27)*. "Thou wilt shew me the path of life: in Thy presence is fulness of joy; at Thy right hand there are pleasures for evermore" *(Psalm 16:11)*. And thanks be to the Lord Jesus we can even be found faultless in His presence. "Now unto Him that is able to keep you from falling, and to present you faultless before the presence of His glory with exceeding joy" *(Jude 24)*. That should be exciting to us all!

This document will help give us a greater desire to be in the presence of the Lord, by heightening our awareness that His presence is the place where our spirits are ignited into the action of effectual prayer and true communion unto Him. The sad thing is we spend time with people and even God in accord with what we can get out of the time invested. We tend to desire and need things from them more than we desire building relationships where we solely need to be in their presence.

It is truly not the aim of this document to tell us that our request and needs are immaterial. Yet, it is aimed at engaging us to understand and believe that no issue, trial nor trouble is more important than merely spending time with the Lord our God. This is one of the greatest blessings gained. The devil will try to make us think differently. He wants us to spend more time focusing on our issues and trials than we do keeping our mind stayed on Jesus. Again, it is not the intent to minimize our need to be delivered of a trial or a suffering, but it is essential that this document press upon our spirits the need to be delivered into being a Christian who seeks God for who He is and not just for what He provides.

The fact of the matter is far too many of us treat our daily relationships the same way we treat the Lord. We tend to spend time with people because of what they can do for us. We treat the Lord in the same manner, for we only call on Him when we need something from Him. As well, our spending time with God has been relegated to our requesting of Him versus our giving unto Him. This is another example of how our vertical relationship with the Lord dictates and is mirrored by our horizontal relationships with others here on earth. More will be spoken of vertical and horizontal relationships within the balance of this document.

What of the fantastic yet archaic idea of spending time with someone simply due to our love for who they are and not for what they can do for us? Treating God merely as a supplier minimizes the spirituality of our fellowship with Him. This is the best way to minimize our blessings, as well. It is the promise of the Lord to never leave us alone. "I will not leave you comfortless: I will come to you" *(John 14:18)*. Yet, He is in no way obligated to sit at our beck and call posing as a genie in a bottle.

This document shall impress upon our spirits the importance of how we are to become filled in the Lord Himself instead of being engulfed in our earthly wants and desires. For some this may seem like a let down of their expectations of the effect of prayer, but trust that the *Elements* and *Progression* within this document will be a greater blessing to us than most things we may entertain in life. Receiving deliverance is great, but there is no greater blessing than loving the Lord for who He is, alone.

That is where our spirit's true blessings occur. It is simple to receive a blessing for our living, but the true increase is in our spirit being blessed. The Lord Jesus made point of our spiritual needs being greater than our natural needs when He forgave the sins of the man having palsy before He healed the man's physical illness *(Mark 2:3-12)*. Our spiritual condition and connection with the Lord is far more important than our earthly needs; whether they are physical, financial, or some other concern.

Our spirits' greatest blessing is to be connected to the very Spirit which created us. It is through this connection that we receive joy. It is in His Spirit where we find increase. It is in our fellowship with God's Spirit where we even find deliverance from our desire to want things other than Him. Many earthly desires are of the flesh and have no part in His Spirit. It is in the Spirit of Christ where we gain the desire to be filled with the Father's presence. What shall we have when we leave this Earth? It is hoped that the answer for us all is communion with His Spirit. So let us get into desiring communion with Him now, so we can enjoy the fullness of His joy here on earth, in addition to Heaven. There is where we have our everlasting here on this Earth as well as in the there after. There we have the prosperity many think is connected with things of this Earth. As I always say, "The prosperity is in Jesus Christ." The Lord Jesus proclaimed in John 10:10, "The thief cometh not, but for to steal, and to kill, and to destroy: I am come that they might have life, and that they might have it more abundantly." It is easy to miss this, just as most have in the past. Remember the fullness of His joy is in His presence. This is the very presence we need in our prayers in addition to our general living.

It is in the intimacy of the fullness of the Spirit where we can receive directions, as well. "And Jesus being full of the Holy Ghost returned from Jordan, and was led by the Spirit into the wilderness" *(Luke 4:1)*. Our destinies are connected with and through the Spirit of the Almighty. Our very destinies are made evident through our desire to be in His presence and through our gaining access unto His presence in truth of Spirit.

In the early Church days those who were chosen to do the Lord's work were full of the Spirit. Sad to say, many in this modern age have turned to the Gospel as a business opportunity. "Wherefore, brethren, look ye out among you seven men of honest report, full of the Holy Ghost and wisdom, whom we may appoint over the business" *(Acts 6:3)*. The same should apply to today's officers of the Church, and it also should be found of those who seek the Lord in prayer and relationship. We have gotten away from this precept in some of today's Churches, whereas officers are chosen according to their willingness to be led, not by the Spirit, but by the nose. Fact remains, there can be no spiritually profitable relationship with the Father where the spirit is lacking. There can be no communion where the spirit is unwilling. There can be no connection with the Holy Spirit by any other means than by our faithfulness in spirit. Woe unto the persons who call themselves children of the Most High Father but are not filled with the energy and Spirit of His Son Jesus.

This is the fullness John speaks of in I John and II John. We should love on the Lord because He first loved us, not that He has or will do anything else for us. Any other love is contingent upon Him continuing to perform acts of kindness. A mature believer has come to realize a prosperous and fruitful relationship with the Lord does not always feel so kind. If our fullness is connected to God blessing us with treasures, what then happens to our fullness when the treasures do not exist? In the same way what happens when our blessings come in a form that is not tangible nor measurable?

It is urged, dear brothers and sisters, to be full with the Spirit of the Lord Jesus. Be full with the presence of the Father of Lights. Be full with none other than an eagerness to spend time with the Creator of all things good. May our hearts, minds, spirits and souls be opened by the Spirit in order to receive of these _Progression of Prayer Elements_. In this way let us begin to live in the fullness of His presence. In that place, my brothers and sisters, is our true blessing. Open your tent doors, Oh Israel. Open your gates, Oh ye Jerusalem. Receive of Him and be blessed in your living and your prayers, alike.

Honesty in Prayer

One thing I wish to make perfectly clear from the beginning is that we must not use cliche's and worn-out statements when we pray to God. The Lord our God is looking for our honest and heart felt words. He is not looking for you nor I to feebly attempt to impress Him with verbiage of the saints, per se. Instead, the Lord is looking to hear from us in such a way that will increase our relationship with Him. This begins by our telling the truth of who He is to us individually. There are even many scriptures that are as cliche to us; whereas, they tell of who God is to the writer, but are not necessarily reflective of who He is to us. We shall be blessed of the Lord's presence and His attentiveness unto our prayers if we pray with honesty in heart felt words. May our words be an honest expression of our spirit's condition and our relationship with the Lord. May our words reflect that which is truthful and meaningful, which in turn will bear blessed fruit in our spirits and in our living.

Honest communication bears great fruit as the communicators become further acquainted one to the other. We must view the Lord as our greatest confidant in order to free our spirits unto being honest and up front. Anything short of being totally honest with God will render our communal experiences ineffective and less than blessed. It is *key* that we are honest unto the Lord, respectful of who He is, and truthful about who we are and who we are not.

Let us be mindful and not forget He is still the Creator all the while we are showing ourselves friendly and submissive unto Him. Acting a little too familiar with the Lord will move us into a realm of disrespect. I am often leery of those who say they are on a first name basis with the Lord, for it is in this type of posture where we begin to take on a spirit of disrespect instead of a spirit of humbled submission. The focus of prayer remains to be the Lord's will in our lives, although we may be praying unto Him about our circumstances and situations. Do not get it twisted – as the young folk say. He is still God, and we are forever His servants, given stewardship only, and for just a moment's time.

It is not even a fine line between honesty and respect. Both must reside within a healthy relationship of any kind. It is often through healthy respect for another that a person can begin to be honest. Our acknowledgment of who we are, truthfully, renders our spirits honest about our positions, places and problems in life. Those who lie, steal and cheat are not respectful of the other party involved. In those very situations there is a breakdown in respect which then inhibits one, or both parties from bearing the fruit of a sound relationship. Proverbs 26:28 proclaims, "A lying tongue hateth those that are afflicted by it ..." It pains my heart to think any of us hate the Lord in the manner of distrustful worship and tainted fellowship. Remember, if someone does it to you, they do it unto God, assuredly.

Dishonesty and Disrespect

Understand, quoting cliche's and age-old statements of hot air unto the Lord is a dishonest attempt to impress Him, which truly illustrates our disrespect for Him. A dishonest worshiper is a disrespectful worshiper. Make no mistake about it. Many people go into prayer in dishonesty of worship in an attempt to steal a blessing from a Savior who would gladly give it unto them if they would only go unto Him in honesty. "... for the Lord searcheth all hearts, and understandeth all the imaginations of the thoughts: if thou seek Him, He will be found of thee; but if thou forsake Him, He will cast thee off for ever" *(I Chronicles 28:9).* "He that speaketh truth sheweth forth righteousness: but a false witness deceit" *(Proverbs*

12:17). Be honest and respectful in prayer, so to witness the blessings of prayer. We do serve a truthful Lord who desires us to replicate His character and Spirit in our worship, prayers and relationships with Him. This document attends to the very center of each of our spirit's conditions.

Included in this document, among many other fruits, is our spirits preparation for the coming of the Son of God. One hundred thousand new prayer warriors will come about through the reading of this document and through their applying these *8 Elements* within their prayer lives. Those same warriors shall have a great advantage in the days that are currently upon us and that are to come. The Lord Jesus spoke of these days in the Olivet Discourse. "Watch ye therefore, and pray always, that ye may be accounted worthy to escape all these things that shall come to pass, and to stand before the Son of man" *(Luke 21, esp v36)*

This document shall illustrate how our prayer lives can strengthen us of God, make us more sensitized to His will, and free us from many of the chains which clamp us down in life. Being strengthened of God through our prayers assuredly helps us in our daily walk called life. It is the tumultuous days before us which demand we be strengthened of God by way of our prayers.

Binding Force Rightly Applied

Make no mistake about it, prayer is a binding force of our witness unto Christ and of our strength in being. With little prayer there is little power. With great prayer there is great power. Many of us falter and faint through even minute parts of life because we lack in prayer. It will be senseless to complain about concerns in our lives after this document empowers us to live, pray and have our being in the Spirit. Far too many who call themselves Christians can recite His Word, but surely do not know His Spirit, and surely do not live within His Spirit in prayer. In this way they miss out on the fruitfulness of communion with God.

Operating outside the Lord's Spirit is a dangerous and sorrowful state. The most sorrowful affect is how we become as carnal Christians, partly due to our living unto the flesh instead of being moved by the Spirit. These very folk even misapply the Word of God, taking it out of context as they live fleshly lives, with the Spirit of Christ void from their hearts and prayers.

The Word of God misapplied can surely render our spirituality ineffective. A major way to ward off this ineffectiveness in living is by strengthening our prayer lives in order that the Spirit of Christ may rest upon us, prompting our spirits to the truth of God. Then, and only then, will we become true witnesses of His great power in our lives. Only then will we be able to stand strong in times of trouble and in moments of despair. Only then will we be able to make mountains move. "And Jesus said unto them, because of your unbelief: for verily I say unto you, If ye have faith as a grain of mustard seed, ye shall say unto this mountain, Remove hence to yonder place; and it shall remove; and nothing shall be impossible unto you. Howbeit this kind goeth not out but by prayer and fasting" *(Matthew 17:20-21)*.

Please do not make the mistake of taking lightly our strength nor our weakness in prayer. If we do take our position in prayer lightly, it will show in our living and it will prove us ineffective and sorrowful in the days of His return.

Pray for Yourself

Our increased spiritual strength is paramount, so as you enjoy this document I write unto you, still be mindful to internalize the basis of these *Prayer Elements* that you may make your living most effective unto the Lord. Put into action the *Elements* within these pages and shout the victory, for your life will now and forever be changed. It's ok to have others to pray for us, but after reading this document we will no longer be dependant on others to get a prayer through on our behalf. We will now be able to pray and not worry who's not praying for us. This document shall bring alive the strength of scriptures into our prayers and our living. As an example, many of us rely on others to intercede for us in prayer when we should be relying on the Spirit of God to intercede on our behalf. "Likewise the Spirit also helpeth our infirmities: for we know not what we should pray for as we ought: but the Spirit itself maketh intercession for us with groanings which cannot be uttered. And he that searcheth the hearts knoweth what is the mind of the Spirit, because he maketh intercession for the saints according to the will of God" *(Romans 8:26-27)*.

The Bible does indicate how we are to make intercessions one to another, but no longer will we be tethered to leaving all our concerns and request on someone else's prayer list. Some of us need to pray that the persons in whom we left our prayers can themselves pray and get an answer. Best believe not everybody can pray for us. Some people merely endear the title and thought of being prayer warriors, all along they lack the true ability to get into the presence of the Lord. This document will equip us with the ability to decipher between those who can pray for us and those who we dare not ask to pray for us.

A Soul's Connection

We will have such a joyful increase in our spirits after a time of instituting this _Progression of Prayer_ into the pattern of our prayer lives. It will be like finding a new friend whose actually our soul-mate. Soul-mates not only know one another intently and spend quality time in fellowship, but they are in tuned with one another, as well. Are we in tuned with God enough to consider Him as our soul-mate? Many a folk have God as a Friend, Father and a Provider, but few can truly consider Him in the category of soul-mate. He greatly knows us, but the converse is not true.

This _Progression of Prayer_ can truly help us to become more in tuned in spirit with God. Enjoy the ride for it is truly a joy, an exciting joy, to be in tuned with and led by His Spirit through prayer. Oh, you truly should be excited! I am excited for you.

The Order of Worship and Progression

I find it is important not to skip any steps in this _Progression of Prayer_ to begin, in order to build a foundation of fellowship. This building process enhances our sensitivity to commune with God and increases the probabilities of our receiving answers from Him. Skipping steps may make the prayer experience shallow and framed. Understand, this document maps a _Progression_ and not a structure. Allow this _Progression of Prayer_ to become a part of the fabric of our individual communion with the Lord. It is important to follow this _Progression_ in order to come into a heightened spiritual awareness of what it truly means to pray.

The Word tells us, "God is a Spirit: and they that worship him must worship him in spirit and in truth" _(John 4:24)_, so how much more should we be in the spirit of Christ Jesus while praying? It is essential that we accept our obligation to worship the Lord in our prayers. Also, recognize that all of prayer is a combined worship unto God as we submit our spirits unto Him; showing reverence and honour. Prayer, in itself, is a mode, method and form of worship unto the Lord. Included in that worship experience is the show of faith necessary to even get on our knees to pray. This is a foundation of strength in our prayers which evolves from that very reverence and worship unto the Lord. In other words, our prayers are less effective when we do not originally have a spirit that proclaims prayer as worship. Prayer warriors realize that prayer is most about God and less about us! It is at that point where prayer is accepted as worship unto God. An objective of this document is to prompt believers to realize we cannot effectively pray until we can effectively worship. _Powerful Prayer Progression for Prayer Warriors_™ is a worship experience!

Many of us meander in our lives simply due to our meandering in prayer. It is shameful that many do not pray, but just as regrettable is a large percentage of those who do actually pray do so in an aimless and wandering fashion. Now let it be known that I am not a proponent of a certain structure of prayer, nor is this book designed to box persons into a specific frame for praying. That would be in a sense the same as babbling prayer, which the Bible speaks out against. "But shun profane and vain babblings for they will increase unto more ungodliness" *(II Timothy 2:16)*.

What this document is geared to create is a spirit for praying, a foundation for communing with God, and a platform for success in prayer. Those who know me well know I am avid about having strong foundations; without which everything built upon it thereafter is shaky at best. Our Lord Jesus spoke of foundations when He spoke the parable of the sower and the seed in Matthew 13:1-9. These verses conclude in saying, "But other fell into good ground, and brought forth fruit, some an hundredfold, some sixtyfold, some thirty fold." This document shall set forth a base for a lifetime of victories in prayer. A footing fruitful upon which the Spirit of Christ will rest. A foundation for a spirit receptive of God's answers.

Let us be mindful how God desires us to communicate and commune with Him on a regular basis. Far too many of us reach out to God only in times of need and trouble. This document will feed us with power to urge and entice us to speak to the Lord on more of a regular basis. Actually, speaking to the Lord on a regular basis will help to minimize those troubling times in our lives, as prayer affords unto us God's directions for wholesome living. It is through prayer that we live unto the Lord and do His great will. How can we do His will if we do not know of His will? As well, how might we know of His will lest we hear from Him through His Word and through our prayers? Hence this document.

Overall Increase

Also, it is hoped that our entire living receive the increase through this *Progression of Prayer.* These *Elements* shall renew our focus on engaging our spirits into communion with God in all that we endeavor. We will further come to realize we are nothing without His Spirit's movement in our lives, and admit poor decisions are made when we stand outside the Holy Spirit's aiding and guiding. Improper directions are taken in life simply due to our relying on our own knowledge rather than our leaning on God's Spirit. Upon reading this document we will learn to coincide our spirits with His Spirit in order to ensure the best results of our actions. One hundred thousand new prayer warriors having spirits leaning upon the Lord will effect an entire generation to turn unto God with unfeigned contrition and confession for mercy and grace. It is through them that the world shall see miracles of a True and Living God.

The strongest components of this document are the very elements we most recognize as God – Spirit and Word. The main objective of this *Progression of Prayer* is to release us into a spirit realm which will enable us to best commune and communicate with our God. "For it is in him we live, move and have our being ..." *(Acts 17:28).* Let us remember, "God is a Spirit: and they that worship him must worship him in spirit and in truth" *(John 4:24).* The Truth of Jesus Christ and His Word.

I am so excited to deliver this document unto you as it is given unto me by His Spirit. This is such a spirited read that you should be prepared to "Get-your-shout-on" even as you read and digest these *Prayer Elements and Progression.* If only you will grow in great excitement to receive such a gift that will entitle your spirit to commune with the Lord on a heightened level of truth and love!

This document goes beyond that of attempting to help us pray unto God. It is the motivation of the Spirit, and my obedience unto Him, to reveal *Elements and Progression of Prayer* that will fortify our spirits unto His. This fortifying will not only increase our strength of prayer, which is probably the main reason many of us made this purchase, but will strengthen our vertical relationships with the Lord, also. In addition, our horizontal relationships shall receive overflow, just as our general faith walk shall be further empowered. Oh, what a blessing it shall be in having one hundred thousand or more strong warriors of prayer transforming a generation, in the witness of Heaven and Earth. God's timing is always perfect as our world is in such great need of truthful prayer.

So often we are taught to pray through ineffective means and unsound theological positions, which render us incapable and helpless in times of trouble and moments of storms. Far too many are made powerless and left needing after being taught fruitless habits. Those fruitless habits have rendered many Christians useless to help others and even themselves in times of need and peril. Far too many of us couldn't get a prayer through to God if our lives depended on it; let alone hear an answer back from Him. Let it be known our lives do depend on us hearing a word from the Lord. Why else might we come to the realization that there are so few true and powerful prayer warriors! Oh yeah, there are many who claim to be prayer warriors, but when push comes to shove they are not hearing from Heaven.

This document will not only give us the tools to more effective prayer, but it will also illuminate what we must do in order to render our prayers most effective in the eyes of the Lord. So many of us cannot get a prayer through because we, ourselves, render our prayers ineffective. This document will illustrate how prayer is not just about getting on our knees and calling out to the Lord. The pages to come will explicate how effective prayer begins with effective and consecrated living unto the Lord. Just as we are writing our obituaries through our daily walk, so too our prayer's successes begin with us long before we ever get on our knees.

Let me give a little tidbit of what this document offers. There are even some of us who are actually prayer warriors, but still cannot and may not ever get a prayer through. You ask, "Why can't a prayer warrior get a prayer through?" God may have set them apart to be prayer warriors, but their noxious and sinful living cancels their prayer's effectiveness. Here is where quite a few folk set down this document, only to return later after a few moments of shedding apologetic tears unto the Lord. This document will be an eye-opener and a blessing for all who take the time to read and digest its contents. Reading it a second time will surely be a necessity in order to receive of the portions we did not receive through the tears and high spirit of our first reading. Allow this document to become a part of our libraries and night-stands just as it becomes a part of our very living. Allow it to give our lives overall increase.

Not of Science, but of Spirit

First and foremost, there is no set way to pray. These *Prayer Elements* should be received, first, of the spirit, then second, as assisting designs versus diagrams of exactness. Unlike other books on prayer, this document and *Progression of Prayer* is designed to elevate our spirits, which will increase the likelihood of our prayers being heard, received and answered by God.

Those who institute these *Progression of Prayer Elements*™ will gain an eagerness to pray and live within the will of God. Many people pray in a monologue fashion not discerning of the Lord's Spirit speaking back to them concerning His will. Discernment is further illustrated in the *#5 Element of the Prayer Progression.*™ It can be said that some of our failures in prayer can be attributed to our not discerning, nor accepting, the Lord's will for our lives.

One of the main points of using these *Elements of Prayer Progression*™ is to grant us better access to the Lord's Spirit. Once we have access, not just His attention, we then minimize and often eliminate our immature babblings which so hurriedly demand failure from the onset. So many have failed in the midst of trying hard to succeed during prayers, as they merely end up babbling. Let us receive of these _Progression of Prayer Elements_™ so we may be able to best commune with God.

We will joyfully find how each _Element_ prepares us to progress to the next _Element._ For example, by the time we have _Acknowledged (#1)_ who God is in <u>our</u> lives, we are most prepared to then _Praise (#2)_ Him for who He is in <u>our</u> lives. Natural _Progression._ Thus, by the time we have given the Lord _Thanksgiving (#3)_ for all He's done for us, we are then most spiritually prepared to make a _Request (#4)_ of Him. This document's _Progression_ will also sift our request. That is to say, by the time our spirits have so joined with His Holy Spirit many of our proposed requests fizzle away, simply due to our realizing we have already received all that we need from God. As further example, the desire for the fur coat we were about to request of God dwindles away after thanking Him for the parka and leather coats He's already provided unto us. Or maybe the caviar we were poised to request becomes obsolete after we have just thanked Him for the pork & beans we ate the night before. The _key_ is for us to pray in His Spirit! "Ye ask, and receive not, because ye ask amiss, that ye may consume it upon your lusts" _(James 4:3)._ "But the natural man receiveth not the things of the Spirit of God: for they are foolishness unto him: neither can he know them, because they are spiritually discerned" _(I Corinthians 2:14)._

One thing I will warn you of this very moment is that as you grow in tremendous leaps and bounds in this _Progression of Prayer_ you shall be transformed into, not only a prayer warrior, but a believer who diligently seeks the will of God. And this be the warning: as you become stronger in seeking the will of God through powerful prayer, I highly recommend you be mindful of those things for which you pray. The Bible tells us, ".... for we know not what we should pray for as we ought ..." _(Romans 8:26)._ In your experience and living you should already know and trust this to be absolutely true. As prayer warriors we must submit to the very fact we are nothing without the Spirit's intercession, thus we must depend more on the Holy Spirit's direction in our prayers. For more on direction, read the _#5 Element of Discernment_ and the _#8 Element of Meditation._

As we develop as prayer warriors, it is also suggested that we end many prayers with, "But bring me Your grace and Your mercy;" especially for those prayers that we are not too positive of the outcome of the item requested. This serves as a kind of disclaimer to God, acknowledging we know not what to truly pray and that He knows best. This disclaimer can serve to protect us from God potentially putting-it-on-us; or shall we say, God may grant our request even though He knows we are not ready to receive of it. Make no mistake that God will put-it-on-us. He may protect us from certain harms, but He just may allow us to go through a certain thing, if only to make us more fully understand how much we need to wait on His answering prayers in His time.

Transformation Through Submission

As one can see, even thus far, being a prayer warrior is not just about getting a prayer through, but it is much about our submission unto God. Our submission is what grants us the power to be conjoined with God's will, which then solidifies our prayers and gives them a greater chance of being answered. Our submissiveness unto the will of God strengthens our relationship with Him, as well. Sounds rather elementary, but the distressing number of people who do not submit unto the Lord is alarming. Why else might we have so many issues in our society?

Can I make this a little clearer. Many folk think they can change God's mind, and/or change His course for their lives through prayer. On the contrary, prayer warriors know our minds and spirits are changed to that of Christ's Spirit through prayer, therefore lending us to pray and speak of those things preordained and predestined by God. This is a major *key* for the development of our prayer lives. What saith the Lord? This happens so our prayers and Christian lives are mysteriously transformed to reflect what God so wills in the first place. As an example, Joseph's prayers and visions were reflective of what God had already willed to occur, versus what Joseph saw fit *(Genesis 37-50)*. This is a key we must digest and believe in order to walk the walk of a true prayer warrior.

God's will for our lives is that which we must eagerly seek through prayer, ultimately performing it in our living. It must be our spirits' thinking that it is better to have a penny in our pockets while doing God's will rather than have a million dollars in the bank while sowing to the flesh. The Bible tells us in no apologetic form, "For what is a man profited, if he shall gain the whole world, and lose his own soul? or what shall a man give in exchange for his soul?" *(Matthew 16:26).* There are many who are weeping at this very moment having just realized they previously made packs with the accuser, and are fully in need of true repentance. Even so, someone should be blessed by this document, already. I cannot wait for us to proceed into the rest of this document, written unto all who have ears to hear and wanting to be elevated in spirit and in living unto Christ Jesus. This is just the *Forward Message*, so buckle the seatbelts and receive power from on High as we proceed.

Humble Beginnings

My personal prayer life began at approximately age 8. This is the time I began to pray and meditate on my own. At that early age I heard the Pastor say something in regards to "Going into your prayer closet." Well, I took the statement literally, since I was unschooled of the difference between literal and figurative languages used in the Bible. As we all know, children most often take things rather literally, thus I would actually go into the extremely cluttered closet of my bedroom, shared with my sister, to pray unto the Lord. Thanks be to God, this was the beginning of my personal prayer life with the Lord. From that day forward I was never the same. There was an unexplainable power that came upon me which has guided, built and strengthened my life ever since.

There have been times in my life where I sorely and apologetically abandoned getting on my knees to pray, but thankfully as a child I came to understand it was possible to pray and meditate unto God without actually kneeling. How many can attest to praying while standing in the face of an enemy, boss, or child who plucked your last nerve? I know there are many witnesses. Praying without kneeling was difficult to digest at first, since I thought it to be the highest reverence unto God to get on bended knees to pray. I had to grow to realize how imperative it is to show God great reverence at all times, even as troublesome days call for us to pray at all times and in all positions; standing, sitting, eating, jogging, working, etc.

We must learn to pray at all times, even though there will be moments we may not be able to actually get on our knees, or go into any closet. The Bible says, "Rejoice evermore. Pray without ceasing. In every thing give thanks: for this is the will of God in Christ Jesus concerning you" *(I Thessalonians 5:16-18).* Oh, the great power we receive when we live in the Word and not just move our mouths to man's ungodliness.

I can remember one of my first and most powerful prayers, which was at eight and some months old. I was a very perceptive child who saw that the world listened to persons who had riches. Of course I knew nothing about Solomon's prayer and his wealth, but I did pray, verbatim, "Lord make me rich like a King so people will listen to me talk about You." A prayer I shall never forget. Oh, what a prayer, especially for a child of such an age. This is a prayer which made me later realize how God will answer prayers and supplications in His time and His own way. He has given me a richness in the truth, spirit and context of His Word; thus people with a truthful hunger are eager to listen to me talk about Him.

As just mentioned, you must watch what you pray to receive when you become a prayer warrior, because you not only may receive it, but it may not come the way you think. Yet, I am ever so thankful!

Submission: His Grace and His Mercy

The second most powerful prayer I prayed not too long after the first was, "Show me everything there is about life." Oh boy! The remembrance of that prayer hit me like a rock as my life went through trials and tribulations in childhood and in my young adult years. The grateful lesson learned about prayer and God was that as a child of God, whom God bends ear toward, I must be careful of those things for which I pray. Amazing that I did not have to be told of that life-aged adage once I had grown to be a young adult. I personally learned the lesson of that adage as God granted numerous prayer requests only to later find I was ill-prepared to receive of them, or they turned out to be things I did not truly desire after all. Many of us can attest to regretting receiving of some things we have asked, just as I grew to realize I did not want to see all this world had to offer. The Lord will show His providence and His eminence even to the tune of our hind sight; which we know to be 20/20. Amazing how God will reveal Himself and His Word to those who diligently seek Him with a pure heart. "Blessed are the pure in heart: for they shall see God" *(Matthew 5:8).*

I have since recanted on that prayer, asking for God's great mercy. I truly had no idea of knowing for what I had prayed, but as time went on I truly found out just how dangerous it can be to pray; quite painfully at times I might add. Again, this is why I've found it so essential to ask for God's grace and mercy upon praying, so as to inform the Lord that we are submissive unto His will and that we truly do not know for what to pray. It essentially says to God, "This is what I ask, but give me Your grace and mercy by not granting it unto me if I'm not ready, or give me Your grace and mercy if You decide to put-it-on-me."

So understand, I have been a prayer warrior for some time; and even more profoundly from the age of ten. My desire today is to do God's will by empowering you, His people, to become prayer warriors while moving you closer to Him relationally and spiritually. These *Progression of Prayer Elements*™ are designed to do that very thing. They are pregnant with power, but you must do more than just read in order to gain the power. You must institute these *Prayer Elements* into your prayers and your living in order to transform both. The later is often more crucial than the former, yet both are important just the same.

Finding a Community's Transformation

In a quest to increase faith and worship unto God, diligence was given to find and digest the wisdom which gives clear direction toward greater fellowship with Him. The quest left me with little more than additional definitions along with non-scripturally supported and out of context theologies of those who clearly lacked strong and affecting personal relationships with the Lord.

There I seemed befuddled as I became aware of a reason the current state of the Church continues to weaken and falter amidst scholars who continue to impress us with liturgical knowledge void of much applicable substance. So much of our community and Christian education has been based upon a mentality of, "I've got mine, now you have to get yours." The Spirit then led me to believe that not all educators and teachers have purposely withheld pertinent empowering information. Instead, some solely understand the Biblical concepts, but lack the application knowledge needed to convert the information into sheer spiritual power and wisdom. It reminded me of Romans 10:14-15a, "How then shall they call on him in whom they have not believed? and how shall they believe in him of whom they have not heard? and how shall they hear without a preacher? And how shall they preach, except they be sent?"

The sad thing is that some leaders do withhold information from those who desire to get closer to the Lord, so to sustain their supposed power; in attempts to be gods themselves and without discerning the Lord's body. The Bible tells us, "For as the body without the spirit is dead, so faith without works is dead also" _(James 2:26)_. So, here the Spirit presents this document, intended not only to inform the reader, but to empower the believer with a spiritual renewal. A spiritual renewal and strengthening to make the devil mad and quake in his boots. A strong prayer warrior will give fear to the devil. There's not many things more dangerous to the devil than a prayer warrior who has a strong tie and submissive connection with the Almighty.

We ought give God thanks in advance for the blessings that shall be bestowed upon our living and our prayers. Oh, I personally praise His holy name for the great increase that awaits our hearing within these pages. Oh, the blessings He is going to rest upon us.

We live in a church climate where there are so many who want to have strong faith but do not see the fruit within the existing structure of Biblical teachings, nor do they see strength in the current forms of worship. I do not necessarily fault those who seek the Lord by circumventing what they do not currently believe, and I do not necessarily lay blame to those who have faltered in their teachings. That being said, I truly believe the issue is that the old stuff, as some would call it, does actually work, but persons have lacked the ability and/or the spirit to convey the power within. God stands ready to bless those who seek Him in truth and not in fashion. The fashion for the day is not always what is right. "The Lord looked down from heaven upon the children of men, to see if there were any that did understand, and seek God" _(Psalm 14:2)._

Fact is, every time something does not first work for some of us we tend to automatically resort to starting something new, or try diligently to change what exist. The same happens in the Church, whereas people who do not see the fruit immediately, either, jump ship to start something new rather than seek the truth and the power within what exist (the old), or they will viciously and wickedly war to change what exist. We need not start anew nor fight to change what exist. We need to learn how to use the old stuff. Let me say it again. We need to truthfully find out how the old stuff works, before we go starting new stuff. The problem lies in the fact that most of us do not know how to apply the old stuff to our lives; thus we falter and we fall. This document is intended to reveal some of the power of the Gospel so we may correctly apply the Word to our living and our prayers. New is not wrong in some instances, but let us take a full examination of all we have missed in the context of what currently exist within the foundation of Biblical truths and what God set forth.

Spirit led Success!

This document is heavily based in scripture and spirit, of course. Being so based is not only right for everything we do, but such a basis will connect the readers to God's great Holy Spirit. It is in this connection where believers gain the power, not just for knowing, but for the putting into use or application. Today's world is filled with so many who lack strength and hope, which includes even those who call themselves believers in Christ. Many times we cannot tell the difference between those who merely claim to believe in Christ and those who do not, simply due to their similarities of their lacking in power and in hope. These persons have an inability to hope which transfers into their incapability to perform greater works, as well. Our Lord and Savior said, "Verily, verily, I say unto you, he that believeth on me, the works that I do shall he do also; and greater works than these shall he do; because I go unto my Father" _(John 14:12)._ Sadly, many of our works are rendered hopeless and minuscule for a lack of spiritual power. Is it any question why this generation has not seen great works? It can be mostly attributed to our lack of power based in scripture and our lack in spiritual hope or faith.

So many supposed believers in Christ have absolutely no power to make it through even the smallest of crisis. If we as believers are to be the light and salt of the earth, please tell me why our spirits are more dimly lit than fading car headlights operating on a drained battery and spent alternator? If I may answer the question by simply saying, they sorely lack in the spiritual linkage that gains believers access to the victories of life. I am so absolutely sure that each person reading this document desires to have more victories in their lives. Don't we all! Oh, I surely desire more victories as well. There are not too many things better than a victory or "W."

This document will enlighten readers how to have the victory every time! So, buckle that seat belt and pray for God to open your heart, mind, spirit and soul to receive this empowering document and the *Progression of Prayer Elements* ™ Go ahead and say it now, "devil get behind me." The accuser satan cannot do a thing about the power you are about to receive by the Spirit of God. Communicating with God can be boring or exhilarating, depending upon our approach. It is the design of this document to transition readers into a spiritual excitement for communicating with God. We should be excited to talk with God and hear from Heaven. Oh, the blessing in hearing His voice. Oh, what great blessing it is to receive direction from our Saviour and His Spirit. The joy to be in His presence! Oh, the great joy. We may already be dead if we cannot get excited to converse with God. How can we not get excited about going into fellowship with the One who created us? How can we not burst at the seams excited to go into communion with a Lord and Saviour who laid down His very life for us? "Greater love hath no man than this, that a man lay down his life for his friends" *(John 15:13)*. "For when we were yet without strength, in due time Christ died for the ungodly. For scarcely for a righteous man will one die: yet peradventure for a good man some would even dare to die. But God commendeth His love toward us, in that, while we were yet sinners, Christ died for us" *(Romans 5:6-8)*. In knowing this very fact, how can we not shout His glory and be ecstatic to enter into His presence? It is the duty of this document to evolve the readers into prayer warriors who are on fire to walk with God! "So shall my word be that goeth forth out of my mouth: it shall not return unto me void, but it shall accomplish that which I please, and it shall prosper in the thing whereto I sent it" *(Isaiah 55:11)*.

The Holy Spirit: the Charger for Our Change

A child of God should not be at ease if they have not heard from the Master. The Master is the charger to our spirit's battery pack. A child of God's Spirit is truly weakened and often times made to be dead when not hearing from the very Spirit of God. That Spirit of uplift. That Spirit of revival. That sustaining Spirit. Oh, just to hear a word from Him. Just one word from the Master changes everything. Best believe we all can use some change in our lives. A transforming change is what we all stand in need, if nothing else. King Hezekiah came to understand this fact, as can be read in II Kings 20:1-6. He was about to die, but prayer was made unto God and everything changed. The Lord heard the cry, and sent Isaiah back to the king to tell him God was adding 15 years to his life. Not only did God add the years to his life, but He also blessed his living by removing an enemy threat and defending the land and the people.

Best believe a word from God changes the dead into life. Just a word from Heaven changes darkness into light. A blessed word from the Lord changes midnight into day. Tears into joy. Meandering into purpose. For our change alone we should be excited to communicate with the Almighty. His Spirit is excitement. He is still in the miracle working business and He truly has compassion for His children. The Word tells us, "For the eyes of the Lord run to and fro throughout the whole earth, to shew himself strong in the behalf of them whose heart is perfect toward him" *(II Chronicles 16:9a)*. He is willingly enthused to come see about our situations, so how much more should we be excited to prop our ears to hear from Him? Our transformation will not occur until we have submitted unto His will and began to eagerly seek His word in truth and in spirit.

Oh, I get excited to know He hears my faintest cry. "For the eyes of the Lord are over the righteous, and his ears are open unto their prayers ..." *(I Peter 3:12).* It's a blessing in itself for believers to truly know we have someone who is attentive to our cries. Many of our lives are void of a person who we can truly call on and who can truly do something about our situations. On top of that, there are those of us who may have folk who will listen to our cries, but surely not willing to do anything about our situations. We live in a society where every calamity has Viral Video potential, versus ministering possibilities. Still and yet many others we may call on for help have volumes of their own issues and do not have the capacity to add our concerns onto their long list of issues. But God! But God! God not only has a long list, but He is long suffering. He is also omnipresent. As He is now helping our neighbors, His arms are more than long enough to outstretch in our situations, as well.

The question of the hour is, "How can we effectively pray to God without being in the Spirit to pray?" It's truly befuddling that many think its possible to drop a quick or thoughtless prayer unto God and still expect Him to respond in their favor. If I could drop a pen here for a moment. We discuss discernment and direction in *Element #5* where it is illustrated how we need to be respectful of the Lord's "No's" and His "Maybe's." That being said, the bulk of our frustrations that arise out of our prayers occur when it seems God does not answer or when He simply says no. We must be discerning of God's attributes and nature in order to minimize and possibly eliminate our falling out of love with Him. We discuss God's attributes and nature after the chapters of the *8 Elements of Prayer.* There is nothing wrong with how God responds to our prayers, for He is God. The issues arise out of our lack of knowledge of God's attributes, which would otherwise give us a greater capability to accept all of His various answers to our prayers; likewise, giving us victory in any case.

It was mentioned in an earlier paragraph that we can gain victory every time we pray! Our knowing God's nature and attributes is the major foundation for such a rate of success in prayer. This document will provide us with the wisdom and the spirited increase to be able to find victory even through the "nos," "maybes" and the "waits" set forth by God. Many do not accept God as He is, or wholly, simply due to their not knowing who He is through His nature, attributes and character. Many others are atheistic in their views as their disbeliefs are often rooted in their personal experiences with God being less than what they expected. Fact is their expectations and experiences with God would be transformed and improved if they truly knew who He is and how He operates through His character. If we knew the Lord's character we would realize and accept things like His being immutable; as He never changes. It is due to our lack of knowledge of His character that we become disappointed in our faith walks, then we begin to forsake Him, thereafter. Do not forsake the section on God's attributes, character and nature, for the section will profoundly prepare the spirit for much of what is taught in this document.

Now, back to our point about quick and thoughtless prayers. Not to say it takes a certain amount of time in prayer in order to hear from Heaven, but I will profess boldly that it does take being in the Spirit. Sometimes hearing from the Lord does take a bit of time, whereas it always takes effort. The time it takes truly depends on the existing condition of the believer's spirit and relationship with God. A weak spiritual and devotional relationship with God demands more time and effort to hear from Him in prayer. Anything less may not bear fruit nor blessings. A devoted spiritual life makes it easier to be in the spirit while praying, but never is it totally easy. Do not make the mistake in thinking that prayer does not always take effort and heart.

It pains me to know the amount of people who lack the ability to effectively pray. People would be more diligent in prayer if they only knew the power prayer warriors hold in their combat war chest. It would seem easy to most, as many writers on the topic of prayer have done, to take up the breadth of this book to give illustrations of prayers prayed and prayers answered. On the contrary, it is the Spirit's desire that this document produce 100,000 strong and true prayer warriors instead of merely giving praise reports of how others have been successful in their prayers. This document will site illustrations and Biblical characters in regards to prayer, but more importantly readers will be given foundational basis, keys and precepts to build their strength in prayer. A quest of this document is to develop you, yes you, as a prayer warrior, strong and productive for the Kingdom of God. Half-hearted and ineffective prayers are what this document seeks to remedy, along with increasing reader's general spirituality with the Lord. Understand, prayers are often rendered ineffective simply by our ineffectual spiritual conditions. Throughout this document we shall reiterate, "God is a Spirit; and they that worship him must worship him in spirit and in truth" *(John 4:24).*

Hope Makes all the Difference

This document of prayer is so necessary and on time, for we live in perilous times. Daily we are confronted with ordeals and circumstances that test our nerves and grieve our spirits. Many of us have fallen short of sustaining through trying times simply due to an inability to pray. The electronic age has miniaturized our world and left us less patient with all of life and less eager to take precious moments to pray. Likewise, the quality of life has increased for a majority of us, while our spiritual lives have continued to diminish. This statement can be proof testified by surveying the lack of hope that permeates every age group and every corner of our society. A life lacking in prayer is often a life lacking in hope. Much of this society's turmoils have stemmed from individuals lacking hope that there is a bright side somewhere. The hopeful and spirited in Christ Jesus may not be able to physically see where the light is shining, but they have faith in knowing that it is shining, or going to shine, somewhere. We all need to develop that "somewhere" type of spirit in order to become stronger in our prayer lives. Let it be known here today, there are times when the only way to get to the "somewhere" is by first having hope that the "somewhere" truly exist. See, if our faith does not tell our spirit that "somewhere" truly exist, our hope will lack the ability to sustain until "somewhere" comes about. This plight we face in the depths of our hope is especially true amongst today's children who are growing in a me-ism society. This is a me-ism society which continues to displace God and prayer into a corner called "Inconsequential."

Simply put, we have lost faith in answered prayers. The wars that continue to plague our streets and countries seem, at least to the naked and spiritless eye, bigger than any God and loom larger than any prayer. But, I am here today to declare that God is still in full control, and He has not left the throne of grace! Too many so called Christians have fallen pray to the wiles of the devil because they first lost their faith and hope in "somewhere." Becoming a prayer warrior demands that we have hope that believes in victory when the circumstances scream of impossibilities. This is a strong *key* for us all. As prayer warriors we must have ingrained (7) in our spirits, minds and souls, "But Jesus beheld them, and said unto them. With men this is impossible; but with God all things are possible" *(Matthew 19:26).* As prayer warriors we must have entrenched into the fabric of our faith, "For with God nothing shall be impossible" *(Luke 1:37).* We will have a difficult time becoming of the 100,000 strong prayer warriors if we are lacking in hope in any way, shape or fashion. But, God has a way of fixing that condition as well.

Our metaphorical "somewhere" represents our vision of tomorrow and beyond. As prayer warriors we must have hope. Not just any hope, but a hope built upon faith in the Lord. A hymn writer penned, "My faith is built on nothing less, than Jesus blood and righteousness." The "less" is our having faith in ourselves. What happens on those days when we are feeling less than able? The Bible says, "And Jesus answering saith unto them, Have faith in God. For verily I say unto you, That whosoever shall say unto this mountain, Be thou removed, and be thou cast into the sea: and shall not doubt in his heart, but shall believe that those things which he saith shall come to pass; he shall have whatsoever he saith. Therefore I say unto you, What things soever ye desire, when ye pray, believe that ye receive them, and ye shall have them" *(Mark 11:22-24).*

To believe in our meager abilities outside of our mere ability to pray will leave us inept each and every time we are in need. On the contrary, if we put our trust in the Lord, our hope shall receive power and sustainability. It's easy to see how little faith some people have in God by seeing how little hope they have in their tomorrow. Faith in God and hope for tomorrow are connected at the hip. "Now, faith is the substance of things hoped for, the evidence of things not seen" *(Hebrews 11:1).* It's impossible to truly have faith in God and not exhibit hope in tomorrow. Prayer is built upon our faith and hope in the Lord's power and in who He is. Mastering this document's *8 Elements of Prayer Progression*™ will make it easier to have a spirit of faith in communicating with God.

Our hope is not only built upon our strength in the Word, but it is more so dependant on our strength in the truth of the Word. In other words, we would have stronger hope if we would wrap ourselves in the truth of His Word and not be concerned with only reciting His Word. I am even speaking to those preachers and teachers of God's Word who minister the Word unto others by voice, but their ministry by actions speak of a different language. Hear me on this. Many people, even those who are carnal, can recite God's Word; for some people truly have good memories, while others simply have bad intentions from the start. But, let the wind start to blow and the waves begin to bellow and those very folk turn high tail to the hills, weeping and crying and gnashing their teeth. This occurs mostly because the Word was not securely affixed to their spirits; thus hope was a fickle care wisped away like tumble weed in a western desert. "And when he sowed, some seeds fell by the way side, and the fowls came and devoured them up: some fell upon stony places, where they had not much earth: and forthwith they sprung up, because they had no deepness of earth: And when the sun was up, they were scorched; and because they had no root, they withered away. And some fell among thorns; and the thorns sprung up, and choked them:" *(Matthew 13:4-7)*. Take this moment to pull out your Bibles and read the short verses of Matthew 13:1-30 so you may get a greater understanding of the type of seed and ground you may be harvesting.

This document will later speak on how our churches are bent on learning the Word without any regard to the believer's spiritual condition. Fact is, we can learn the Word verbatim from Genesis to Revelation, able to recite every jot and every tittle, yet our spirits can be in total disarray or simply jacked up. Such a spirit obliterates and makes useless all the memorizations and verse studies. There must be a change for us to make changes.

Hope will demand that we truly affix the Word of God unto solid ground within our spirits. Hope will encourage our spirits to say, "And again, I will put my trust in him" *(Hebrews 2:13a)*, and "But thanks be to God, which giveth us the victory through our Lord Jesus Christ" *(I Corinthians 15:57)*. Our hearts and mouths cannot truthfully shout of those victorious words without having hope in Him who gives all things good. Likewise, our prayers will remain shallow and ineffective until we fill our spirits with the hope of Christ successfully working in us, and through us.

The Hope to Have Vision

Most prayer warriors are given visions before, during and/or after we pray. Believers will indeed be driven to be more attentive in prayer once we firmly believe we will be given visions upon praying. It should be our greatest hope that God will give us a vision or direction to help us in our living and/or current situation. It is this ability to see a way through which builds hope. Hebrews 11:1 was mentioned just a moment ago, thus we are not now speaking in contradiction to the Word. No sir and no ma'am! This sight that we now speak of is a seeing through a spiritual connection with God; seeing that He is able, capable and willing to come see about our circumstances, conditions and needs.

Prayer warriors have spiritual eyes stayed on the power and will of God. God gives prayer warriors glimpses of things to come. Those glimpses alone can strengthen our hope in ways beyond comprehension. "But as it is written, Eye hath not seen, nor ear heard, neither have entered into the heart of man, the things which God hath prepared for them that love him. But God hath revealed them unto us by his Spirit: for the Spirit searcheth all things, yea, the deep things of God" *(I Corinthians 2:9-10).* Likewise, this *Powerful Prayer Progression for Prayer Warriors*™ has been given unto me by the Spirit of God in order to reveal a few mysteries of His great power available to all who believe and live in hope of His power.

100,000 Making Effectual Changes

Parents and adults alike have begun to give up on controls and morals that kept us safe and out of harms way in the past. Many of our officials and leaders have even accepted societal ills and their personal corrupt ways as the norms for today. So where do we turn? The answer is, there is only one direction to turn. We must turn unto the Lord in prayer. "Is anything too hard for God?" *(Genesis 18:14a).* Surely not, thus we must turn to Him for healing of the perversive ills of today.

Those who pray effectively and effectually have the ability to change the ways of a world gone savage. Effectual prayer has the ability to change everything in our lives. Make no mistake a prayerless life is a powerless life. People often wonder why their lives meander without cause, blown in the winds of today's plights. Well, hear me now. There is power available to help direct our lives, and that power resides in effectual prayer. Many of us even sing, "Prayer changes things," and yet nothing ever changes in our lives. Our lives will continue to move aimlessly when we pray ineffectually.

On the other hand, prayer warriors pray with a purpose. We must go into prayer with a purpose and a plan. That plan, for a prayer warrior, is to get into the presence of the Almighty and gain His attention upon the matter we bring forth. "The effectual fervent prayer of a righteous man availeth much" *(James 5:16b).* The "effectual" portion of the verse speaks of our zeal, passion and eagerness to enter into the presence of the Lord in pursuit of a purpose, while the "righteous" part refers to our living at a standard of morality that is acceptable unto the Lord. This document addresses both matters with the intent to elevate our prayers and our living to a level of great power and strength. Yes, this document is gonna make the devil mad, but he can't do a thing about it. The power is being released and the saints are being empowered for battle. The Lord has given me a vision: effectual prayer being conducted by 100,000 strong warriors; miracles and extraordinary occurrences coming forth; a glimpse of the Lords power revealed; the Earth avowing its purpose; the Lord's glory sounding with great brilliance. Let you be of the number who are powerful and effectual.

Dependence and Subjection

Entering into prayer shows our dependance on the Lord and demonstrates how much we are subjected unto His desires. When we pray, if praying in the spirit, we reveal our need for God's hand in our lives. This subjection can also be termed as a "turning ourselves and our situations over to God." The healings, the deliverances and the blessings do not truly begin until we allow our lives to be directed by God, and God alone. We must be subjected unto God while in prayer and in living, otherwise we will position ourselves outside His desires, unable to effectively hear Him speak.

We surely become connected more closely to God when we pray with submissive spirits and hearts. It is through this type of submissive union that we even become more sensitized to His speaking. Oh, to hear from the Lord. The more we submit unto God, the more our hearing is heightened and sensitized. The more we hear His voice the greater our interests join with His desires. The blessings will flow through our lives as sweet honey within such a distinctive communion. Chapters within this document shall further help us get into the spirit of submission, with gladness in our hearts.

How might we be directed by God less we can hear from God? We are to open our hearing by becoming sensitized through our subjection unto God. So often, Christians and the unsaved alike, claim that God no longer speaks to this world. But, I am here to declare that God still speaks even in this evil day. The issue has become that we are not sensitized to the level needed to hear Him speak. The Lord continues to speak through many people, means and vessels, but people of today refuse to release control of their very beings unto Him. Our world and its people have become so centered on individualism that we lack the will to live within God's plan. "Furthermore we have had fathers of our flesh which corrected us, and we gave them reverence: shall we not much rather be in subjection unto the Father of spirits, and live? For they verily for a few days chastened us after their own pleasure; but he for our profit, that we might be partakers of his holiness" *(Hebrews 12:9-10)*. Too many people feel its not cool to not be in control. It seems not in style to permit someone else to drive our car called life; the very car we so think we own. The sooner we realize that our lives are not our own, the sooner we will be able to submit unto God's control; thus become better connected to Him. This is a *key* which will release God's power within our lives.

Know and understand God created us, gave us all we possess and has the power to decide all that we shall become. Before we pray we ought to truly understand and commit to believe He is God and God alone. Once we begin to truthfully believe that fact we shall then begin the necessary step of submitting unto Him in spirit. We must believe in order to submit. We must submit in order to pray. And, we must pray in order to be blessed. This is another *key* we must secure within our spirits this very moment. It is difficult at best to move forward in strong prayer without this key being settled in our spirits. "Submit yourselves therefore to God. Resist the devil, and he will flee from you. Draw nigh to God, and he will draw nigh to you" *(James 4:7-8a)*. We shall shout glory to God for the deliverance and victory made possible by our dependence upon Him.

Excitement to Walk With the Lord

I am so excited for all to read and receive the blessings of this document. We all shall be blessed in our faith walks, and in our prayer lives after digesting this document. I truly get elated and overjoyed when I think of all the ways we shall be blessed in our walks with God. We all should be excited to see the change in our world once 100,000 true prayer warriors take position. What a glorious day it is going to be when the face of this world shines eager to pray in all of life.

This writing will not only increase the fruitfulness of our prayer experiences, but it will motivate our faith walks, also. We will not only be motivated to get closer to God, but we will be further stimulated to walk with Him. See, many of us do not mind getting closer to the Lord, but most of us do not want to then walk with Him. Walking with Him takes a larger commitment than just getting closer to Him. Let me make this a little more plain. Too many of us want to get just close enough to receive a blessing from Him, but will not take His hand thereafter. Taking His hand calls for us to change our ways and change our walk.

This document shall truly give us an eagerness to want to take the Lord's hand and walk with Him in spirit and in truth. If we are to worship Him, why not worship Him in the way the Bible prescribes and even commands of us? Half-hearted worship may not even benefit us with half-hearted blessings. Our true blessings are in our having strong relationships with the Father, and not necessarily in the so called "things" He provides unto us. We promote the blessings of His joy, peace, love and providence in our lives when we worship Him in spirit and truth. Just to have His presence in our lives ought truly be our goal! This document goes into further depth as to what should be constituted as real blessings. The elevation of our spirits to recognize true blessings is alone a huge deliverance for our prayer lives. In that recognition we are sure to find a blessed transition in our faith walks, just as we are sure to witness increase in the rate of victories in our prayer lives, as well.

The Approach of an Introduction

Here we say "Introduction" with a two-fold approach. First, introduction to this document, which shall bless our prayer lives and spiritual living, alike. This document shall introduce *Elements* that will elevate our spiritual beings and strengthen our relationships with the Lord. Second, this document presents to some an introduction to prayer, and to others a strengthened level of prayer. Most of us know of prayer but do not truly live in prayer. Big difference. Just knowing of something does not constitute living within it. Just as many know of the Lord, but some do not truly live within Him; nor He in them. Just as we are called to practice our faith we must put into practice prayer lives strong unto the Lord. Practicing the faith is stimulated by a prayer life that is reliant on the power of the Lord. Faith built in the knowledge of our Lord having all power to do all things stimulates believers to communicate with Him on a regular basis. In essence, we have often asked the question, "What would I do if I could not speak to the Lord?" If you have never asked that question, it is the duty of this document to drive you toward the asking. For all who have asked that question, this document shall further solidify and strengthen your need to call on the name of the Lord in prayer.

It does not take a Master's Degree in Quantum Field Theology (Physics) to know that far too many of us just do not pray, and those of us who do pray do not spend enough quality time in actual prayer. I would be remiss not to mention, there are even others of us who spend time in prayer, but are ineffective therein. That ineffectiveness is partly due to us not having been taught how to pray; so we babble in prayer and we falter in life. How essential must prayer be if the disciples made a point to ask Jesus to teach them how to pray? "And it came to pass, that, as He was praying in a certain place, when He ceased, one of His disciples said unto Him, Lord, teach us to pray, as John also taught his disciples" *(Luke 11:1)*.

Understand, the disciples had prayed previously, but there came this point when they realized the difference between a babbling prayer, which benefits little if nothing, and that of effectual prayer that is life changing. How long must we also live lives of babbling unto the Lord before coming to the realization that our spiritual lives are being rendered ineffective by an inability to fruitfully communicate with Him? There is so little fruit in some of our lives as result of our impotent prayer lives. It is this document's aim to change the face of the way we pray, so the many who have waited desperately to get a prayer through to God can now pray with purpose, power and success. Now is the time to learn the *Powerful Prayer Progression Elements*™ that follow within this document. In doing so, we shall embark upon a new and strengthened fellowship with God aimed at bringing about changes and victories. I can envision God's joy as this document is being poured unto a new generation of prayer warriors; the young and the older.

Having Excitement for Prayer

Prayer is a great communal experience with the Lord. We should be ever so excited to go unto Him with a heart full of joy. Yes joy! No matter the concern which drives us into prayer we should have great joy in our hearts and spirits about our entering into communion with the Lord. First of all, there is no greater exercise to embark upon. Some may refute this from the bowls of their fleshly compassions, but what can be better than to have a little talk with Jesus? It should bring a shout of glory to our spirits. Just to speak to Him makes most things alright. Many are the pains that would dissipate and even disappear if we would simply remember to have a little talk with the Lord. The comfort in knowing He is listening is in itself great relief. The pleasure to know He cares and stands near is reassuring to the soul. To stand in His presence is to have great consolation and encouragement, as well. Do you remember the last time you had something that weighed heavy on your mind, and found that it all faded away as soon as you took it to the Lord in prayer? Your tears were then dried. Your heart became calm. Your smile returned.

The Bible declares, "Thou wilt keep him in perfect peace, whose mind is stayed on thee: because he trusteth in thee. Trust ye in the Lord Jehovah is everlasting strength" *(Isaiah 26:3-4)*. What better way is there to keep our minds stayed on Him than that of entering into His presence for communion? It is so exciting to know when the devil gives me a fit I can in turn give him a fit by entering into the presence of the Lord to capture perfect peace.

It is every intent that this document give increase to your excitement to communicate with the Lord, just as it has totally enthused me while receiving it from Him. I can truly say my heart did burn *(Luke 24:32)* as this was poured unto me, and it is hoped that you will exclaim the same upon your reading.

The Pain of Not Calling on the Lord

The fact is, we need to remember it is so very important to carry our concerns to God more quickly during our trials and tribulations. The trials may not be rectified immediately, but the headaches, migraines, eyelid pressures and heart palpitations can be minimized and eventually eliminated by merely conversing with the Lord. "Oh what needless pains we bear, just because we do not carry everything to God in prayer." The writer of this hymn does not say anything about the trials themselves, necessarily. We can more so construe this stanza as speaking of the pains associated with the trials; such as the agony, heartache and distress that often wreck the body, heart and mind. These are the effects of the trial. Often the release of the agony and distress is enough to bide us some additional mental and physical freedom until we get through the actual trial.

Let's make it a little more plain. The trial sometimes is not the true pain. Sometimes it is the stress that is attached to that trial which breaks us to our knees. The trial caused the effect (pain) which in turn caused the headache and the stress. In affect, praying unto the Lord then affords us a cushion of mental and physical relief by having His comforting hand upon our situations. For most of us there have been times when the Lord has had His calming hand upon our hearts and minds long enough that we did not lose it all in the meanwhile of Him working out our actual trial or tribulation.

We all need a little relief sometimes; for the devil will attempt to push us beyond the edge of despair. The devil's every attempt is to harm us, whether it is by his hands, his mouth or by us doing his dirty work for him. We do hurt ourselves at times by allowing our situations to get the best of us. That is the reason it is so important to imperative that we stay connected to the great Comforter through prayer. The great Spirit of God is passionate about our well being. He knows we do not have the ability to secure our own comfort and joy, so He makes Himself available; especially in and through prayer.

Comfort - the First Order of Business

A prayer warrior does not hesitate to call on the Lord; whether day or night, rain or shine, low or high. Calling on the Lord is the first order of business for a prayer warrior in any situation. He or she knows that the Lord's covering of comfort is needed while He puts His plan of action upon their concerns. They do not underestimate that the Lord's timing for deliverance or blessing may not be immediate, yet they are faithful to believe the great covering of God will appear at any moment once they go into prayer to hand the situation over to Him. Some folk would harm themselves if God's sedative (comfort) was not provided for the headaches that come with some issues. Some folk would have heart attacks if God's sedative (comfort) was not applied to soothe their chest's eruptions until the storms pass. Others would simply give up on fighting the good fight of faith *(1 Timothy 6:12)* if God's sedative were not abundantly, unfailingly and constantly available to all who call upon Him in prayer and to all who wilfully receive of His Spirit.

It is so imperative to understand how important it is for us to call unto the Lord in prayer initially for the comfort. Yes, we all want and need deliverance, but we will not survive till the deliverance comes if He does not first cover us with comfort for our souls, spirits and bodies. This is a *key.* As prayer warriors, let it be our prayer's first mention that the Spirit bring comfort. Do not forsake this key and precept, so troubling times will be less painful and less traumatic; for most trauma comes from being uncovered by His comfort.

Let me further explain why it is so essential to immediately ask the Lord for comfort. There are great blessings awaiting us all, but there are some things we must go through in order to receive them. I Peter 5:10 says it best, "... after that ye have suffered a while, make you perfect, stablish, strengthen, settle you." Most of us want the prize, but we want to avoid the pain. I can imagine we would better bear the pain if we knew the price, time frame and full extent of the pain. For example, if someone gave you the chance to endure ten minutes of pain to receive ten million dollars, you could condition your mind and body to handle it. Yes, come back to reality, cause neither the time frame nor the pain's extent is known in most situations; just as the prize is often vague, as well. Not knowing is a part of what makes the pain and trial a little tough to handle.

I Peter 5:10 does explain that we will — let me repeat — we will go through some times of suffering in order to reach some victories. This may sound far fetched for some disbelievers, but I Peter 5:1-11 sounds, to me, like that ten minutes for ten million dollars. If you receive that you surely have faith the size of a grain of a mustard seed *(Matthew 17:20)*. My faith tells me the treasures of the Lord far outweigh the gold and silver of the earth. My faith tells me the Lord Himself is my ten million dollars even while going through the ten minutes of pain; and there it is!

Nehemiah is a good example of how we should pray for the Lord to help us make it through, instead of praying to be immediately delivered out of the situation or task. Nehemiah had a task to accomplish even amidst all the persecutions, lies and attacks. He prayed, "Now therefore, O God, strengthen my hands" *(Nehemiah 6:9b)* instead of requesting that God provide a way out. He had to go through his metaphorical "ten minutes of pain" to ensure the completion of the wall being built; thus God's will being done. There are some things we, just as Nehemiah, are simply going to have to go through in order to see the victory. The Lord Jesus said it this way unto His disciples, "... Pray that ye enter not into temptation" *(Luke 22:40)*. As the disciples and Nehemiah found, it is not always easy walking on the Lord's side. Therefore, we must ask Him up front for comfort and strength to make it through till the deliverance or blessing comes into fruition; and sometimes thereafter, as well.

Empowering

This document will empower our prayer lives as well as strengthen our spiritual living. Oh, its gonna be a blessing, so let us open our tent doors, oh Israel, to receive a great blessing that is going to transform our lives! How might we otherwise live in the way our Lord proclaimed unto His disciples and us, "Do not enter into temptation?" Someone who babbles in prayer will most times fail tests presented unto them in their living. This document is presented unto us by the Spirit of God so we may be able to withstand the wiles of the devil and sustain through the trials that will surely blow strong and destructive winds in our lives. Woe unto the man or woman who is unable to become empowered by the Spirit of Christ through prayer.

I truly shed tear for all who have been left unarmed and exposed. We cannot fight the good fight of faith without our most powerful weapon. Many claim the Word as their most powerful weapon for warfare, and thus they spend a spiritual lifetime memorizing scripture and learning those coined phrases of a fair weathered Bible toting church member. I present to some and introduce to others that it is the Word who is our most essential weapon: the Word our Lord Jesus the Christ. It is the Lord who is our most essential warfare weapon. Most of the dramatic battles that come our way will not be fought by us. Hear me on this. Not one of us is so strong that we can fight against those major ordeals that kick up the most dust and turmoil. Those very battles, and others, will be defeated by the hand of the Almighty on our behalf. So, how might we have success against those tremors and earthquakes if we lack the ability to effectively call on the Lord for our empowerment and deliverance? It is the Lord's Spirit's distribution of this document's precepts that shall empower us to have victories beyond thought and beyond imagination.

More Time Spent on the Mainline

It can be asked of many of us "Where is your faith?" _(Luke 8:25a)_. Many of us are weak in our faith as an effect of our lack in prayer. Our faith would be much stronger if our prayer lives were much stronger. Little prayer produces little power and little faith. This "little" spoken of is what causes our lives to meander between belief and disbelief, just as it causes our living to so shift and sway. Our lives would be transformed and our spirits empowered if we would only spend more prayer time with the Father. Churches large and small preach their congregant's increase in faith, yet never give the direction nor the empowering tools to accomplish that very daunting task. This document stands in the gap to empower and encourage. So, open your tent doors and receive from the Lord.

Prayer is our mainline communication with God and must not be taken lightly. Our lives have been rendered ineffective and this world continues to become more corrupt due to the inadequate amount of time we spend in prayer. "If only my people, which are called by my name, shall humble themselves, and pray, and seek my face, and turn from their wicked ways; then will I hear from Heaven, and will forgive their sin, and will heal their land" _(II Chronicles 7:14)_. The degradation of our spirits, bodies, minds, lands, communities and society will continue until we see the need to commune with the Lord on a more regular and more deeply spiritual basis. The Lord is not at all happy with a generation of people who seek this world more than it seeks His presence.

Not only must we take the time to pray, but we must truly spend quality time with the Lord. Communing with Him takes more than just carving out some time from our schedules to give unto Him. It takes more than having a scheduled hour of ritualistic murmurings and expressions. To the surprise of many, it even takes more than simply opening the Bible and reading scriptures. That is not the type of quality time we speak of here in this document. Quality time with the Lord begins with our allowing the Lord to open our hearts, minds, spirits and souls. It is then made full when we are moved by His Spirit.

A few minutes of speaking with the Lord each day will not cut it! To tell it all, thirty minutes per day is borderline not enough and close to shameful. "But I don't have thirty or more minutes a day to allot to prayer," is what many are now saying. How would you feel if the Lord said the same thing to you? To make it a little clearer, many of us ask for more blessings each day, yet we refuse to give God more time in prayer each day. I'm not shy to say this is simply shameful. The only occasions we tend to spare more time for God is when we are sick and in need of a healing, or when our pockets are empty and we need a bill paid. What if at those very moments the Lord told us He did not have the time to spare to come see about our needs?

Our lives have become so busy with so many things other than God. Someone is now saying, "What will I give up in order to make ample time to pray each day?" Wow! This is amazing since we should be planning our day around God, rather than planning time for God somewhere within the busyness of our days. God deserves our first. Too few of our churches today take the time to teach congregants the principles of First Fruit. "My schedule just will not allow me to spend that much time in prayer," is another statement we often make; as we still claim to love the Lord. That's the trick of the devil who makes our lives appear to be so busy that we then shift God to second, third or even twelfth on our list of things to do. How can we truly love Him when we spend so little time with Him? The simple truth is we all spend time doing those things we enjoy most. It is natural that we give more time to those people who take priority in our lives. This is one of the main reasons this document speaks so heavily on the key of our being in the spirit of prayer.

The natural man has great difficulty in switching attention away from the world in order to focus more on the Lord. We all must decide right now to give way to our spirit man; causing us to desire greater communion with the Lord. If not, we will continue to make excuses and feed the desires of our natural man. A change is in order.

Is it true that we spend so much time with others, but spend so little time with the Lord? Is it true that we spend so much time enjoying the things we are blessed to possess, like our cars, homes, families, friends and jobs; yet we spend so little time with He who bestowed the blessings upon us? Is it true that we forsake the One who has blessed us, at the same time that we heavily entertain our possessions? How can it be that we are blessed with twenty four hours in a day to enjoy all that the Lord has granted us, but find it difficult to spend at least one of those hours with the One we should love the most? It cannot be true that we love possessions and people more than we love the Lord. That statement's answer is revealed through the amount of time we spend with God versus the time we spend with the things of this world. It is as simple as it sounds.

The Bible says, "He that loveth father or mother more than me is not worthy of me: and he that loveth son or daughter more than me is not worthy of me. And he that taketh not his cross, and followeth after me, is not worthy of me. He that findeth his life shall lose it: and he that loseth his life for my sake shall find it" *(Matthew 10:37-39)*. In other words, we are not worthy to enter into the Kingdom of God if we place these things on this Earth ahead of He who created Heaven and Earth. "He that loveth his life shall lose it; and he that hateth his life in this world shall keep it unto life eternal. If any man serve me, let him follow me; and where I am, there shall also my servant be; if any man serve me, him will my Father honour" *(John 12:25-26)* What is it we love more than spending time with the Lord? I implore us this day to eliminate all those things from our lives that so distract our time and attention from the Lord.

We must be mindful to realize God may eliminate those very things we adore more than we honour Him, if we refuse to remove those things ourselves. I'm sure someone reading this today can testify to that happening to them. "Now therefore thus saith the Lord of hosts; Consider your ways. Ye have sown much, and bring little; ye eat, but ye have not enough; ye drink, but ye are not filled with drink; ye clothe you, but there is none warm; and he that earneth wages earneth wages to put it into a bag with holes. Thus saith the Lord of hosts; Consider your ways. Go up to the mountain, and bring wood, and build the house; and I will take pleasure in it, and I will be glorified, saith the Lord. Ye looked for much, and, lo, it came to little; and when ye brought it home, I did blow upon it. Why? saith the Lord of hosts. Because of mine house that is waste, and ye run every man unto his own house. Therefore the heaven over you is stayed from dew, and the earth is stayed from her fruit. I called for a drought upon the land, and upon the mountains, and upon the corn, and upon the new wine, and upon the oil, and upon that which the ground bringeth forth, and upon the men, and upon cattle, and upon all the labour of the hands" *(Haggai 1:5-11)*.

We must all grow to a point where we realize we serve a God who has control over everything; including time. Best believe the Lord will multiply our time where it is needed, if we would simply and faithfully spend more time with Him in prayer. We must commit to believe that fact right now; not later, but right now. Many of us do not spend large amounts of quality time with God because we do not truly believe in our hearts that He will make a way in all the places we seem not to have enough time. It's a faith walk. We must have more faith in God's power to provide. Another trick of the devil is he will make us believe we can control the destinies of different parts of our lives if we would simply spend more time attending to them; rather than spending that time in devotionals with the Lord believing He will give us ample time and more than enough resources to take care of those other areas and all our living.

Someone can truly testify how you have spent extra time with God, knowing some other things needed to be accomplished during that period. For the longest time thereafter you resigned to the fact that you would just have to pay the price for the things you did not get done due to the extra time spent with the Lord. But, wasn't it amazing how you later found out God had already worked things out on your behalf in regards to what you thought you should have done instead of spending that extra time with Him! The Lord has a miraculous way of taking care of all our wants and needs when we give due diligence to spend time with Him.

The more time we spend doing the Lord's will the more He provides for all the other things in our lives. "With the merciful thou wilt shew thyself merciful, and with the upright man thou wilt shew thyself upright. With the pure thou wilt shew thyself pure, and with the froward thou wilt shew thyself unsavoury" *(II Samuel 22:26-27)*. In other words, the Lord will be faithful to us if we are faithful to Him. Many of us miss out on the fullness of His faithfulness simply because we are so unfaithful to Him.

Some have questioned why God has not shown up in their situations. Some have been going through some situations for quite a while and they feel as though the Lord has still failed to show up on their behalf. Let it be known here today, it may be because the Lord knows they have not shown up for true prayer and devotionals in quite some time. In secular situations we tend to believe, "You get out what you put in." We feel the same about our relationships, friendships and marriages. So, why do we not recognize how little we devote into our devotional time unto God, while expecting greater outputs from Him? Wall Street has an acronym of ROI, which means Return On Investment. It is known on the metaphorical "Street" that there is no return if there is no investment. Let the question now be asked, "What have we invested in our relationships with the Lord, and what are we expecting as a return on our investments made?"

The next time we say, "Help us Lord," take time to ponder over what we have invested that gives us the right to call on His name. There should be a strong conviction in our spirits if we know we have not made the proper investment of time; amongst other investments. On the other hand, we can go to God in prayer with confidence and strength knowing we are not strangers to Him, if we have truthfully spent quality time with the Him. It is in that very moment that our prayers gain in power, having faith in knowing we already have the ear of the Master, because we have obediently spent ample time with Him. There has to be a moment of doubt in the minds of those persons who call out to God, but had not previously spent quality time with Him. They must have doubts that God is even available or even willing to listen to their requests. They must have doubts about their prayers being attended to by God, since they know in their hearts they have not been doing right by Him all along.

It is another trick of the devil to try to make us think we do not have to get close to God in order to get an answer from Him. The devil would have us to believe God is required to answer all our prayers. This shall be said again within the balance of this document − God is not required to do anything, so do not allow the devil's tricks to keep us separated from our God.

The Lord tells us, "If ye have faith, and doubt not, ye shall not only do this which is done to the fig tree, but also if ye shall say unto this mountain, Be thou removed, and be thou cast into the sea; it shall be done. And all things, whatsoever ye shall ask in prayer, believing, ye shall receive" *(Matthew 21:22)*. How can we finish a prayer in belief if we first doubt that the Lord even bends His ear toward our voices, due to our not holding up our end of the bargain called faithfulness? It is a sad day and a dead prayer when the person enters prayer with doubts and disbelief. It's hard enough walking in the faith when the thing we pray for is tough, but how much harder is it to believe in getting a prayer answered when we first enter prayer with doubts that the Lord is even available unto our voices. This document will further discuss additional portions of things we, as children of God, can do to strengthen our belief and prayer power. This document is surely for all who want power!

The Lord demands that we take the time to develop a relationship with Him. At one time or another we will give the Lord the attention He deserves, whether it is of our own doings or by the effects of our trials. Let me say it another way. Many of us go through trials longer than we ought, even though we go to God in prayer at the onset of our trials. The reason for our delayed deliverance is that God takes advantage of our need for Him during our trial. The Lord makes full benefit of our trial when we have neglected to spend quality time with Him previously. Someone may say this is against our free will, but that is not the case. The simple fact is God could not get our attentiveness unto Him until we ran into a little trouble. So, the Lord allows the trouble to run a little longer than normal just so we can get the greater benefit of spending some quality time getting closer to Him. Yes, the added time in pain is for our benefit. We may see it all as a conglomerate of pain, while God sees it as growth for His children.

A parallel can be made to our bodies shutting down when we run them ragged. We refused to get rest and pay attention to our health, until our bodies demanded we get needed rest. It was for our own good that our bodies shut down, demanding rest before we had a true collapse or even came to death. In the same way our God does not want us to die physically nor spiritually; thus He shuts us down for additional moments in order that we get proper rest in Him. Fact is, we all can use a little more rest in the Lord. Paul said, "Most gladly therefore will I rather glory in my infirmities, that the power of Christ may rest upon me" *(II Corinthians 12:9b).*

In this type of scenario and life situation we bring upon ourselves added durations of pain, simply due to our not taking it upon ourselves to spend regular quality time with the Lord in prayer. I'm not sure how each reader feels, but I'm going to spend time with God so He does not delay my healing, blessing or deliverance when I seek Him. Recall the scripture where the Lord says, "... I know you not whence ye are: depart from me...." *(Luke 13:27).* Understand, He will not reject us when we pray, but He may delay the healing or the breakthrough for a spell until a relationship is first kindled; and why not, since God knows that our greatest deliverance is our having a quality relationship with Him.

I have often taught that the extent of a Christian's prayer and devotional life can be seen through their living and how they treat others. The fact is, we will have a better appreciation for others here on Earth (horizontally) after we begin to show more appreciation for God (vertically). We show this appreciation by spending ample quality and spirited time with Him. Those who do not show respect unto the Lord will not show respect for their fellow man. The horizontal is truly reflective of the vertical. Make no mistake about it. If you disrespect others and treat others poorly and lowly, it is almost a shoe-in that you, in some way or another, treat God in the same manner. You may not want to believe it, but it can almost be guaranteed that your respect level for others is mirrored in your respect level for the Lord. Instead of reiterating that statement, I will simply direct each of us to read it a second or third time in order to grasp its seriousness. This document will speak more about how our vertical relationship affects our horizontal relationships.

We must spend ample and quality time with God to render affect unto our living and spirits. We have heard it before, "There is a process." We must respect the process and allow it to take its course. It is called sanctification and we are all at different levels within it. We all have the same level of salvation, yet we are all at different levels in the process of being changed and purified. So, not only are we to respect the process, but we must activate the process, as well. It begins and is made manifest with our spending quality and sufficient time with the Lord.

Do not misunderstand this point about time spent. Deep devotionals and prayer that renders effect does not always call for our being in prayer for an extended period of time. Proper *Prayer Progression* will enable us to produce the depth of spirit needed to cultivate rich communication with God without needing to spend an exorbitant amount of time in devotionals and prayer. We all shall see how much prayer truly works when we begin to spend quality and ample time in spirited communion with God. True prayer warriors desire spirited time with the Lord, knowing how it results in God revealing Himself. It is a blessing to be delivered and healed, but the true magnificence is to see the Lord actually show up in our situations. Maybe it will be best understood by saying, the Lord's presence in our lives is more important than anything else we may desire, want or need.

There are No Excuses for Any of Us!

The amount of time we spend with the Lord should be dictated by, not only our portion of faith given by the Holy Spirit, but our place in the process, also. It's rather simple. If we are hellions, a larger amount of time with the Lord is necessary. Conversely, those with less drama in their lives may not need as much time to develop a spirited connection with the Lord in prayer. But, it surely does not excuse those who are more kindly and loving from spending in depth time with the Lord; for the Spirit has much work to perform in us all. Truly know here today, no one, absolutely no one, is exempt from spending quality and ample time with God. Let me speak to the Bishops, Pastors and Deacons for a moment. You are not exempt either! You even more so must spend x-amount of time with the Lord to then be able to live in accord with the Spirit and in order to minister to others in the spirit.

Some of the issues we have in the church begin at the top, due to a lack of quality time spent with the Lord. Of course this is not true in your Church, but there are congregations that consume too much of the Pastor's and Deacon's time, whereby ample time is not made available for them to spend with God in devotionals, study and prayer. On the flip side of the coin, many who grace the desk for preaching and teaching often get to the point where they think they know it all. They take for granted devotional and study, thinking they know every story and every theological point, position and criticism. Ministers must realize their sanctification process has not ceased, either. Pastors are to be the number one voice through which God speaks unto the Church; thus they, more so than most, must yield unto the Lord through plentiful devotionals and prayer; not the television. The Lord our God is not in the business of making Pastors, but of developing saints. The Lord desires to build us all as saints who are faithful unto Him, and strong in ministry unto His will and purpose.

There is no rightful excuse for any of us to not spend ample time in prayer unto the Lord. What will you say when Jesus returns? Will you say, "Sorry Lord but I was too busy to truly get to know You?" Will your excuse be, "There were so many pressing issues that kept me from spending quality time with You Lord, so please forgive me?" Let us explore what the Lord currently reveals unto us as His response to our many ineffectual excuses; by way of our truthfulness, or the lack thereof. The Bible says, "Every knee shall bow and every tongue shall confess that Jesus is Lord" *(Isaiah 45:23, Romans 14:11, Philippians 2:10)*. The Word also declares, "And it shall come to pass, that whosoever shall call on the name of the Lord shall be saved" *(Acts 2:21)*. Many of us lean on these scriptures and others that are similar, thinking we have all the time in the world to get right with God; assuming He is required or obligated to receive us if our lips part those words. This is similar to our thought about our prayer lives, whereas we feel we can run throughout the world and life doing everything we think we are big and bad enough to do, then run to the Lord in prayer when things do not quite work out as we planned. We then expect God to fulfill the scripture which declares, "And whatsoever ye shall ask in my name, that will I do, that the Father may be glorified in the Son" *(John 14:13)*. Our spirits have deceived us and our hearts do testify against us. Why do we attempt to hold God to the iron on His Word, when we refuse to hold ourselves to the iron of acting as though we are saved? There are often conditions to receiving the fruit.

The truth is our hearts become even harder the longer we live with wicked hearts and evil spirits. Those are the same hearts which the Lord will read in the last day and even reads today when we pray unto Him. Hebrews 4:12 proclaims, "For the word of God is quick, and powerful, and sharper than any twoedged sword, ... and is a discerner of the thoughts and intents of the heart." This tells us that a hardened heart will testify against the lying lips of the deceiver who attempts to come in through the back door. We all must enter in by the strait gate *(Matthew 7:13-14)*. At the end times the Spirit of God, being a discerner of our intents, will know whether we are calling on the name of Jesus only to escape hell's fire or to glorify His name in love and praise. No one will want to see hell fire, of course; as that lake will be at hand for many.

that lake will be at hand for many. "For with the heart man believeth unto righteousness; and with the mouth confession is made unto salvation" *(Romans 10:10)*. Our hearts are testifying against us now just as they will in the last day. That is a truth most don't know, while a few others refuse to minister; fearful of losing members who refuse to change.

We must sincerely ask ourselves the question, "What are my truthful intents in my relationship with God?" Whether we are truthful or not, the intents of our hearts are reflected in the amount of quality time we spend with God in prayer. Our hearts may not have to testify against us if our lacking devotionals already vow of our unfaithful spirits and illegitimate intents. Will the Lord continue to not answer our prayers due to, both, our not truthfully seeking Him and our dishonestly and periodically knocking on the door of communion? The righteous heart cannot be hidden, just as the wicked heart is transparent unto God. Although deceivers will claim Jesus' name, He shall still demand they depart from His presence because He shall read their hearts. Their mouths shall surely call out His name in prayer and in the final day, but their hearts shall condemn them. Listen!

The Lord made it perfectly clear when He declared, "Not everyone that saith unto me, Lord, Lord shall enter into the kingdom of heaven; but he that doeth the will of my Father which is in heaven. Many will say to me in that day, Lord, Lord, have we not prophesied in thy name? and in thy name have cast out devils? and in thy name done many wonderful works? And then will I profess unto them, I never knew you; depart from me, ye that work iniquity" *(Matthew 7:21-23)*. In this sense, why do we question that our prayers go unanswered today? It is that same hardened heart which testifies of our wayward desires! Let us then draw back the excuses of why we lack in our relationships with God, and draw nigh unto Him with renewed spirits desiring to glorify His deity.

This document will not only help to strengthen our spiritual lives and our prayer lives, but it will prick our spirits to change our ways, as well! Let's take to heart these *8 Elements of Prayer Progression*™ so we may become more spirited in prayer. We must first know to what and to whom we must be faithful, before we can attempt to do what it takes to be faithful. That is rather straight forward. The knowing comes from not only His written Word in the Bible, but from His Spirit unto us through prayer, as well. We get only half the message of what we must do to become faithful if we merely study His Word while neglecting to spend time with His Spirit in prayer. In prayer we receive encouragement, strength and answers for concerns, in addition to gaining directions for faithful living unto Christ. Psalm 48:14 for the Sons of Korah said it this way, "For this God is our God for ever and ever: he will be our guide even unto death."

What do Others See?

The lack of visible spiritual fruit in the lives of believers is often more than enough reason for non-believers to continue to doubt that the Lord is true and living. However it may seem in the minds of disbelievers, we as believers have a responsibility to do our best to represent Christ. Our lack in devotionals is evident through several things: our unrighteous living; our lack of faith in things unseen; a lack of power to do the impossible; and our lack of abounding joy. These conditions would change and more people would be convinced that our God lives and is fully able to do all things, if we would spend more quality time building our faith and spirit in devotionals with the very Spirit of God.

The Bible says, "And I, if I be lifted up from the earth, will draw all men unto me" *(John 12:32)*. Here the Lord was truly speaking of His mode of death, being resurrected and ascending unto the Father, while we often include the point of us lifting up His name in praise, honour and glory. We must glorify the Lord with our living so others will believe in His power and likewise be drawn unto the Father. Far too many of us exalt ourselves and entertain evil which muddies the waters and turns men, women and children away from the Lord our God. We are then looked at as hypocrites as God appears as a liar. Maybe many of us do not lift Him up because we have neglected to get to know Him through spirited prayer and devotionals. It is hard to lift up someone who is unknown to us.

Our living would be more reflective of the manifestation of Christ if we spent more time hanging around the Spirit. We, as Christians, would walk more uprightly and confidently in faith if we got closer to the power of the Lord in devotionals. The Church would be able to make mountains move by the Lord's power working within us, if we would spend more personal time in the power of His presence in prayer. We would have that great joy no man would be able to refute if we would get to know the Creator of joy, personally. "These things have I spoken unto you, that my joy might remain in you, and that your joy might be full" *(John 15:11)*.

Then and only then will the Church see the increase of persons being saved unto the Lord's great righteousness; as it should be. Folk can tell if what we propose for them is not even working for us. This thing called faith is not working for many of us, as many of us refuse to spend enough quality time with God for His Spirit to make a difference in our lives. Someone asked me just yesterday, "Ty, when was it that you finally felt the change in your life?" I joyfully explained how it happened over a period of time and through a process of spending quality time with the Lord. I stressed to him it did not happen overnight and is still occurring.

We must do more than simply remember to spend personal time with the Lord if we are to effect the resonating power of Christ. We must activate His being manifest within us by wilfully spending extra quality time in devotionals and prayer. "He that hath my commandments, and keepeth them, he it is that loveth me: and he that loveth me shall be loved of my Father, and I will love him, and will manifest myself to him" *(John 14:21)*. We do not show the love if we do not spend the time.

We must make it personal. The Bible tells us, "Not forsaking the assembling of ourselves together..." *(Hebrews 10:25)*, whereas it is in the personal quality time spent with the Lord that individually benefits us with the greatest increase in His Spirit. Just as the Samaritans besought the Lord to tarry with them, according to John 4:40, we must invite Him into our lives through practicing consistent and healthy devotional prayer lives. Do not just invite Him in, but spend some time with Him, as well. We all have been taught to invite Him in, yet we are not urged to spend actual time with Him. Howbeit we invite a friend to our home, yet spend time doing other things rather than entertaining that friend? Remember Martha and Mary? The same goes for our shouting invitations for God to reside within us, yet we refuse to take respectful time to commune and fellowship with Him. Make time and He will cleanup our natural beings.

It is when we spend quality time with the Lord that we will see the greatest increase, accomplishing two things. First, it will enable us to truthfully proclaim to know the Lord for ourselves, and second, others will witness the power as they shall come to believe the Lord can work in their lives also. "And many more believed because of his own word; And said unto the woman, Now we believe, not because of thy saying: for we have heard him ourselves, and know that this is indeed the Christ, the Saviour of the world" *(John 4:41-42)*. It is sad to say many of us should never have claimed to know Him since we have never truthfully invited Him into our lives nor have we taken the time to sincerely and faithfully fellowship with Him. But, let it now be said we will truthfully turn unto the Lord with all power and conviction, seeking the greatest benefits of His will and desires.

We learn a magnitude of the corporate when we assemble with other believers, but we more so learn of, and grow in, the character of Christ' Spirit during our personal time with God. It is in that personal quality time that we are individually transformed to be like the Son Jesus through the filling of His Spirit, love and power. I am quite sure most Christians desire to be filled by the Lord. We must understand the filling comes by way of the quality time we spend unto the Lord. Therefore, where there is no quality time spent, there assuredly is no spirit transformation. I do not know about you, but not only do I desire to be filled, but I hunger to be ultimately transformed into the likeness of Christ. "Now the Lord is that Spirit, and where the Spirit of the Lord is, there too is liberty. But we all, with open face beholding as in a glass of glory of the Lord, are changed into the same image from glory to glory, even as by the Spirit of the Lord" _(II Corinthians 3:17-18)._ "And be not conformed to this world: but be ye transformed by the renewing of your mind, that ye may prove what is that good, and acceptable, and perfect, will of God" _(Romans 12:2)._ This likeness was ordained by God in Genesis 1:26-27, and enjoyed by Adam and Eve before The Fall. Let us all fight the good fight of faith _(I Timothy 6:12)_ until we are fully transformed and glorified when Jesus returns.

I declare today, we cannot be transformed without being absorbed by that very transforming agent called the Holy Spirit; and I do mean absorbed. We cannot get absorbed just in shouts of praise. We must get absorbed in the truth of who He is, the truth and context of His Word and the truth of personal fellowship in prayer. That is where and when the power begins to take hold in believers. That is where and when others begin to receive the overflow. That is where and when non-believers step out in the faith of believing, "If He can deliver you, He can surely deliver me."

This transformation occurs in His presence. In His presence there is healing of spirit. In His presence there is great joy of fellowship. In His presence there is deliverance through His power. His power transforms us in His presence when we pray effectually. Many of us are as evil as we want to be, due to our refusing to spend truthful quality and spirited time with the Lord. Many of us want to simply study the Word (book), but wince away from worshiping in the spirit of the Word (Son). There ought be some type of visible evidence that we have been, and are being transformed. It is not that we must always jump and shout throughout our homes, churches or streets, yet others should be able to witness the power of Christ within us. I once heard a preacher say, "I'd rather see a good sermon than to hear one, any day." We will see the overflow of His Spirit and Word at work in the lives of others after we allow the Lord to work in and through us. If we desire to see scripture fulfilled, let us begin by seeking the Lord through prayer and devotionals that are spirited.

Put in the Work

As we athletes say, "You've got to get it in. You've got to put in the work." Oh yeah, it is work; something many of us shy from and shun. The truth is we put in the work at our jobs, so why not put in the work with God? Do not be mad at me for bringing this to light, for I am merely a messenger who must live II Timothy 4:2 which demands, word; be instant in season, out of season; reprove, rebuke, exhort with all longsuffering and doctrine." Our true deliverance comes by way of our having a sustaining quality fellowship with the Spirit of Christ. Life becomes clearer and more full as our personal time with Christ increases. How can we feel comfortable giving time and work to this world and refuse to give it unto God? We should feel great conviction in our souls for putting in work at the job, but not putting in work with the Lord. Much of the work we put into our fellowship with God is through prayer.

Simply put, we are not putting in work if we are not spending quality time in prayer. Oh, there is no mistaking that fact. If we do not put in the time, we are not putting in the work. Do not give to the world that which we should be giving to the Lord. Many of us truly ought be ashamed of how we give to the world what belongs to God. Are you hearing me on this? After reading this document, we shall not be comfortable to render unto Caesar and not render unto Christ. We should say to ourselves everyday, "Got to put in the work." Read Matthew 22:21.

We should desire to have a second job. That is to say, we all should have jobs of spending quality time with God. How many of us have a second job? Many of us have second jobs that give us pay-checks at weeks end, but far too few of us have second jobs that pay us glory each day. The whole of *The 8 Elements of Prayer Progression*™ is about putting in work with the Lord. One hundred thousand believers shall put in the work and become mountain moving warriors who desire to give God glory.

Many of us seek glory but we do not seek Jesus through prayer and communion. He alone is the glory that we seek. He is the joy we desire. He is the peace we are wanting. The Lord says, "But seek ye first the Kingdom of God and his righteousness, and all these things shall be added unto you" *(Matthew 6:33)*. We all know of that scripture but we fall short in teaching the context of the verses that precede it. Jesus tells us in verses 25-32 not to worry about being arrayed by what we can do for ourselves. He tells us to be blessed by the clothing of the Almighty God. In other words, some of us should trade in our secular part-time jobs for putting in more work with the Lord through personal fellowship. Let me tell you, no job pays like the Lord. I am in no way prescribing anyone to go out and quit their job. What I am saying is we must show more love for the Lord by spending more quality time with Him. It is my prayer that we cease showing this world that we love it more than we love our God.

Fact is, more work with the Lord may not even pay you an increase financially, but it will pay a spiritual increase that is unmatched by any finances any of us could possibly acquire. It is better to have a peace with

God than any piece of this world's gold or platinum. It is better to live in God's shining glory than to live attached to the approval of fickle man. It is even better to possess wisdom from God than to acquire all the positions of man. "Then Peter said, silver and gold have I none; but such as I have give I thee: In the name of Jesus Christ of Nazareth rise up and walk" *(Acts 3:6)*. Do you have any, "In the name of Jesus" in your life? We have heard it and/or said it before, "Nobody can do you like the Lord." Now we should live it! Oh, to know the power through living it. Live it so to see the transforming power of the presence of the Almighty.

(11) Here is where the true blessing comes in. The true blessing flows when we convert our job with God from a part-time or second job into our first job. This is a *key* for us all. This is where we begin to realize the truth of first fruit and all its benefits. The increase of all things good in our lives becomes manifest when we begin to first give unto God. The Lord is the biggest proponent of first fruit and His desire is for us to make Him our number one job. We must seek Him first by spending quality time in prayer if we desire to see great increase and provisions in our lives.

We can witness the fullness of His provisions if we would only first seek Him full-time instead of part-time. Put in the work and watch how the Lord places us upon a rock, as written in Psalm 27:5-6, "... he shall set me up upon a rock. And now shall my head be lifted up above mine enemies round about me ...." Make it a point to put in the work today and every day. We all should ask the question of ourselves, "Did I get my work in today?" Our spiritual power in living will be reflective of the quality time spent with God in prayer; or the lack thereof. Not only will others be able to tell how much time we spend with God, but our spiritual level of strength will be evident even to God as we pray. In addition, our level of spirituality with God in prayer will even be reflective of the quality time we have spent in His Spirit leading up to the next time we pray. Another way of looking at it is many of us render our own prayers ineffective by putting in so much part-time work with God, refusing to place Him first.

As we all know part-time workers do not carry the same benefits as full-timers. The same is with our communion with God; whereas we cannot expect to be covered with the Lord's assurance (insurance plan) if we insist on carrying part-time hours with Him. It is not as though there are no full-time positions available with God, for the Bible says, "... The harvest truly is plenteous, but the labourers are few" *(Matthew 9:37)*. I'm not saying that everyone is to desire to be on staff at the church, but what I am saying is far too many of us place God on the back burner in our lives, in quasi rejection of Him, yet we expect Him to accept us twenty four hours a day and seven days a week; or just when we are in need or in trouble. A true warrior is not interested in simply praying to God. He or she, more so, desires to abide with God rather than simply present their concerns and wishes. There is this bound spiritual union with God which must occur, if we are to effect change in us and in our surroundings.

Can I make it personal to you? The fulfilling of your needs and wants are dependant upon your spending quality time with God. There are blessings waiting to be poured unto you from God, but you have continued to live in weak fellowship and diluted prayer unto Him, to the point that you have no power to ask, receive nor sustain the blessings He has for you! Later chapters within this document will speak on how we often stand as our own biggest road blocks to success. No greater way do we block our paths to success than to simply refuse to join our spirits with the Lord's. We cannot receive what is laid up for us until we first put in the work with the Giver. "Every good gift and every perfect gift is from above, and cometh down from the Father of lights, with whom is no variableness, neither shadow of turning" *(James 1:17)*. Then, how is it that we continue to vacillate and waver with our fellowship with Him, yet ask daily for everything under the sun lit sky?

I truly do not know of anyone who does not desire to have their prayers answered, but the fact remains, I witness daily many people who refuse to put in time with the Lord. Many superficial professors refuse to put in the time needed to, both, sustain fellowship with God and reap the benefits of strengthened spirituality. To their defense, far too many believers have never been taught the truth about prayer. On the parallel, the majority of us have not been taught the truth about faithful living that's in accord with the Lord's truths. We talk about truth and preach on related subjects, but we never actually attend to the truth of the matter that will effect change in our living and prosperity in our prayers. At the nuts and bolts of a thing, the actual truth may be taught at times devoid of the application. There it is! Wherefore, this document.

Many of us have been told how to live, but not taught how to live! The simple reasoning for this quandary is those who teach often do not know themselves how to apply truth to their lives; thus the repetition of ignorance and powerlessness becomes cyclical and generational. I am not one to greatly get into generational curses, but folk do often curse their own family lines and church lineage (congregations) by teaching the same powerless practices that render their own lives fruitless and immature in faith. This is reason enough to be mindful of the ministry we follow and lead, so we do not end up as superficial professors lacking spiritual wherewithal and lacking the truthful spiritual power needed to help others. I beseech us all to look at the fruit, or the lack thereof.

I shall reveal unto you some mysteries and wisdom through this document by the power vested unto me by the very Spirit of God. With your willingness of spirit this document shall reveal keys which will unlock the greatness God has already bestowed unto you through His indwelling Spirit. It is a *key* in itself that we must be willing to receive of the principles and directions God awaits to give us. We all have been given our own measures of faith, so it is now the objective of myself and this document, through the workings of the Holy Spirit, to tap into your well of faith, so the Spirit of truth can pour overflows through your prayers and unto your living.

This document removes the remaining excuses we have for not praying effectively. These principles are truly needed for the coming days, so allow the Lord to open our spirits in order that we may be girded, armed and prepared, thereafter. "Then opened he their understanding, that they might understand the scriptures." *(Luke 24:45)*. Thus this document. The Lord is going to use this document to bring readers, and those indirectly touched, into a greater spirituality. In addition, those who truly receive these principles shall be empowered by God and given strengthened abilities to get answers to prayers. I do declare at this very moment, there shall be 100,000 truthfully empowered prayer warriors to come forth from the Lord using this document. Let one of them trustingly be you! One of life's greatest blessings is to be able to get answers to prayers.

How We Request (Time, Blessings, Directions)

How can we ask to receive of the overflow God has stored for us unless we know how to request it? Here is a *key* for many of us. God knows if we are ready to receive something by the way we ask for it. That is a simple yet potent breakthrough for someone here today. The Lord can very well tell if we are ready to be blessed with the overflow just by how we ask for the very thing. Scripture tells us, "Ye ask and receive not, because ye ask amiss, that ye may consume it upon your lusts" *(James 4:3)*. How blessed are we when we stick with the context of the scriptures. Let me say it again, the Lord knows if we are going to ruin a blessing just by how we ask. This document shall assist us in even the way we request of God. Yes, the Lord knows our hearts, and this document attends to the condition of the heart in connection with our spirits and mouths. There is a funny yet appropriate commercial about an inspector testing cheese before it reaches production, which gives example of how our mouths express the condition of our spirits. Let it be understood that God is our inspector (Potter) and we are the cheese (clay), as the Bible has it. "But now, O Lord, thou art our father; we are the clay, and thou our potter; and we all are the work of thy hand" *(Isaiah 64:8)*.

How we ask is reflective of our time spent with God and our living unto His character and His will. We will continue to "ask amiss" if we do not spend quality time with the Lord. As we have read, the scripture tells us we shall not receive if we ask amiss. It is just that simple. Why else have we yet to receive that which we know has been stored up for us? Let this be as increase for our deliverance. Do not feel alone in this matter for many who will read this document, and others who will not, are in the same drifting boat, but to God be the glory for the insights unto His Word.

In addition, we cannot sustain what God has given us lest He prepares us and gives us direction on how to sustain and maintain the very thing. We very well know in our spirits we have squandered some blessings in our day, simply due to our inability and lack of knowledge. Some folk even come into great wealth only to lose it within a year or some other short span of time. Some of us have lost a lot of things before we even ever reaped of its benefits, because we had no clue on how to keep it, nor maintain it. The *#5 Element of Discernment* speaks heavily on how we are to receive directions from God for how to sustain the blessings He gives.

God's Word teaches us what is right and wrong, and His Spirit gives us directions in accord with His Word. The more time we spend getting to know the Lord, the more sensitized we become to hear and receive His Spirit's directions. I do pray our spiritual antennae become raised to their highest peaks to receive all that will be taught within this document; as we become readied for the coming days. This document should be read, not just once, nor twice, but it should be kept near for easy reference and continual sharpening. You shall know better by and by!

Learning these *Elements* will provide a strong foundation for prayer, since they are constructs that help us best understand the Spirit's flow within prayer. *Progression* from one *Element* to the next is important in order to gain deeper access to the Spirit of God. Transition to successive *Elements* becomes easy and obvious once we have been diligent in each previous *Element.* John, Ty or anyone else may teach how to pray, but the Holy Spirit is the change Advocate who gives directions in prayer. It is the Holy Spirit who will progress us through this document with power and deliverance. "Thus saith the Lord, thy Redeemer, the Holy One of Israel; I am the Lord thy God which teacheth thee to profit, which leadeth thee by the way that thou shouldest go" *(Isaiah 48:17).* In turn, it is imperative that we have a strong desire to be taught these principles and receive the Spirit's directions.

Are You Ready?

No Faking It Till You Make It!

Let it be fully known and understood that these _8 Elements of Prayer Progression_™ will not work as something magical, as if you can spue or blurt them out of your mouth to make things happen in a witch like whim. These words are true and they are power unto your prayers and your living, but they will not come into fruition if you are not of the Spirit of God. Let me say it again and with more emphasis — this will not work by some magical power, but only by your being connected to the Vine — Jesus. The Bible gives us great example of how persons may try to misuse and fraudulently claim the power of Christ within. Acts 19:11-22 speaks of such an occurrence when the sons of a preacher (priest) were leapt upon by evil spirits in response to their untruthful and non-spirited use of the word and name of the Lord Jesus. Verse 15 explicitly says, "... Jesus I know, and Paul I know; but who are ye?" Let not it be you who are lacking in His Spirit and torn from flesh to bones by evil spirits who recognize a powerless fraud. I urge you not to play with the Word of God nor His power within these mysteries revealed; lest ye find yourself as an offspring of Sceva, badgered and wounded.

It is your spirit's connection with the Lord which gives these principles the true power and authority to claim anything in the name of the matchless Jesus; the One and only True and Living Saviour. Greater is the child with large amounts of faith and is truthfully connected to the Spirit of God, than the man who knows every word and verse, blurting empty epithets without the Spirit of Christ within. He it is who appears as holy, but it is the child whose loins are truthfully built in Christ Jesus who has the power of thousands with the Spirit as anchor. The Lord Jesus proclaimed, "I am the vine, ye are the branches: He that abideth in me, and I in him, the same bringeth forth much fruit: for without me ye can do nothing" _(John 15:5)_. Nothing!

What Can Be Expected

The order of these _Elements_ will become distinctively obvious by the end of reading this informative devotional prayer document. By no means is it intended for these _Progression Elements_ to constrain anyone's prayer pattern. Contrariwise, the important thing to remember is this document is meant to teach believers how to pray and teach them to allow the Holy Spirit's directing within and through prayer. As will be illustrated, this _Progression of Prayer_ was used heavily in Biblical days but is in no way constructed as handcuffs upon our spirits. The essential thing for all believers to do is strongly embrace the Spirit's movement in prayer.

These *8 Elements of Prayer Progression*™ will surely help to eliminate babbling and increase our spirit to pray, but it is the Holy Spirit who shall reveal the most important fruit through our investing the time in prayer.

There are many inferences throughout this document denoting the horizontal and vertical relationships we bear. It is a blessing of how this document will bear fruit in our prayer lives, but it will first bear fruit in our spiritual lives. One may ask, "How can that be the order when this is a document on teaching how to pray?" Well, a prayer life will be weak and ineffective without a strong spiritual life as the driving force; a simple, yet neglected truth. It is our strength in spirituality that drives and promotes a healthy prayer life. A spiritual life heavily directed by the Spirit of God commands and demands prayer and communication with the Father. Just any type of communication will not be sufficient for those believers who seek the presence of the Father in all their living. A life filled with the Spirit of the Almighty demands not only wholesome living, but necessitates attentive listening unto Him, as well. Minimal listening to God has granted many of us weak and defenseless. The Bible even tells us, "For we wrestle not against flesh and blood, but against principalities, against powers, against the rulers of the darkness of this world, against spiritual wickedness in high places" *(Ephesians 6:12)*. Much of our lack of success in life is a response to our weak spiritual living with the Lord. It is a weak spiritual life which proves ineffective in our prayers. It behooves me how many of us pray to God without effectively connecting with Him in spirit. In effect, this document will strengthen both our spiritual living and our spirit to pray.

It is a purposed attempt to not be overly technical nor too deep with this document of learning so readers of every spiritual level will receive of its fruit. Jesus is the Master and He was a master at making precepts easy to digest. His earthly ministry was filled with His great strives in breaking down concepts of spirit and law so the masses could receive of them. Let it be in that same spirit that this document makes things plain so the largest possible number of people come into a greater saving knowledge of Him who sent this.

It is not within the technical that we are delivered. On the contrary, it is in the spirit and in the truth where we are healed, blessed and set free. Far too many teachers and preachers attempt to be so technical about the Word of God in attempts to impress others, while all along they miss the blessings for themselves and they miss the mark in conveying the blessings to others. It is my desire and the Lord's will that we receive of His blessings rather than any technical boastfulness. I love learning the technical portions of doctrines, but that is for another time and another personal place. I have not been called to write this document to "wow" you with doctrinal truths beyond understanding, that you would look upon me as some masterful instructor. I have been called to present this document so you may receive of its fruit, be blessed by the power of God's Word, and receive of some mysteries revealed. "All this, said David, the Lord made me understand in writing by his hand upon me, even all the works of this pattern" *(I Chronicles 28:19).*

Now turn to the next page and begin your life as a strong prayer warrior, able to effect change in your life and in your environment. Pray now that the Lord open your heart, mind, spirit and soul in order to receive of the principles that are to follow. Accept now that your life as a prayer warrior shall never be the same. Give God the glory due His name. The day has surely come, and is, that prayer warriors will rise in order to thwart the roaring evil which pervades our air, land and neighbor's flesh.

"But as it is written, Eye hath not seen, nor ear heard, neither have entered into the heart of man, the things which God hath prepared for them that love Him. But God hath revealed them unto us by His Spirit: for the Spirit searcheth all things, yea, the deep things of God. For what man knoweth the things of a man, save the spirit of man which is in him? even so the things of God knoweth no man, but the Spirit of God. Now we have received, not the spirit of the world, but the Spirit which is of God; that we might know the things that are freely given to us of God. Which things also we speak, not in the words which man's wisdom teacheth, but which the Holy Ghost teacheth; comparing spiritual things with spiritual. But the natural man receiveth not the things of the Spirit of God: for they are foolishness unto him: neither can he know them, because they are spiritually discerned. But he that is spiritual judgeth all things, yet he himself is judged of no man. For who hath known the mind of the Lord, that he may instruct him? But we have the mind of Christ" (I Corinthians 2:9-16).

Passion for Prayer

Forward Message About Prayer

Exercises

INSTRUCTIONAL

1. Take a sheet of paper and pen and write all the reasons (excuses) you can think of that are currently denying you access to the Lord's overflow in prayer. Keep this sheet on hand until you finish reading the whole of this document. Add to the list along the way if need be. Review this list at the end of your reading this document, then with a pair of scissors cut it into little pieces and throw them into the trash can.

   BENEFIT:
   Realization that there are no more excuses for your not entering into the fullness of God's presence and overflow.

PERSONAL

1. From the contents page on *Forward Message About Prayer Progression*™ select one of the headings that may seem to be a roadblock to your current success in prayer. Openly discuss this with a small group of three to four persons; talking over the why's and the how's.

   BENEFIT:
   To openly bring into the forefront of your spirit and mind the hurdles you may not have been able to leap in the past. Open communication often permits a person's spirit to begin to vigorously and honestly tackle concerns and trials.

Forward Message About Prayer

General Questions

1. What should be our first request in prayer since we may have to wait for our breakthrough, blessing or deliverance?

2. In what are prayer warriors most interested if they are not interested in simply handing over their concerns unto God?

3. Are prayer warriors interested in changing God's mind through prayer? Provide explanation with the yes or no answer.

4. What must we do after inviting the Lord into our living?

5. It is very necessary for the Holy Spirit to make intercessions for us, but what is better than our having our neighbor to make intercessions for us?

6 What are two reasons it is important to first follow the order of *Progression* patterned within this document?

7. What is the major two-part warning given to those who are to be prayer warriors?

8. How can we increase our abilities to accept all of God's various answers to our prayers?

9. What are the two verses prayer warriors must have ingrained in their spirits, minds and souls, in order that they may believe in victory when circumstances scream of impossibility?

10. It is imperative that prayer warriors have hope; great hope. In what two things is their hope built upon?

Forward Message About Prayer

Advanced Questions

1. Do our prayers begin when we take posture or position to pray; such as getting on our knees? If so, why? If not, when?

2. What does it mean to "Put in the work?"
    Write a short paragraph on the benefit of putting in the work.

3. Write a short paragraph as to why prayer warriors must have hope in the Lord's power instead of in their own abilities?

Acknowledgment

Pray this prayer with me:
A Prayer for Acknowledgment

""Blessed and glorious God, how I do praise You with every bit of strength in my spirit. Oh, how I praise Thee. I call You power! I call You faithful! You alone are my every need, and I stand thankful to be Your child and servant. Bless my spirit now Father with added understanding of how to give You the greatest acknowledgment. Have this chapter's words empower my prayers and my living unto You. Bless me that I not only receive increase, but have it to be that Your name is glorified all the more, as well. I now give shouts of pre-praise knowing in my heart You shall bless me greatly and magnificently. This I do pray with the Spirit of Christ resting upon me, as it is in His gracious name — Amen."

This section is to better enhance our understanding of the Biblical reasons for who should give acknowledgment, how should acknowledgment be given, why should acknowledgment be given, what should be given acknowledgment, where should acknowledgment be given and when should acknowledgment be given. Our study of acknowledgment will be further enhanced if these verses are read previous to moving onto the chapter material; as this format will indeed better prepare our spirits to receive of the chapter material.

1) **WHO should give acknowledgment?**
   - I Kings 8:33, 35; II Chronicles 6:24 — Those who have sinned
   - Isaiah 33:13 — Those who are near the Lord
   - John 5:23 — Those who honour the Father
   - John 9:21-23 — Those of age; the touched by the Lord
   - Philippians 2:10-11 — Every tongue; everything in Heaven, Earth and under the Earth
   - Hebrews 11:13 — The saved; strangers to the Earth; those who the promise was made unto
   - I John 2:23 — Those who love the Father
   - I John 4:2-6 — Those of God
   - I John 4:15 — They that have God (love) dwelling within them
   - II John 7 — Those who are not the deceiver nor anti-christ
   - Revelation 3:5 — Overcomers; the saved; those in the Book of Life
   - Revelation 19:7 — The Bride of Christ

2) **HOW should acknowledgment be given?**
   - I Kings 8:35 — Towards Heaven (***** some say towards the east)
   - Job 40:14; Psalm 32:5 — Unto God; Unto the Lord
   - Psalm 66:2 — With singing and praise
   - Proverbs 3:6 — In all your ways
   - Proverbs 3:9 — With thy substance and first fruits
   - Isaiah 29:13 — With mouth, lips, heart and in fear of God
   - Matthew 15:8 — With your heart, not just your lips
   - John 5:23 — Honour the Son as you honour the Father
   - John 9:22 — Unashamedly and through persecution
   - Romans 10:9-10 — With your mouth and believing in your heart
   - Romans 14:11 — With your tongue and bowed knees
   - Romans 15:9 — Singing unto His name
   - Philippians 2:10-11 — With your tongue and bowed knees
   - Colossians 2:2 — With comforted hearts and with full assurance
   - Hebrews 12:28 — With reverence and godly fear and grace
   - I John 4:14 — Testifying
   - Revelation 19:7 — With gladness and rejoicing

3) WHY should acknowledgment be given?

- I Kings 8:33-35 — To be forgiven of sins
- Psalm 32:5 — For forgiveness
- Proverbs 3:9-10 — So thy barns may be filled with plenty and thy presses shall burst
- Isaiah 3:30 — To be honoured of God
- Isaiah 33:13 — To acknowledge His might
- Matthew 10:32 — For Jesus to confess you before Father in Heaven
- Luke 19:40 — The rocks would otherwise cry out
- Romans 10:9-10 — Because you believe He is Lord and was raised from the dead; for salvation
- Romans 14:11 — To confess Him as Lord; it is written; the Lord says so
- Romans 15:9 — To glorify God for His mercy; it is written
- Philippians 2:9 — God exalted the Son; He has a name above every name
- Philippians 2:10-11 — To glorify God the Father
- Hebrews 12:28-29 — For God is a consuming fire
- I John 4:14 — God sent the Son
- II John 7 — So you are not deceived

4) WHAT should be given acknowledgment?

- Job 40:14 — That He can save
- Psalm 32:5 — Sins and transgressions
- Isaiah 9:6 — That He is wonderful, Counselor, the mighty God, the everlasting Father, the Prince of Peace
- Philippians 2:11 — That He is Lord
- Colossians 2:2 — The mystery of God, the Father and Christ
- I John 4:15 — That Jesus is Lord

5) WHERE should acknowledgment be given?

- II Chronicles 6:24 — In prayer and in the Church
- Jeremiah 3:9 — Before all the nations of the Earth
- Isaiah 29:13 — Drawing near God
- Matthew 10:32-33; Luke 12:8-9 — Before men
- Luke 19:30 — Amongst the multitude
- Romans 15:9 — Amongst the Gentiles
- Revelation 21:23-24 — In the Light

6) WHEN should acknowledgment be given?

- Revelation 21:24 — When you are saved; when you come into the Light

"In all thy ways acknowledge him, and he shall direct thy paths"
Proverbs 3:6

To acknowledge (to show honour, appreciation and respect) God for who He is in our lives does not consist of calling Him by a name by which our mothers, fathers or grandparents claimed of Him, per se. No, no, and no! If we do so, we are sadly mistaken of how to worship God in Spirit and in Truth, and our prayers begin on the wrong track. We all should know there is nothing worse than an incorrect beginning with anything; even more so in communing with God. It is all the more difficult to have a successful ending when we begin incorrectly and/or dishonestly.

Who is God to You?

The plate of grace is correctly set when we honestly acknowledge God for who He is in our individual lives. Calling God by the name we have personally experienced of Him accomplishes several things at the onset:

1) It sets our spirits in a mode of remembrance for who God truly is in our individual lives.
2) It grants us deeper access into the Throne of Grace by getting God's attention more readily; unlike babbling names with so much personal insignificance.
3) It more naturally prepares us for the next *Element* in the *Progression of Prayer;* for how can we show Him truth in adoration lest we are truthful about who He is to us personally?

The Spirit to Pray Always

Prayer is about having faith that God is not only who He is - The Creator, God alone, The Alpha & The Omega, and more, but it is about the spirit of the matter, also. The act of praying boils down to being in the spirit of prayer. Many times the devil will be on our backs so much that we may not even feel like praying. There are times we are not in the mood nor spirit to pray, yet we must pray no matter how we feel; as we very well know. Although the devil is a liar, he poses times and difficulties that make it essential to pray and put our faith and trust in God.

We must be diligent to pray even more when we do not feel like it. We can propel our faith and relationship with God to another level if we push through to pray and worship Him during times when our spirits seem lacking. It is in those very times that our faith is increased voluminously, because we have persevered and stretched our efforts in faith.

Physical, mental and spiritual exercise are best served in the times when we do not necessarily feel like doing it. "Stick-to-it-ness" and perseverance are by-products of a spirit that grows weary at times, but does not faint.

A Renewal from Weariness in Prayer

A cure for weariness in prayer is to acknowledge the Lord for who He actually is in our lives versus falsely claiming coined cliches of old and statements made by others. Not too many things are more uplifting than to be reminded of what God truly means to us. We all should be able to proclaim who He is without even reciting scriptures. It is the elementary believer who needs to shout scripture after scripture to relay who God is to them. We all must grow out of our juvenile level of Christian faith and living. This is one reason it is so essential to develop a close and personal relationship with the Lord. We truly and truthfully must know Him for ourselves to be able to get spiritually refueled from exclaiming who He is to us individually.

The down side and the up side to this fact is we must go through some trials, with God along side us, in order for Him to have a personal place in our spirits. Oh, the pain but spiritual prosperity of trials and tribulations; transitioned into Gods deliverance, covering and power to sustain. At these moments we can begin to more so understand and appreciate James 1:2-4 which proclaims, "My brethren count it all joy when ye fall into divers temptations; Knowing this, that the trying of your faith worketh patience. But let patience have her perfect work, that ye may be perfect and entire, wanting nothing." How amazing and profound it is that the Book of James begins with that bit of wisdom. Let us too take those words to heart and unto our living, through the practice of our acknowledging the Lord for who He is to us personally.

The best way for us to get into the spirit to pray is to first recall and recite all those things God has done. These things should permeate in our spirits so to excite us into prayer and into a strengthened connection with the Lord. Remembrance! The simple fact is, in this remembrance we must acknowledge God for who He is in our lives, and not in the lives of other folk. (This will be additionally discussed in *Adoration Element #2*). Truthful acknowledgment unto the Lord properly sets the table for giving Him adoration. We have heard the term and probably shouted it a few times ourselves, "When I think about all that the Lord has done for me." Well, within that acknowledgment is the defining portion of <u>who</u> He is to us in our <u>individual</u> lives.

If God delivered you out of a tight situation, He then is your deliverer; so acknowledge Him in prayer as your Deliverer. If He has protected you from things unimaginable, which is the story of us all, then acknowledge Him as Protector. Please do not miss this point. It may seem mundane to some, but the truth of the matter is we overlook the simplest and most foundational items. In our lives we seek the bling only to later realize the foundational items would have granted us access to the excitement of all the matter. There was no excitement in classes such as Statistics and Calculus for those who did not receive the base in Basic Math, Algebra and Trigonometry. The same is true for receiving the excitement of prayer. Prayer may not be too exciting for those who do not first read and digest the *Elements* of this document.

Likewise, the foundation of prayer, or the setting of the plate, cannot be sound unless it first begins with the truth of who God actually is in our individual lives. That is the beginning of our communications with Him. This is important, not only in our prayer lives, but also in our general faith walks, as well. As mentioned in the introduction, these *Prayer Elements* are meant to build us up as prayer warriors, but more so these elements will build up our relationships and living unto God. There is a beginning, and that beginning starts with acknowledging God in specifics of those things He has actually done for us. At this point, someone may say that is too technical or too much work. Please remember and truly understand, God never said it would be easy, but the Bible tells us in many verses, "... if thou seek him, he will be found of thee...." *(I Chronicles 28:9)*. It is not technical, it is spiritual, and the main importance is that it is truth — the basis of it all. The mere fact is, there would be more prayer warriors throughout this earth if it were an easy process, or an easy act. It takes effort. The ease comes through our being truthful in acknowledging who He is to us on a personal basis. If the Lord has taught you some important values, then call Him your Value Teacher. If God has sustained you in the worst of times, then by all means call Him your Sustainer! Call Him what He is — to you! Yes, He is the Alpha, but you were not there with Adam nor Eve at the early moments of Earth as they knew it. Yes, He is the Omega, but you have not seen the end as the Apostle John saw it through the power of the Holy Spirit. In other words, both our praise and our witness lose power when our acknowledgment unto God is based upon something other than His living within us. The Bible is truth in telling us God is Alpha and Omega, yet it helps us all the more in our spiritual walks when we proclaim that which we have personally experienced with Him. We tend to want to shout the things Biblical characters and church elders shout because we want to appear to be super-sanctified. You can have the prestige, just give me the power of His Holy Spirit working upon me by way of truth. Make it personal and it will generate power!

Let me get a little closer to some and make it a little more painful for others. Some of us call out "He is my Morning Star" and/or "He is the Bright in the Morning Star." The Lord Jesus said, as proclaimed by the apostle John in his vision, "I am the root and the offspring of David, and the bright and morning star" _(Revelation 22:16b)_. The word is translated as "day star" or "son of dawn" and can also be found in Numbers 24:17, Revelation 2:28; 22:16. Albeit, the reference can also be found in Isaiah 14:12 where the words refer to the fallen angel Lucifer; signified as "light bearer" and "planet Venus." The Lord Jesus made reference to this in Luke 10:18. Now I direct us to open a dictionary to the word "Lucifer" to see what may be found. There we will find him defined as "the morning star," "light bearer," "devil," and "planet Venus." So, I ask the question, to whom is your neighbor shouting when they call out "He is my morning star?" In the same way I ask, who are you calling unto when you proclaim that name? Help us God! Just imagine calling out to the morning star and Lucifer shows up to your doorstep and says, "What's up, you called?" For the reason of this example, and others, I urge believers to know in what we speak, as well as, simply acknowledge the Lord our God as who He is truly known to be in our individual lives. Be leery to shout names heard proclaimed by others. Just remember those we imitate may sound great, yet they may be closet satan worshipers or they may be worshiping Lucifer unaware of the true condition of their own spirits. Let it be understood that even some of our out-of-context traditions have kept many of us weak in our relationships with God, and continue to keep us unable to truly assume the power vested in us.

See, one thing we must do in this walk called faith is remove all the mundane statements that are out-of-context and/or not applicable to our relationships with the Almighty. Some proclamations may even be true to someone, yet they may not get to the heart and truth of the matter for others of us. Some of us fail to be blessed this day because we have failed to worship God in the Spirit and Truth that is proclaimed in John 4:23-24 and Psalm 145:18. Take the time to see and know what things really mean before shouting them to a God who knows better and knows all. Can I make it a little more plain? Some of us come up short in our prayers and in our walk of faith simply due to our speaking to God in references that we and God know of which we have no true knowledge nor personal attachment. Let each of us be truthful in our walk and talk.

This document will also illustrate the fact of many folk still being on milk. That's partially ok since we all develop at different times, in different areas and at different rates of speed. Much of our religious atmosphere and lives are based on knowing and reciting scripture alone; so we are taught. If we are unfamiliar with the context of what God was telling the original writer than we may be no better off than the keepers of the Law who knew the letter of the Law, but did not know the spirit of the Law — the basis of much of Jesus' teachings. In that, we are on milk.

To bring it full circle, we may have heard someone call God, "A shield in the middle of a storm." Yet, how can we be so bold and inattentive to speak to God in such terms if we have never been in a storm? This document will not go so far as to call anyone a liar in regards to their acknowledgment unto God, but it shall be said that sort of disregard in acknowledgment is the type of disharmonious spirit that may have God to say, "You really do not know me in those terms, thus why should I answer your prayer?" The Bible proclaims it this way, "Thou shalt not take the name of the Lord thy God in vain; for the Lord will not hold him guiltless that taketh his name in vain" *(Exodus 20:7).* The Hebrew indicates "vain" as false and lie. The New International Version translates to "misuse."

That moves us to the next illustration. How better to close, shut off, or disconnect a conversation with someone than to call them out of their name? This is the base of this *key.* "Boo" might be their name according to someone, like their significant other, husband or wife, but don't you dare call them by that name and expect a warm reception. In the same respect, you better not call your wife by some name in which she is unfamiliar, unless you plan on sleeping on the couch all this week. Maybe that illustration sunk in a little deeper. Please get this point however you may; for much of the strength of our spiritual faith walk is built upon it. It is so instrumental that we recognize that the same horizontal rules in which we live are dictated and first governed by our vertical relationship with the Almighty. We cannot possibly get the full effect of calling someone by a childhood nickname when we did not grow up with them to know how and where the name originated. It may smooth over later, but the main point is it creates a barrier or stumbling block which delays progress and, at times, disallows a successful outcome. Delay is one of the last things we want when it comes to prayer.

How better to get God's attention than to call Him by a name He knows we truly know Him as? God remembers when He sheltered us from the storms of life, so our calling Him "Shelterer" may very well make His eyebrows go up, His ears pop up and His blessings shower down. God may very well say, "That's my child I sheltered from the floods of life." So, why take the forbidden chance of calling Him by an unconscionable or personally unrecognizable name? Some folk are so phony that they do not realize it is fully exposed in their walk with God. We must become better exalters of our God, since acknowledgment is a part of exaltation. Many folk call themselves praisers, but for the life of them, they cannot truly exalt and extol God. This is primarily due to their inability to worship God in Spirit and in Truth, as they continue to recite those things of God that others have come to know Him as. It is a painful reality that many folk just do not praise God in accord with their own experiences and through their own walks with Him. This is a wicked truth that most of us have fallen into; if we were to tell the truth.

Simply put, individually we do not spend enough personal time with God in order to acknowledge who He truthfully is to us. This bears out in our inability to joy in our sufferings; events where we come to know Him better and truthfully. We come to know that He is our Deliverer by the way He brought us out of situations. We come to know that He is a Comforter by the way He never leaves us when times get tough. We come to know that He is a Healer by the way He removed sickness out of our bodies when the doctor found no cure. That's when the greatness of our relationships with God turn into truthful praise and worship. Then, we can truthfully acknowledge the Lord as we go to Him in prayer.

Oh, there is nothing greater than to know for yourself the fact that the Lord is faithful. What a joy to be released into the realism of knowing He is faithful and will never leave you alone. We would never come to know of His faithfulness unless we had gone through a few trials and witnessed the Lord showing up to deliver us. Many people cannot elevate to our level of spirituality, for reason they do not want to go through what you and I have gone through. So many of us, and rightfully so, diligently try to avoid issues and problems in our lives. It is true that we simply do not embrace the growth that comes by way of trials. We want a pristine life, void of trials, void of sufferings and void of mistakes. Paul proclaimed to joy in sufferings so to take part in the spiritual increase.

"Therefore being justified by faith, we have peace with God through our Lord Jesus Christ. By whom also we have access by faith into this grace wherein we stand, and rejoice in hope of the glory of God. And not only so, but we glory in tribulations also: knowing that tribulation worketh patience; And patience, experience; and experience, hope: And hope maketh not ashamed; because the love of God is shed abroad in our hearts by the Holy Ghost which is given unto us. For when we were yet without strength, in due time Christ died for the ungodly. For scarcely for a righteous man will one die: yet peradventure for a good man some would even dare to die. But God commendeth His love toward us, in that, while we were yet sinners, Christ died for us. Much more then, being now justified by His blood, we shall be saved from wrath through Him. For if, when we were enemies, we were reconciled to God by the death of His Son, much more, being reconciled, we shall be saved by His life. And not only so, but we also joy in God through our Lord Jesus Christ, by whom we have now received the atonement" (Romans 5:1-11).

Again, let it be understood this document will give us increase in our prayer lives along with increase in our worship experiences unto God. Our relationships with Him will forever be changed and renewed.

"I beseech you therefore, brethren, by the mercies of God, that ye present your bodies a living sacrifice, holy, acceptable unto God, which is your reasonable service. And be not conformed to this world: but be ye transformed by the renewing of your mind, that ye may prove what is that good, and acceptable, and perfect, will of God" (Romans 12:1-2).

Oh, somebody ought shout right now, "I want to be renewed. Oh, Lord renew me. Renew this broken body. Renew this broken spirit. Renew, Renew, Renew!" Come on back now. Come on back! Understand and digest this point. We cannot be renewed on our own, nor by our own power. We cannot be renewed of anything by our own might nor strength. The only way we can truly receive of this renewal is by the Spirit of the Living God working within. "... Not by might, nor by power, but by my Spirit, saith the Lord of hosts" *(Zechariah 4:6).*

Why Acknowledge the Lord's Deity at all?

Why acknowledge God at all? Mmmm. One answer to this question is two fold. First, God can recognize our faith in His deity by way of our hearts, our living and our acknowledgment of Him. In other words, we should let God know that we are truly aware of who He is, and that we strongly believe in who He is. This firms our union with Him, as does any union become strengthened when each party is formally acknowledged. He acknowledges who we are throughout scriptures, so why do we find it difficult to acknowledge who He is in our hearts? As an example, we give strength to our relationships with our parents when we announce them as Pop, Mom, Father, Mother, etc. Just imagine how much the relationship would be diminished and stricken if we called them Pam, Joe, Nancy or Mike. Truly understand there are many broken child-parent relationships which are representative of the children addressing their parents on a first name basis, rather than addressing them by their rightful and respectful parental titles.

We surely do the same in our relationships with God when we fail to speak of His deity. We tend to diminish our proper connection with God when we fail to acknowledge Him as the Author of our faith and the Creator of our very being. What worse way to begin our prayer than by starting on the wrong foot through our improperly acknowledging the Lord? Here is where a few folk may say, "Praying to God should not be so much of a systematic event." Of course this is a true statement, but those who say such have missed the point. The point is how we acknowledge God is the beginning of our being ushered into the right spirit of prayer. Make no mistake about it, we cannot get into the spirit of prayer through misrepresentations and perversions. How can we figure to call someone out of their name then expect a positive outcome of our experience with them? Can a student call their teacher by their first name and not expect to be chastened? How could we not expect that relationship to be rocky in the thereafter? Even so, productivity in that relationship will surely be diminished because one of the parties failed to promote the spirit of the relationship through proper acknowledgment. Conversely, there are many on the face of this earth who seek degrees and positions just so they can be called by a certain title, versus their being recognized as such. Know the difference and be blessed. This is another example of how important it is for us to <u>acknowledge</u> God for who He is and not merely call Him by title alone.

Second, our spiritual awareness is elevated when we duly and rightly acknowledge the Lord as Father, Deliverer, Healer and other names that more so represent our relationships with Him. Our spirits are then elevated into a realm of respectability and blessings that tend to promote a spiritual increase. In other words, we become more sensitized to our Lord and His Word when we are submissive unto His deity and dominion.

Let me pause here for just a moment to say, many of us are so stuck in a rut with our faith walks, simply due to our not being submissive unto God. Many of us think we are all that and a bag of chips and think we alone are responsible for our successes. Others of us continue to falter in our faith because we tend to minimize the spirituality of our faith walk with the Lord. We read the word in John 4:24 which tells us, "God is Spirit and they who worship him must worship him in spirit and in truth," and say we believe this verse, yet we refrain from living this verse. The Word is power, but it will not work if we do not impregnate that very Word with our faith and our truthful walk.

Most of us have been asked the question, "How's it working for you?" In response some of us have sat idly complaining that it is not working. Imagine that. Complaining that the Word is not working, yet refusing to live and pray in the spirit of the Word in order to make it work effectively. Please don't miss this, for this is the breadth and expanse of this document. The keepers of the law missed this very point and thus refused to receive our Lord Jesus. The same plight haunts us today, whereas we subvert the sanctification process within us and reject renewal by not worshiping the Lord in spirit. It is an empty worshiper who attempts to worship our Lord with the mind only.

Acceptance and Appreciation

Acknowledgment is a form of showing appreciation, and vice versa. We will not acknowledge someone for something we surely do not appreciate of them. We surely do not call our enemies "friends" when they truly are not such. Nor might we be able to honour our parent with the term "Father" if they were never present in our lives. As humans, we have a tradition of acknowledging others through titles as to how we accept them or appreciate them. You may acknowledge your supervisor at work as "the" Boss if you do not care for him or her, whereas, you may call him or her "my" Supervisor if you accept them and their position. We treat God in the same manner. Those who have an intimate relationship with Him tend to address Him with endearing and meaningful names, whereas, they who spend less time with Him may simply call Him "God." Those who have moved a little closer to Him call Him names which are even more endearing to them than Friend, Savior, Love, Joy or Provider; if one can imagine. Our acknowledgment of who He is ought to graduate and become more spirited and personal, as we accept Him more and more into our living.

Some carnal Christians have come to know the language of church worship and thus babble words that are true of God, yet not indicative of their relationships with Him. This is more prevalent than we may think since the importance of properly acknowledging God is not taught in all places of worship. Therefore, I declare to you here today, proper acknowledgment is of the utmost importance in our having a healthy and prosperous relationship with the Lord. He already knows who He is to you and what He has done for you, so you might as well be truthful and walk into the blessings of a powerful relationship spawned by your truthful praise and acknowledgment of Him. It is through your truthfulness that many of your blessings shall come into fruition.

Someone at this point may ask, "Well Reverend, how do I come into knowing these truthful terms by which to acknowledge the Lord?" I answer, it all begins with spending time with the Lord in everyday living. We must accept Him in our living then watch how He works in and through our lives. He works in different ways in all of us. Be sensitized to know He is in control of all that goes on in our lives, then pay attention to how He directs things. Then and only then will we be able to truthfully acknowledge who and what God is in our lives, personally.

Only you can testify of the first hand accounts of God's greatness in your life. Others may be able to eyewitness what He has done in your life, but only you can personally attest to how He has individually touched your life! Your deliverance may be different than my deliverance. Your healing may be greater and more profound than my healing. In saying this, we all should be mindful of the truth of who God is in our individual lives in order for us to best worship Him in spirit. It need not be a historical name and it need not even be something dramatically original, but it truly needs to be described in your heart, permeated in your spirit, and indicative of your living with God; less you fall short in extolling who He truly is — to you!

The Bible gives us a great example of acknowledging the Lord through David's instructing Solomon in I Chronicles 28:9. The New International Version translates "know thou the God" as "acknowledge the God." David goes on to express a list of items to Solomon, but he proclaims acknowledgment as the first item of business; which further stresses its importance. We may not possess the faith to serve the Lord if we do not acknowledge Him as Lord of our lives. We may have difficulty devoting our lives, time, talents and hearts to the Lord if we do not acknowledge Him as the God who entrusted us as servants with God given talents. We surely will not be willing to turn our everything over to Him if we do not first accept and acknowledge that He is in full control, all powerful (omnipotent), and all knowing (omniscient).

Driven by Faith

Acknowledgment is a bi-product of our faith in knowing God is; not the other way around. We must grow to realize shouting unrealistic or non-personal statements unto God does not increase our faith. On the contrary, it's our increase of faith which prompts us to acknowledge who He is. Many of us sadly continue to try to accelerate our faith by shouting the names of God, in every attempt to consciously or unconsciously fake-out ourselves, God and the brethren. The spiritual _Progression_ is that our faith drives our willingness, servitude, devotion and acknowledgment of who He is. It is our faith in Him that gives us the willingness to say, "Though he slay me yet will I trust in him..." _(Job 13:15)._

God can view through our hearts whether our motives are driven by faith in Him — The Creator; as explained by David. Let it be known that our willingness to acknowledge and serve the Lord should be driven by our faith and our love for Him, rather than driven by our desires to receive only blessings from Him. So few of us are willing to bless His name in faith rather than in wading for some form of reciprocation. The Word is a reader of hearts, "For the word of God is quick, and powerful, and sharper than any twoedged sword, piercing even to the dividing asunder of soul and spirit, and of the joints and marrow, and is a discerner of the thoughts and intents of the heart" *(Hebrews 4:12).*

We should have it in our hearts to seek the Lord with faithful spirits and not spirits solely desirous nor spent on receiving anything from Him. Let us have it in our spirits to want of God's presence in our prayers, and not just want of the blessings He can provide through our prayers. Seek Him first and all the other things we stand in need shall be provided; for He is a provider and rewarder. "But without faith it is impossible to please him: for he that cometh to God must believe that he is, and that he is a rewarder of them that diligently seek him" *(Hebrews 11:6).* This scripture does not reference for anyone to diligently seek the things, nor does it direct us to seek Him for those things. The scripture is quite distinct in directing us to solely seek Him and to not be concerned for what we shall eat or drink, for He even provides for the raven *(Job Chapter 38)* and the sparrow *(Matthew Chapter 10).* Yes, the Lord is truly a provider, but He is a provider first unto our spirits and souls, then He is a provider unto our living and other parts of our being. Let us recall Luke 5:17-26 when the Lord Jesus first forgave the sins of the man with palsy before He healed his body. The Scribes and Pharisees were perplexed and vexed of the Lord's actions. We must be counter to those disbelievers and be mindful that the Spirit is mostly concerned about our spirit's condition. Do not be as the keepers of the law; be like Christ.

Many of us are afflicted with the plight of seeking God for things instead of seeking Him for our spirits' increase, first. We all want to pray the prayer of Jabez. "And Jabez called on the God of Israel, saying, Oh that thou wouldest bless me indeed, and enlarge my coast, and that thine hand might be with me, and that thou wouldest keep me from evil, that it may not grieve me! And God granted him that which he requested" *(I Chronicles 4:10).* Few of us want to pray as Peter prayed, "Thou hast made known to me the ways of life; thou shalt make me full of joy with thy countenance" *(Acts 2:28).* Believers should be excited to enter into the countenance (presence and approval) of the Lord. Everyone wants things, yet not everyone truly wants God. We all talk and pray of wanting stuff. "I want this and I want that," is the catch phrase of our day, but how about us first wanting God and God alone? Oh, what a joy to just want Him. Oh, what greatness and fullness of joy to just want Him. What power unto thine spirit to just desire Him. To seek that which last throughout all eternity. Oh, what a blessed joy!

Surface Value Acknowledgment

Our mode of acknowledging the Lord is often just a surface value type of acknowledgment. Our acknowledgment unto the Lord remains on the surface of giving Him credit for what He has done for us, rather than for who He is in all creation. He is much bigger than what we often give Him credit. Recognizing Him as the Creator of all things normally does not give us great excitement, and so we tend to omit it all together. The truth is our faith would increase if we would learn to acknowledge His greatness based on who He is, alone. We are so accustomed to giving Him credit for how great He is based upon what He does for us, which lends to a spirit attached to the possessions rather than to Christ Jesus. Glory and great blessings go unto the heart which honours Him for who He is rather than for just what He has done.

We will better honour our parents, our children, our spouses and our neighbors for who they are, if we first learned to acknowledge and honour the Lord for who He is. See, we acknowledge God solely based on what He has done, so we acknowledge our friends, family and neighbors in the same fashion. Again, a correct vertical relationship with the Lord will dictate fruitful horizontal relationships. Simply check your own heart to understand how great you would feel if someone loved and acknowledged you mostly for who you are, rather than for what you can do for them. This point must be digested, for we must truthfully seek and acknowledge God and not just seek and acknowledge the things He can provide.

Now, many may be saying it seems as though I am teaching people not to pray for things. This is far from truth. This document is designed and presented in such a fashion to give us and our prayers the best chance of success. It all begins by preparing our spirits for what is expected of us by God. We are in the best position to have our prayers answered positively by God and our spirits immensely blessed by the Holy Spirit, once we best understand what is expected of us and once we have received changed hearts. This document shall fully clarify this point.

Heart is Fixed

Our hearts must be fixed whenever we enter prayer. Not fixed on our request, but fixed on the Lord and who He is. Far too many of us need a heart fix. That heart fix comes by way of fastening our hearts on the Lord and changing our mentality towards communing with Him. As believers, we are famous for fixing our hearts on those things we need or want, while at the same time fixing our hearts on God only as the provider of those very things we want or need. We would be greatly blessed and we would more so glorify God if we would fix our hearts just on Him being God alone. "My heart is fixed, O God, my heart is fixed..." *(Psalm 57:7).*

For the most part we should fasten our hearts and spirits on the fact that He is our Creator and Father. Instead, we woefully concentrate on God as a bank machine or a prosperity concession stand. It can be said that our hearts are so often in the wrong places. Yes, the Lord is a provider, but better be it that we are preoccupied about Christ being the Son of an Almighty God and the Savior of our salvation. God surely wants us to be blessed, but He truly wants us to realize He alone is our greatest blessing. We often say, "As long as I got King Jesus, I don't need anything else." Yet, we are often asking for things other than He alone. I do pray someone is receiving the fullness of this, for it is a *key* for us all.

Please do not misunderstand this. I am not prescribing that we not ask the Lord for a new car or a new house. What I am declaring is that we have our hearts stayed on Jesus, then the car and house shall be added unto us. The Lord is faithful to provide our hearts' desires when our hearts are fixed on Him. He knows all we stand in need, and He knows we first stand in need of Him. I repeat. He knows we first stand in need of Him! If we say, "As long as I got King Jesus, I don't need anything else," then let it be testified through our faith of living accordingly, as our true intents glorify His Holy and righteous name. I do declare this moment there is no blessing greater than to know He is God alone and that we stand in need of His very presence in our lives, above all else.

We cannot acknowledge God to the best of our abilities without having our hearts fixed on who He is. It is great to label Him and to know Him as Merciful, Provider, Shelter, Rock and Supplier of all our needs, but much greater is it to fix our hearts and spirits on Him as Savior, Lord, God and King. Let me make it a little more personal. Would your heart shine if you knew your spouse and children loved you for you alone instead of their loving you for your purchasing them gifts weekly? What happens when your money ceases and the gifting depletes? Then where goes the love? Does their love for you leave along with the fading and temporal resources? Our love, adoration and acknowledgment for the Lord can be examined under the same analogy and premise. Will our devotion unto the Lord cease if He were to stop showering us with gifts?

As we see it is essential for us to actually acknowledge Him for His Lordship alone, lest our spirits' joy for Him wisp away at the turning of a foul wind. We are not the first to come into this awareness that our souls' greatest desire ought to be for the Lord alone. In the Book of Ecclesiastes Solomon gave reflection of the vanity of prosperity in his life, whereby he concluded, "Let us hear the conclusion of the whole matter: Fear God, and keep His commandments: for this is the whole duty of man" *(Ecclesiastes 12:13)*.   King Hezekiah proclaimed in prayer unto the Lord, "... thou art the God, even thou alone, of all the kingdoms of the earth; thou hast made heaven and earth" *(II Kings 19:15 see 19:14-19)*.   Hezekiah acknowledged God as Lord rather than as Deliverer.   He was surely in need of deliverance, yet he kept his heart fixed on God as Lord.   God's answer to his prayer entailed, "But I know thy abode, and thy going out, and thy coming in, and thy rage against me" *(II Kings 19:27)*, illustrating God knew the whole of the situation; hence the Lord God favorably answered Hezekiah's prayer as written in verses 34-35.   Isaiah 37:14-38 also speaks of Hezekiah's prayer, and how the king acknowledged God for who He was and not for what He had done.

Acknowledgment vs Thanksgiving

It is important to recognize all that the Lord has done for us, but the proper place for speaking of the things He has done for us is in our giving thanksgiving versus acknowledgment. Our primary focus in the *Element* or mode of acknowledging the Lord is on "who" He is rather than "what" He has done. Yes, there are times when the who is defined by the what, but fact remains that our major focus during *Acknowledgment* is on He alone.   There is coming a point in prayer where we speak of the great works (the what) of His Spirit and hands, but acknowledgment is about lifting Him up in name and position. At this point in prayer it is all about who He is. It is fine to blend thanksgiving and acknowledgment while praying but it is essential that our spirits do realize the difference and pray accordingly. We shall surely be blessed additionally if we realize the difference and put into practice the act of acknowledging the Lord for who He is alone.

Upon reaching this greater level of acknowledging God we will attain blessings unknown by most. This is a level that inspired the original writers. This is a level which kept David through all the storms and battles. A level which empowered the early Church to sustain and stand through persecutions. We must seek and acquire this level so we can become empowered beyond ordinary fellowship with the Lord and so we can attain the greatest blessing. The Bible says, "Delight thyself also in the Lord: and he shall give thee the desires of thine heart" *(Psalm 37:4)*, and "But seek ye first the Kingdom of God, and his righteousness; and all these things shall be added unto you" *(Matthew 6:33)*. We shall eventually come to realize, just as Solomon, that the Lord is our greatest heart's desire. The sooner we grow to acknowledge that fact the sooner we shall be blessed beyond measure and beyond compare. Let it be so as it is.

"A Story of Acknowledgment"

I Samuel chapters one and two tell a story of a strong prayer warrior, Hannah, who proclaimed great words of acknowledgment unto the Lord. She was once a barren woman married to a priest named Elkanah, who had another wife, Peninnah, a provoker of Hannah, because she was without child. The Bible tells us Hannah prayed continuously *(v1:12)* and she poured out her soul *(v1:15)*; for she had a strong relationship with God. In verses 2:1-2 Hannah prayed powerful words of acknowledgment unto the Lord, "And Hannah prayed, and said, my heart rejoiceth in the Lord, mine horn is exalted in the Lord: my mouth is enlarged over mine enemies; because I rejoice in thy salvation. There is none holy as the Lord: for there is none beside thee: neither is there any rock like our God." These words, so strongly spoken, illustrate that Hannah knew the importance of acknowledging God for who He is in addition to what He was able to do *(v2:4-10)*.

The power of Hannah's prayer relationship with God is partially revealed through her words spoken in acknowledgment. She acknowledges the Lord's deity through mentions of His power, acts, characteristics, providence and sovereignty, just to name a few. It would behoove us to follow her example, since she has characteristics of a strong prayer warrior; like obedient, sold-out, patient, promise keeper and others.

In addition, Hannah used acknowledgment as not only a means by which to worship the Lord, but she also used the power of truthful acknowledgment to renew her weariness in prayer *(v2:2-10)*. She had gone through some ups and some downs to see the salvation of the Lord. She had even gone through the rededication of the very blessing she prayed to receive − her new born son. Here she also demonstrates how prayer warriors are to keep covenants; as will be illustrated within this document. She came to a time in her faith when she could powerfully acknowledge God and be renewed in spirit, therewith. If ever there is a need for renewal, it is just after we have done something which requires big faith and great spiritual fortitude *(v1:24-28)*. Her acknowledgment unto the Lord had truly set the table for adoration unto Him. Finally, Hannah's acknowledgment unto the Lord also illustrates the fine line that can exist between acknowledgment and thanksgiving. We can thank the Lord without actually saying the words thank you, but it is imperative that we recognize the difference between the two *Elements* so we may more strongly receive of His presence and His Spirit's directions.

I get excited each time I read from this text, for it is of great encourage-ment to witness, albeit through pages of text. Oh, the power of faithful prayer and the fruit that comes about by spending quality time with God. There are many who prayed to God throughout the Bible, of course, but none too much stronger in acknowledgment as in the grass roots and heart felt prayer given by Hannah. The Bible makes it perfectly clear through the telling of this story, fervent prayer and a seeking heart are rewarded with God's presence and with His mighty works. What more can we ask?

It is not until we pour out our soul and spend time with the Lord, such as Hannah, that we shall be able to receive fruits ripe and sweet. Hannah prayed and her prayers were answered by God because she exhibited the characteristics of a truthful and unashamed prayer warrior. Her acknowledgment of God is a great example of just what it takes to be that prayer warrior God desires each of us to become, even in this modern day.

Focused on Communion

NAMES OF GOD

Below is a list of names of God most of which we are all familiar. Again, it is hoped that we acknowledge God with names we personally familiarize Him as in our individual lives, so to best heighten our communion with Him.

NAME OF GOD	MEANING	SIGNIFICANCE
Elohim	God	Refers to God's Power and Might
Yahweh (Jehovah)	The Lord	Proper Name of the divine person
El Elyon	God Most High	He is above all gods. Most Sacred
El Roi	God Who Sees	God Oversees all Creation and Affairs
El Shaddai	God Almighty	God is All-Powerful
Yahweh Yireh (Jehovah Jireh)	The Lord will Provide	God will Provide our Real Needs
Yahweh Nissi (Jehovah Nissi)	The Lord is my Banner	Remember God for Helping Us
Adonai	Lord	God Alone is the Head over All
Yehweh Shalom (Jehovah Shalom)	The Lord is Peace	God gives us Peace So We need not Fear
El Olam	The Everlasting God	God is Eternal He will Never Die

ACKNOWLEDGMENT — *Progression of Prayer Element #1*

Exercises

INSTRUCTIONAL

1. Pair with a friend or classmate to discuss the section on "Who is God to you?" Re-read this short section, then verbally share your acknowledgments of who God truly is in your lives. Ensure neither of you uses cliche's to acknowledge God.

   BENEFIT:
   This is an exercise to help drive us to be honest about our acknowledgment of who God truly is in our lives. Truthful acknowledgment shall strengthen our spirits union with the Lord through prayer.

PERSONAL

1. At the beginning of your daily devotionals read scriptures listed at the front of this chapter concerning the how, why, what, and when. Do this for at least a week's time.

   BENEFIT:
   To have devotionals in regards to these four items will strengthen your parent-child relationship with the Lord; as your spirit becomes more in tuned with your position and place of submission unto Him.

ACKNOWLEDGMENT — *Progression of Prayer Element #1*

General Questions

1. What are the three basic essence' of setting the plate of grace?

2. What are the three things we should fix our hearts upon when entering prayer? What should our hearts be less fixed upon? And why?

3. What is one reason it is essential to develop a personal relationship with God?

4. Is it best to acknowledge God by the name someone else has proclaimed Him as? And why?

5. What are the two reasons why we should acknowledge God?

6. Of what is acknowledgment a bi-product?

7. According to scripture where should we acknowledge God?

8. How can we be renewed in our prayer lives?

9. What is the essential difference between acknowledgment and thanksgiving?

   Why should prayer warriors be aware of the difference?

10. How do we obtain a "heart fix?"

ACKNOWLEDGMENT – *Progression of Prayer Element #1*

Advanced Questions

1. Choose three Biblical characters and list one name of God acknowledged by each character.

   Site one reason for each as to why others should refrain from proclaiming these names of God?

2. By what name do you normally acknowledge God?

   Why?

3. How is acceptance and appreciation connected to acknowledgment?

   What does our horizontal appreciation reflect?

   Why?

Adoration

Pray this prayer with me:
A Prayer for Adoration

"All seeing, all merciful, all blessed, all powerful, all knowing, all gracious and glorious God! How I do praise Your wonderful name. I adore You Father for who You are, above all else. You alone are God. My Holy God, worthy of all honour, glory and praise. Hallelujah! You are the praise in my heart and the adoration on my lips, and I thank You for the very ability to shout Your name glory. Thank You God. Now I pray that You bless my spirit with more wisdom of how to greatly adore You. Let me praise You all the more after the reading of this chapter. Have these principles move me beyond merely getting Your attention and into a heightened spiritual connection with You. Fix my heart on praising You, for You alone are worthy of high praise. Let Your name be glorified and magnified. This I pray in faith in Jesus Christ my Lord and in the Spirit of Your presence — Amen."

This section is to better enhance our understanding of the Biblical reasons for who should give adoration, how should adoration be given, why should adoration be given, what should be given adoration, where should adoration be given and when should adoration be given. Our study of adoration will be further enhanced if these verses are read previous to moving onto the chapter material; as this format will indeed better prepare our spirits to receive of the chapter material.

1) WHO should give adoration?

- Exodus 15:2 — All who claim the Lord as God; strength and salvation
- II Chronicles 29:28 — All the congregation
- Nehemiah 8:6 — All the people
- Psalm 45:17 — The people
- Psalm 66:4 — All the Earth
- Psalm 74:21 — The poor and the needy
- Psalm 89:5 — The Heavens and the congregations of the saints
- Psalm 119:175 — The living
- Isaiah 38:18-19 — They who are alive and not in a pit nor grave (the living)
- Isaiah 42:10 — The inhabitants of the sea
- Isaiah 42:11 — The wilderness and the cities
- Isaiah 66:23 — All flesh
- Jeremiah 17:14 — Those who are healed and saved
- Matthew 21:16 — Babes and sucklings
- Luke 19:37 — His disciples
- Hebrews 1:6 — The Angels of God
- I Peter 4:11 — All things
- Revelation 19:5 — His servants and those who fear Him; both small and large
- Revelation 22:9 — They who keep the sayings of the Book

2) HOW should adoration be given?

- Genesis 24:26 — With head bowed down
- II Kings 17:36 — With fear
- Nehemiah 8:6 — With your face to the ground
- Psalm 29:2 — In the beauty of holiness
- Psalm 34:1 — With your mouth
- Psalm 63:4 — With lifted hands
- Psalm 71:8 — Filled mouth and all day
- Psalm 95:5 — Exalt Him
- Psalm 95:6 — Bow down, kneeling
- Psalm 100:1-2 — With singing and joyfully
- Psalm 149:3 — In dance; timbrel and harp

2) HOW should adoration be given? *(Continued)*
- Psalm 150:4 — With timbrel, dance, stringed instrument and organs
- Psalm 150:6 — Everything that hath breath
- Isaiah 42:10 — Sing a new song
- Joel 2:26 — Unashamedly
- Matthew 15:7-11 — Not in vain
- Mark 5:6 — Running (eagerly)
- Luke 19:37 — With a loud voice
- John 4:23-24 — In spirit and in truth
- I Corinthians 14:15 — With your spirit
- I Corinthians 14:25 — Falling on your face (prostrate)
- Hebrews 13:15 — With sacrifices, your lip's fruit and continually
- James 5:13 — With singing
- Revelation 4:10 — Casting crowns before His throne

3) WHY should adoration be given?
- Exodus 15:2 — The Lord is our strength, song, salvation and God
- Judges 5:2 — For the Lord being avenging
- I Chronicles 16:25 — The Lord is great, greatly to be praise and to
          be feared above all gods
- Psalm 45:17 — To make His name remembered in all generations
- Psalm 95:5 — For He is Holy
- Psalm 147:1 — For it is good; it is pleasant; it is comely
- Psalm 150:2 — For His mighty acts and excellent greatness
- Isaiah 61:3 — To glorify the Lord and to be called trees of
          righteousness (the planting of the Lord)
- Jeremiah 17:14 — Because He is your praise
- Luke 19:37 — For the mighty works you have seen
- Luke 23:47 — Because of all He has done
- Revelation 4:11 — Because He is worthy to receive glory, honour
          and power; He created all things for His pleasure

4) WHAT should be given adoration?
- I Chronicles 29:13 — His glorious name
- Nehemiah 8:6 — The great God
- Psalm 5:13 — For His mercy
- Psalm 89:5 — His wonders
- Psalm 95:6 — The Lord our Maker
- Isaiah 12:2 — Jehovah
- Isaiah 42:10 — A new song
- Joel 2:26 — The name of the Lord our God
- Acts 24:14 — The God of our fathers
- Revelation 4:10 — He that liveth forever and ever

5) WHERE should adoration be given?
- Psalm 99:5; 132:7 — At His foot stool
- Psalm 100:2 — Before His presence
- Psalm 100:4 — Entering into His gates and into His courts
- Psalm 149:1 — In the congregation of saints
- Psalm 150:1— In the firmament of His power
- Isaiah 42:10 — From the end of the Earth; down to the sea and
  isles
- Isaiah 42:11 — In the wilderness and the cities; from the mountain
  top
- Isaiah 42:12 — In the islands
- Isaiah 61:11 — Before all the nations
- Luke 14:10 — In the presence of them that sit at meat with thee

6) WHEN should adoration be given?
- Exodus 15:2 — When He saves you
- I Chronicles 23:30 — Every morning
- Psalm 34:1 — At all times
- Psalm 45:17 — Forever and ever
- Psalm 63:4 — As long as you live
- Isaiah 66:23 — From one new moon to another; from one Sabbath
  to another
- Jeremiah 17:14 — When you are healed and saved
- Luke 18:43 — When you are delivered and when you follow Him;
  when you witness God's delivering power
- Luke 23:47 — When you see all He's done

"I will bless the Lord at all times: his praise shall continually be in my mouth"   Psalm 34:1

Adoration (act of expressing honor to glorify, worship, extol and show reverence) should come rather easily after we have acknowledged who God is in our lives, personally; as each *Element* in this *Progression of Prayer* is dependent on the previous *Element*. Here, our praise and adoration unto God is elevated by the mere recognition of all the who and the what God is in our lives. I do not know about you, but when I think about all He is to me! Oh, I can immediately begin to give Him praise. King David said it this way, "When I consider thy heavens, the work of thy fingers, and moon and the stars, which thou hast ordained;" *(Psalm 8:3)*. That exaltation hugely speaks of God's deity. This is why I often say, "It does not take much for me to shout His glory;" for I truly can remember what He means to all that I am in this life.

Truthfulness is one thing we must be mindful of throughout this document. In speaking, adoration and praise come naturally after giving the Lord honest acknowledgment. It is our honesty and truthfulness which grant us the spirit to move powerfully from one *Element* to the next; ultimately giving us benefit of answered prayers.

His Deity

The *Progression* of this document from acknowledgment to adoration suggest that we more so give God *Praise* for who He is, instead of only for what He does for us. It is a glorious thing to bless the name of the Lord for the great things He has done *(Job 37:5; Psalm 71:19)*, but let us grow to the next level of communion with the Lord by expanding our adoration to express who He is. The Lord is pleased that we acknowledge the results of His works, yet He is declaring to us this day how He shall rejoice all the more for our praising who He is. There is a power behind the "what He does." That power is the "who He is," and it goes beyond the names we give Him; like Provider, Shelterer, Healer and Deliverer. Oh yes! He is a great provider. The greatest provider anyone will ever find, yet His deity alone is far greater. It is *key* that we digest and live upon this precept which demands us to commune with the Lord in accord with who He is. Our power in prayer and in living depends on our grasping this major *key*. Make no mistake of this document's reiteration of this precept, for it is far too important for us to miss. This precept is wisdom, empowerment and contentment rolled into one.

There is a contentment spoken of in the Bible which emanates only by our being strongly settled in the fact that He is our God and beyond that nothing else much matters. Yes, we have good concerns and loves we are to attend unto, but a prayer warrior acknowledges that their greatest blessing is to know that He is God and God alone. Many of our prayers seem to fail due to our improper focus. Focusing on God's deity will automatically render our prayers successful, due to a change in our mind-sets and spirits. Paul said it this way in Philippians 4:11, "Not that I speak in respect of what: for I have learned in whatsoever state I am, there with to be content." In verse 13 He speaks of the power that resounds from such a spirit, "I can do all things through Christ which strengtheneth me."

Then, Paul proclaims in I Timothy 6:6-7, "But godliness with contentment is great gain. For we brought nothing into this world, and it is certain we can carry nothing out. And having food and raiment let us be therewith content." He goes on in verse 9 to say how we fall in our living and spirits when we fail to be content. I declare this very day this contentment begins with our diligence in acknowledging and praising God for His deity above all other things. If we recognize Him, we shall recognize what everything else is not.

I Know Him for Myself

If for a moment we could mention how important it is to acknowledge God, in *Element #1*, in regards to who He truly is in our individual lives. If we acknowledge Him as being our deliverer when times got tough, we should not have a difficulty in *Progressing* to *Element #2* of *Adoration and Praise*. As a matter of fact, persons often skip adoration in prayer, simply due to their never truly acknowledging God for who He actually is in their lives. This is repeated for emphasis. Make no mistake about it, truthful acknowledgment gains us greater access unto the presence of God. We cannot truthfully shout His glory if we claim the Lord as something we have never experienced. Woe unto the one who exclaims hollow shouts to imitate the praise of others.

Similarly many folk lack spiritual strength because they attempt to worship the Lord based upon things they have heard rather than things they have experienced. Worship, praise and spirituality are first matters of personal experience with God; past and present. We cannot truthfully praise God on a personal level by imitating the adoration and the witness of someone else. We can celebrate with others as they praise God in their personal witness, but we must be truthful to develop our own adoration unto God so our praise is made personal. This adoration we speak of in this part of the *Prayer Progression* is about our personal knowledge and experience with the Lord. We may be able to experience corporate worship in regards to what others have experienced with God, but each of us must be able to worship and praise Him in accord with our own personal relationships with Him. "Let everything that is in me praise ye the Lord," can only happen if all our entire beings acknowledge who He truly is in our individual lives, rather than praising Him according to what others have proclaimed. The 100,000 prayer warriors who will come forth through this *Prayer Progression* will indeed praise the Lord with power built upon truthful acknowledgment of their personal experiences with Him. A mature, strong and fruitful relationship with God is impossible if we operate on a "fake it till we make it" mentality. We cannot fake out God when it comes to anything; including the truth of the praise that is in our hearts and that comes out of our mouths. As stated in the introduction, it is hoped that our prayer lives become elevated through this document's *Prayer Progression*, while our spirituality unto God is blessed, as well. We should find it difficult not to praise God more and more each day after reading and experiencing these *Elements of Prayer Progression.*^{TM}

Getting God's Attention – a bi-product

If acknowledging God is the meat on the plate of getting His attention in prayer, then adoration and praise are the potatoes. There is nothing better than a hearty meal to get someone's attention. After setting the plate with the meat of recognizing who He is in His great splendor, it is then time to serve the compliment dish. Now take heed to this. Our objective is not necessarily to get God's attention, per se; for in spirit we truly praise Him for who He is rather than shouting untruthful felicitations for the mere intent of getting His attention. It is merely natural to want to get someone's attention when speaking with them. Conversely, it is greatly spiritual to speak with someone with no ulterior motives. Sounds mundane, but truly understand acknowledgment is all about who God truly is in our lives. Praying is not so much about knowing the language, as it is about being in the spirit and in the presence of the Lord. Fact is, the more we concentrate on God in our prayers and focus less on our own wants and needs, the more we get His attention. That is the point and *key.* The Bible tells us in no uncertain terms, "The Lord is nigh unto all them that call upon him, to all that call upon him in truth" *(Psalm 145:18).*

Lets be perfectly clear, we are not praising Him as an exchange for His attention. Do not get it twisted and do not mistaken the fact that God knows our hearts. "... and serve him with a perfect heart and with a willing mind: for the Lord searcheth all hearts, and understandeth all the imaginations of the thoughts: if thou seek him, he will be found of thee; but if thou forsake him, he will cast thee off for ever" *(I Chronicles 28:9).* We should not waste our time trying to coerce God into giving us His attention. We should automatically praise Him and acknowledge who He is as a matter of relationship. Our relationship with Him ought to generate praise for Him. Our Love for Him ought to produce praise for Him. Our history with Him ought to make us acknowledge Him for who He truly is in our lives. Our faith in Him ought to drive us to pray unto Him for answers, guidance, peace, fellowship and strength.

Solomon was aware of this truth as can be read in II Chronicles 7:1-11, where he went about his business of praising the Lord and offering sacrifices. God showed up thereafter saying, "... I have heard thy prayer, and have chosen this place to myself for an house of sacrifice .... Now mine eyes shall be open, and mine ears attent unto the prayer that is made in this place" *(v12-15).* Prayer warriors must offer sacrifices of praise.

Prayer warriors know a major focus of prayer is to commune with God. Most times we need answers to our prayers, but even in those instances communing with the Lord should still be a major root of our prayers. Prayer warriors are grown Christians who will often pray to God with no intent to ask Him for anything. Many prayers of the warrior are simply to commune with the Lord and give Him adoration. We may not be the prayer warriors we think we are, if we cannot find great joy in communing with Him without making a request nor thanking Him. Hear me and be blessed. Graduate to this level and receive a great spiritual benefit and increase. This document is designed through the strength of the Spirit so to take us to another level in prayer. I am so excited to know the Lord shall produce thousands of prayer warriors from this key alone.

The fact of the matter is we gain God's attention by the mere fact that we love on Him so much that we are compelled to praise Him. We should be compelled to praise Him for who He is and not just for what He can do for us. Simply put, He has already done more than enough. He's done more than enough for us that we should have a praise in our spirits, a shout in our mouths and an acknowledgment from the truth of our hearts that truly represents His living in our lives. After all, He sent His only begotten Son to die on our behalf so we may have a right to the Tree of Life. For that alone we ought to praise Him in all His glory!

Please understand, gaining God's attention is a bi-product of our praising Him with all intents of showing Him love, honor, glory and respect. We are called to praise Him, not to swindle Him. First of all, we cannot swindle an all-knowing, all-seeing God. There are those of us who speak His Word, but do not truly believe His Word. It is evident that some folk do not truly believe His Word for it shows in their living. So many persons who claim they believe His Word still try to swindle Him into giving them things through prayer, rather than their giving Him truth and spirit in prayer. Too many people attempt to gain God's attention through hollow prayers, which are merely attempts to swindle Him into blessing their lives. What about the verse that tells us, "I will bless the Lord at all times: his praise shall continually be in my mouth" _(Psalm 34:1)_? There are many verses that give us joy in knowing God will bless His children, yet we fail to realize the conditions for our being blessed by God have not changed. The conditions were and are that we give Him glory, honor and praise. The conditions are that we seek Him first. The conditions are that we keep His commands and live according to His will.

Self-centered attempts to get God's attention are like having the childish behavior of a toddler who has his or her communication skills built upon selfishness and me-isms. By now we ought know that, on a whole, spirit and life are not about us; they are about the Lord. At one point we must grow from milk onto meat. Our relationships with God are based upon His Word and His Son, driven through and driven by His Spirit.

The blessing that comes from our worshipping and praising the Lord in the spirit of His love is the access granted unto His presence! That is where the fullness of His blessings abide — In His presence! We should be eager to enter into the fullness of His presence. We would be ushered into His presence by the Spirit, if we would only praise Him with all our being and with truth. Much of our praying comes to fruition when our spirits connect with His Spirit. Prayer is not a monologue directed in our personal choirs. Prayer is surely the fulfillment of a communion and an open communication with God, wherein we speak to Him and He speaks to us. We must hear His answers and directions just as He hears our request. More will be spoken on dialogue in the _Element of Meditation._

The word adoration is of the root word adore. The words reverence and admiration are verbs or action words associated with adoration. Let's speak of a few scenarios of which all of us are most familiar in order to make the point of how much we should adore the Lord. We have all had an outward expression towards someone we admired from a distance; such as a singer, a movie star or as in a schoolmate crush. There may have been feelings and emotions in our spirits which made us eager to outwardly express that which we felt on the inside. We all surely can remember the first crush we had as children. Within us was a stir of emotions which often kept us up at night, unable to sleep due to the swelling activity within our spirits and hearts. That action swelled within us to different heights and levels each time that special person came into our thoughts and our presence. We all can remember how we wished the thought of them and that stirring within us would go away; at least long enough for us to get our chores done, be able to eat something and even possibly get some sleep at night. The thought of that person often consumed us and, if we were to be honest, it almost made us sick on our stomachs. That sense of being sick with adoration tended to elevate the person we adored up an imaginary ladder called "How great she/he is." The starry-eyed looks. The dreamy visions. The can't eat a thing cause my stomach is too twisted with emotions; and so on.

This same, if not more, adoration and emotion should be felt for the Almighty God; especially when we remember all He is in our lives. Truly no one can do us like the Lord. No greater love has ever, nor will ever, be shown by anyone that can compare to the love the Lord gave us by going to that old rugged cross on Calvary. No greater sacrifice and no greater care for another shall ever be shown until He returns for His Church. For that alone we should boil over with adoration and praise for Him. Mind you, this is apart from the things He does for us on a daily basis which also warrant our praise unto Him. He is a jealous God and desires us to adore Him as much, and more, than we adore others on the face of this earth. Others should get upset with the way we love Him more than we love them. Maybe we don't love Him but so much, if no one is mad.

Each night we should retire with our spirits truthfully aware that we owe Him praise for all He is to us and for all He's done for us. Someone reading this document can testify that it was a blessing from God that He even opened their eyes this morning. Someone else is overwhelmed with joy for God in knowing He was the one who healed them when the doctors, some family and even friends gave them a direly negative report. I can shout His hallelujahs knowing He kept food on my table when I had only three dollars and sixty-five cents to my name. No matter our individual cases and testimonies we all should be head over heals about our Savior. We should be so head over heals that there is no reluctance nor emptiness in our praise for Him. Jeremiah exclaimed, "But his word was in mine heart as a burning fire shut up in my bones ..." *(Jeremiah 20:9b).* You have heard it said many times before, "If it had not been for the Lord who was on my side!" For that we ought praise Him.

How easy is it?

The ease of giving the Lord adoration depends upon what is already in our spirits prior to entering into prayer. What is our level of love for

God? How much of our lifes' events do we credit to the hand of God? Are we faithful saints or fair weathered singers? What is the extent of our knowledge of God's attributes and how they work in accord with our living? The answers to these questions and others become the basis for our giving the Lord strong and truthful adoration in prayer. It is of no debate believers must give God adoration, thus it becomes essential that we truthfully attend to repair and/or enhance our spirit's conditions.

We will have a difficult time praising the Lord if our spirit of love and adoration for Him is broken or torn. We must truly be in love with the Lord in order to truly adorn His name with the adoration and praise it is due. It is already difficult enough to continue to praise the Lord when going through bad times, but much greater is the difficulty when our spirits are unsettled with God in the first place. We must have our hearts and devotion settled in the Lord before we even enter into prayer. We must be convinced and persuaded that He is King of all and in full control prior to going to the Throne of Grace. I praise the Lord so much because I am convinced of who He is. Are you convinced? Our heart's answers to that question will surely show in our praise no matter what our lips spue. We ought not need for God to first answer our prayers before we believe He is Lord of all. The fact still remains He is God no matter how, when or if He answers our prayers.

A portion of the blessing of this document is the *Progression* of how the *Elements* tie together. In this instance, it is good for many of us to *Praise* the Lord *(#2)* before making a *Request* unto Him *(#4)* so our adoration and praise can remind us of how convinced we are that He is Lord; thus empowering our faith to make a request and know we shall receive an answer. Some of us carry doubts caused by the pains and sufferings of our days, but through our praise we can be delivered into a realm of assuredness that He is, always has been and will forever be, Lord. I am not sure if we can remember a day when we had some doubts, but we should also remember how all doubt left once we began to praise Him. At that moment of adoration and praise we were reminded of just how great is He. Praise will help our remembrance even through the shortness of our humanistic memories.

Something about Praise

There is just something about praise that sets our souls right. Praise unto the Lord lifts the spirit and soul to such a place of heightened communion with the Lord. King David had doubts at times, but oh how he became encouraged when he began to praise the Lord. I once preached a sermon entitled "How Long" from Psalm 13. David had doubt and grief when he began this communion with God. He proceeded to imagine God hiding His face and not hearing his voice, while all along he cried out to God, "How Long?" David then continued with words filled with suffering, and tears, doubting he would even survive the attacks of his enemies. Then David began to praise the Lord; rejoicing and singing! His spirit lifted and his trust in the Lord was restored. This Psalm was recorded around the same time, 1018 B.C., as II Samuel 22 and 23, which also pour of great praise and even much acknowledgment. Like David, we must recognize how essential it is to celebrate and praise God for who He is. Failure to properly praise the Lord can set us up for failure in prayer. He is worthy of all our praise and He remains to be a jealous God.

The Example of David

Psalm 8 illustrates, as do many other Psalms, how David gave the Lord praise for what He had already done for him and man as a whole. Verses 1 and 9 give praise unto the Lord for who He is. Verses 2 through 8 also praise the Lord for blessing man with greatness and for God being Creator. We must likewise embrace praising the Lord, for He is worthy of all our praise. "Rejoice in the Lord, o ye righteous: for praise is comely for the upright" *(Psalm 33:1)*. The Hebrew states comely as beautiful and suitable, (naveh). It is a beautiful thing when the saints go up for praise. We should not only be Christians in belief of the Lord, but we should be actual praisers of Him, also.

King David, one of the greatest praisers who will ever live, gave one of the strongest praises in I Chronicles 29:10-19. Verse 10 illustrates how David was not ashamed to praise God in the midst of others. Verses 10 and 11 shout of the Lord's deity. Verse 17 tells of how God tries the heart and how we are to have willing spirits. Verse 13 even goes as far to give us illustration of David's prayer *Progressing* from *Praise (Element #2)* to *Thanksgiving (Element #3)*. Mark this praise scripture, as it shall give illustration of other *Progression Elements*, as well. A large majority of David's writings are filled with praises unto the Lord, as he is a great study for, both, all those who are lacking in praise, and all those who desire to go to another level in praise. It is urged that we do not merely imitate His words, but we should more so digest his mode and spirit of praise into our praise and worship. Allow the truth of his praise to inundate our faithful words unto the Lord, with power, conviction and authenticity. Through the studying of this document 100,000 prayer warriors shall come forth as Davids of this modern era, with truthful praises upon their mouths in a spirit of power.

Knowledge of God and Devotional Praise

This I suggest to anyone who may be weak or lacking in praise and worship: study the Book of Psalms for the next twelve months as a part of daily devotionals. Let us become Davids (men and women after God's own heart) by increasing our truthful praise spirit. We must get into our spiritual systems just how important it is to praise the Lord. Just having knowledge of the Lord is just not enough these days. We must be like David and be praisers, as well. Like David, we must become praisers who give God truthful adoration along side our having knowledge of Him. Let me tell you, to know the Lord is to be elated and even ecstatic about praising Him. God Himself said, "Thus saith the Lord, Let not the wise man glory in his wisdom, neither let the mighty man glory in his might, let not the rich man glory in his riches: But let him that glorieth glory in this, that he understandeth and knoweth me, that I am the Lord which exercise lovingkindness, judgment, and righteousness, in the earth: for in these things I delight, saith the Lord" _(Jeremiah 9:23-24)._

One reason God loved David so much was because David patterned his devotionals and praise according to his knowledge of who God was to him. God loves us, for we are His children, yet we too can go to another level of His loving us if we would simply and truthfully praise Him in regards to, and in conjunction with our truthful knowledge of Him. David knew the Lord, as was reflected by the plethora of praise he gave in many of the Psalms. These writings were not only Psalms of praise, but they were illustrations of David's knowledge of who God was to him, also. Psalm 81:1 describes the Lord as strength. Psalm 91:2 speaks of God as Refuge and Fortress. Psalm 99:1-2 shout that God reigns and He is great. Psalm 107:1-2 exclaim of God as merciful and Redeemer. Psalm 117 and 118 give praises to God as merciful, good, strength and salvation. We could go on and on. One can even see within these Psalms how our acknowledging the Lord is a forerunner of, and can be integrated with our praise. If we can acknowledge who He is, then it should be easy to give Him the praise He deserves and demands.

A spirit Connection of Praise to Prayer

There is a reality about the connection between praise and prayer. If our hearts are not set on praising God, our spirits may not be right for praying unto Him. Please understand this point. Our spirit's condition is the catapult or stumbling block for many of our prayers. This is a _key_ for us all. "As the fining pot for silver, and the furnace for gold; so is a man to his praise" _(Proverbs 27:21)._ The Lord stands ready and willing to positively bless the prayers of each who's spirit's condition is right. Far too many of our prayers have gone unanswered because of this fact. Let me make it a little more plain. If our spirits are not right for praising the Lord, our spirits surely will not be right for giving Him the glory and honor once our blessings are delivered unto us. This is a simple fact of which God is fully aware. Many of us will claim we will praise and honor God once we are delivered, but we are only fooling ourselves. Having a tough time giving the Lord praise has already rendered our hearts unable to give Him post-praise, honor and glory. We have more than likely done it many times in the past — received our blessings then forgot from whom they came. It was not our intention to forget, yet the conditions of our hearts were not such that the praise unto Him abounded.

A True Blessing

Let us get our spirits right so we can receive our blessings. Let us truly understand that getting our spirits right is a blessing within itself. Make no mistake about it. There are many children of God who receive a change in their spirits, then realize they never really needed the things they were praying to receive in the first place. They come to realize the "spirit fix" is one of the greatest blessings anyone can receive. Hear me!

The spirit's Condition

The condition of our spirits can bless our entire lives and not just our prayers. The very outlook we have on our lives may improve once our spirits' conditions are improved. As stated in the Introduction, this document is written not only to bless our prayer lives, but to bless our general living, as well. For that matter, we who have changed spirits come to have a different outlook even upon the prayers we speak. Some of God's answers to our previous prayers have been frowned upon by us, until we have later had a change in our spirits' conditions. This change altered our view on what is truly a blessing. This is a *key* to our being blessed by our prayers and by our communing with God. Many folk have later realized their past prayers had actually been answered in a mighty way by God. A change in our spirits can change our very outlook on even the answers God provides unto us. As an example, we who have a common roof over our heads should feel blessed, but we still have an outlook of dissatisfaction because we are not earning at least six figures every twelve months. Oh, how the folk less fortunate would love to have the blessing of a roof, alone. We tend to take things for granted until we have a change in spirit. The Lord will help with our change, if we ask and allow Him. So, let us not wait for the change to be instituted by way of God removing blessings from our lives so to alarm us to better appreciate what we already possess.

We ought pray today that God grant us spirits receptive of His answers and His ways. Truth is, most of us need a change in our spirits' conditions before we can entertain becoming prayer warriors. A change in the condition of our spirits will further bless our abilities to submit to the will of God. Please understand this point. We will not accept His will in our lives if we do not first have spirits able to submit to His answers and ways. This document speaks heavily about having a submissive spirit unto God, and it is my hope we adhere to the power.

The condition of the spirit of a prayer warrior is refreshed and revived with each answer God gives through prayer. It is not something we can force ourselves to do, but it comes naturally to those who have the right spirit receptive and connected unto God. We can be trained to improve our spirits' conditions through diligent and faithful prayer lives and through the learning of these *8 Elements of Prayer Progression.*™ These *Elements* are designed and presented so the condition of our spirits improve at least prior to the point of request.

Do not take lightly the fact that the condition of our spirits lend unto God a peak at our motives, desires and grounds for praying. Believing that God sees and knows everything makes it easy for us to see the fruitfulness of I Samuel 16:7, which proclaims, "But the Lord said unto Samuel, look not on his contenance, or on the height of his stature; because I refused him: for the Lord seeth not as man seeth; for man looketh on the outward appearance, but the Lord looketh on the heart." Later in verse 13 David is anointed by Samuel, for his spirit was rather found in right condition.

Let it be that God stops at our prayers' front doors to answer because He finds the condition of our spirits to be right. I am faithful to believe the Lord anointed me to be blessed with His pouring this document because He first found the condition of my spirit to be receptive for the task. None of us is perfect, yet each of us must strive to have an improved spirit's condition so the Lord may be able to use each of us in mighty ways. "And he that searcheth the hearts knoweth what is the mind of the Spirit, because he maketh intercession for the saints according to the will of God" *(Romans 8:27).* It is known that our mouths can testify against us, but I believe too that our hearts more so testify against us, revealing our true intentions, motives and thoughts.

Fixed and Set

Fixing the condition of the heart must be an elementary priority of a person who desires to be stronger in prayer. There must be a change in our hearts unto God before we can commune with Him in any manner of success needed for today's perilous times. Anyone can pray to the Lord, but these times call for prayer warriors with hearts receptive of, and conditioned to God's voice and will. We all must commit to the change.

Are we ready for a heart fix? The answer must be an emphatic "Yes," not from the mouth, but through the action of our spirits. Join the few who have spirits conditioned for the workings of the Holy Spirit, enabled to consistently have prayers answered by the Father on high. "O God, my heart is fixed; I will sing and give praise, even with my glory" *(Psalm 108:1)*.

A change in the condition of our spirits will enable us to praise and worship Him in spirit and in truth. Much of the praise many of us give today is neither in truth nor in spirit; thus many fall short of praying in the power of a true prayer warrior. "And might not be as their fathers, a stubborn and rebellious generation; a generation that set not their heart aright, and whose spirit was not stedfast with God" *(Psalm 78:8)*. Let us settle in our spirits today that our praise and adoration onto God will be heightened by the elevation within our hearts. Pray to the Lord to fix the heart if it seems afar. God will surely bestow it upon us; as He knows the truth of our intentions.

> A way in which to check our spiritual conditions before entering prayer is to ask ourselves the following question: "Who and/or what will be edified by the reason I am entering into prayer at this time?"

A Biblical Illustration of Praise to that of Progression

I Chronicles 17:16-27 gives us a great illustration of how King David was aware of the importance of *Prayer Progression*. Verse 16 tells us that David sat before the Lord, then gave God praise and adoration through verse 23. It was not until verse 24 that David requested anything of the Lord. How much more should we be mindful of the *Prayer Progression* if a man after God's own heart exercised fixing his heart and spiritual condition before making a request? God will bless us just as He blessed David if we have spirits bent on praising Him. David even goes as far, in verse 24, to profess that the Lord shall be magnified above all else. David succeeded in his prayers due to his desire to have a fixed spirit and due to his desire to give God great honour, praise and adoration. Let it be our desires to do the same, so we may likewise see great victories in our families, communities and relationships with the Lord. It is the duty of 100,000 strong prayer warriors to have a condition of their spirits and hearts fixed in the Lord.

ADORATION – *Progression of Prayer Element #2*

Exercises

INSTRUCTIONAL

1. I Chronicles 16:23-26 is a great praise prayer exclaimed by David, which includes thanksgiving given unto the Lord. Read these verses then choose two precepts from this chapter that illustrate how David was a strong prayer warrior. Write a short paragraph in support of your choices.

BENEFIT:
To enhance your awareness of God's being worthy of appreciation.

PERSONAL

1. Praise the Lord each morning for who He is alone. For seven days do not praise Him for anything He has done. He knows your heart is full of praise for His mighty acts, so He will grant you reprieve for your willingness to go to another level in praising Him. Proclaim words that recognize His deity.

BENEFIT:
It is essential for your spirit to grasp the need to acknowledge and praise the Lord for who He is. All strong prayer warriors praise God mostly for His deity. You will never be the same after truthful realization of this precept, as it will take you to another level in Christ.

ADORATION — Progression of Prayer Element #2

General Questions

1. What can be said about gaining God's attention?

2. What makes adoration easier for us to give during prayer?

3. What should we do if we are lacking in praise?

4. What does acknowledging God in truth grant us?

5. Yes, often times prayers are about receiving an answer in some form or fashion, but what should be a prayer warrior's main focus in prayer?

6. Where does the fullness of God's blessings abide?

7. What is the catapult or stumbling block for many of our prayers?

   Why?

8. How can we change the way we view God's answers to our prayers?

9. Is prayer a dialogue unto God?

   Why?

10. At what point in the *Progression of Prayer* should we be sure to have a changed/right spirit's condition?

ADORATION – *Progression of Prayer Element #2*

Advanced Questions

1. When it comes to adoration, why is it so essential to properly acknowledge God in the *Progression of Prayer Element #1?*

2 Why is it so essential to give God adoration according to our own personal experiences rather than in accord with what we have heard others proclaim?

3. Write a short paragraph on why you think God gives more attention unto our prayers when we are focused on who He is instead of being focused on receiving from Him'?

Thanksgiving

Pray this prayer with me:
A Prayer for Thanksgiving

"El Elyon and Yahweh Shammah, I do glorify Your beloved name. I lift my voice in acknowledgment unto You, shouting glory! Hallelujah! I do acknowledge You as my One, True and Living God; giving You honour and praise. My heart screams of thanks and my spirit is overjoyed with Your presence. There are never enough words to illustrate how much I thank You, yet I pray now that You bless me with the writings of this next chapter so I may know how to better appreciate all You are unto me. Allow me to enter into Your presence during this reading so these words may be fruitful unto my prayers and unto my living. Lift my spirit and strengthen my submission unto You, wherein I shall elevate thanks for all You have done. All that You have done Lord! Bless Your name. This I submit unto You with the power of the Lord Jesus working through me – Amen."

This section is to better enhance our understanding of the Biblical reasons for who should give thanksgiving, how should thanksgiving be given, why should thanksgiving be given, what should be given thanksgiving, where should thanksgiving be given and when should thanksgiving be given. Our study of thanksgiving will be further enhanced if these verses are read previous to moving onto the chapter material; as this format will indeed better prepare our spirits to receive of the chapter material.

1) WHO should give thanksgiving?
- II Chronicles 5:13 — The trumpeters and singers
- Nehemiah 11:17 — The leaders
- Nehemiah 12:31 — The companies (choirs)
- Jeremiah 30:18-19 -- Those who were captive
- II Corinthians 4:15 — They of increase

2) HOW should thanksgiving be given?
- Leviticus 22:29 — Willingly
- I Chronicles 16:8 — Call upon His name
- I Chronicles 23:30 — Standing
- II Chronicles 5:13 — As one; as one sound
- Nehemiah 12:27; Psalm 147:7 — With singing and gladness; cymbals, psalteries and harps
- Psalm 26:7 — With the voice
- Psalm 116:17 — Offer it up
- Isaiah 51:3 — With melody, joy and gladness
- Romans 1:8 — Through Jesus Christ
- II Corinthians 9:12 — Abundantly
- Colossians 2:7 — Abounding
- Colossians 3:15 — With the peace of God ruling in your heart
- Revelation 7:12 — Unto our God

3) WHY should we give thanksgiving?
- I Chronicles 16:8 — Make known His deeds
- II Chronicles 5:13; Psalm 136:1 — He is good and His mercy endureth forever
- II Chronicles 20:26 — Because He fought our battles
- Psalm 26:7 — To tell of His wondrous works
- Psalm 30:4, 97:12 — Remembering He is holy
- Psalm 51:3 — Because of His comfort and works
- Psalm 69:30 — To magnify Him
- Psalm 75:1 — For His name is near; His wonders declare
- I Corinthians 11:24; Luke 10:21 — Jesus gave thanks
- I Corinthians 15:57 — Because He gives us victory through Jesus

3) WHY should we give thanksgiving? *(Continued)*
- II Corinthians 4:15 — To the glory of God
- II Corinthians 9:11 — Caused by bountifulness
- II Corinthians 9:15 — For His unspeakable gift
- Colossians 3:15 — Because you are called into one body
- I Thessalonians 1:2 — For others in our lives
- I Thessalonians 5:18 — Because it is the will of God in Christ
           Jesus concerning you

4) WHAT should we give thanksgiving unto?
- Leviticus 22:29 — Unto the Lord
- I Chronicles 16:8; Psalm 100:4 — Unto Him and His name
- I Chronicles 16:35 — To His Holy name
- Romans 1:8 — For you all
- I Corinthians 15:57 ; II Corinthians 9:15 — To God
- Philippians 1:3 — Upon every remembrance of others
- Philippians 4:6 — While making request unto God

5) WHERE should we give thanksgiving?
- I Chronicles 16:8 — Among the people
- Nehemiah 11:17 — In prayer and among the brethren
- Psalm 35:18 — In the great congregation and among much people
- Psalm 95:2 — Before His presence
- Psalm 100:4 — Entering into His gates
- Philippians 4:6 — In prayer

6) WHEN should we give thanksgiving?
- I Chronicles 23:30 — Every morning and every evening
- Psalm 30:12 — Forever
- Philippians 1:3 — When you remember others
- Philippians 4:6 — When making request unto God
- I Thessalonians 1:2 — Before you do anything else
- I Thessalonians 5:18 — In everything
- Revelation 7:12 — Forever and ever

"Thanks be unto God for his unspeakable gift."
II Corinthians 9:15

Giving thanksgiving (expressing gratitude for something received) to God for the things already received is quite instrumental in getting into the spirit of prayer and communion. Think of someone, like your children, approaching you to ask of some request and they never thought for a moment to thank you for what you just provided for them last month, last week, or even just this morning. How would you feel if someone was so unappreciative of the things you gave them in the past? Then, how would you feel about them approaching you later in asking for something else? Most likely you would think it to be just something else the person would not be thankful to receive.

Well now, place yourself, humbly, in the shoes of our gracious God in regards to this same subject matter. How might He feel when you disregard or omit giving Him thanks for things He has done for you in the past? Might He not be as receptive to your present prayer request as He may have been had you been thankful for all He had done in the past?

As you may now see, this matter is a large portion of the area we must grow in our prayer lives. We need to be humbly thankful and in a spirit of appreciation unto the Lord as we enter unto the Throne of Grace. We should appreciate Him if we love Him as we say we love Him. What better way to show our appreciation in prayer than by our giving Him thanksgiving?

This *Prayer Element* should be easy to effect after accepting and putting into practice *Element #2 Adoration and Praise.* Upon giving God adoration our minds should automatically reflect upon those things we are thankful He has blessed upon our living and spirits. I do not know how you may feel about this, but I surely feel quite uncomfortable about asking anyone for something, especially when I know I never thanked them for what they had done for me in the past. We all have a need to feel appreciated. It is only human and logical to feel a sense of being appreciated when you have done a good deed for someone.

Appreciation is in Order

In Matthew 6:1-4 the Bible tells us not to look for our rewards from man, but that our Father in Heaven shall grant us our just rewards. These verses address the fact that there is a natural tendency for persons to desire appreciation from others. Anyone with half a heart will desire to know others appreciate them. We all enjoy being acknowledged and/or appreciated, and we should only imagine God desires the same from His children. That is the point. We should look for our spiritual rewards from God, as we lift up our appreciation unto Him.

Again, this lends us to understand and more fully be mindful that our vertical relationships with God dictate our horizontal relationships with others here on this earth; not the other way around, as some tend to think and live upon. Many of us do not appreciate our neighbors simply because we never began to appreciate God. This document shall help many people in their relationships all together. This is a document to further strengthen our prayer lives, but truly understand that prayer and general spiritual living are so intertwined and connected that one emphatically feeds off the other.

We must realize in this walk called faith we shall begin to grow as children who are more like Christ, if we take more time to be mindful of the basics and foundational truths of our faith. "I am crucified with Christ: nevertheless I live; yet not I, but Christ liveth in me: and the life which I now live in the flesh I live by the faith of the Son of God, who loved me, and gave himself for me" *(Galatians 2:20)*. In this so called modern day, we are so bent on being so super-spiritual and overly intelligent that we so often neglect the foundational truths which give us the most spiritual strength and power. Many of us tend to overemphasize the intellect of faith and minimize the truths that make us who we are to be in Christ Jesus.

The *Progression Elements* in this document shall truly increase our abilities to get a prayer through to God, and they shall elevate our relationships with Him and with our neighbors, also. Keep in mind life on a whole often begins with how we approach things in our spirits; including the spectrum between issues and joy.

What has He Done for You, Not for Your Neighbor?

We are truly indebted unto God for all He has done for us. If nothing else we should know and truly believe, "God so loved the world that he gave his only begotten Son, that whosoever believeth in him should not perish, but have everlasting life" *(John 3:16)*. In light of which, this *Progression Element of Thanksgiving* should be made very personal just as was done with the *Acknowledgment Element*. We should truly thank God for the exact things He has done in our lives and not attempt to shout and mimic claims spoken by others.

We all have some reason to be thankful unto God, whether we illustrate it or not. Fact is, He has blessed each of us in some way or another. Overwhelming trials can loom over our spirits at times, causing us to have to dig a little deeper than other times in order to remember something for which we can give Him thanks. As prayer warriors, we must keep fresh in our minds those things for which we can give God thanks, so we are able to proclaim as did David and Israel in 1058 B.C., "If it had not been the Lord who was on my side ..." *(Psalm 124:1)*. We like to shout it when times are good, but let us put it into action when times are not so good. I am not urging us to remember the pain of the bad times, per se, although we must recall who covered us while in the bad times and who brought us out of those very same times. This we must do for the sake of our rendering thanksgiving unto God, if for no other reason.

One thing which is of utmost importance about these *Elements of Prayer* is that they instruct how to more fully and more energetically be clothed in the Spirit of Christ so to best pray and live unto the Father. We should be mindful that speaking of those personal things we know God has done for us will more assuredly grant us access to a higher spirited moment of prayer and living. Let me again make it more plain, since this is so instrumental in our success within the *Progression of Prayer* and in our faith walks with God. If God has never delivered you from something, why thank Him for being your deliverer? If you have never gone hungry a day in your life, why thank God for feeding you when you were hungry? Get the point? <u>Much of our spiritual walk is based upon the extent to which we are truthful about who He is to us, individually</u>. In doing so we must refrain from many of those overused Christian statements and verses that are not applicable to us individually and that are often taken out of context. Hear me when I say, if you are out of context you are not in the Word; no matter how much you read, study, minister, preach, teach, shout, sing and/or dance. Otherwise, it's artificial.

Praying and living in the spirit also suggest we be ever so mindful of not rambling nor muttering in our prayers. "O Timothy, keep that which is committed to thy trust, avoiding profane and vain babblings, and oppositions of science falsely so called: which some professing have erred concerning the faith. Grace be with thee. Amen" *(1 Timothy 6:20-21)*. Speaking those things which are applicable to you and your living is one great way to eliminate the tendency to babble while praying. If the Lord just made a way for your bills to be paid, you then ought to address Him as Way Maker and Bill Payer, then thank Him for the same. Do not just recite the things and thanks you have heard others say, like, "He made a way out of no way;" unless you truly know and believe that there was no other way. It may be true and applicable in your life, but many of those statements we often hear then copy have been so overly used, abused and misused. I cannot imagine these replicates of babbled statements get God's attention as fully as stating things in exact and in truth.

The shoe being on the other foot, how would you feel if someone came to you and thanked you for something you know you did not do for them? Let me make this plain. Wouldn't you be reluctant or less apt to listen to those things which are stated by that person thereafter? Your feelings of that person may be that either they did not know you too well, or they were disrespectful of you enough to not be mindful of getting their facts correct. So, how might God feel about our thanks when we babble statements made by others; including statements made by the non-saved? Treat God with the respect He is due by being truthful and exacting in thanking Him for that which He's actually done for you, and refrain from spouting what you have heard said by others.

Be mindful and remember those things which God has already done for you, and be thankful. "Only fear the Lord, and serve him in truth with all your heart: for consider how great things he hath done for you" *(1 Samuel 12:24)*. Be thankful unto Him who has delivered you, healed you, covered you, strengthened you, fed and gave you increase. I Samuel 12:25 suggest, in giving thanks unto the Lord we may be able to stop from sinning against Him. Some of us, just like the Israelites, forget who God is and so go on sinning against Him over and over again. We do have less of a tendency to sin against Him when we fear Him and when we truthfully remember who He is. In other words, our relationships with Him are strengthened by our remembering who He is, fearing who He is and serving His will.

If the truth were told, most of us are often less thankful than we ought. Of course, this is nothing new to most of our ears, for even our ancestral Israelites were ungrateful for many things God provided for them. Historically humans have a tendency of feeling weak or less apt as persons if they were to thank others. Let it be known today that thankfulness is one of the best forms of showing appreciation and strength, yet it is something we tend not to give unto others. How much more should we give thanks to the Almighty! As you see, that last sentence was left in an exclamation rather than a question mark; for it's no question whatsoever that we should give God thanks for all He has done.

How can we not show great appreciation to the supplier of all our needs and some of our wants? Many of our horizontal relationships continue to falter and fade, mostly due to our inability to show others appreciation. If someone has a difficulty of showing their fellow man appreciation, best believe they probably have a great difficulty of showing true appreciation unto God. "If a man say, I love God, and hateth his brother, he is a liar: for he that loveth not his brother whom he hath seen, how can he love God whom he hath not seen?" *(I John 4:20)*. How can we believe in someone we do not appreciate? Understand, we cannot be strong in prayer lest we believe in the power of Him in whom we pray. "But without faith it is impossible to please him: for he that cometh to God must believe that he is, and that he is a rewarder of them that diligently seek him" *(Hebrews 11:6)*. There is no way we can truly know who God is and not give Him appreciation. It is just not possible to know such a thing of His power, love, grace, mercy, covering, guidance, etc., and not show Him appreciation. It is just not possible. I emphatically reiterate in the truth of spirit, it is just not possible to know Him, I mean really know Him, and not show appreciation unto Him and all His creation! One of the highest forms of appreciation is giving thanks. Let us try it now. Go ahead and say, "Thank You God! Thank You God!"

In the Church we are often told to praise Him, but far too few times are we told to truthfully thank Him. We shout thanks, but not in the truth of who He is. I am not only talking about thanking Him for what He's done for us. Oh, many of us are good at that. We can thank someone all day long and not have true appreciation for who they are. We have all done it ourselves. In the past, someone with an evil spirit has done something nice for us and we thanked them, even though we still did not think too highly of them. Maybe it was someone who had harmed us in the past and they had enough nerve to speak to us or give us something. We thanked them, but we still did not appreciate them. Afterwards, we may have even called one of our best friends and cursed about that very person who had the nerve to ever speak to us, let alone give us something for which we had to superficially thank them. "Can you believe what so and so did just now!" Oh, you know you have done it. So understand, we can thank someone but still harbor bad feelings and not truly appreciate them in our spirits. The sinful thing is some of us do the same thing to God.

We can thank someone and still not show appreciation because we never truly appreciated <u>who</u> they are. We tend to show appreciation for the act, or thing given, but miss out on the true blessing of showing appreciation for the giver. This is a *key* to implement. Please understand the distinction between the two: appreciation for the giver versus for the gift. Yes, we are still talking about being strong in prayer, but it is much of our living that must coincide. There are many distinctions and strong truths spoken/written in this document which are instrumental to take us to the next level in prayer. This *key* is one of those distinctions.

You are well on your way to becoming a strong prayer warrior if you can grasp and institute this and other distinctions, truths, and keys proclaimed in this document. If it is difficult to grasp any portion of this document, immediately pray unto God and ask that He reveal it. He is faithful to give understanding. It may not be at that very moment, but He will keep His Word. "Ask, and it shall be given you; seek, and ye shall find; knock, and it shall be opened unto you. For every one that asketh receiveth; and he that seeketh findeth..." _(Matthew 7:7-8)_. It is only natural to show appreciation for persons we trust and believe. How about that! That may be like a new revealed and foreign action for those of us who tend not to show appreciation and love to others; nor unto God for that matter.

Sure we appreciate that which God does for us, but how much do we truly appreciate who He is? The main reason we often do not thank God is because we never appreciated who He is in the first place. Here are a few other reasons we tend not to give God truthful thanksgiving: we think we are entitled to receive; we think someone owes us; and we are a self-centered people in a selfish society. Let's further explore these reasons.

Unfruitful Entitlement

The first of the three reasons mentioned is that some believers tend to have a spirit of entitlement (a sister to covetousness). This type of spirit can truly harm a person's relationship with God, and others, if that person is not sound in the foundation of their faith from the beginning. A huge part of our spirits' foundations is to not only know who God is through His attributes and characteristics, but to know the extent of our entitlements as Christians, as well. God's attributes and characteristics are extensively discussed in the last chapter of this document.

Yes it is true, as Christians, we are entitled to many things. We are entitled to the Tree of Life if we live holy and righteous. We are entitled to be sons, daughters and joint heirs with Christ Jesus. We are entitled to live in the promises made to us as children of God; as written in the Word of God. We are even entitled to the Kingdom of God in the after life. Here are a few verses which indicate the things we are entitled (inherit):

- Matthew 5:5 (inherit the earth)
- I Corinthians 15:50 (flesh and blood will not inherit)
- Colossians 1:12 (inheritance shared)
- Hebrews 9:15 (inherit the promise - eternal)
- John 10:10 (life more abundantly)
- Jeremiah 50:20 (pardon of sins)
- Exodus 23:22 (the Lord will fight your battles)

It is easy to accept our positive inheritances, but not so easy to receive the haters and enemies we inherit. Jesus tells in His Word, just as they hated Him they will surely hate those who truthfully follow Him. "And ye shall be hated of all men for my name's sake: but he that endureth to the end shall be saved" _(Matthew 10:22)_. "If the world hate you, ye know that it hated me before it hated you. If ye were of the world, the world would love his own: but because ye are not of the world, but I have chosen you out of the world, therefore the world hateth you" _(John 15:18-19)_. That is an inheritance I do not see many of us shouting His glory over.

There are promises made by God of what we shall receive as His children, but our having an arrogance thereof is surely not included as part of those promises. The Bible tells us, "And the Lord shall make thee the head, and not the tail; and thou shalt be above only, and thou shalt not be beneath; if thou hearken unto the commandments of the Lord thy God, which command thee this day, to observe and to do them:" _(Deuteronomy 28:13)_. Take notice the Bible says nothing about having an arrogance in acting as if we are entitled to it just because we are His children. Several verses in the Bible do tell us we should be bold: Proverbs 28:1; Ephesians 3:12, 6:20; I Timothy 3:13; Philemon 8; Hebrews 4:16, 13:6. Whereas, in II Corinthians 11:16-22 Paul declares that we act boldly, but we are to be mindful of both our boldness and that which we edify.

Our inheritance is in Jesus, thus we must refrain thinking we are entitled to anything less Christ. We come boldly knowing that all we inherit is through Christ and not of ourselves. He gave a ransom that we may have a right to the Tree of Life. "I am the Alpha and Omega, the beginning and the end, the first and the last. Blessed are they that do his commandments, that they may have right to the Tree of Life, and may enter in through the gates into the city" _(Revelation 22:13-14)_. "Even as the Son of men came not to be ministered unto, but to minister and to give his life a ransom for many" _(Matthew 20:28)_. It is the Lord and the Holy Spirit who gives us the strength and words to speak boldly. "And now, Lord, behold their threatenings: and grant unto thy servants, that with all boldness they may speak thy word" _(Acts 4:29)_. "It is of the Lord's mercies that we are not consumed, because his compassion fail not" _(Lamentations 3:22)_.

All that was stated and all those scriptures quoted to say the following. As Christians we do have a great inheritance through Christ Jesus, but it is no way a means of entitlement to act as if God the Father grants us anything just because. Make no mistake there are great rewards and blessings in Christ Jesus, but they do not entitle us to get the "big-head!" A big-head of arrogance comes from our thinking we deserve what we receive just because we are His children. Sounds like spoiled children to me. Jesus has spoiled us of the great hope of His soon returning, and of the Holy Spirit never leaving us alone. Albeit, we should not act like brats choking on the plenty and the pleasures given us as favor. Let it be that we have bold appreciation for, both, that which God does for us and in who He is.

Who Owes What to Whom?

Let's now examine the second reason mentioned: despair can create a feeling of something truly being owed to us. Many of us feel we have been down so long, or without certain things we think we deserve, that a "you owe me" attitude develops. This is opposite to the feeling of entitlement, since the lack promotes the feeling of being owed something. There is a difference between claiming something we may have worked to receive and that of claiming entitlement due to position or placement. Fact remains, they are equally destructive to a sound fruitful relationship.

To have a feeling of being owed something lends one to take on a posture of lording over another. "You owe me, thus I stand over you." "The rich ruleth over the poor, and the borrower is servant to the lender" _(Proverbs 22:7)_. Or, we often develop a mentality of "You do as I say." Can you see the danger of taking these postures in our relationships with God and in prayer? Oh, it becomes clear of how scripture tells us to lend without thought of receiving in return. "And if ye lend to them whom ye hope to receive, what thank have ye? for sinners also lend to sinners, to receive as much again," says the Lord in Luke 6:34. "When thou dost lend thy brother any thing, thou shalt not go into his house to fetch his pledge" _(Deuteronomy 24:10)_. Yet those who owe and have received should be diligent to repay! "The wicked borroweth, and payeth not again: but the righteous sheweth mercy, and giveth" _(Psalm 37:21)_. Truly the Lord owes us nothing since He is the creator of all things. He only grants us stewardship over a few things, and for that we should be more than thankful. Let us all assume the spirit of stewardship. A spirit of stewardship will grant us a heart of thankfulness and appreciation unto the Lord. This is the spirit which will bless our prayers and our living more than we can image. The Bible says, "... thou has been faithful over a few things, I will make thee ruler over may things ...." _(Matthew 25:21)_.

That which is said here gives spirit to understand how our relationships fail due to our eagerness of heart to receive that which we think we are owed. "You owe me," becomes the catch phrase in our so called friendships, replacing the truth of being your brother's keeper. "And the Lord said unto Cain, Where is Abel thy brother? And he said, I know not: Am I my brother's keeper?" _(Genesis 4:9)_. The Lord is truly our keeper yet He does not cry bloody murder for all we owe Him. At this point someone should recollect all God has done for them which has yet to be repaid and appreciated. We could never repay God for all He has done for us, yet some of us take on a posture that He owes us something. Oh, how wicked a people and with such short memories. We too should be called modern day Israelites, since we are often so unappreciative and wicked. Make no mistake about it, it is wicked to think God is indebted unto us.

This mentality of feeling someone owes us anything hinders our abilities to be thankful. I surely know and many can attest how hard it is to free our minds when we think someone owes us. It is hard to shake our spirits from wanting what we metaphorically call "ours." Do not forget that all we have is God's. We are to be good stewards over that which He grants us, yet the fact remains it is all His. The sooner we faithfully wrap our minds and living around that very fact, the sooner we will move into a greater realm of spiritual power capable of praying unto God with thankfulness in our hearts and spirits. We cannot be thankful unto Him as long as we think He owes us something. That is the point!

I even now edit this completed document during the blizzard of 2010 thankful for the candle light God has provided, but in hopes that the electricity be restored soon. Dare I think God owes me the light of day nor electricity by night simply because I am doing His will in speaking His words unto you, His people. Dare I think for all I continue to do for Christ' sake places God in a position of subservience unto me. Lest I be sadly mistaken, my words and living should always reflect that I am forever indebted to Christ. "For when we were yet without strength, in due time Christ died for the ungodly" *(Romans 5:6)*. He truly died for me. My being thankful unto God makes my relationship as His servant more fruitful. As well, He gains trust in knowing He can use me as I remain thankful even through trials, difficulties and pains. How else might I have had this testimony for these very pages? For there are many who know that I do not complain of the many trials. Oh! The many trials that most of us would dare not entertain to sustain. I am so thankful!

"Owing something," has nothing but bad connotations. Even denotatively it speaks of something still being outstanding and not yet paid. The last I knew, Christ Jesus already paid the price for our sins, and redemption. What more could the Godhead owe anyone? It was only by grace, the Son Jesus, that we are even redeemed unto the Father. For all that, we should truly find ourselves thankful unto Him. Thankful! Oh, just to be thankful!

That word "owe" is too close to the word "own," and we should not be involved in such matters. As stated, God owns it all and we dare not stand in lordship over Him. Is anyone understanding what I am saying about this thing called owe? It is we who owe Him and not in reverse. Other words in context of owe include: obligation; having an attitude; deserving; unsatisfied. Wow! Let me ask the question, "Is anyone unsatisfied with Jesus?" This truly makes this point more potent. To think in any sort of way that someone owes you something is, in retrospect, to be dissatisfied with them. Let me make this a little more plain. If someone you love owes you something, the very love you have for them should wipe the debt clean. Am I talking about Jesus? "But God commanded his love toward us, in that, while we were yet sinners, Christ died for us" _(Romans 5:8)._ The love you have for someone should override any, so called, obligation or debt. First and foremost, there never was a debt God owed to us. I'm trying to help all those who live in a world of debt payments. As mentioned, this document has been written to help not only His children become stronger in their prayer lives, but to strengthen their spiritual relationships with Christ, also. In addition, this document shall help with believer's relationships with their fellow man, as well.

I am merely trying to help someone move from a point of being held captive by this world of things, to a truth of spirit realm of being stuck on Jesus. It is our spirits' conditions we need to change. Oh, hear me when I say, change our spirits' conditions and we will change our mind about many things. This is a _key_ spoken of at greater length in the _Progression_ (21) _of Prayer Element of Adoration._ May this document help to make that very change through the workings of the Holy Spirit. "Make a joyful noise unto the Lord, all ye lands. Serve the Lord with gladness: come before his presence with singing. Know ye that the Lord he is God: it is he that hath made us, and not we ourselves; we are his people, and the sheep of his pasture. Enter into his gates with thanksgiving and into his courts with praise: be thankful unto him, and bless his name. For the Lord is good; his mercy is everlasting; and his truth endureth to all generations" _(Psalm 100)._

Thankfulness is another form of appreciation and praise unto the Lord. We do give His name praise by giving Him thanksgiving. We should always find it in our hearts and spirits to give God praise through our thanks unto Him. He is worthy of all our forms of praise.

Self-Centered? It's Not about You

Many others of us still abstain from giving thanks to God and to others due to our being so self-centered. We live in a world of me-ism. Our society has unfortunately become based in "What's in it for me?" Many of us are far too consumed with our own needs, desires and wants, which has created a society bent on making sure self is ok. We should ensure to take care of ourselves and all those we are responsible unto, to the best of our abilities, but who can attest and proclaim that it was the Lord who truly has kept us through the good and through the bad? It has been the One who sits at the right hand of the Father who has made intercession for our comings and our goings. "Who is he that condemneth? It is Christ that died, yea rather, that is risen again, who is even at the right hand of God, who also maketh intercession for us" *(Romans 8:34)*. "Likewise the Spirit also helpeth our infirmities: for we know not what we should pray for as we ought: but the Spirit itself maketh intercession for us with groanings which cannot be uttered. And he that searcheth the hearts knoweth what is the mind of the Spirit, because he maketh intercession for the saints according to the will of God" *(Romans 8:26-27)*.

God Himself, in Ezekiel 36:22-38, proclaims it is not about us. Verse 22 says, "I do not this for your sakes." Then He follows in verse 23 with, "And I will sanctify my great name..." The NIV writes, "I will show the holiness of my great name..." There are many "I's" within these verses, yet not one of them is a pronoun for anyone other than God. We all should read these verses at least once every few weeks, or so, in order to grasp the point that He does most things for His name's sake; not ours. All that we are and everything we shall do should be for His sake. What the Lord performs may be for our good, but it is ultimately for His glory.

How can anyone be so stuck on themselves and their own concerns to not realize it is not about them? Too many of us, so called believers, still strongly think it is all about us. We walk around from one place to the next, one situation to the next, and one thought to the next, with the opinion that life and death rest upon us. This self-centeredness clouds our minds so much that we find it hard to be thankful unto others. Enough is enough! Do you know anyone like that? What you did for them today is never enough to make them happy tomorrow. They are always taking. Always needing more. In doing so they move into the realm of never having thanks for anything. You can break your back for these types of folk and they will never once say thank you. Many of us have even worked and/or served under supervisors, bosses and even leaders in ministries who act that very way. These types of people set illegitimate examples of thankfulness. God sent manna daily so the Israelites would depend on Him alone and be thankful daily. Our Lord and Savior even included this precept in the prayer He taught the disciples, "Give us this day our daily bread" *(Matthew 6:11)*.

God gives us blessings daily; of which we should be thankful. He wants us to depend on His sending things our way so we can live in the essence of being thankful. Not being thankful will give rise to an evil spirit within us which will smother the light of appreciation and love. How can we love someone we do not appreciate, and how can we appreciate that of which we are not thankful? It all ties together and is an essential point we must grasp on our way to becoming prayer warriors. Again, we must first fix our spirits' conditions to allow the fullness of God to resound in our living and prayers. True warriors spend most of their prayer time praying for others; not themselves. That is a leap for many of us, but we can get there with thankful hearts and the Holy Spirit's help.

You will become a prayer warrior if you follow this document of *Prayer Elements* and have the right spirit. This I do proclaim and declare right now, in the blessed name of Jesus. The mission of this document is to develop numerous prayer warriors who will be needed for the days ahead. For some of us it may seem like the theme of this document vacillates from prayer to that of living. Fact of the matter is we must digest faith and spirit precepts into our living so we may act them out in our prayers. This is all in the realm of fixing the spirit's condition. If you can live in the spirit, you then can pray in the spirit. The reverse is more remote, although we can pray for a spirit fix prior to living in the spirit. Strong truthful prayer in Christ often results from strong truthful living in Christ.

Our becoming prayer warriors will not come into fruition because of our desire to be prayer warriors. Oh no, on the contrary. Our desire to pray for others comes about through our strength of relationship with God. See, it is not a desire to pray for others that is at the forefront of the life of a true prayer warrior. It is the praying for others that is a result of the relationship we have with God. We must first understand that prayer warriors have such strong relationships with God that have germinated from their thankfulness unto Him. Also, they tend to believe and realize the truth that God knows their hearts' desires and all they stand in need. Not to say they think it unnecessary to pray for themselves, but they realize two things: it is not about them and their focus should be on the blessing that is Christ Jesus. That is the true blessing which drives prayer warriors. Not that they want others to know them as prayer warriors, but because their desire is to do God's will and minister unto others. There are far too many who call themselves prayer warriors simply because of their selfish desires to be known or dubbed as prayer warriors. The truth is they could not get a prayer through even if they paid someone. Sorrowfully, they are more concerned about how they appear to others and less concerned with the will of God for the lives of others. That is where a lot of the rubber then meets the road.

It is not a cute act praying healing for others. It is not sterile touching the infirmities of others in body nor in spirit. It is anything but fashionable laying your will before the presence of God in supplication and mercy knowing that God is not pleased with the sinfulness of those for which you pray. Being a prayer warrior is an obligation. There is that word "obligation" in correctness of spirit. Being a prayer warrior is a painful experience not truthfully shared by many. The truth of the matter is there are not enough prayer warriors on the face of this earth; although many claim to be. This document will expose many people for their lack of authenticity and lack of true prayer power. Call that prophetic if you may, but I call it God speaking truth through His servant.

Truly I have not been willed to write this second document to call out those who are not as they claim. The mission of the Spirit is to empower some to be strong prayer warriors, others to increase in their faith in prayer, and all to be strengthened in their spiritual walk with the Lord. For truly God does not necessarily desire to make preachers, teachers nor prayer warriors, yet it is His will to make us all stronger Christians fighting the good fight of faith. "But thou, O man of God, flee these things; and follow after righteousness, godliness, faith, love, patience, meekness. Fight the good fight of faith, lay hold on eternal life, where unto thou art also called, and hast professed a good profession before many witnesses. I give thee charge in the sight of God, who quickeneth all things, and before Christ Jesus, who before Pontius Pilate witness a good confession" *(I Timothy 6:11-13).* That command was not just to be a leader, but to be a Christian; strong and faithful unto God. That charge I give unto you this day that you think not of yourself, but of that perfect will of God through Christ Jesus our Lord. It is not about you; it is about Jesus. It is about the will of our Father, the Creator of all things good.

I do beseech you today to study these *8 Elements of Prayer Progression*™ to become not only a strong prayer warrior, but more so to become a Christian who lives holy and powerfully unto Christ. God desires you live Christ-like unto Him and others, then through that type of living He shall make you a strong prayer warrior. Oh, buckle your seat belts again, for the chains are coming off and the wheels are revving. In that you ought be thankful.

We cannot be all about ourselves in prayer nor in our living unto the will of God. God cannot use us appropriately when we concentrate just on our own will or desires. God is not self-centered and we must find ourselves being like Him. He is a gracious, kind, just, loving and merciful God, but He is in no way self-centered. He is all powerful, righteous, truth, faithful and immutable, but there are no signs of His being self-centered.

I find myself in this walk called faith knowing and believing it is all about Him, although He does not necessarily carry it that way. My thinking it is all about God keeps my focus off me, and off other things of this earth which would render me carnal and weak. Throughout the Bible scripture lays claim to God's undying concern for His children and the lost. We must lay claim to this same focus in our spiritual walks. We must have a spiritual focus on God and the needs of others. Just imagine a world where people thought less of themselves and more of others. What a place that would be! Let me say, "What a place that shall be!" I'm talking about the glorious Kingdom of God and our inheritance in Glory. Oh, bless the name of the Lord. Oh, when we make it to Glory!

In the meanwhile, can I bring you back? We must refocus our attention on those things of Christ and stop focusing so much on ourselves. That is the place where God is then able to use us with power and conviction. That is the place where souls are saved and wholesome living begins. Oh! Somebody ought be ready for the change. People are waiting for your change to take place so they may then be reached by the Spirit of Christ working through you. That change begins with not just you learning how to become strong in prayer, but through your becoming a stronger Christian unto Christ, as well. It is not necessarily where you end up, but as the sailor says, "It's more about the journey in getting there!" Thank You Lord for the process. In that you should be thankful. Go on and thank Him!

Prayer warriors have a vision, directed from the Father and spoken through the Spirit. That connection is broken when our thoughts are all tied up in ourselves. Me-isms and living for Christ are contradictions that never marry. Me-isms appose the very fabric set forth by Jesus. What room is left to think of others if thou are thinking so much of thyself? How can the Spirit use us to deliver others out of bondage if we are still locked in chains? Let us get up off ourselves! Release the power of the Almighty by centering our thoughts on Christ and others. There is no other way. There are some things we will have to let go and release in order to move into this power God has for us. Letting go of me-isms is one of those things we must release.

Thanksgiving unto God must not be taken lightly. The ramifications of an ungrateful and unthankful spirit are catastrophic. There is nothing gained through not being thankful. We can truly have many different characteristics and potentially everything will still be fine in our lives, but being unappreciative unto God is not one of those characteristics that will render things to be ok. Why would anyone respond to someone who has not been grateful? Cannot imagine many people jumping at the chance to bless someone a second, third or fourth time if that person never thought it of themselves to say, "Thank you," for things done for them previously.

Most of us are not into emotional nor physical pain, especially that which is subjected unto us by others; and rightly so. Why might we think God can be at all happy with our disregard for all He's done for us? How might an all giving, all loving, but just God feel about our never giving Him thanks for those things He has done for us in the past? I truly know how I would feel, but of course I am not God. The conviction of the matter is what's important here. Let's metaphorically and emotionally put ourselves in the shoes of He who is all things to all people. After doing so we may begin to understand how important it is to thank someone for those things they have done for us; and likewise be thankful unto God.

It is a sad shame how many of us have gone to God over and over, and time and time again, without once saying, "Thank You for yesterday's blessings." How many of us can truly say we have taken a moment in prayer to thank God for what He had already granted unto us, even before we began to request anything else of Him? We all surely have something to be thankful for each day. We all should be able to count our blessings. The Bible tells us of His mercies, "They are new every morning: great is thy faithfulness" *(Lamentations 3:23)*. King David put it this way, "How precious also are thy thoughts unto me, O God! how great is the sum of them! If I should count them, they are more in number than the sand: when I awake, I am still with thee" *(Psalm 139:17-18)*.

A person may be dead in spirit if they cannot count their blessings. Air, food, limbs, walking, sight, and speech are just a few things we ought be ever so thankful to possess. It is a daily blessing to possess the basics of life. Far too many of us continue to take for granted those basic things while requesting the stars. The reality is the stars are often in the basics.

In His Presence

Thanksgiving on our hearts and lips puts us in the spirit of submission, appreciation, communion and dependence upon God's will. Thanksgiving takes us to another level of relationship with God necessary to fully enter into His presence. How might we pray effectively lest we fully get into the presence of the Lord? Oh, to be in His presence. Far too many of us try to gain access into His presence, but always stop at praise. That is when many of us get upset as we find ourselves falling short in prayer. Psalm 16 exemplifies this point as David added praise with counting his blessings in order to gain access into the fullness of God's presence.

Thanksgiving is emphasized in Psalm 95:2 also, "Let us come before his presence with thanksgiving, and make a joyful noise unto him with psalms." The sad but true fact is many people, including some preachers, often minister and fellowship in accord with cliches which often do not include the true context of verse. The Old and New Testament characters found strength in the Lord by using the truth set forth by the words and Law given unto them by God. There is no good reason for us here today to not do the same, lest a person desires a half-hearted relationship with the Lord. In other words, so many of us are comfortable with shouting God's praises, but we are not too familiar with giving Him true thanks. As believers we would refrain from asking the Lord for many things, if we would submit ourselves to being truthfully thankful for all He's already done for us. What a mighty shame it is that many of us are discontent with, both, who we are and with what we possess; evident through our ungrateful characters, and thankless spirits. Most of the world's drama would be eliminated as well, if persons were more whole-heartedly thankful for their blessings already received.

Let it be understood that the epitome of a thankful spirit is one that does not frivolously desire things outside of that which is already in one's possession. Do not get me wrong on this, healthy desire is ok, but frivolous desires are spoken against in the Bible. The Word tells of how we have not because we ask amiss _(James 4:3)_, and how we often lose the inner war _(Romans 7:13-15)_. Let me say it this way, the closer we get to the Lord the further we get away from the world's system of beliefs. Our spirits then begin to direct our thoughts and minds upon things eternal and less about things of the flesh. Let it be understood that only a grown spirit in Christ is thankful for its today and hopeful for Jesus' sake in tomorrow.

Again, the direction of this document is not to change our minds to not want to make request in prayer, but it is the vision that all who receive of this knowledge will grow into a closer relationship with the Lord and progressively acquire a heightened ability to receive answers to their prayers. That is the goal. Oh, to hear from Heaven and have the Lord answer our prayers on our behalf!

This I say as well, as we become stronger in prayer we then will better understand Romans 8:26 which tells us how we do not know for what to pray. We will have more understanding of how our desires and prayers must align with God's will as these mysteries are revealed unto us and as we begin to live within them. As an example, it is only heart felt that we would pray for someone's healing, but a strong prayer warrior wants to know God's will in the situation. What is the bigger picture the

Lord is painting? That is the mode where this document is designed to direct and guide our spirits.

Submission is Strength

The truth of thanksgiving cannot be had without having a submissive spirit. Our spirits must submit to the fact that thanksgiving is deemed necessary. Some folk do not even think it necessary to thank others, let alone thank God. These persons often say, "Well you know I am appreciative," or "You know I appreciate you." I say this, "Well, if that be the case, say it." Fact is, thanksgiving is often not in someone's spirit if they have difficulty parting their lips; even though on the other hand people can say thanks but not truly mean it. Nevertheless, we must do all things in spirit and in truth in order to worship our Lord *(John 4:23)*.

The Bible strongly speaks on submission. "Furthermore we have had fathers of our flesh which corrected us, and we gave them reverence: shall we not much rather be in subjection unto the Father of spirits, and live?" *(Hebrews 12:9)*. It is so true that many of us submit unto those who have the most to offer us. Few of us tend to be submissive unto those who arc of the most spiritual benefit to us. Of course, this is not something new for most of us; for this pattern began in childhood. We learned as growing children to gravitate towards the people who held their fleshly giving hand towards us, as we shied away from chastening and wholesome hands. "Let every soul be subject unto the higher powers. For there is no power but of God: the powers that be are ordained of God. Whosoever therefore resisteth the power, resisteth the ordinance of God: and they that resist shall receive to themselves damnation" *(Romans 13:1-2)*. Live we must in the spirit and in the will of God Almighty. The Lord Himself said, "For whosoever shall so do the will of my Father which is in Heaven, the same is my brother, and sister, and mother" *(Matthew 12:50)*.

Submission unto God grants us access unto the Spirit, which in turn enables us to thank God in truth. Submissive carries with it a "letting go" of oneself. God being Spirit, how then can we expect to gain access unto Him without being submissive unto His Spirit? Disobedience unto others and unto God tends to forbid us from turning over spiritual authority unto those very same persons. Submission has a lot to do with surrendering and yielding control to another, which is massively difficult for they who are self-centered. The difficulty takes residence in our inability to get into the fullness of God's presence; thus aborting some of our prayers. If only we could fully surrender unto Him we would then get more prayers through. If only we would give it to Him. We continuously give Him our issues, but we refuse to give (surrender) our submission unto Him.

The act of "giving it over to God" does not solely involve handing over our concerns and issues. Let it be known here today that the major part of "giving it over to the Lord" is our having a submissive spirit unto Him. It is our spirit God desires and not just our issues. He already knows of what we stand in need before we even pray. "Be not ye therefore like unto them: for your Father knoweth what things ye have need of, before ye ask Him" _(Matthew 6:8)_. It is our spirits' submission He desires. A true father, let me say it again, a true father, always desires to be close with his children. There are many donors in this land who never desired to be close to their offspring, but God our Father is faithful. He desires nothing better than to be in total communion with His children, even to the point of His abiding in us. Jesus said, "Abide in me, and I in you. As the branch cannot bear fruit of itself, except it abide in the vine; no more can ye, except ye abide in me" _(John 15:4)_. In verse 11 He speaks of that abiding which grants us the fullness of joy.

The Lord does not desire us to rely on Him for our needs, alone. He also desires we be in touch with His Spirit. So many of our concerns will pale and fade away as we further abide in His Spirit. If I can truly make it plain, many of our issues and concerns have been created by our not abiding in the Lord. You fully know your problems never would have begun if you had only kept your eyes stayed on Him and not on that flesh of a thing. "Thou wilt keep him in perfect peace, whose mind is stayed on thee: because he trusteth in thee" _(Isaiah 26:3)_. Oh, but as soon as you took your eyes off Jesus! As soon as your spirit was dislodged from the power source! Then is when your troubles started.

Again, as you can see these _8 Elements of Prayer Progression_™ are not only for powerful prayer, but for powerful living, also. We cannot gain full access unto the thrown of grace until we have first truthfully connected with His Spirit. Surely I am not suggesting God does not listen to those of us who are not totally committed to Him, but as it is written in Romans 13:1-2 we must be subjected unto Him. I'm just pressing upon our spirits what the Word says. If that verse be so, how much less shall the Lord tend to the prayers of a non-submitted spirit? Therefore my brothers and sisters, I do urge us to submit ourselves unto the Lord as He is ready to receive of our spirits' communion. For those of us who did not know, submission involves compliance, humility, surrender and obedience. It also entails a large amount of not resisting God, while persistently resisting the devil. The Bible says it this way, "Submit yourselves therefore unto God. Resist the devil, and he will flee from you" _(James 4:7)_. Sometimes the devil we should flee is ourselves. For some of us that is hard to accept, yet reality testifies we get in the way of our own abilities to submit, at times.

Maturing Appreciation

After coming into full submission unto the Lord, we can then truthfully appreciate not only what He's done and is doing in our lives, but we can more fully appreciate who He is in our lives, also. The latter being more important than the former things. Most of our living in faith can align properly with the Holy Spirit through our appreciation for who God is more so than for what He's done. We will surely appreciate the things He's done if we would first appreciate who He is. Yes, we're still talking about thanksgiving unto God.

Appreciation for who someone is, rather than for what they do, sets the tone for healthy and truthful thanksgiving horizontally and vertically. Far too many of us are in relationships with folk we do not appreciate which causes dissension and grief every step of the way.   Our relationships with God tend to follow the same pattern of bearing grief, sorrow and let down. This happens from our unwillingness to appreciate Him for who He is as well as for all He's done. If we would just straighten up and fly with the Lord we would not be in danger of flying over those no fly zones aptly called "Disappointment" and "Disobedience." The Lord can pilot our spirits and our living in such a way that our pains will be minimized. We shall never be void of all pains, but we can surely minimize them by willingly showing appreciation unto the Lord for who He is.

God reads our hearts, thus He knows the truth of our appreciation. "And He said unto them, Ye are they which justify yourselves before men; but God knoweth your hearts: for that which is highly esteemed among men is abomination in the sight of God" *(Luke 16:15)*. We falter in many of our horizontal relationships because we try to fake out other persons into thinking we are appreciative of them. Oh, and sometimes we do a pretty good job of it. We then apply that same mode of action to our vertical relationships with the Lord, yet we wonder why our connections with Him are not as strong as other believers have with Him, nor as strong as we would like. Jesus said, "But I know you, that ye have not the love of God in you" *(John 5:42)*. In other words, we cannot fake out an omniscient God, yet and still there are those who try.

This is why it is so very important to learn, digest and live in accord with the attributes and character of God. If we truly digest His attributes, we will come to truthfully show Him appreciation, and we will come to a fullness of living with Him. Make no mistake about it, there are no paradoxical worshipers. Hear me! We treat others the same way we treat God. Likewise, we tend to treat God the same way we treat those around us. Some try to say they have more deference for God than they have for their neighbor. They say, "He is God and they are not." The truth is no one is able to turn on and off the love of God nor the Spirit of Christ within.

Many still claim, "Well you are you and He is God." But the Bible says, "Let your moderation be known unto all men. The Lord is at hand" _(Philippians 4:5)_. Our spirits release only that which is known to it: evil or love. If our spirits are righteous, righteousness will emit. There is no vacillating! The wicked at heart may think he or she can treat God differently than they treat mere man, but it is not possible to vacillate so easily from hatred to love. Only in the mind are such character flaws, I mean character sways, justified. Only in the mind of the wicked can it be reasoned. "Ye are of your father the devil, and the lusts of your father ye will do. He was a murderer from the beginning, and abode not in the truth, because there is no truth in him, when he speaketh a lie, he speaketh of his own; for he is a liar and the father of it" _(John 8:44)_. He is a liar who says he treats others comparatively different than the way he treats God. He it is who, over a period of time, has convinced himself that it is possible to do such a thing. All in all it still remains to be a lie.

A good-hearted person can attest to this supportive fact. It is even difficult to truly hate someone who has done you wrong, when you are a Christ-fearing and Christ-loving person. You may dislike what the person did to you, but the love for Christ within drives you to still do the right thing. A person of evil will not see it that way, and will immediately want an eye for an eye. Again, what is in your spirit comes out in your character towards God and towards others, in equal fashion. No one really knows how you treat God behind closed doors, although this document declares that your treatment of God is evident through how you treat your neighbor. The Lord Jesus said it this way, "Then shall he answer them, saying, Verily I say unto you, Inasmuch as ye did it not to one of the least of these, ye did it not to me" _(Matthew 25:45)_.

If someone treats you poorly, best believe they treat God poorly. For a contrite and lying spirit has no ability to treat God well. If they, in some possible way, have the ability to treat their horizontal relationships any differently than they treat their vertical relationship, they ought be committed to a hospital with white padded walls and jackets that strap around the back. We are so foolish in some of our thoughts and ways till it becomes real to us. We are to love Christ through loving others. This document is to awaken you to facts, truths and some mysteries of God; albeit, it is our duty to apply them to our spirits and living, so we can become effective in prayer and fulfilled in life. We can be empowered by this document, but we must receive of it and act upon it, first.

A deeper sense of thanksgiving and appreciation for someone surely comes from having knowledge of that person and an acceptance of who they are. We may like God's grace more than His justice, but both must be appreciated just the same. We may endear His mercy and love more than His chastening, but in receiving one we must receive the other. "But he said unto her, Thou speakest as one of the foolish women speaketh. What? shall we receive good at the hand of God, and shall we not receive evil? In all this did not Job sin with his lips" *(Job 2:10)*. It is all a part of who He is. We will fail at becoming stronger in prayer until we appreciate God for all of who He is. Listen! We pray our most potent prayers when they are in accord with His attributes and character. Not speaking of prayers that get others shouting, necessarily. I'm speaking of prayers that get answered by God; thus, the reason you are reading this document.

Appreciation Through His Word

If we lack in appreciation for God then we are void of an appreciation for His Word! If we cannot appreciate His Word then we will not pray in His Word; especially in the truth of His Word. There is power, deliverance and healing in His Word; among many other things. Still, we cannot appreciate what God is accomplishing in His Word, if we do not show appreciation for who He is and for what He has done for us. I love His Word so much because I appreciate He who wrote the Word. I try diligently to live in accord with His Word, because I appreciate what He is trying to do through me, and in me, by means of His Word. I pray in appreciation for His Word because I have faith in Him.

As prayer warriors we must appreciate God for His Word. Cannot imagine a person praying to a God in whose words they do not trust nor believe. In trusting His words there should be a strong appreciation for who He is. It should be quite easy to give God thanks for His Word alone if we are true believers. An ability to give thanks to God for His Word converts into strong faith in prayers unto Him. It is this thankfulness which translates into an appreciation that pours out to Him in prayers and through living. It all originates from a belief in Isaiah 55:11 which declares, "So shall my word be that goeth forth out of my mouth: it shall not return unto me void, but it shall accomplish that which I please, and it shall prosper in the thing whereto I sent it." If we do not believe that verse we will not pray in accord with His Word nor promises; as will be illustrated in the next *Element of Request*.

There is a great power that is secured for all who give appreciation and thanks for the Word of God. Prayer warriors will be the first to declare the power that is built upon giving God thanks for His Word. Best believe prayers are rendered weak and fruitless without having thanks for the Word of God sewn in our hearts and on our lips. There is a spiritual power that is connected to our ability to be thankful unto the Lord for all He has proclaimed and declared in the Bible. I am speaking of a natural state of spirituality and power that expresses itself through thanksgiving and through effective prayer. This document can teach us some things in regards to being thankful, but at the base of it all only the Lord can place the thankfulness and appreciation upon our spirits and hearts that is required of prayer warriors. As mentioned in several parts of this document, a close relationship with the Lord is the only way to receive great spiritual powers.

There is nothing magical about having a strong relationship with God. It all becomes solidified through our appreciation for Him. We ought show God the appreciation He truly deserves. It is for our good. Much of what God has us to do is solely for our good, and for His glory. He alone is already good. You know someone once asked the question, "Is He good?" Best believe, God is good. As a matter of fact, He is great! How many can truthfully testify of that fact?

Appreciation Through Communion

Entering into communion with the Lord often begins with and is strengthened by our showing Him thanksgiving. Thanksgiving sets the table of fellowship and worship with God, whereas, many of us think worship stops at praise. "Enter into his gates with thanksgiving, and into his courts with praise: be thankful unto him, and bless his name" *(Psalm 100:4)*. Again, praise is great, but many of us miss out on the fullness of His blessings by omitting to give Him thanks for who He is and for the blessings already given unto us.

The spirit of any fruitful fellowship is founded upon a level of intimacy with someone. This fruitful fellowship and rapport cannot exist without showing the other party appreciation, just as communion on a spiritual level cannot exist without thanksgiving. Evil may be able to have a rapport with evil, but a truthful spiritual communion exist only within thanksgiving. "If ye were of the world, the world would love his own: but because ye are not of the world, but I have chosen you out of the world, therefore the world hateth you" *(John 15:19)*. In other words, it is difficult at best for us to have communion with the world when we are of God's spirit, and it is even more difficult for us to have communion with God when we are of the world. Both parties have little appreciation for the basic foundations of who they each assert to be.

We can surely commune with anyone and in any type of way; that is if we are not concerned about the results and the fruit thereof. On the contrary, as believers we must be concerned about the outcome of our prayers. Prayer warriors have intimate appreciative relationships with God which help to produce fruitful results in their prayers. How we commune with the Lord is so much a spirit matter that it cannot be taken lightly, if we expect to be successful in prayer.

Giving thanks unto the Lord does so much in helping to connect our spirits with His Spirit, that to omit thanksgiving is to subvert the intimacy. Praying to the Lord is a fellowship that cannot be had at a distance. Not communing with the Lord lends our prayer experiences to that of long distance telephone calls, or even text messages. When it comes to communication, texting and long distance calls are two of the most impersonal forms that exist. Since when do we send a text to ask God of anything? Communion! Communion! Communion!

We must appreciate spending time with the Lord. As mentioned in the introduction, we cannot commune with the Lord only in times of need. The thought of speaking to Him only in times of need is unimaginable and so impersonal. We all have our testimonies of persons who show up at our doorsteps only when they are in need. What better way to show the Lord appreciation and thanksgiving than by spending quality time with Him in times other than when we are in need? Communing with the Lord on a regular basis will show Him thanks and appreciation. If we do not spend ample quality time with Him we may not truly appreciate who He is. Entering someone's presence only in times of need illustrates how we appreciate the things they do, but not necessarily appreciate who they are. We should not show God's deity such disrespect and disregard. Show greater appreciation for spending quality time with the Lord then watch how our prayer lives expand to greater heights.

Eager to Get Into His Presence

That brings us to another point about rapport in prayer: getting into the presence of God. We have already spoken in part about getting into His presence, but here we mention how we must be eager to be in His presence. Eagerness illustrates a heightened degree and in-depth willingness for communion. We will be less effective in prayer if we lack a desire to be close to Him. We can get meager prayers through to God while staying at a distance, but prayer warriors pray for some serious concerns and issues which necessitate being close and personal with Him. It is more than just calling a meeting with God. It is more like how the first settlers of the Americas, the Indians, would call for a pow-wow!

To hold a pow-wow was and is a serious matter. Major decisions are considered and concluded in this type of communion. No less serious should we take the matter of communing in prayer with our Father who delivers us from all concerns.

Giving thanks unto God sets our spirits in a mode of earnest, as it pricks our spirits to not take lightly who the Lord is to us and all He has done for us. We have missed the boat if we take thanksgiving in prayer lightly. For all who take lightly being in the presence of God, it is good to remember what the Lord told Moses, "Thou canst not see my face: for there shall no man see me, and live" *(Exodus 33:20)*. So, best believe it is a serious matter to go into the presence of God. We should not be fearful to come unto Him, but we should have a healthy fear in reverence of Him. "The Lord taketh pleasure in them that fear him, in those that hope in his mercy" *(Psalm 147:11)*.

As we give thanks to the Lord we show Him we are sober and solemn about coming into His presence. If prayer is crying out to the Lord, then why do many pray playfully? Not only does it not make sense, but it does not work, either. Let us bless ourselves, our communion with God, and our prayers, by giving the Lord truthful thanksgiving. "Let us come before his presence with thanksgiving, and make a joyful noise unto him with psalms" *(Psalm 95:2)*.

THANKSGIVING – *Progression of Prayer Element #3*

Exercises

INSTRUCTIONAL

1. Select a verse from the "How" Scripture Section at the beginning of this chapter. Write a short paragraph on how this verse relates to showing appreciation unto the Lord.

   BENEFIT:
   To enhance your awareness of God's being worthy of appreciation.

PERSONAL

1. Think of three blessings which the Lord bestowed upon you on yesterday. Think back five years to the date the Lord blessed you with something in particular. Truly think of the year and the date. Now, think back eight years and do the same. Take a moment to thank Him for all the above blessings. Counting our blessings is a simple exercise in which we should engage more often.

   BENEFIT:
   To convey the fact that we all have something for which to thank the Lord; we need only to take the time to count the ways, times and occurrences. Also, this will reinstate the act of counting blessings into our prayer lives. Every now and then most of us forget this simple, yet fruitful exercise. We do have much for which to thank Him.

THANKSGIVING – *Progression of Prayer Element #3*

General Questions

1. What is the opposite to the feeling of entitlement?

2. What is a contradiction to living for Christ?

3. Having thanksgiving on our hearts and lips puts us in the spirit of what four (4) things?

4. What grants us access unto the Spirit of God?

   What does it then enable us to accomplish?

5. Who should give thanks unto the Lord?

   What is one Bible verse which supports that answer?

6. For what does the Lord desire we rely on other than our needs?

7. What must we accomplish in order to fully gain access unto the Thrown of Grace?

8. What can be said of those who are not thankful towards their fellow man?

9. What is the concern of mimicking the thanksgiving others give unto the Lord?

10. What is one of the best forms of showing appreciation unto God?

THANKSGIVING – *Progression of Prayer Element #3*

Advanced Questions

1. How can our living in faith align most properly with the Holy Spirit?

   Give a brief description of how this most affects our thanksgiving unto the Lord?

2. How is it one person can thank another yet still not show them appreciation?

3. This document makes mention of people who stake claim they can treat God with love while showing disregard to their neighbors. Write a short paragraph stating your position on this point?

   Give a Bible verse as support to your answer?

   What was the Lord Jesus' response to a similar scenario?

Pray this prayer with me:
A Prayer for Request

"Divine and faithful God. Creator of both Heaven and Earth. Great in power and perfect in all Your ways. Shouts of praise unto You pour from every part of my being; as there is no one great like You. Thank You Lord for not only being my Jehovah Jireh, but for being my Jehovah Nissi, as well. Thank You even at this moment for blessing my heart with spirited praise, in order that I may enter into Your presence with the fullness of joy upon me. Bless Your name God! I now pray You help me to better understand the *Element of Request* in prayer. Grant unto me a fresh spirit to glorify Your name in my requests, as those very appeals align more with Your Word, Your promises and Your will for my living. All the while I shall remain mindful that You alone are the answer to all my prayers, and there is nothing I stand in need outside of my need for Your presence in my life. Glory! Allow my spirit to be more sensitized to Your will, then let me ask for that. Bless me and I will be blessed. In this I pray in the name of the Father, the Son and the Holy Spirit — Amen."

This section is to better enhance our understanding of the Biblical reasons for who should make request, how should request be made, why should request be made, what should be requested, where should request be made and when should request be made. Our study of request will be further enhanced if these verses are read previous to moving onto the chapter material; as this format will indeed better prepare our spirits to receive of the chapter material.

1) WHO should make request?
- Judges 20:18 — The children of Israel
- Jeremiah 23:33 — The people, the prophets or priests
- Matthew 7:8 — Everyone
- Luke 11:10 — Everyone

2) HOW should request be made?
- II Chronicles 20:4 — Seeking the Lord
- Psalm 78:18 — Not tempting God
- Psalm 106:15 — Being mindful of what you ask
- Matthew 6:33 — First seeking the Kingdom of God and His righteousness
- Matthew 18:19 — Two touch and agree
- Matthew 21:22 — Believing
- John 14:13-14 — In Jesus' name
- John 15:7 — Abiding in the Lord
- John 15:16 — Of the Father in Jesus' name
- John 16:23 — Ask the Father in Jesus' name
- Romans 1:9 — Always and without ceasing
- Romans 8:26 — With the help of the Spirit (intercession and groanings)
- Ephesians 3:16 — According to His riches in glory
- Ephesians 3:17 — Rooted and grounded in love
- Philippians 1:4 — With joy
- Philippians 4:6 — Not be careful for anything; by prayer and supplication with thanksgiving; unto God
- James 1:5 — Ask of God
- James 1:6 — In faith, not wavering
- James 4:3 — Not amiss and not to consume it upon your lust
- I John 3:22 — While keeping His commandments; while doing those things that are pleasing in His sight
- I John 5:14 — In confidence in Him; according to His will

3) WHY should request be made?

- I Chronicles 4:10; Job 6:8 — That God would grant the request
- Psalm 2:8; Matthew 7:8, 21:22; I John 3:22 — To receive
- Psalm 107:13-14 — To be saved and delivered
- Proverbs 30:8 — So not to deny Him nor take His name in vain
- Jeremiah 18:13 — The Lord said to make request
- Jeremiah 30:6 — To see
- Matthew 6:8 — The Father knows what we need before we ask
- Matthew 18:19 — It shall be done for you of the Father in Heaven
- John 14:13 — That the Father may be glorified in the Son
- John 14:14 — Jesus will do it
- John 16:23 — He will give it to you
- John 16:24 — That your joy may be full
- Romans 1:10 — That it be God's will
- Romans 8:26 — We know not what to pray
- Ephesians 3:16 — He will grant it
- Ephesians 3:17 — That Christ may dwell in your heart by faith
- Ephesians 3:20 — He is able to do exceedingly and abundantly
- Philippians 4:7 — Have the peace of God; keep your heart and mind
- James 1:5 — God gives to all men liberally and upbraideth not
- James 4:2 — You will not receive if you do not ask
- I John 5:14 — He hears you

4) WHAT should be requested?

- Judges 20:18 — Counsel of God
- I Kings 3:11 — Not long life, nor riches for thyself, nor the life of thine enemies; to discern
- I Chronicles 4:10 — Enlarged coast (territory); that His hand would be with you; keep you from evil; that it may not grieve you; to be blessed indeed
- II Chronicles 20:4 — The Lord's help
- Psalm 2:8 — The uttermost parts of the Earth for your possession
- Proverbs 30:8 —Neither poverty nor riches; food convenient foryou
- Isaiah 7:11 — A sign
- Isaiah 45:11 — Of things to come concerning the Son and the work of His hands
- Matthew 7:11 — Good things
- Matthew 18:19 — Anything
- Matthew 21:22 — All things
- John 15:7 — What you will
- John 15:16; I John 3:22 — Whatsover
- John 16:23 —Asking Him nothing
- Romans 1:9 — Mention of others

4) WHAT should be requested? *(Continued)*
- Romans 1:10 — For safe travel
- Ephesians 3:20 — Above all that you may ask or think; according
        to the power that worketh in you
- James 1:4 — Wanting nothing
- James 1:5 — For wisdom

5) WHERE should request be made?
- Judges 20:18 — In the house of God
- Jeremiah 18:13 — Among the heathen
- Isaiah 7:11 — Either in the depth, or in the height above
- Matthew 18:19 — On the Earth
- Matthew 21:22 — In prayer
- Philippians 1:4 — In every prayer

6) WHEN should request be made?
- Psalm 107:13 — When in trouble and in distress
- Jeremiah 30:6 — Now
- Matthew 21:22; Philippians 1:4 — While praying
- John 16:26 — At that day
- Philippians 4:6 — In everything

"And whatsoever ye shall ask in my name, that will I do, that the Father may be glorified in the Son. If ye shall ask any thing in my name, I will do it."   **John 14:13-14**

First and foremost, a request (act of asking or making an appeal) unto God in prayer is not in the form of a demand. We should not and surely cannot demand anything of our God, the One who created Heaven and Earth; including you and I, of course. A request in prayer is asked; never demanded. As scripture tells us, "... make your request be made known unto God" *(Philippians 4:6)*. We can surely make it known, but there is no demanding anything of the Lord. Let us be quite clear, He already knows a thing before we pray, anyhow. By this time in prayer our hearts and spirits should be fixed unto the Lord. The first three *Elements of the Prayer Progression*™ prepare our spirits for this very moment of request. A request should never be made until we have first fixed our heart's condition and ushered in the presence of the Holy Spirit. As will be discussed, the first three *Elements* help to shape and revamp our request. A request without preparation can be made to be hollow and unfruitful; something we want to avoid at all cost.

What are You Asking: Need or Desire?

It is great that God already knows what we stand in need before we pray, for it is true we know not what to pray for in the first place. The Bible tells us, "Likewise the Spirit also helpeth our infirmities: for we know not what we should pray for as we ought: but the Spirit itself maketh intercession for us with groanings which cannot be uttered" *(Romans 8:26)*. The "ought" portion of this verse is made manifest by these *Elements of Prayer Progression*™ within this document. For example, by the time we finish acknowledging who God is in our lives, praising Him for who He is, and thanking Him for what He's done in our lives, our spirits should be in such an elevated place that our focus then changes and we may no longer desire that which we originally sought to ask.

Let this be clear and dear to our spirits. Often, we pray for unnecessary things due to our not first being in the Spirit of Christ. Our selfishness, no matter how small or minute, tends to steer us toward things of desire versus things of necessity or things of God's will. We often realize the impractical nature of our request when we are elevated in the Spirit of Christ. If we are true to our thanking God for who He is and for what He's done in our lives, we will then come to realize how blessed we are of God already. Also, we then will truly realize how God has provided all our needs and sustained our very existence. Too often we forget just how God has covered us from those things seen and those things unseen.

Let us be mindful of the progressive nature of the *Prayer Elements* presented in this document and allow that very progression to move us into a realm filled with God's Holy Spirit. Personally, I often reach the request portion of prayer and do not request one thing of God. Although I first have every intention of asking Him for a certain thing, the Spirit will often move me to a place of heightened spirituality where my only desire is to have the Lord. To be even more frank, those prayers were the most spirited and most rewarding prayers of all, even though I did not take the opportunity to ask for anything. After the first three elements of acknowledgment, adoration and thanksgiving, I become so in tuned with the Spirit of Christ that the "I" within my prayer is no longer important. The manifestation of Christ by way of the first three elements draws me to a place where I desire Him and Him alone. We all will accept that God is all we need when we realize His great presence in our prayers.

To have the Lord's Spirit heavily abide within our prayers will enter us into a place where we realize God was all we have ever had, and God is all we will ever need. When our prayers become more engaged with the Spirit of the Living God, we then will more fully appreciate Luke 12:33, which indicates only what we do for Christ will last. Please do not misunderstand, this *Prayer Progression* is surely not directing believers to forsake making request of God. Absolutely not! The Word tells us, "Ye lust, and have not: ye kill, and desire to have, and cannot obtain; ye fight and war, yet ye have not, because ye ask not" *(James 4:2)*. What I do infer is that our requests and our motivations in prayer should and will surely change during this *Progression of Elements*. There will surely become less thoughts about "me" and more thoughts about "He." Well, isn't that where our minds and spirits ought to reside in the first place?

Our prayers are truly all about the Father and are so little about us. The more we tend to His will the more He tends to our comings and our goings. I thank the Lord for placing upon my spirit at an early age the concept of, "I take care of you and you take care of me, and neither of us will have a need to become self-centered; for our needs will be supplied by the other person at all times." This is a concept unto which we all should adhere for good health in all our relationships. This is a concept which God spews to us throughout His Word, including, "Seek ye first the Kingdom of God and His righteousness; and all these other things shall be added unto you" *(Matthew 6:33)*. As we see, this concept is not so novel; its just not known by most and surely not taught by others.

The Fruits of Progression

Lets go a little deeper into a few strong patterns of praying. Listed below are some powerful ways in which to make our request unto the Lord:

1) That His will shall be done.
2) In accord with His promises and covenants.
3) That our receiving the blessing requested will bring Him glory.
4) That others will receive salvation through Jesus Christ. Pray that whatever is received from God will in turn have others to come into a saving knowledge of Christ Jesus, and that others will be eager to claim Him as Lord.
5) That others will receive the overflow of blessings. Pray that we receive a blessing so we may be used as vessels to bless others.

As we can surely see, power in prayer is a matter of taking the "selfish you" out of the equation. We must remove self if we want to be blessed and if we desire to be truthful prayer warriors. The Lord intends on blessing us, but His plan is to use us to bless others. So, let us get connected to His power by praying in accord with the above list which consist of prayer patterns to which the Lord responds most readily. If you look closely you will see how the list does not concentrate on the wants of the person who is praying.

The Will of God and our Request

We should find our most successful prayers to be those which concentrate on the good and perfect will of God, His nature and character. This is another *key* to being a strong prayer warrior. It is not always as though a prayer warrior has special powers to pray. Most often what makes the warrior effective is his or her willingness to pray according to the will of God. Hear me on this. This is why it is so essential to not only know the attributes of God, but it is so crucial to want to see the will of God come to fruition, as well. We will not become a part of the 100,000 strong prayer warriors until we master this essential point. Far too many persons call themselves prayer warriors, claiming to be capable of getting a prayer through to God in regards to anything, anyone, and anytime, yet they lack the knowledge of praying according to the will of God. These persons are fake in their spirits and false in their claims. We must call it what it is in order that we can get to where we all need to go.

Let us go a little further in this point to the tune of someone's deliverance. The people to whom we reach out for prayer ought to be those people we know want to see God's will done. <u>This is our criteria for asking someone to pray for us.</u> The criteria is less about their position in the church and more about their spiritual submission unto God's will and nature. Also, let it be known that someone who is not living according to God's will and Word is not someone, more than likely, who submissively seeks the will of God in prayer; thus, don't ask this fashion of person to pray for us, for their prayers are for gain in areas other than for God's will to be done. We must allow this key to truly saturate our spirits that we may receive of the deliverance.

We do not ask someone to pray for us because we think they have special magical powers to get prayers through to God. The fact is God hears all the prayers of the righteous *(Proverbs 15:29; James 5:16)*, yet whether He answers specific individual prayers is whether the prayer is in accord with His will and His character. It is true we can live and think unto righteous-ness and still our prayers may not be what God wills for our lives. Living righteously means we are living according to God's law and not necessarily according to where God wants us to go and what He wants us to do with a blessing He has given. That is the point where many of us become disgruntled and dismayed about the faith, just as we do with prayer. We tend to think our living should automatically be blessed just because we are living righteous lives. This thinking is a reflection mainly of how most of us have been taught. Fact is, it's the Lord's will which comes forth. Many of the things we have learned have come via teachers with no power to empower. The simple stay simple and teach likewise for they know not of Him who is the Creator of all power. This document has been delivered unto us that we may be empowered by our getting closer to the Lord in truth so we may live in the power of His will, thereafter. Let me speak on this for just another moment. There are even leaders who do not want us to follow God's will for fear that our following God's will results in their having less control; making them less than kings and little gods. These are the very same leaders who have continued to diminish the power of the Church from within; causing others to seek things that are not eternal. God's will is eternal.

In Biblical days people sought the prayers of faithful servants such as David, Ezekiel and Jeremiah, not because they had special powers of their own, but due to their having special relationships with God which prompted them to want to see His will done. Folk submitted to their words because they knew they were in essence submitting to the will of the Father who sent them and spoke through them; no matter the pain nor persecution that would follow. David prayed to the Lord saying, "Teach me to do thy will; for thou art my God: the spirit is good; lead me into the land of uprightness" *(Psalm 143:10)*. He also prayed, "Shew me thy ways, O Lord; teach me thy paths. Lead me in thy truth, and teach me: for thou art the God of my salvation; on thee do I wait all the day" *(Psalm 25:4-5)*.

Jeremiah remained faithful unto the Lord for 40 years preaching the message of repentance, because he had a binding relationship with the Lord. The strength of his relationship with the Lord and his desire to do the Lord's will can be seen in Jeremiah 26:2-7;

"Thus saith the Lord; Stand in the court of the Lord's house, and speak unto all the cities of Judah, which come to worship in the Lord's house, all the words that I command thee to speak unto them; diminish not a word: If so be they will hearken, and turn every man from his evil way, that I may repent me of the evil, which I purpose to do unto them because of the evil of their doings. And thou shalt say unto them, Thus saith the Lord; If ye will not hearken to me, to walk in my law, which I have set before you, To hearken to the words of my servants the prophets, whom I sent unto you, both rising up early, and sending them, but ye have not hearkened; Then will I make this house like Shiloh, and will make this city a curse to all the nations of the earth. So the priests and the prophets and all the people heard Jeremiah speaking these words in the house of the Lord."

Subsequent verses illustrate how some persons came against the words of the Lord spoken by Jeremiah, yet Jeremiah continued to do the will of the Almighty, proclaiming what saith the Lord. "What saith the Lord," may not seem to be in the favor of us nor others at times, but His will must still be sought and done just the same.

Twelve years after the above was spoken Jeremiah was seen still doing the will of God as the people sought his words in order to know "What saith the Lord," as written in Jeremiah 42:1-3, "Then all the captains of the forces, and Johanan the son of Kareah, and Jezaniah the son of Hoshaiah, and all the people from the least even unto the greatest, came near, And said unto Jeremiah the prophet, Let, we beseech thee, our supplication be accepted before thee, and pray for us unto the Lord thy God, even for all this remnant; (for we are left but a few of many, as thine eyes do behold us:) That the Lord thy God may shew us the way wherein we may walk, and the thing that we may do."

As further illustrations of this point: Noah was found to be a righteous man, but it was his submission unto God's will which moved him to build the ark; Abram was a man of faith and righteousness, yet it was his obedience unto God's will which moved him to a land God would show him; Paul became upright in his ways after he received the Lord Jesus, but it was his submission unto God's will which moved him to open churches throughout the land and amidst much persecution; Jesus was and is the most righteous of all, yet it was His desire to do the Father's will which sent Him to this earth to save that which is lost *(Matthew 6:10, 12:50; Luke 19:10).*

Understand, God cannot use us mightily if we are more concerned about our own selfish desires than we are about doing His will. I will make it plain in a painful way. It is human to want to see someone healed, but it is heavenly to want to see the Lord's will done no matter the outcome. This I tell folk, "Be mindful coming to me for prayer if you do not accept God's ultimate will in the situation." What's best for us is what God wants for us. This is a submission point many of us will not accept. Even they who claim to be prayer warriors have a difficult time dealing with the pains that sometimes come with doing the Lord's will.

For a moment, let's use Psalm 105:15 to illustrate the strength in, both, submission and God's power working through us: "*Saying*, Touch not mine anointed, and do my prophets no harm." There is a close connection between God and believers who diligently seek to do His will. When tough situations arise, many of us ask the question, "What would Jesus do?" Contrarily to the milk fed, meat eating believers have spirits tethered unto God's will, so they speak the actual words of God when those tough situations arise. God is able to speak and act through those believers due to the strong connection which is bound by His will. In this fashion the believer (prophet) may speak a curse and/or facilitate the very actions God sees fit for the situation; just as Jesus cursed the fig tree *(Mark 11:11-14, 20-21)*. Powerless is he who is unbelieving. Here it is made plain − if a person comes against a servant of God, who diligently seeks to do His will, is as if that person is coming against God Himself. For, if in anger a servant/prophet speaks against that person, the prophet's anger may be so tethered to God's wrath and to God's concern about the situation, that the outcome will surely not be favorable for that person. Prayer warriors must be similarly so wrapped in God's will and Spirit so we may boldly speak and pray truth for things present and future. No other way may Romans 4:17 work through us; "... even God, who quickeneth the dead, and calleth those things which be not as though they were." It is not we who speak words of ourselves, but it's the power of God's will and character speaking through us and through our prayers.

We must submit unto the Lord, and live and pray that His will be done, in order for us to become prayer warriors and in order for us to pray prayers which receive favorable answers. We must have spirits that strongly desire to see God's will done no matter how difficult it is to accept. Those who find this point to be less than digestible may have a difficulty in transferring their prayers into power. For example, most of us find it unbearable to see someone wrecked in pain and/or in the process of dying, but prayer warriors stand tall and strong in faith believing God knows best for the situation. As well, we truly cannot save the world from what God inevitably has for us all, yet many praying people whom claim themselves warriors run around thinking they have an 'S' on their chests able to slay all the biggest and baddest issues at the drop of a hat.

Now, I do not say "We cannot save the world" in negative connotation. What I am saying is our personal power will not grow exponentially until we accept that we are better off in the long run after going through some trials, if it is God's will that we do so. "And not only so, but we glory in tribulations also: knowing that tribulation worketh patience; and patience, experience; and experience, hope; And hope maketh not ashamed; because the love of God is shed abroad in our hearts by the Holy Ghost which is given unto us" *(Romans 5:3-5)*. It is great power unto our spirits and our prayers to know God's will is perfect in every respect.

How then might we say, "The Lord is doing some marvelous things in our lives," lest we first have faith in knowing He is perfect in all His ways? We truly cannot know, nor understand, all that the Lord is doing in our lives. We must only have faith to know and have submissive hearts to believe He is in full control and able to do all things but fail. This is where a prayer warrior lives in spirit. This is where a prayer warrior resides in heartfelt acknowledgment of who God is. This too is why a prayer warrior moves beyond thought of the pain and suffering of any direction God passes down as final.

We do not request for the Lord to change His will; for God is immutable (unchanging), as written in Malachi 3:6. "Jesus Christ the same yesterday, and today, and for ever" *(Hebrews 13:8)*. Many of us go into prayer thinking, for some twisted reason, we can change the Lord's mind and/or alter His plans for our lives. Isaiah 45:9-10 proclaims God's words, "Woe unto him that striveth with his Maker! Let the potsherd strive with the potsherds of the earth. Shall the clay say to him that fashioneth it, What makest thou? or thy work, He hath no hands? Woe unto him that saith unto his father, What begettest thou? or to the woman, What hast thou brought forth?"

A prayer all of us should practice praying is, "Lord, help me this day to be more in tuned and connected with Your perfect will for my life and for the direction of my day." Our main focus in prayer ought truly be that we become more in sink with the grand plan set forth by an all knowing and all powerful God. It is when we are in tuned with the Lord's plans that our lives are blessed in tremendous ways. "If my people, which are called by my name, shall humble themselves, and pray, and seek my face, and turn from their wicked ways; then will I hear from heaven, and will forgive their sin, and will heal their land" *(II Chronicles 7:14)*. This verse says nothing about what it is you nor I want and desire. This verse is pregnant with references of how we are to get in accord with who God is, what God wants and what God desires of us. For the most part, these verses direct us to "seek" God in order to get in accord with Him.

The situations and circumstances in our lives would be healed if we would simply submit unto the Lord's will through our prayers and through our living. It is all about the Lord and His will for His creation. It makes no sense to pray to God with the intent of changing His mind, since He is all powerful (omnipotent), all knowing (omniscient) and everywhere (omnipresent). In reality we should change our minds to fit into God's master plan. This may sound mundane, but it still reigns true that He knows everything about everything, and that "everything" is more than you and I will ever know in twenty lifetimes to infinity. It lends me to ask, "Why would we pray to change the Lord's plans?" His plans are perfect, although sometimes those plans may take us through a little pain and suffering. We must believe His plans ultimately result in our growth and added blessings. Overall we should focus on getting closer to God to do His will, instead of trying to fit God into our selfish desires.

We should pray that God's will be done, not ours, and that He bring us His grace and mercy through it all. Jesus said in Matthew 6:10, "Thy Kingdom come. Thy will be done in earth, as it is in Heaven." What makes us so intelligent to think any differently than Jesus' command for us to pray the will of the Father? Maybe this is why the scriptures tell us we surely do not know for what to pray. Even Joab understood this concept while in the heat of battle as he said, "And let the Lord do that which is good in his sight" *(I Chronicles 19:13).*

This document is meat for all who want to be delivered into a realm of living and praying that goes far beyond the norm and the powerless. There are times coming when they who have truly digested this material will be needed to forge ahead in power and strength. In the times to come there will be people who will need the help of warriors who understand and live in accord with these *Elements* and God's will. May it be you who stands firm upon the Word and the unlocked mysteries of God. "And we know that all things work together for good to them that love God, to them who are called according to his purpose. For whom he did foreknow, he also did predestinate to be conformed to the image of his Son, that he might be the firstborn among many brethren. Moreover whom he did predestinate, them he also called: and whom he called, them he also justified; and whom he justified, them he also glorified" *(Romans 8:28-30).* So, be of good cheer and allow God to give us the increase. The Lord shall grant us the increase from our request, only after He builds us to live according to His will.

We must begin to understand how our living and even our request should be connected to and directed by the nature and attributes of God. Here we arrive at the meat and potatoes of a thing. So many of our prayers are never answered in our favor for one simple but contrite reason: the requests we make are not in accord with God's will and character. Be aware that this is not the only reason our prayers go unanswered, for there are several reasons behind unanswered prayers. This document addresses some of those reasons later in this chapter and in other chapters. Here we shall give short illustrations of how some prayers are automatically made ineffective because they are outside God's will, nature and character.

Let me explain it this way. We cannot pray that a person dies *(I Kings 3:11)*, for we are to live and pray in accord with His attribute of love. There is no love in hoping that someone dies; not even our enemies. "This I command you, love one another" *(John 15:17)*. "But I say unto you, Love your enemies, bless them that curse you, do good to them that hate you, and pray for them which despitefully use you, and persecute you" *(Matthew 5:44)*. Fact is we are not to gloat over the demise and brokenness of our enemies. Proverbs 24:17-18 says, "Rejoice not when thine enemy falleth, and let not thine heart be glad when he stumbleth: Lest the Lord see it, and it displease him, and he turn away his wrath from him." Edom gloated over Judah's destruction and was then punished by God *(Obediah 12-15)*. Similarly, we cannot request to hit the lottery, since God, as Yahweh Yireh, wills us to have faith in His providing our every need. "But my God shall supply all your need according to his riches in glory by Christ Jesus" *(Philippians 4:19)*. It is not by luck nor by chance that God provides all the needs of His children. So, let it truly be understood that prayers, or request in prayers, are fruitless lest they are joined with the character and will of God. Some of us get unnerved by our prayers getting "nay" answers from God, thinking He does not care for us. It's not true that God does not care for us, yet it is true He's not all that favorable to our asking for things that are outside of His will, character and nature.

Let me clarify this another way, as well as give clarity of scripture. John 14:13-14 tells us, "And whatsoever ye shall ask in my name, that will I do, that the Father may be glorified in the Son. If ye shall ask any thing in my name, I will do it." This verse speaks heavily of how God's will is to be done in our lives; such that our doing the will of God is the only way our actions will glorify the Son. Anything done outside the will of God surely will not glorify the Son, the Holy Spirit, nor the Father. We must ask of things which are in His will in order to edify His Kingdom. Those things of which we ask are to include those things He has planned for our individual lives. Be mindful that we may even pray for some things that are within His nature, yet not be in His will for our individual lives. The best way for us to even partly know His will for our individual lives is for us to be sensitized unto His Spirit's speaking and by our continually aspiring to be in right relationship and in consistent fellowship with Him.

We can go a step further by referencing Matthew 21:22, "And all things, whatsoever ye shall ask in prayer, believing, ye shall receive." This verse is a favorite for all the "name it and claim it" and "tag it and bag it" folk. Yet many of these same persons' faiths are shaken to the core when they have believed all day, all night and even all year without results. There are many Christians who have bold, strong and enduring faith, but the reality is this — they may continue to live righteously and pray every day in the name of Jesus, yet their prayers will not come to pass if they are not in accord with God's will for the path He has for their lives.

I know truth may be painful for a lot of us to digest. Someone may be exclaiming how we have free will, which I do not refute at the least. God also has the will and the power to not give fruit to our prayers if they are not in accord with His desires for us. Our free will over God's will and blessings? Hmm! He may allow some things to occur in our lives which are not in accord with His will, yet He will not participate in the aiding and abetting of our wayward partakings. I'm not claiming anyone is committing a spiritual felony, although there are some choice words that describe those who neglect to do God's will. The sooner we realize and accept that much of prayer is not about us, the sooner we will begin to actualize the principles and elements that empower our prayer lives.

Many of us do not want to accept any form of predestination in our lives, as we often reach back and proclaim of our spiritual freedoms. Oh yeah, we have free will. Make no mistake about it. Notwithstanding, we should truly know and believe in our spirits God has some great plans for our lives, and those plans are in accord with His will. We all want the blessings God has planned for our lives, yet we do not truly want to participate in the plans God has patterned for our lives. We cringe to accept the fact that in order to receive of the blessings we must walk along the path God has designed. Can I make it even more plain? Our lives are often a mess and in disarray simply because we get off His path, out of His will and so very far from His plan for our lives. We may be good persons by nature, yet still not walk in accord with God's plans for our lives. This causes conflict in our relationships with God and results in unanswered and/or denied prayers. We are no different from quite many characters in Biblical times who found it difficult to walk constantly in the will of God. As example, Jonah spent a moment of his life in turmoil and in the belly of a large fish. Why? Simply due to his unwillingness to do as God willed. Jonah was to proclaim repentance unto the Ninevites; whom he thought to be too wicked to deserve God's blessings. Let this story speak unto us as we also admit and accept Isaiah 55:8, which states, "For my thoughts are not your thoughts, neither are yours ways my ways, saith the Lord." Best believe God's will for our lives is a more excellent way. The word "is" is used here instead of the word "are" because there is only one way, and that way is Jesus the Christ wanting us all to be saved.

Let us go a little further with this point on believing and receiving. Truly understand, we can believe a thing all we want, but we may find ourselves turning blue in the face before some of our prayers come into fruition, if they are not in the will and character of God. The "whatsoever" in Matthew 21:22 surely does not imply whatsoever man conjures in his/her thinking. It simply infers the magnitude of asking in the name of the Son Christ Jesus, who makes intercessions for us at the Right Hand of the Father; giving further reason that our request ought to glorify the Son.

Handling Disappointments in Request

Some folk exited the faith, partly for no reason other than their prayers, supposedly, went unanswered. They were compelled to relinquish the even slight connection they had with the Lord instead of trying to discern their mode of prayer. These believers, turned doubtful, never took into consideration the things for which they asked were so not in the fabric nor make-up of a sovereign God. I recently spoke to Shelly, a High School and College sister, about an issue I had with one of my computers. I asked if she had ever encountered a certain issue that I was facing. She simply replied with laughter and brevity, "I think what you have is a common issue of operator error." Her statement is so profound of how we presently operate in our faith, as well. We surely should not be disgruntled and say our prayers falter due to God's err. Rather, it can be said that our faltered prayers are the result of the way we operate our faith. Too many of us simply do not know how to operate our faith; thus the reason for and objective of this document. Many of our disappointments in prayer can be minimized and/or eliminated by changing our outlook. First, we should remember God is in full control and He knows what is best for us. This is something we proclaim but fail to live by faith. Second, it is essential to truthfully examine our motives for our request. The Lord may delay or deny our request based on our motives behind the appeal. Our request can be on point and in-line with God's will yet our hearts may remain tainted. More of this is discussed in other parts of this document. Third, we must be patient and realize God's timing is perfect. We will grow in character through patience, so to be equipped to receive of the answered prayer's blessings.

This document is to equip the saints as proclaimed in Ephesians 4:12, "For the perfecting of the saints, for the work of the ministry, for the edifying of the body of Christ:" Not only are we going to be blessed with great abilities to make requests after digesting of this document, but we shall be spiritually strengthened to handle the different answers God may give, as well; which is sometimes more important than the former.

Many of our congregations are held captive in disgust of their prayer's answers. This occurs as leaders shout of freedom but without themselves realizing Isaiah 61:1-3, "The spirit of the Lord God is upon me; because the Lord hath anointed me to preach good tidings unto the meek; he hath sent me to bind up the broken-hearted, to proclaim liberty to the captives, and the opening of the prison to them that are bound. To proclaim the acceptable year of the Lord, and the day of vengeance of our God; to comfort all that mourn; To appoint unto them that mourn in Zion, to give unto them beauty for ashes, the oil of joy for mourning, the garment of praise for the spirit of heaviness; that they might be called trees of righteousness, the planting of the Lord, that he might be glorified."

Fact remains, many of us know so little about prayer and its answers due to half-hearted leaders who make selfish attempts to comfort the masses, while all along their self serving causes chain the spirits of the unaware. Unto all of them I speak of Ezekiel Chapter 34, and ask, "Should not the shepherd and teachers care for the flock, drinking clear water of their own, while muddying the waters and fields of the rest?" Dare not saith the Lord, and woe unto them who continue in their wolf-like dealings. Hear. It is this document's purpose to free every heart from the negative emotions that result from the many types of answers given for our prayers. We should never be disappointed by any answer God gives. It is the spiritual duty of a prayer warrior to find the blessings in all the directions and answers given by God. Remember, the answers to our prayers are to benefit us and glorify Jesus. No matter how we were taught to receive of our prayer's answers, let it now be received that we are to bend our living unto God's answers, versus God bending His answers to fit our desires. Much of our power in prayer is our having power to receive all of what God gives as answers; not in part, but in whole.

Much of this teaching is so new to many of us for two simple, yet sad, reasons. First, there are those who are void of the Spirit who would otherwise give them knowledge of how to equip the saints. Second, there are those who refuse to equip the saints for fear that doing so would eliminate the need for them and put them out of business. A huge part of the equipping issue is far too many view the Church solely as a business opportunity. On the contrary, this document's business is to equip the reader with power from on High to best magnify our most high God. "How dare we hear from Heaven," is the mentality of some who do not want us to hear God's voice. Some who have never heard from God would rather we listen to them to learn how to hear from Heaven. How dare we listen to that sort of nonsense, and how dare we rely on them to then teach us how to handle God's answers to our prayers? The Lord came to this Earth to release us unto Himself; thus the gain of this document is to assist in that releasing.

Disappointments in our prayers and faith walks would subside if only we lived in the truth and context of scripture, and if we relied less on mystic type thinking to substantiate our faith walks. Mystical theology expresses spirituality from excitement, more so, than from authority of scripture. This I say, what remains after all our excitement is gone is God's truth and the authenticity of His Word; as breathed unto the original writers.

Stating His Promises to Make the Appeal

Use God's promises and declarations made in His Word in order to make appeals to Him and in order to get His attention more fully. This is one of the simplest yet a most potent _key_ for prayer warriors, because we serve a promise keeping God. "So shall my word be that goeth forth out of my mouth: it shall not return unto me void, but it shall accomplish that which I please, and it shall prosper in the thing whereto I sent it" _(Isaiah 55:11)_. As an example we can pray, "Lord, You tell us in Your Word You will not leave us nor forsake us. Right now I feel forsaken. So, Lord please reassure my spirit to know You are still with me and that You are fighting this battle on my behalf." This key is a release for the majority of us. Those who do not receive this now will truly receive of it in the time allotted to their faith by God our Father. Nonetheless, I do pray this very moment that we all receive the power of this key as soon as possible so each of us may move into a deeper realm of prayer.

Appealing to God in accord with His promises and the Word's declarations adds power to our prayers. This key is available to us only if we have belief in God's attributes and have knowledge of the true context of His Word. Otherwise, our faith in the fulfillment of our requests will be rendered ineffective and impotent. The Lord has made promises. Mention His promises in prayer and know in spirit and in faith He will not forsake His own Word. Here is another similar example of how to pray in accord with His promises. Instead of praying the words, "Lord come help me," our prayer should be "Lord You said You would never leave me alone, and Your Word declares that I should not fear, for You will strengthen me, help me and uphold me with Your righteous hand."

Here is a short list of just a few promises, assurances and declarations made unto us through God's Word, of which we should mention in our prayers:

- "I will not leave you comfortless: I will come to you" *(John 14:18).*
- "And let us not be weary in well doing: for in due season we shall reap, if we faint not" *(Galatians 6:9).*
- "But they that wait upon the Lord shall renew their strength; they shall mount up with wings as eagles; they shall run, and not be weary; and they shall walk, and not faint" *(Isaiah 40:31).*
- "For the Lord God is a sun and shield: the Lord will give grace and glory: no good thing will he withhold from them that walk uprightly" *(Psalm 84:11).*
- "Thou will keep him in perfect peace, whose mind is stayed on thee: because he trusteth in thee" *(Isaiah 26:3).*
- "Bring ye all the tithes into the storehouse, that there may be meat in mine house, and prove me now herewith, saith the Lord of hosts, if I will not open you the windows of heaven, and pour you out a blessing, that there shall not be room enough to receive it" *(Malachi 3:10).*
- "Saying, Touch not mine anointed, and do my prophets no harm" *(I Chronicles 16:22 & Psalm 105:15).*
- "To me belongeth vengeance, and recompence; their foot shall slide in due time: for the day of their calamity is at hand, and the things that shall come upon them make haste" *(Deuteronomy 32:35).*

Let's go a little deeper. We must not only know the Word in its context, but we must also believe the Word in order to command the power of those promises. Our prayer's words become as sounding brass unto the ears of God if we do not believe in the very words we exclaim as His promises. "... I am become as sounding brass, or a tinkling cymbal" *(I Corinthians 13:1).*

God is immutable, and He is faithful to His promises. This document is unlocking several mysteries, but it is no new thing to pray in accord with His promises, nor is it new for prayer warriors to gain in faith and power by exclaiming how His promises are connected to our prayer requests. King David often prayed in accord with the promises made by God just as Solomon prayed believing God to be a promise keeping God. Solomon proclaimed in I Kings 8:23-24, "And he said, Lord God of Israel, there is no God like thee, in heaven above, or on earth beneath, who keepest covenant and mercy with thy servants that walk before thee with all their heart: **Who has kept with thy servant David my father that thou promisedst him: thou spakest also with thy mouth, and hast fulfilled it with thine hand as it is this day.**"

Speaking God's promises in prayer was a practice of old, and our today's prayer experiences need not be anything different nor new; in light of a world that wants to create new denominations and new forms of worship, praise and church. We merely need to tap into the true power of the Word, as did numerous Biblical characters who prayed in faith and strength. In doing so, we will gain in power and we will begin to actualize our own increased spirituality.

Not enough of us, who are called to minister God's Word, have the ability to unlock the mysteries which empower ourselves and others; thus many continue to suffer while seeking idol and alternative forms of worship. Alternative forms need not be established in the name of new age, since there is nothing new under the sun *(Ecclesiastes 1:9)* and the Lord is the same yesterday, today and forever *(Hebrews 13:8)*. Why do we, in our humanistic intelligence, find the need to create something which is unproven and none contextually based? I remember someone once said, "If it worked for Momma, it will work for me." Well I declare to you today, if it worked for the faithful in Biblical times, I am sold out in believing it will work for us today.

Hear my words. I do pray these *Progression Elements* and *keys* are found to be plain unto us, for it is of the Lord's will that we receive this document in its fullness, as a blessing unto our souls, living and prayer lives.

Praying According to His Promises and Word.

If we are to be strong prayer warriors we must use God's very Word, nature and attributes to communicate with Him in prayer. In Psalms 31:3 we can see how the writer, David or Jeremiah, illustrates how we should pray God's promises unto Him. Here the writer exclaims how God's helping him would bless and/or benefit His Holy name; insinuating that anything less may bring shame to His servant and to Him. This is a major *key*. David appealed to the Lord by the use of His promises by proclaiming, "For thy people Israel didst thou make thine own people for ever; and thou, Lord, becamest their God. **Therefore now, Lord, let the thing that thou hast spoken concerning thy servant and concerning his house be established for ever, and do as thou hast said. Let it even be established, that thy name may be magnified for ever**, saying, The Lord of hosts is the God of Israel, even a God to Israel: and let the house of David thy servant be established before thee. **For thou, O my God, hast told thy servant** that thou wilt build him an house: therefore thy servant hath found in his heart to pray before thee. And now, Lord, thou

art God, and hast promised this goodness unto thy servant: Now therefore let it please thee to bless the house of thy servant, that it may be before thee for ever: for thou blessest, O Lord, and it shall be blessed for ever" *(I Chronicles 17:23-27).*

Praying His Promises Encourages Us

God truly knows all things before we pray them, nonetheless our spirits are strengthened when we pray in accord with His promises and Word. In our living it encourages our spirits to rely on a God who is faithful unto His children and unto Himself, and in the same manner we receive an indirect blessing of encouragement, reassurance and power unto our prayers when we rely on Him by proclaiming His Word in His presence. His Word is given unto us not only to follow and obey, but by which to be encouraged, also. One writer said unto God, "Remember the word unto thy servant, upon which thou hast caused me to hope. This is my comfort in my affliction: for thy word hath quickened me" *(Psalm 119: 49-50).*

The truth is our pain sometimes makes us forget the very promises made by God. Remembering His promises can be tough when the enemy has leapt on our necks in his every attempt to destroy our very being. It is difficult enough to merely sustain through the attacks of the enemy, and even more difficult to muster any remaining strength, energy and spirit to recall the promises of God, all while being attacked. Although tough we must remember God's promises and remember to proclaim them.

Another Level in The Word – Promises versus Conventional

In our attempts to come out of a trial, sometimes, it is not enough to simply remember His Word. In truly difficult times we often must go to another level of faith by remembering and reciting His promises; not just conventional verses. Mind you, God's Word is in no way conventional in the truest sense of the word "conventional," yet this word is used simply to make differentiation.

God's Word in its conventional form, if we may say such, can help most times, but His promises take us to another level of blessed assurance and faithfulness that can help us get through those truly tumultuous times. The difference between conventional verses and promise verses is simply that conventional verses do not include declarations for expectation. Examples of conventional verses include praise, exaltation, song, thanksgiving, history, etc. Some folk lean on praise in tough times, which can help to an extent of each individual's faith level, whereas, standing on God's promises gives us more power and blessed assurance to stand tall.

We all can attest that there are times in our days and lives when we need just a little more in order to make it through. If that is not believed just keep on living and there will come a day when saying, "I will bless the Lord at all times: his praises shall continually be in my mouth" *(Psalm 34:1)* just won't get it done. What may more so get us through those tougher times is to proclaim such promises like, "Lord You said You would never leave me nor forsake me" *(Joshua 1:5 and Hebrews 13:5)*. If He said it we ought believe it, and we ought mention it in our prayers; especially in our times of great despair and mounted trouble.

In times of trouble it is ok to shout, "He alone is my Rock and my Salvation; he is my defense; I shall not be greatly moved" *(Psalm 62:2)*, but more power can be received from, "Lord You said in Your word '...Touch not mine anointed, and do my prophets no harm' *(I Chronicles 16.22)*, so come see about me now Lord, for I am Your servant." Oh, understand the difference and receive of its power. These very principles are revealed unto us from on High so to give us sustaining power for the times to come; for there shall come days long and nights dreary. We can stand and stand strong by this power God is bestowing upon us. Let's lift our heads and be encouraged, for the Lord is a promise keeping God.

Promise Keeper

Unlike ourselves and other mere humans, God surely keeps His promises. He kept His covenant with the Israelites even through their wickedness, and He shall keep His promise unto us, His children, although we too are less than perfect in our ways. If you do not remember anything else, remember God is a promise keeper. The Apostle Paul too spoke of having strong faith in God's promises, "And being fully persuaded that, what he had promised, he was able also to perform" *(Romans 4:21)*. Keeping His promises has less to do with you and I, and more to do with His being immutable (never changing). Not only will He not forsake His children, but above all He will not forsake Himself. He has a reputation that He will uphold and surely sustain. In this we can depend!

To God be the Glory!

Another strength and *key* in prayer is to mention how God's name shall (25) be glorified and magnified by the success of our prayers. So many of us mention His glory unintentionally when at home and in church, but not so many of us actually pray that the Lord receive the glory and honour. It is one thing to mention His glory in just, but it is another thing to actualize the sentiment through our actions and prayers. Asaph said it this way, "Help us, O God of our salvation, for the glory of thy name: and deliver us, and purge away our sins, for thy name's sake" *(Psalm 79:9)*. King David's similar proclamation of prayer was, "For thou art my rock and my fortress; therefore for thy name's sake lead me, and guide me" *(Psalm 31:3)*. *(At this moment our hearts should burn more for God's word, just as we should never look at verse the same in future days)*. When will we grow to be more concerned that God receive the glory rather than our being overly zealous that we receive a blessing? It is in that day of growth when we shall be indirectly and even inadvertently blessed of God in many tremendous ways.

King David gives us another great example of strong prayer, where he emphasized the connection between his answered prayer and God receiving glory because of it. "Let it even be established, that thy name may be magnified for ever, saying, The Lord of hosts is the God of Israel, even a God to Israel: and let the house of David thy servant be established before thee" *(I Chronicles 17:24)*. Many of us shout of His glory only because it seems vogue and sounds correct in the face of our brethren. "Give God the glory," is probably shouted at least once in every Sunday church service throughout the land. Question is, do we truly want the Lord to be glorified through our answered prayers, or are we solely concerned with how we appear and with what the answered prayers will do for us? I painfully proclaim the later to be true for most of us.

We should think of prayer in terms of, "What's in it for the Lord?" This is a way of thinking and believing that can become ingrained in the fabric of both our prayers and our living unto God; only if we give diligence to practice it. I can often be heard saying, "It is not about us. We have already been saved." Giving God glory should become a major purpose and drive of our prayers, as written by one psalmist, "Save us, O Lord our God, and gather us from among the heathen, to give thanks unto thy holy name, and to triumph in thy praise" *(Psalm 106:47)*. Most of the strong and faithful leaders in the Bible can be found to have sought God's glory through their living and through their prayers. No different was the faithful leader Joshua as He spoke with God while grieving over Israel's loss, "... and what wilt thou do unto thy great name?" *(Joshua 7:9)*. The Lord immediately answered him and gave him directions! Likewise, in order for us to become, both, strong prayer warriors and faithful children of the Most High God, we too must seek His glory over our selfish request and over our sometimes outright foolish desires.

If those examples do not touch our spirits, as they should, let us spiritually mention God's stance on His receiving glory from our answered prayers. God proclaimed in II Chronicles 7:16, "For now have I chosen and sanctified this house that my name may be there for ever;

and mine eyes and mine heart shall be there perpetually." This proclamation was made in response to Solomon's prayer *(v12)*. God truly desires to receive all the glory. The Lord Jesus made it plain in John 8:50, "And I seek not mine own glory: there is one that seeketh and judgeth." He speaks of God the Father receiving the glory.

The essential strength of our fellowship with the Lord is empowered when we truly desire that God be glorified through answered prayers. The fruit of our desires is made evident by our living unto the object for which we pray, or by how we transform our living unto Christ after we receive our request. In other words, a faithful Christian first seeks to give glory to God through prayers, whereas, immature and fleshly Christians shout God's glory in attempt to coax Him, unsuccessfully by the way, into answering their prayers. These *Elements of Prayer Progression*™ shall transform us into faithful prayer warriors who often resign our desires in order to best seek God's will. I do declare in the spirit of prayer and in the power of the Holy Spirit, we will endear our spirit's urges to truthfully get closer to God after digesting this key and others within this document.

If we desire to have our prayers answered, we must truthfully seek to glorify God. As we shall see, we will often choose not to present our original request unto God after our spirits are changed by the *Elements of Prayer Progression*™ *#1, #2 and #3*. The very essence of these elements, combined with the truthfulness of our spirits, makes it almost impossible to continue to think selfishly in our prayers. As a matter of fact, our original requests may be scrapped and we may end up praying something more fitting like, "Lord if You bless me this day, bless me with Your presence; for I know I have all I need in Your presence." The first three *Elements* are designed to increase our desire for God over anything else. Well, isn't that the way it is supposed to be? This is an essence of what the writer of Hebrews stated in v13:5, "... and be content with such things as ye have: for he hath said, I will never leave thee nor forsake thee."

A Spiritual Shift in Prayer

We should resign to a couple of facts by the time we progress through the first three *Prayer Elements*. First, we should resign to the fact that God is still in full control. This can be made evident through our spirit's recognition of how the Lord has brought us thus far along the way; as an example. Second, we should resign to the fact of how senseless and/or unnecessary the item is that we had planned to request of God. Often times we turn-down our plate of request after we have come to realize how thankful we ought to be for all the Lord has already provided. There are many things we all truly stand in need, but these *Elements of Prayer*

Progression™ shall help to weed out the unnecessary prayer requests. This blessing will occur as these *Prayer Elements* heighten our spirits in Christ Jesus and as they strengthen our communal experience in prayer. The closer we get to the Lord in spirit the further we will get from needing things worldly. At which time we will love others and worship God more faithfully and honestly. This is what God desires as our growth, and it is made possible through digesting these *Elements of Prayer Progression.*™ The power of this document shall strengthen our awareness of how essential it is to be about the Lord's business and less focused on selfish desires. Then, we will truly say we live for God's sake and not for our own desires. Isn't that true glory and honor unto the Lord?

Saving Knowledge of God

Stating prayers in the form of the Lord receiving glory and honor is great, but let me explain what else is heavenly to pray: the Lord's good and perfect will that everyone be saved. "For God sent not his Son into the world to condemn the world; but that the world through him might be saved" *(John 3:17)*. "And he is the propitiation for our sins: and not for ours only, but also for the sins of the whole world" *(I John 2:2)*.

In other words, praying over (for) something with the attachment of "someone coming to the saving knowledge of Jesus Christ," adds power to our prayers. Power is added to our prayers through this *key* by the mere fact that we are then praying in the will of God and in accord with His nature. Listen, this is especially effective with regards to our enemies. We must be mindful to pray in accord with God's nature, will and attributes if we are to be of the coming 100,000 powerful prayer warriors. "... For this is good and acceptable in the sight of God our Saviour; Who will have all men to be saved, and come unto the knowledge of the truth ...." *(I Timothy 2:1-8)*. We shouldn't pray that our enemies die, but we can pray they be chastened of the Lord in such a way that by the end of their suffering they will come to truly know the salvation of the Lord. A way in which we can pray that they die is to pray that they die to their sinful ways. Again, this is praying in accord with His will and in line with His character.

Hear me on this and be extremely blessed. What greater blessing could we give unto our enemies than to pray a prayer which ignites their salvation? What greater way could we "get an evil person back," per se, than to have them change the very wicked ways they love so much; thus the Lord's vengeance? The Bible tells us to do right by our enemies; "If thine enemy be hungry, give him bread to eat; and if he be thirsty, give him water to drink. For thou shalt heap coals of fire upon his head, and the Lord shall reward thee" *(Proverbs 25:21-22).* This I give unto you this day, what greater coals can we possibly pour upon the heads of our enemies than the fire of change; a change by way of the Holy Spirit and salvation? This pouring we can ignite by praying that they come into a saving knowledge of Christ Jesus. "... Vengeance is mine, I shall repay, saith the Lord" *(Romans 12:19).* So, let us do our part in praying for the greatest vengeance of all: the salvation of wicked people who are being used heavily by the devil. What reward, or crown, may we receive for that act of civility? As my dear cousin always says, "I'm just saying!"

As we can read, this *Elements of Prayer Progression*™ document is truly meat; meat we surely must digest as we continue to usher in the Spirit of God. I say again, do not attempt to use these precepts for filthy lucre or any other ill-gotten gain, for they will not work in such a manner. God knows our true intents, and demons can recognize from what spirit or Spirit we are hewn. We must have true spiritual connections with the Lord, along with strong faith, in order for these precepts to work on our behalf.

Overflow of Blessings and God's Greater Glory

The Lord desires that we act as vessels who are great blessings to others. The Lord, most often, is not direct when He blesses us. Surely He could bless us all directly and individually, but He desires a few things: First, each blessing reach many people; Second, He receives the most glory and honour; Third, we become more giving in spirit as He uses us as vessels; Fourth, His amazing works connect people in a fashion that His presence is unquestionably evident. Let's examine each of these now.

First, praying that the Lord use us as vessels for overflow unto others is one of the strongest ways to increase the likelihood of our prayers being answered; since He is interested in blessing many with little. It is not that the Lord is cheap in handing out blessings. On the contrary, He is very giving and desires to bless the most people. As well, He desires the greatest glory, which comes about when less is used to bless multitudes. For this to occur we must act as willing overflow vessels. Do not cut off the blessings that God so designs to reach the masses. This is a *key* we should be heavily mindful to remember and institute into our prayer lives. The Bible tells us how the Lord does great things (Psalm 111 and many other verses), of which many have been, are and will be accomplished through those of us who act as willing vessels. This truth is exemplified in many Biblical occurrences where God the Father, the Lord Jesus and the Holy Spirit used little to bless many; including Matthew 14:13-21, where the Lord fed five thousand plus with five loaves and two fishes.

Second, the Lord is always interested in His receiving optimum glory, of course; thus, He wisely chooses to use one vessel to overflow unto others. This bears truth when no individual can then lay self claim to their being the source of their own blessing. We may attempt to take the credit for our blessings instead of giving God the glory and honour if He were to always bless us directly. Some of us are less blessed today because He knows we have the propensity of taking the credit ourselves. In addition, He also knows others of us refuse to receive from they who are being used by Him to bless us. Not accepting growth and blessings by way of others can cause grave disorders that harden the heart and develop personality characteristics stilted with control issues. Sounds like someone you know? We should simply give God the all-out glory, accept His blessings by way of others, then watch more blessings flow.

The third desire of God becomes evident when we submissively become more giving of our spirits and our living; so acting as true overflow vessels. We take on a Christ-like character when God allows us to witness first-hand His manifold greatness at the same time He allows us to participate in the process of blessing others. This is that realm where Christ manifest Himself within us as proclaimed in Romans 16:25-27. John 14:21 speaks of this manifestation of Christ Jesus within us, as well. God desires us to be like Him and His Son Jesus — giving of ourselves and being thoughtful of others. Prayer warriors recognize this truth and seek opportunities to pour overflow unto others whenever they receive blessings from God. Can God depend on you to keep the blessings flowing? Or, will you clinch your fist, choking the blessing that may have been intended for hundreds and maybe even thousands of others?

Fourth, overflow unto others often relinquishes people to say truthfully, "Only God." Often, we shout, "Only God" in every attempt to convince ourselves and others into believing God is working in our lives. For many of us our religious walks are merely acts to convince, rather than acts of faith. Here's how we can often tell of God's involvement in the blessing. The blessed evidence occurs when all parties involved exclaim how they were moved of God to do a certain thing at a certain time, which brought them all together to witness and/or share in the blessing. The greater blessing is their seeing the presence of God at work in their lives, rather than their receiving of the tangible blessing that was bestowed between them. In this event each person usually has little or no idea of the other person(s) need, yet their obedience to God's directing brought them together at just the right time so one of them, or both, received the needed help or blessing. In other words, there was no doubt that God had orchestrated it all, because by no other means would they have known nor traveled that way.

Here is an example to better explain. There was a man who needed to pay his mortgage through wire transfer by 12:00 midnight or he would lose his home. The man left an evening church meeting at 10:30 pm not having a clue how he would save his home, so he resigned to the fact that it would be lost. Twenty minutes later a friend phoned him, asking if everything was alright. He replied that all was fine. She exclaimed that God placed upon her heart to call him and ask that very question. So, she asked again, "Is everything alright? Well, this went on for about 10 minutes before the man finally told her of the pending foreclosure and the time restraints. She, being the great friend she was said, "Man I knew God had me to call you for a reason, and you wasted valuable time denying anything was wrong. You know God's timing and directives are perfect. Let me get off the phone and make something happen." This lady lived every bit of thirty minutes across town, yet she called another friend to pool resources, then called the man back and met him with the full payment amount. The man paid the mortgage payment at 11:58 p.m.; two minutes before losing his home.

That is a case where "only God" is appropriate to exclaim. The fantastic blessing was not really that the mortgage was paid on time, but that the presence of God's hand could be seen in the situation. Yes, it was a blessing that the mortgage was paid, but the greater blessing was to witness the movement of God in truth. God could have blessed the man directly in any number of ways, but He got more glory by working through other willing vessels, as there was no mistaking that it was His hand which made it all possible.

Let's further illustrate this point with a couple of Biblical examples. First, the story of Elijah and the widow who's food was multiplied from a handful of meal and a little oil _(I Kings 17:8-16)_. The Lord told Elijah to go, as neither the woman nor Elijah were aware of one another. Only God! To add to the overflow glory, neither of them could understand how they all were to eat, given the limited resources available. They both had to submit to being willing vessels, leaning on the Lord for a successful outcome. Only God! As another example, Ananias was to lay hands on Saul (Paul) to restore his vision. The only way Ananias and Saul knew this encounter was to occur was by the voice of God. Saul was given the vision by God, while Ananais was given directions by God. Their paths crossed because of their willingness to be used as vessels. All who witnessed this healing and blessing gave the Lord more honor than He may have received had He simply opened Saul's eyes directly.

These are great workings of God's overflow through His willing vessels. Not that they are such amazing occurrences, but because there is no way to mistaken them as being caused or directed by anything other than the hand and presence of God. The Lord desires to use us in the same fashion, as He is still in the blessing business. In such circumstances all He ask is that we be willing vessels so He can receive the greatest glory.

NOTICE:

Let this serve as notice that if ye pray to be an overflow vessel, best believe ye better use the overflow received for the blessing of others and not hoard it for personal use. Let's not be tricky in our dealings with the Lord. That which we pray is that which we do. God is a covenant keeper and we must keep our promises and covenants, just the same. Do not block present and future prayer blessings by breaking covenants made yesterday and today. Trust that it will not go over well with the Heavenly Hosts. As well, be mindful that overflow does not always appear as extra. Far too many of us want to give others out of our extra. Just be careful not to always expect overflow to come as a package marked "Extra Blessings." Overflow from the Lord may come by way of His giving us something we wanted and/or needed for ourselves, yet the blessing is bestowed upon us as a test to see if we will either hoard the blessing for ourselves or if we will be faithful unto our prayers that He use us as overflow vessels.

Be mindful, says the Lord, that we do not think we must be wealthy in order to overflow unto others. The fruitfulness of this point can be made evident only through our sensitivity unto the Spirit of God as we follow His directions to bless others.

In the Name of Jesus — In the Spirit of Jesus

We all have been taught and even directed by the Bible to pray in the name of Jesus Christ, and in such we do fine. Yet, many of our prayers continue to go unanswered because we do not pray in the Spirit of Christ Jesus. This is a *key* to being a prayer warrior. We tend to pray with His name on our lips, but void of His Spirit in our hearts. Lord only knows in what spirit some of us actually pray. God knows in what spirit we speak the name of Jesus, just as evil spirits too recognize; as illustrated with the sons of Sceva written of in Acts 19:11-17. To pray in His name requires only a movement of the lips, but to pray in His Spirit demands a movement of the heart and soul. We previously mentioned how necessary it is to get into the presence of the Lord. In addition to all that was stated, be mindful that praying in the Spirit of Christ grants us even further access into the presence of the Father.

Communicating with God involves levels. Levels which most of us have never ventured. Levels of trust. Levels of maturity. Levels of wisdom. Levels of fellowship and levels of spirit. It is the level of spirit and fellowship which grant us the deepest access unto the presence of the Lord.

At this point, it is essential to say praying in the name of the Lord will get the Father's attention and fulfill scripture, but it may leave us in a surface level of prayer; depending on our spirit's condition. Whereas, doors begin to open unto levels of greater fellowship with Him, as we tap into His Spirit at the same time of praying in His name. It is in this greater access where we get healing, deliverance and receive more power. Yes, there are blessings on the surface, but it is in the fullness of His Spirit where we receive the overflow. Most of us have heard of believers talking about the overflow. Well I declare this very day, we shall be ushered into the overflow if we allow the writings of this document to elevate our spirituality. To enter into the presence of the Lord is a great blessing; beyond what many shall obtain in truth. But, hallelujah to His holy and righteous name for granting us access into the overflow. Overflow in His Spirit will be further discussed in the *Prayer Element of Meditation.*

It is essential to pray in the name of the Father, the Son and/or the Holy Spirit, but I declare today that it is necessary, and all important, to pray in the spirit of the Father, the Son and/or the Holy Spirit. In other words, it does not matter in what name we pray if our minds, hearts, and spirits are not right. We must dwell in the spirit in order for the name to work for us. Throughout most of Jesus' earthly mission He told people how it was by their faith in which they were healed, delivered and saved. We unlock the power of prayer when our spirits are in tune with the greatness of His Spirit. Jude 19 and 20 proclaim it this way, "These be they who separate themselves, sensual, having not the Spirit. But ye, beloved, building up yourselves on your most holy faith, praying in the Holy Ghost."

As example, many of us talk of how we grew up in the Church, but on-lookers scoff at how we act so worldly and present ourselves as though the Church never grew up in us. The same goes for many of us praying in the name of Jesus, when we never allowed Jesus to take hold within us. On the contrary, after digesting this document there shall come forth 100,000 strong prayer warriors steeped in the Spirit of Christ Jesus and able to strongly and truthfully pray in His name.

His Abiding Spirit

Faith to Believe

These _Elements of Prayer Progression_™ elevate our spirits to supernatural levels where we shall possess the faith to believe each of our request will be answered. The Lord says, "And all things, whatsoever ye shall ask in prayer, believing, ye shall receive" _(Matthew 21:22)._ Sorrowfully, many of us do not truly believe. We may shout and dance like we believe, putting on a show, but our unanswered prayers testify against us. Our prayers may be on point and in the very will of God, but they still end up failing because we fail to believe our request will come to fruition. Some of us are quite unbelievable in our unbelief.

Jesus Himself proclaimed a generation unbelieving, "O faithless generation, how long shall I be with you? how long shall I suffer you? bring him unto me" _(Mark 9:19)._ This was a Biblical time where the disciples were unable to cast out a dumb and deaf spirit from the child of a scribe. We too must act in the same level of faith it took for the father to say, "... Lord, I believe; help thou mine unbelief" _(v24)._ This man knew it was his doubt that could hold back the blessing, and he was aware that God would help by first removing that doubt. That is a blessing in itself.

There are great blessings to be bestowed unto us if we would simply endear the power of belief. It doesn't take much on our part, for the Lord will do the rest. If we would only believe! "Unbelief" is a New Testament Greek term who's Biblical reference is first seen in the Books of Matthew and Acts. The Lord Jesus spoke to the disciples about their unbelief in regards to the devil-possessed boy, proclaiming the power to move mountains through having faith the size of a grain of a mustard seed _(Matthew 17:14-20)._ The Apostle Paul spoke of unbelief as he taught of the grafting into the faith of new branches and the breaking off of them who do not believe _(Romans 11:11-24)._ Hebrews 3:12 speaks strongly about this disbelief as it proclaims, "Take heed, brethren, lest there be in any of you an evil heart of unbelief, in departing from the living God."

The amazing thing about our belief, or lack there of, is that we are not required to necessarily believe in our own abilities. Please receive of this **29** _key._ It is difficult to imagine moving mountains with our human deficiencies; as we have fallen, stumbled and failed at things innumerable. At times it is impossible for some of us to conceive moving a small pebble, let alone a mountain. Trials and tribulations can jump on our backs in such a way to make us want to surrender. There are even times when sufferings compound sufferings to no relief, causing many of us to wince at the next slightest troubled wind. But, thanks be to God, we serve a Lord and Savior who has all power to do all things but fail! We've heard that before, but we fail to apply that very fact to our prayer lives. It is not "we" who do anything. Apostle Paul exclaimed, "I am crucified with Christ: nevertheless I live; yet not I, but Christ liveth in me: and the life which I now live in the flesh I live by the faith of the Son of God..." *(Galatians 2:20)*. We of ourselves can do nothing; absolutely nothing. For this reason we must believe in Christ Jesus and His power to lift up, strengthen, deliver, and perform greatness in our lives.

Things are out of our hands once we give them over to God in prayer. The Lord may decide to use us somehow to bring about the blessing's success, but things remain to be out of our control. If we were to be truthful about it, we would be thankful things aren't in our hands, since we know how to mess up things. It is by the Lord's hands we are able to even see the light of a next day. "For in him we live, and move, and have our being ..." *(Acts 17:28)*. Many so called powerful people live in unbelief simply due to their inability to have trust and faith in someone else's power; no less the Lord's power. We must wrap our hearts around the fact that our power comes about through having faith that His power is all that's needed. Someone once said, "I found out the Lord was all I needed, when I saw that He was all I had." His permissive will allows some trials to collapse the pride we have in our own abilities, so we can then come into the saving knowledge of His power to do all things but fail.

Sorrowfully, some of our prayer lives reflect this inability to believe in Christ, as our requests continue to fade like dust in the wind, unresolved and seemingly unanswered. We fail to realize our prayers are often fruitless mainly because we doubt the Lord's power. Woefully, some of us believe in ourselves entirely too much, even to the point of harming the results of our own prayers. Far too many of us are too haughty for our own good. It is fine to have confidence, but that confidence must be rightly centered in Christ and not in ourselves. Our boldness must pronounce our faith that Jesus is the source of strength and power of our whole existence. Our fearless assurance must proclaim our belief, as Paul told Timothy, "For God hath not given us the spirit of fear; but of power, and of love, and of a sound mind" *(II Timothy 1:7)*. We ought be bold in Christ, but it is a boldness of who He is and not who we think we are.

As believers we even have a history of saying things like, "The Lord will," "I know He will," and "God will." We holler so many claims through hollow shouts and playful affirmations. These things sound good, yet we fail to transfer that belief into our prayer lives and into our general faith walks. This is proven by one simple fact: we have problems of truthfully giving God pre-praise for all He is about to do. Pre-praise will be further discussed in *Pre-Praise Thanksgiving Element #7*.

We should never have a difficulty believing in the Lord's abilities, since He has such a long track record of deliverances, miracles performed, and times He has shown up right when we needed Him. We all surely would have been devoured had it not been for the Lord who is on our side. "It is of the Lord's mercies that we are not consumed, because his compassions fail not. They are new every morning: great is thy faithfulness" _(Lamentations 3:22-23)._ We have more than enough proof to render our belief strong. Our prayers must be impregnated by faith knowing He can, He will, He shall and He must. Our prayers will not work lest we ignite them with, both, our belief in the Creator of all things good, and our faith in knowing He is willing to show up and show out. I don't know about you, but I am excited to know not only will the Lord show up in our situations, but He will also show out! We must have faith in all of who He is and in all of what He can and shall do.

I Chronicles 22:11-13 gives us illustration of how our success comes from the Lord and not from ourselves. David tells his son Solomon, "Now, my son, the Lord be with thee; and prosper thou, and build the house of the Lord thy God, as he hath said of thee. Only the Lord give thee wisdom and understanding, and give thee charge concerning Israel, that thou mayest keep the law of the Lord thy God. Then shalt thou prosper ..."

Having Need for the Lord

"The Lord is my Shepherd; I shall not want" _(Psalm 23:1),_ speaks volumes to our matter. We can truly shout and know we want for nothing other than He alone when we truly and truthfully know He is our Shepherd, our provider, our covering, our joy, our peace, our sustainer, and our getting up in the morning. Oh, what a release to not have want for the things of this world, but to truly have want for the Lord. This spiritual increase is a major release by way of this document.

In this document we find the added power and strength to have need for the Lord; especially the presence of His Spirit. Our spirits should be elevated greatly after progressing through _Elements #1, #2_ and _#3;_ to a level of spirituality that gives way to a realization that what we are about to request is not as important as our need for Him, and Him alone. How many of us truly have graduated to a level of spirituality where we seek God first and above all things? How many of us can attest to have grown to a spiritual level where the Lord's presence in our lives truthfully has become our main desire? It will be a blessed joy for each of us when we come to realize our most potent prayers are actualized when our spirits are eager for Him and less concerned of things of the flesh and things of this world.

James 1:4 tells us, "... be perfect and entire, wanting nothing." Let it be known here today, the only way to be patient and want for nothing is to have a heart content in the presence of the Lord. A healthy and strong need for the Lord is the only thing that can make our spirits desire less of earthly things. It's only natural for us to want for some things, but our spiritual power depends on our foremost need for the Lord. Through this need we then shall see the fruit of Matthew 6:33. Most of us know a healthy need for the Lord will minimize and maybe eliminate desires for the earthly. Shamefully, we forsake Him in order to continue to feed our fleshly desires. Prayer warriors must truthfully and wholly abide within, "For in him we live, and move, and have our being ..." _(Acts 17:28)._

So many of us call ourselves prayer warriors, unbeknownst of what it truly means to be such. Anyone can speak to God in prayer, but few of us can speak for God in prayer; meaning, we submit to the Lord's speaking truth through us while in prayer. Simply put, prayer warriors speak God's truths in prayer. On one hand, people often babble all sorts of things when speaking with God, while on the other hand, warriors speak of God's truths and desires. This is not to say we are necessarily prophetic in prayer, but it is that we are so desirous of God's will that we then pray of heavenly things that are of God. Some people think being a prayer warrior is about just quoting some scriptures, reciting some names on a prayer list, and inciting vigor in the voice saying things like "In the name of Jesus," and "Amen;" as if to gloat suggestive nanny goat inflections. Praying in such a spirit will render results unto potluck rather than consistent spiritual victories. Potluck is not the posture nor spiritual thinking of a prayer warrior. Consistent spiritual victories begin with our having a need for the Lord that's greater than our need for things worldly.

Prayer warriors have an understanding that success in making requests involves several key principles. I shall briefly list a few at this time only to make the point that many of us are so totally unfamiliar with being true prayer warriors. A few of these aspects include living justly, praying in accord with the Lord's character, consecrating oneself, and having a submissive spirit while praying. These principles and others are discussed in different portions of this document. A good number of us are not looking upon this short list for the first time, yet a large number of us continue to lack the spiritual DNA of those principles. We may choose to receive or reject this point, however, the principles still remain true; unmistakably. In order to become the prayer warriors we desire, it is best that we receive of these truths now and allow the Spirit to pour the power of this document into us. I say at this point, do not hesitate to re-read any portion of this document. The more we digest this document in truth and in spirit, the stronger shall be our prayer lives and our general faith walks.

Keep His Commandments and Improve the Possibilities

We must keep God's commandments in order to receive of Him through prayer. Many of us cannot receive from God because we are so sick in sin. We are often so deeply rooted in our own wickedness that God would not dare bless our prayers. God wants us to be His children more than He wants us to be bless on this earth. Solomon prayed, "Then hear thou from heaven thy dwelling place, and forgive, and render unto every man according unto all his ways, whose heart thou knowest; (for thou only knowest the hearts of the children of men:)" *(II Chronicles 6:30).* Let me tell you, our true blessing is in Him. We all need to be released unto the knowledge that there is no greater blessing than to have the Lord on our side. There is no greater blessing than to be in the presence of the Lord and know that Heaven is smiling upon us. You can have the king's ransom, just give me Jesus. You can have the jewelry and the cars, just give me the anointing of the Holy Spirit. You even can have a great name, just give me the One who's name is above every name. You even can have a great position, but I just want the Spirit of the living God to fall fresh on me. In order for us to become strong prayer warriors, we must graduate to a spiritual level where we desire to have the Lord's presence over anything else, and where we truthfully desire to keep His commandments. This we must do without want for any gain other than to increase in Him. That's the stance of a true prayer warrior.

What is being said here is, it is a great blessing to live with the Lord and within what He commands of us. It's sad that many of us remain on a small level of blessedness merely from our desire to do things which appose His commandments. For example, the Lord commanded, "A new commandment I give unto you, That ye love one another; as I have loved you, that ye also love one another" *(John 13:34),* yet many of us still choose to hate others for reasons unfounded and groundless, even; still supposing the Lord will favorably answer our prayers. How preposterous can that be? We refuse to do as He commands, yet we want Him to bless our request. Now, let's be honest, how much sense does that make? Let us take it a step further by mentioning Matthew 7:21 where the Lord proclaims, "Not every one that saith unto me, Lord, Lord, shall enter into the kingdom of heaven; but he that doeth the will of my Father which is in heaven." So, if following His will and commands is a prerequisite to our entering the kingdom there must not be any contradiction to the prerequisites to our prayer request' being answered favorably by Him. "He that turneth away his ear from hearing the law, even his prayer shall be abomination" *(Proverbs 28:9).* I'm simply making scripture clear to all!

Let me make it crystal for all who have yet to receive of this point. The Lord said, "If ye abide in me, and my words abide in you, ye shall ask what ye will, and it shall be done unto you" *(John 15:7)*. It is more than a notion that the Lord will grant our request at a higher ratio if we do as He commands. The abiding surely does not mean that the Word simply sits idle in our minds. On the contrary, the Lord is telling us we are to hear and do what He says. We all are familiar with the verse which says, "But be ye doers of the word, and not hearers only, deceiving your own selves" *(James 1:22)*. You're not fooling anyone and you're surely not fooling God. We fail to realize how much we diminish our relationship with God when we neglect to do as He commands. The probabilities of our receiving favorable answers to our prayers is improved when we improve our relationship with the Lord. Our improved relationship can be equated with our renewed willingness to live as He commands. I would like to make a joke or say something light-hearted in order to slacken the seriousness of what's being said here, but it would totally constitute as levity. Fact is, it is no laughing matter not doing as the Lord commands of us. As taught in most hermeneutics classes, there is no Gospel ministry lest it include conviction. Therefore I say, it's almost like a breach of contract that we violate our relationship with God by disregarding His commands. Why then do we expect Him to favorably answer our request? I simply say today, let us do as the Lord commands and we then shall watch the number of positive answers to our request increase.

Living in Sin Negates Prayers

Surely no blessedness can occur if we are up to our elbows in sin. Blessings will not even occur in their fullness if we are up to our ankles in sin. Our ankles alone are sometimes so shackled in lust that we couldn't run to the Lord even if we had the key to the ankle lock. It is a must that prayer warriors be obedient unto His laws. We can know all the caveats of religion and still not get a prayer through to Heaven, simply because our sinful living negates our requests. Many who call themselves Christians can shout a prayer that will set our souls and feet a fire, yet their prayers may still go unanswered by the Lord because their living is unto this world and not unto the Son Jesus.

Prayer is not just about knowing what to say, nor is it just about shouting expressions of scriptural vigor and prowess. No, no, no! Do not be mistaken by the tricks of the devil who would have us to think knowing God's Word is all we need. There are many who can recite the Word of God backwards and forwards, but still are destined to hell fire because the Word was never made manifest in their living. This is a *key* for us all. Right prayer has to meet with right living. Oh, let me say it again, right

30

prayer must meet with right living in order for our prayers to be effective unto Heaven. One of the greatest impediments of answered prayers is sinful living. Hear me on this. Not many things can block our prayers and our blessings like that of sin-sick living. We must perform a diagnostics check on how we are living and make changes in our life-styles so we may be elevated to the next level in answered prayers.

When we are at a place of finding out why our prayers go unanswered, the first place we ought check is the way we are living. When doing a diagnostics analysis of released blessings or the lack there of, we must be truthful to check the vital signs of our righteousness. Is our living unto this world or is it unto the Lord? God does not want us to be blessed without our being a blessing unto Him. "I beseech you therefore, brethren, by the mercies of God, that ye present your bodies a living sacrifice, holy, acceptable unto God, which is your reasonable service. And be not conformed to this world: but be ye transformed by the renewing of your mind, that ye may prove what is that good, and acceptable, and perfect, will of God" _(Romans 12:1-2)._

There are many things that can stop our prayer's blessings from flowing, but none more than unrighteous living and living according to the ways of this world. The Bible tells us, "... no good thing will he withhold from them that walk uprightly" _(Psalm 84:11)._ I John 3:22 tells us, "And whatsoever we ask, we receive of him, because we keep his command-ments, and do those things that are pleasing in his sight." Could it be any clearer as to how our living can affect our prayers? Upon this day we all shall cease thinking answered prayers are affected by the "what" and the "how" we pray, only. We must truly fill our spirits with the fact that our living plays a tremendous part in the answers we receive from God. Receiving a blessing will not get us to live anymore righteously than we have previously, says the Lord. But, if we would only change our ways we shall receive blessings which will abound in our living and our spirits.

Many may be excited to read this _Progression Element #4_, seeking how to make our request known unto the Lord. Those of us even may feel this is not only the meat of prayer, but the very reason we even have come to read this document. Learning how to make a request in prayer is important, but more important to our prayer's success is right living unto the Lord. The Lord is merciful and gracious, and He may not hold against our current prayer how we have lived long ago, but surely the Lord takes into account our current faithfulness. "O Israel, return unto the Lord thy God; for thou hast fallen by thine iniquity" _(Hosea 14:1)._ From this day forward I do hope we do not thwart nor undermine our prayer's requests by living a life sick in sin.

I cannot say we are wasting our time in prayer if we are willingly living a life of sinfulness, for truly prayer changes things and God judges His own matters. Hebrews 10:26 has this to say about it, "For if we sin willfully after that we have received the knowledge of the truth, there remaineth no more sacrifice for sins." In the case of someone willfully living in sin, the fruitfulness of their prayers comes first by way of God's distribution of mercy upon them, rather than their current request being granted. Daniel 9:18 says it this way, "O my God, incline thine ear, and hear; open thine eyes, and behold our desolations, and the city which is called by thy name: for we do not present our supplications before thee for our righteousnesses, but for thy great mercies."

We should not take a chance in apposing God and His Word, whereby testing whether He will bless the prayers of the unrighteous. The Lord Jesus proclaimed, "... for he maketh his sun to rise on the evil and on the good, and sendeth rain on the just and the unjust" *(Matthew 5:45)*. Our prayers are far too important for us to leave it to chance that God may not heed our prayers due to our unrighteous living. Proverbs 15:29 declares this on the subject, "The Lord is far from the wicked: but he heareth the prayer of the righteous." I do not know about you, but I need my prayers answered if it be the Lord's will. I then must give my prayers the best chance of being favorably answered by creating the right platform and atmosphere in my living. I can truly say I'm not perfect, but we all should attempt to live blameless, so our prayers don't go unanswered due to living in wickedness. The Bible proclaims to us "The effectual fervent prayer of a righteous man availeth much" *(James 5:16b)*. Verses previous to verse 16 indicate our sins will be forgiven if we pray the prayer of faith, but verse 16 clearly announces we must live right in order to see great accomplishments from our prayers.

Motives and Pretenses Effect Belief and Affect Prayer

Another sure fire way to have our prayers go unanswered is by praying under false pretenses. Insincerity in prayer will get us nowhere. It is surely a sin to appeal to God with false intentions. It is a sick and wicked mind that would attempt to fool a God who is omniscient (all-knowing). In Biblical days the Lord spoke unto Samuel charging him to annoint another king to replace Saul, "But the Lord said unto Samuel, Look not on his countenance, or on the height of his stature; because I have refused him: for the Lord seeth not as man seeth; for man looketh on the outward appearance, but the Lord looketh on the heart" *(I Samuel 16:7)*. In other words, the answers to our living and our prayers are subject to be scrutinized by God through an inspection of our intents. Let us, therefore, be mindful of why we settle down to pray in the first place.

The Lord reads the hearts of them who come before the thrown of grace; thus, it is senseless to present ourselves and our prayers under false pretenses. How might it be to pray to a God who cannot see the base truth of all things? Would He then not be God? The strength of our faith comes from believing He is. How can He be God in our lives if He cannot know the essence and underlying truths of everything? This is a point where we sorrowfully go wrong in our living and our prayers. We say He is all-knowing, but we do not live and pray as if He is all-knowing. There is a disconnect between our supposed faith and our actual living. Listen intently. This is why it is so important that the faithful and prayer warriors, alike, have their hearts fixed; as spoken in *Element #1 Acknowledgment and Recognition.* Wicked hearts attempt to fool God; to no success. He is all knowing whether we believe it to be true, or not. There's no way around it. Our best blessings in prayer shall result from our truthful claims and honestly stated purposes. This gives reason we must fix our hearts before making appeals.

Along these same lines of false pretenses is that of unintelligible or gibbering prayers. Rattling off prayers that go nowhere and say absolutely nothing may sound impressive in the face of man, but unto the Lord they are pretentious and wicked. This is a place where we can say, "It doesn't take all that." So many who are into the appearance of religion continue to falsify their relationships with the Lord, babbling statements that do not make sense and do not correlate with the truth of their relationships with the Lord. Once again, this shows proof of how some of us do not truly believe He is omniscient. It is easy to see who truly believes in God when you try the spirit by the Spirit. I John 4:1 says, "Beloved, believe not every spirit whether they are of God: because many false prophets are gone out into the world." We see it every Sunday!

People who do not live as though He is God and all-knowing do not believe He is God and all-knowing. That may sound simple, but let us uncover its principles. They may say out of their mouths that He is God, but their hearts testify against them. We should understand, in the face of God our mouths often testify against us just as our hearts tell the truth of our agendas and intents. None-Christ-like attempts to fool the eyes of mere man neglect to realize God sees what man cannot see — the true intents of the heart. We would have a better world if more people believed that simple truth. The world is so far off the hook, for the most part, because we do not believe God is omniscient. This is the basis for why many wicked people will lie directly in our faces. Their pervading wickedness prevents them from realizing God sees and hears all. If a person has such strong audacity to boldly lie in our faces, best believe they do not truthfully believe in God the Father, who is omniscient.

<u>True believers do all things unto Christ.</u> In other words, we do unto our fellow man as we would do unto Christ. See, some would quote the verse which tells us you reap what you sow _(Galatians 6:7)_, or do unto others as you would have them to do unto you, but let us take it to the next level. I give unto you this precept — Do unto others as you would do unto the Lord. Would you lie to the face of God? Would you curse out the Lord Jesus Christ? These are the types of questions we seem not to ponder on a regular basis, if not at all. Prayer warriors must think and live on this next level so their living and prayers are not under false pretenses.

Our prayer lives and our general living must reflect this truth. We must pray in the spirit and in the truth that God already sees our hearts and motives; thus, it's essential we make appeals to Him in truth and without false pretenses. There it is! Anything short of that truth bears witness to our unbelief of our true and living God. Some may attempt to differ, but it still remains true that our faith bears out in our living. The Lord tells us, "... Beware of the scribes, which love to go in long clothing, and love salutations in the marketplaces, And the chief seats in the synagogues, and the uppermost rooms at feasts: Which devour widows' houses, and for a pretense make long prayers: these shall receive greater damnation" _(Mark 12:38-40)._ Paul said it this way, "But shun profane and vain babblings: for they will increase unto more ungodliness" _(II Timothy 2:16)._

The words spoken in our prayers must reflect the truth of our motives. Most of us by choice are not spiritual literati, yet the fact remains our prayers are to coincide with the base purpose of our hearts. Babblings may get us somewhere with the unknowing, but they also may grant us damnation in the greater scheme of things.

Conviction Through Thoughts of Being Chastened

More of us, if not all of us, need to start praying for God's chastening or judgment upon our lives. Hear me on this principle and _key._ Do not get me wrong, for I am not advocating that we seek to have harm come upon us, but in the face of the Spirit I do desire that we thwart our willingness to perform sin and evil by having convicted hearts before we commit sin and not just after the sin has been committed. I am not into inflicting pain upon myself, nor am I into receiving it from others; especially from an Almighty God. I want to avoid pain, if at all possible, which I am sure is the stance of most people; thus this key.

Avoiding sinfulness and avoiding the subsequent pain of our sinning are the points being made here. We often pray for God's mercy upon our lives as if we know the time and the date of the next sin we are about to commit. Whereas, we may become a bit more conscious of trying not to offend the Lord and His Word if we initially prayed for His judgment upon our living. Keep your tent doors open and I will explain further. Too many of us unknowingly depend on His grace and mercy as crutches and supports for sinful living. Let us flip the script and begin to live lives convicted from the outset instead of us being sorrowful only after we have perpetrated the sin. Conviction is the condition of our spirits that most often keeps us from sinning, so let us generate the conviction before we ever commit the sin. Doesn't the Lord desire us to be sinless, and isn't it true that we will participate in sinful activities a lot less if we are convicted from the beginning?

Normally conviction proceeds our sinful act. Instead, let us realize how sinful we can be before the act of sin is ever committed. This is difficult for many of us to swallow and fathom because some of us want to picture ourselves as perfect, while others simply do not want these types of restraints upon our living. "But the natural man receiveth not the things of the Spirit of God: for they are foolishness unto him: neither can he know them, because they are spiritually discerned" *(I Corinthians 2:14).*

Let me further develop this point and explain of the restraints and the conviction. One issue we must counterbalance is our human tendency to get bold and out of control when we become of a certain age. At a certain age we begin to think we are invulnerable to everything, which happens at around the same time we begin to think we can do anything we are big and bold enough to entertain. This thinking tends to grow exponentially if it goes unchecked for an extended period of time, after which it propels us to a character state that unconsciously wishes to oppose the fruit of the Spirit *(Galatians 5:22-23).* This is truth whether we want to accept it or disagree with it. These are tendencies we can neither sustain as children living in the presence of the Almighty, nor can we sustain them as prayer warriors at the throne of grace.

On the contrary, praying to God to chasten our sinful ways will place our spirits in a state aware of our propensity to sin and in a state aware that the Lord will indeed chasten us for our acts of sin. Having an heightened awareness of potential chastening or judgment will result in our having a more bridled spirit unto the Lord. It is through our fear of the Lord that we stand convicted to do right in His presence. And there it is!

One may ask, "How does this benefit our prayers?" Well, in fearing the Lord there is great benefit to both our prayers and our living. Numerous scriptures proclaim how things like our wisdom and knowledge are increased due to our fear of God; all of which bless our living manifold.

Also, our fear of the Lord transforms our spirits to be more submissive, sensitized and obedient; ultimately strengthening our prayer and communal relationships with Him. Plainly said, we seem to want to do right by God only after we forsake Him, as we then become fearful of being in His wrath's line of fire. It is high time we become fearful of God's wrath and chastening at the outset, so we can forsake the sins we would otherwise commit.

It is true there are those of us who truthfully attempt to feel convicted in advance of sinning so not to transgress, but just like new years resolutions those attempts come to naught if God is not a part of them. We are making every attempt with this key to make God the main part of our succeeding to sin less. In praying for His chastening we are in essence calling Him to take part in helping us to avoid sinning. Help us God!

Throughout the ages it has been the case that people feared God only after they had sinned, instead of their being convicted in advance so to have avoided sinning in the first place. Adam and Eve feared God after their sin of eating of the forbidden fruit _(Genesis 3:6-8)_. Paul became fearful of the Lord only after greatly persecuting the early Church _(Acts 9:1-6)_. The Israelites feared God only after each of their transgressions _(Joshua 24:14-24)_, including the time they had chosen to have a King as their leader rather than being led by God _(I Samuel 12:18)_. King Saul turned back to God after he was rebuked for his sinning _(I Samuel 15:24-25)_. Judas Iscariot became heavily convicted of his sin only after he betrayed the Lord Jesus _(Matthew 26:47-51; 27:1-7)_. Let us not likewise nor metaphorically hang ourselves. Rather let us avoid certain ills in advance through having conviction beforehand. We do serve a merciful God, yet His mercies can't compare to the blessings, graces and mercies He will bestow upon us when we make every attempt to be convicted not to sin in the first place.

If we are fearfully made _(Psalm 139:14)_, let us act as though we are fearful of the Lord who made us. Proverbs 14:16 says, "A wise man feareth, and departeth from evil ..." I think we sometimes are more fearful of the circumstances we may get into than we are fearful of God the Father. We even fear what others will say about the circumstances we may get into more so than we fear what will become of our relationships with the Lord in response to our sinning. Hear the Spirit of the Lord and be blessed. Since we are fearfully made we should be more fearful of the One who made us, apposed to fearing other things He has created; even other humans. Two of many Biblical examples include: Moses was fearful that the rumors of his being a murderer would reach the royal family and that they may not respond kindly to him _(Exodus 2:14);_ The Israelites feared other gods as the Kings continued to rule in wickedness _(II Kings 17:7-8)_.

Let it be understood His grace and mercy shall come upon us all the more as a reward for our attempting to thwart sinning from the beginning. As mentioned throughout this document, the Lord reads the intents of our hearts and will chasten us accordingly. Do not be dismayed nor too perplexed by this principle. Believe God will bless us for putting forth the effort to thwart sinning. Let it be understood we must request His chastening in spirit and in truth in order for this principle to take hold in our lives and in our prayers. It's all about our having a change of heart and a change in our fear for the Lord. It shall convict our spirits to sin less if we are truthfully fearful of His chastening. "Let us therefore come boldly unto the throne of grace, that we may obtain mercy, and find grace to help in time of need" _(Hebrews 4:16)._

This is not some new precept, for Biblical characters also petitioned to be judged of God along side His grace and mercy. This principle seems new for some, due to the propensity of Isrealites, Nazareans and Christians, alike, to move so far away from principles that actually take hold on our spirits and help in our living. Truths have become foreign to our ears and repugnant unto our living over a period of time. We continuously forsake all those principles that have the potential of keeping us from desiring the things of the flesh. This document presents precepts that shall return us unto the Lord, if we follow them with truth in our spirits. "Wherefore I am made a minister, according to the dispensation of God which is given to me for you, to fulfil the word of God; Even the mystery which hath been hid from ages and from generations, but now is made manifest to his saints: To whom God would make known what is the riches of the glory of this mystery among the Gentiles; which is Christ in you, the hope of glory" _(Colossians 1:25-27)._

One hundred thousand prayer warriors shall accept these harsh spiritual realities and be blessed with power beyond understanding. We all agree that there is no power without some pain, yet we shun those very processes just the same. Prayer warriors shall be empowered and strengthened in their faith by practicing this precept. It may seem painful to some who are vacillating between milk and meat, and far fetched to others who struggle to get closer to God, but it remains as truth, "And his mercy is on them that fear him from generation to generation" _(Luke 1:50)._ This key and principle on conviction is purposed to build healthy fear of the Lord within us. Most of us are familiar with many of the verses that speak of the fear of the Lord: such as, "The fear of the Lord is the beginning of all wisdom ..." _(Psalm 111:10);_ "The fear of the Lord is the beginning of all knowledge ..." _(Proverbs 1:7);_ "By humility and the fear of the Lord are riches, and honour, and life" _(Proverbs 22:4);_ "... the fear of the

Lord is his treasure" *(Isaiah 33:6);* "He will bless them that fear the Lord, both small and great" *(Psalm 115:13);* " ... and walking in the fear of the Lord, and in the comfort of the Holy Ghost, were multiplied" *(Acts 9:31).* We tend not to want to practice true fear of the Lord; for the sake of fear itself. As stated before, we tend to want the results, yet we shun the processes which grant us those very results.

If we pray in the morning that God chasten our acts of sin, more than likely, we will desperately try to avoid sinning for that day, at least. The fear and conviction of God's potential chastening will constrain most people who have at least a portion of a heart for Christ Jesus. It is great that we will forever be in His graces as long as we proclaim Jesus as Lord, but let us not continue to lean on that fact alone. Let us now go to another level of obedience and communion with the Lord. Let us shine the power of God's love in our lives by avoiding sin in the first place.

Many of us are accustomed to praying certain things that deal more so with the face value of our prosperity. As we can now see, there are request we can make that go deeper than face value and greatly benefit our lives and prayers. For generations we have continued to pray in the standard practice which has kept us powerless and sinful. Let us now move with the great Spirit of Christ and request those things which give us power and grant us the prosperity God intended us to have from the beginning of creation.

Generations after generations have continued to set up calves as idols, just as the Israelites had done in Exodus 32. We carry on the practice of setting up golden calves today due to our lack of advance conviction. In the same manner many people treat one another poorly and with disrespect, simply because they are void of any fear of God's ensuing chastening. The same can be said for the many sins we too commit. This is a tough key for most to digest, but a wise preacher once said, "You gotta holler or swallow!" Nevertheless, we shall be blessed through it all.

What's Good and What's Convenient

We need to better understand the Word in Psalm 84:11 which says no "good" thing. Not everything we pray for is good for us. Some things for which we pray may be ok to have, such that there may be nothing about them that goes against God's law, yet they just might not be right for us individually or collectively. Something might be good for you that might not be so good for me. A simple example is, it might be good for one person to drink wine to cleanse their loins of some infirmities like Paul told Timothy, "Drink no longer water, but use a little wine for thy stomach's sake and thine often infirmities" *(I Timothy 5:23),* whereas a taste of wine may not be good for someone else who has a history of alcoholism. As well, it may be ok for one person who knows how to save to have extra finances, but those extra dollars may not be good for someone who has a gambling problem. Agur, son of Jakeh, said it this way, "Remove far from me vanity and lies; give me neither poverty nor riches; feed me with food convenient for me: Lest I be full, and deny thee, and say, Who is the Lord? or lest I be poor, and steal, and take the name of my God in vain" *(Proverbs 30:8-9).* The Lord surely knows what is convenient for us; thus we must realize that the Lord will not give us everything. It may seem innocent when we asked for a thing, but it may be as destruction unto our living once we receive of it. God knows best in all cases.

Going a little deeper, we must understand God may have another blessing in store for you or for that person for whom you pray. Our finite and feeble minds process things on a smaller scale than does the Lord's. We have greater blessings in store for us if we simply would allow God's will to prevail. Yet, we pray for the same item till our faces are black and blue with thoughts that God does not care. In actuality He cares more than we think and He wants to bless us with more than we can possibly imagine.

Also, we must realize some things are simply not a part of God's grand plan for us. It may be painful to imagine that others may want you to pray that a loved one would recover to good health, but it may not be in God's plan for that recovery to occur. This is why it is so essential for a prayer warrior to be ever so connected to God and His will. We all must learn to accept the Lord's will and plans for our lives. In Biblical days the prophets and prayer warriors, alike, had to contend with those who did not want to hear the truth and/or bad news God was delivering. It is sad and tough to say at this moment many prayer warriors of this generation will have to contend with that same opposition and anger.

It is not fun to have to do the dirty work, per se, yet this is the plight of a true prayer warrior. It is painful to accept the fact that it is not always God's will to heal, deliver or bless someone who appears to be in need, but a prayer still must go forth. In God's eyes the person may be in greater need for something else; just as Jesus forgave the man's sins who visibly appeared to be in need of healing *(Mark 2:1-12).* Likewise, it is no fun having to tell someone the Lord said they must get closer to Him; knowing the person lacks the spirit to receive what they will view as sheer criticism versus spiritual empowerment. All in all, be encouraged that the Lord has a great covering over those who truthfully work and speak as God's prayer warriors and servants. Be encouraged and be blessed!

REQUEST — *Progression of Prayer Element #4*

Exercises

INSTRUCTIONAL

1. Select a Biblical promise made by God. Illustrate whether this scripture is best used as an appeal unto the Lord or as encouragement unto believers.

   BENEFIT:
   To intensify your attention to the power of using the Lord's promises in prayer.

PERSONAL

1. Do not pray any request for yourself nor others for one week. Pray acknowledgment, adoration and all the other *Elements of Prayer* for this week.

   BENEFIT:
   That you digest the spirit of faith that God already knows your every real need and your spirit's desires, and that He will take care of you just as He takes care of the sparrow. In the past we have claimed this faith, but never actually exercised it.

REQUEST – *Progression of Prayer Element #4*

General Questions

1. Name five patterns of request.
   What makes each pattern so essential and different?

2. Name six promises God made in His Word that can stand as base for an appeal unto Him. Then write one appeal to God using one of these promises.

3. What are the two things according to which we are to pray?

4. What is the difference between conventional verses and promise verses? Give two examples of each?

5. How else should we pray while praying in the name of Jesus?

6. What is more essential than making a request unto the Lord in prayer?   Why?

7. What are two things that may prevent our prayers from being answered?

8. Why is it so essential to carry out *Elements #1, #2 and #3* before making a request in *Element #4?*

9. What are two reasons it is important to willingly receive what's convenient?

10. What are three ways to handle disappointments in prayers?

REQUEST — *Progression of Prayer Element #4*

Advanced Questions

1. Write a paragraph on why the Lord finds it so essential for us to remove self from our prayers?

2. What *Elements of Prayer Progression*™ *#4 Request Key* do you find most important for your personal prayer life? And why? (Be sure to mention God or other persons in your answer).

3. In performing spiritual diagnostics why does the Lord want us to be a blessing unto Him, more so, than for Him to bless our request?

Discernment

Pray this prayer with me:
A Prayer for Discernment

"Sovereign, oh so sovereign God. Mighty in battle and strong to protect. Merciful in Your ways, yet just in all Your works. Bless Your name God. Bless Your name God. You alone are the foundation of my strength and my very soul's delight. I thank You this day for blessing me beyond compare and blessing me with maturity, both in spirit and in living. Thank You now for maturing me to seek Your directions in regards to all I have prayed to occur and all I have prayed to receive. It is in Your instructions that all blessings bear fruit. Allow me to have the fruitfulness of Your hand's directing and Your voice's calling. I truly have nothing lest I have Your directions; never failing and never forsaking. Lift me in my spirit's hearing as I pray with the manifestation of Your Spirit and in the name of Christ Jesus — Amen."

This section is to better enhance our understanding of the Biblical reasons for who should have discernment, how we should discern, why we should discern, what we should discern, where we should discern and when we should discern. Our study of discernment will be further enhanced if these verses are read previous to moving onto the chapter material; as this format will indeed better prepare our spirits to receive of the chapter material.

1) WHO should discern?
- I Kings 3:9 — God's servants
- Ezra 7:25 — Leaders
- Job 32:8 — The multitude of years
- Psalm 19:7 — The simple
- Psalm 37:23 — A good man
- Proverbs 1:7; 24:7 — Not fools
- Proverbs 1:22 — Not the simple, nor scorners, nor fools
- Proverbs 9:10 — The holy
- Proverbs 10:14 — The wise and not the foolish
- Proverbs 10:31 — The just and not froward in tongue
- Proverbs 21:12 — The righteous man
- Proverbs 28:5 — They who seek Him
- Ecclesiastes 2:26 — A man that is good in God's sight
- Isaiah 19:11 — The son of the wise
- Luke 12:42 — Faithful and wise steward
- I Corinthians 1:30 — Who are of God and in Christ Jesus
- II Timothy 3:15 — Children
- James 1:5 — Those who lack in wisdom

2) HOW should we discern?
- Psalm 37:23 — With delight in His ways
- Psalm 49:3 — By the mouth
- Psalm 51:6 — Desiring
- Psalm 111:10 — With fear of the Lord; doing His commandments
- Proverbs 1:7 — Not despising wisdom nor instruction
- Proverbs 2:2 — With an inclined ear
- Proverbs 3:7 — Not in your own eyes; with fear of the Lord; and depart from evil
- Proverbs 4:5 — Not declining
- Proverbs 10:5 — Gathering in the summer
- Proverbs 11:12 — By holding your peace
- Proverbs 16:9 — Not by your own heart
- Proverbs 19:20 — By hearing counsel and receiving instruction

2) HOW should we discern? *(Continued)*
- Proverbs 28:11 — Searching for Him
- Proverbs 29:11 — Keep until afterwards
- Ecclesiastes 2:26 — Being sin-less
- Ecclesiastes 7:25 — Seek it
- Isaiah 11:2 — By the Spirit
- Isaiah 30:21 — By hearing; by walking in it
- Philippians 1:9 — Praying
- II Timothy 3:15 — By knowing the scriptures; through faith

3) WHY should we discern?
- Exodus 31:3 — God will fill you with His Spirit, wisdom, under-
standing and knowledge in all manner of workmanship
- I Kings 3:9 — To lead His people; to discern between good and bad
- I Kings 3:10; — To please the Lord
- I Kings 3:13 — To receive above and beyond the wisdom (riches
and honour)
- I Kings 4:29 — To receive from God exceeding much
- I Chronicles 22:12 — That you may keep the Law of the Lord;
only the Lord gives wisdom
- Ezra 7:25 — To teach
- Psalm 16:7 — To be instructed in the night seasons
- Psalm 111:10 — To praise Him
- Proverbs 4:11 — Will be led in the right paths
- Proverbs 4:12 — Will not stumble; your steps shall not be straitened
- Proverbs 11:12 — So not to despise your neighbor
- Proverbs 11:14 — So not to fall; there is safety
- Proverbs 16:9 — The Lord will direct your steps
- Proverbs 16:21 — To be called prudent
- Proverbs 16:22 — Not to be a fool
- Proverbs 16:23 — Lips become learned
- Proverbs 28:11 — Not to have self-conceit
- Isaiah 42:16 — To have the darkness made light; the crooked made
straight; the Lord will not forsake you
- Philippians 1:9 — To have abounding love
- James 1:5 — So not to lack in understanding; God gives it liberally
and upbraideth not; it will be given to you
- James 3:13 — Humility comes also

4) WHAT should we discern?
- Exodus 28:3 — God's filling of the spirit of wisdom
- I Kings 3:9 — An understanding heart
- Job 28:28 -- The fear of the Lord; departure from evil

4) WHAT should we discern? *(Continued)*
- Job 32:8 — The inspiration of the Almighty
- Job 38:36 — Wisdom in the inward parts; understanding to the heart
- Psalm 1:23 — The Lord's pouring out His Spirit unto you
- Psalm 49:3 — Heart of understanding
- Psalm 90:12 — In numbering the days
- Psalm 111:10 — The fear of the Lord; by doing His commandments
- Proverbs 1:2 — To know wisdom, instruction and perceive the words of understanding
- Proverbs 2:5 — To find the knowledge of God
- Proverbs 11:14 — Counsel
- Proverbs 14:24 — Crown of wisdom
- Proverbs 15:33 — The fear of the Lord and instruction
- Proverbs 16:9 — The Lord to direct your steps
- Proverbs 16:22 — A wellspring of life
- Isaiah 11:2 — The spirit of the Lord; the spirit of wisdom and understanding; the spirit of counsel and might; the spirit of knowledge and of the fear of the Lord
- Acts 6:3 — Filled with the Holy Ghost
- I Corinthians 1:21 — Not the wisdom of this world

5) WHERE should we discern?
- Deuteronomy 1:13 — Among your tribes
- II Chronicles 1:6 — The alter before the Lord; in the congregation
- Proverbs 1:20-21 — In the streets, gates, concourse and city
- Proverbs 11:14 — In the multitude of counselors
- Proverbs 15:31 — Among the wise
- Ecclesiastes 2:14 — In the head
- Ecclesiastes 7:4 — In the house of the mourning; not mirth
- Ecclesiastes 7:23 — Not far from you
- Philippians 1:9 — In prayer

6) WHEN should we discern?
- Psalm 48:14 — Till death; for ever and ever
- Proverbs 10:5 — In the summer
- Proverbs 19:20 — In your latter end
- Isaiah 30:21 — When you turn to the right and to the left
- Philippians 1:9 — While praying
- II Timothy 3:15 — Unto salvation

Lord, Direct my Steps

"Give me now wisdom and knowledge, that I may go out and come in before this people: for who can judge this thy people, that is so great? "
II Chronicles 1:10

Making a request unto the Lord can be fulfilling in the light of success, but frustrating and disappointing when our prayers go unanswered. We all tend to think God will answer all our prayers, only to be disappointed when we get no response or even a "no" response. The previous section on the *Element of Request* illustrates some of the reasons our prayers go unanswered. This section of the *Element of Discernment* will strengthen readers in spirit so they will follow-up their request with a heightened spirit that greatly seeks God's voice in prayer, rather than always seeking basic material successes.

It is important to enter into prayer with every intent of gaining victory and success, but more important is the need for us to hear from Heaven on what to actually do with the victory or the so called non-victory of our request. After reading this section it shall be understood that receiving directions from Heaven are of greater importance than to receive a yes or no answer. This section will increase our sensitivity to the act of communing with God through prayer rather than merely increasing our skills to simply call on Him for blessings.

Discernment (the act of discriminating, comprehending and making intelligent application) is of great importance to a prayer warrior's success. Let it be known here today, being a prayer warrior is about more than just having prayers answered by God. This section shall illustrate an importance in prayer that goes far beyond getting the Lord's attention. The proverbial "getting a prayer through to the Lord" is of importance, but that's not the only source of our blessings in prayer.

We must move into a realm of realizing God knows what's best for us and He knows the end before it begins. The Bible tells us, "Likewise the Spirit also helpeth our infirmities: for we know not what we should pray for as we ought: but the Spirit itself maketh intercession for us with groanings which cannot be uttered" *(Romans 8:26)*. For that very reason it is important for us to know to pray in accord with God's character, and be mindful of His good and perfect will. It's almost impossible for earthly beings to know the will of God at each moment, outside of His will for all to be saved; for He is incomprehensible. It's our every hope to be constantly directed by God, although at times we misdirect ourselves due to a disconnect from His Spirit's voice and leading. We truly can only try our best and hope to stay on God's set path, for no man can know every essence of God unless he becomes God himself; which will never occur.

In hopes to remain in the will of God, we are led in spirited attempts to ensure we are requesting that which He would have us to act upon and/or possess. Therefore, after our request is made unto the Lord, we should follow-up by humbly asking the Lord to grant us the discernment to handle the request's answers. This following up is the basis of this *Element;* as it is a binding portion for our prayer life and a catalyst for our spiritual living. This precept can be broken down into the following:

1) Discernment to know what to do with what we requested once it is given to us.
2) Discernment and wisdom to be patient for a time, if we are to wait for our request to be fulfilled.
3) Wisdom to accept our request being either postponed or declined.

What to do with It

Most of us do not have a clue about what to do with many of the things we possess already. To date each of us has acquired and received some things we thought we were privy to how they worked. Later we came to realize just how clueless we were. Reality set in then we spent most of our time trying to figure out how to use what we sought so diligently to acquire. It is a shame how we often destroy things we receive, not on purpose, but solely through our lack of wisdom to discern their proper uses and functions. Persons go a lifetime trying to figure out things in their surroundings, only to come up empty as with a rubics cube brain teaser. This *Progression Element* is designed to rectify and prevent many of our woes of defeat by getting us to act upon directions given by God through our prayers. Even difficult actions and troubling decisions are made clear through having a discerning spirit in prayer. The Spirit of God can reveal unto us the proper directions we should go, ultimately eliminating the pains of poor decisions. We ought know we tend to make some rather poor life choices when our spirits are left unattended.

Again, the Bible tells us, "... for we know not what we should pray for as we ought" *(Romans 8:26)*; likewise we can imagine that we do not know what to do with those things for which we pray once we receive them. It is so important to ask God for discernment as to what to do with what we requested, since we often mess up the very blessings God grants us. We pray for a thing, yet we omit and fail to pray for directions as to the what, the how, the when and the where of the thing requested. What's worse than persons who pray for something, receive it, but not have a clue as to what to do with it thereafter? We ought pray as the Psalmist wrote in verse 119:133, "Order my steps in thy word: and let not any iniquity have dominion over me."

I've had a saying since my teen years, "Those who have, don't have." In this respect, people often acquire things they cannot operate and do not know how to work. They then frustrate the Spirit by not taking the time to become more sensitized to the Spirit's directions. "See then that ye walk circumspectly, not as fools, but as wise, Redeeming the time, because the days are evil. Wherefore be ye not unwise, but understanding what the will of the Lord is. And be not drunk with wine, wherein is excess, but be filled with the Spirit" *(Ephesians 5:15-18).*

If the Creator gives us a blessing isn't it obvious that He not only knows how the blessing should work, but He knows what He wants us to accomplish with the blessing, also? We often ignore the obvious directions because we go about things in our own selfish ways; not discerning the Lord's Spirit. How can we give God glory if we do not do the will of God? The Bible tells us God is pleased when we act in accord with His will, as it also says, "Be not wise in your own eyes ..." *(Proverbs 3:7).*

Seek the Instructions

Anyone who has purchased something from the store is familiar with the fact most packaged items come with instructions, warnings, or some other type of labeling. Too bad our blessings do not come with paper directions forwarded to us by God. What a blessing it would be to have in hand the exact how-to's, where-to's and when-to's for every gift, blessing or deliverance we received from the Lord. How much simpler it would be! We would have far more victories and far less waste in our lives, but we would have less spiritual growth, as well; due to the ease and disconnect. The true issue and difficulty about prayers is they do not come with an attachment of paper instructions. The instructions are provided by God, but they come in a form different to what most of us are accustomed.

The Lord's instructions for blessings He provides come by way of His Spirit. It takes more than merely reading paper instructions to receive God's instructions for blessings. It takes spending time communing our spirits with the Lord's Spirit. Many of us do not receive the instructions because we lack a connection with the Lord. We first must have developed a relationship and communal connection with the Lord prior to attempting to receive spiritual directions from Him. It takes time and sensitivity to be able to, first, hear the Lord's Spirit's voice, then correctly move upon what has been registered into our spirits as directions.

It is highly proposed we have viable and regular devotional periods with the Lord in order to heighten our spirit's sensitivity. Most things in life take practice and time. Sensitizing our spirit to the Holy Spirit's voice is no different. It is more than a theory that the more time we spend in devotionals with the Lord the more our spirits will be sensitized unto His directions. It is a shame many of our lives are so misdirected because we are so disconnected from His Spirit. Those of us who are disconnected spend much time fumbling our way through the application of our blessings. The proper cure for fumbling and mishandling blessings is to first get connected to the only One who gives the proper directions — God the Father, God the Son and God the Holy Spirit.

A blessing is not complete without the correct application to our living. Blessings correctly applied to our living will multiply somewhere; overflow into other parts of our lives or overflow unto others. The fact remains a large number of us do not live in the overflow of life due to our misapplying and mishandling blessings. One part of our lives has been lacking for awhile due to it having to wait for the overflow from the correctly applied application of blessings in another area of our lives. There are small and large blessings we take for granted which could be as overflow. We must understand we can live in the abundance of overflow if we would simply handle the initial blessings according to God's directions. We tend not to realize we are missing out on larger territory increases in additional areas of our lives by misapplying initial blessings. From this point forward it should be plain to know we must be ever so mindful to correctly apply blessings so other areas of our lives and our surroundings may be blessed subsequently.

Correct application can occur only when we adhere to the Lord's Spirit's directions; outside of which we may be blessed, but not to the greatest extent possible. The Lord has an optimum intention for the blessings He bestows upon us. Let it be our spirits which receive those directions, engaging us to properly move upon the blessings. What can be more sad than to have a faithful Father who attempts to give an abundance only to find a disconnected spirit incapable of properly handling the blessing? At the same level of woefulness is a person who prays for abundance never realizing they have continuously squandered the increases by their mishandling of blessings already provided.

It is a discerning spirit connected to the Lord's Spirit which remains in abundant living. Many of us need to get it together spiritually before we cry out to God for blessings we will surely mishandle, otherwise. Believe that it does not take much to get connected, but it does take two things especially: effort and a willing spirit. Call out which of the two you lack and you will have pointed out your road-block to increase and overflow. Improve in that area and you are well on your way to great excess. Extra time in devotionals can grant you greater overflow in all of your living; initiated by an increase in your spirit's sensitivity to God's voice. Funny thing is, so many of us work overtime at the job not realizing extra time in devotionals with God will grant greater overflow through the proper application of blessings already received; thus, potentially eliminating the need for overtime at the proverbial "9-to-5." Question is, "Do you put in overtime in the wrong places?"

Let me elaborate on this example about overtime. We work overtime hours and still squander our earnings because we are so disconnected from the Spirit's directions. We work all those extra hours to never get ahead. How long have you been working overtime at the job, seemingly never to get ahead? Why is it others work less hours yet are more blessed? I can safely say it is most likely that they have a spirit sensitized to the Lord's Spirit, giving them directions on how to apply the little they have received. Why don't you take some extra time with the Lord so you can be abundantly blessed, as well? As you now may realize, <u>overflow is largely about the proper application and less about the size of the blessing itself.</u> Some people get big blessings and are big fumblers, while others can properly apply micro blessings and witness fruitful abundance. It is your choice. Why continue to fumble along in life when you can choose to connect to the spiritual directions that will grant great overflow?

We will not find the directions on the packages (blessings), but they can be found with the One who created the packages. God's blessed directions are designed in ways unlike those found on store bought packages. We must seek Him for the directions. To not seek Him for directions will minimize the overflow that awaits us. Fact is, I would totally be amiss if the Holy Spirit directed me to teach many how to successfully receive blessings through prayer and I not teach the necessity of receiving discernment about the use of the blessing, also. A great shame to have a new population of persons who pray and receive, yet fall short of overflow for lack of discernment. Points like this are the major differences between this document and any other prayer book. A generation of fumblers would, and has, resulted from such lack in wisdom.

Often believers get wrongly caught up in one of my favorite verses, Matthew 6:33 where it exclaims, "... all these other things shall be added unto you." We should all strive for another level in Christ where we seek Him for the directions for all those other things just as equally as we seek Him for the other things themselves. Again, it is God who created us and created the blessings, and it is God who gives the understanding of what to do with the blessings. After we grasp the fullness of this bit of wisdom, we will more fully realize why it is we destroy so many things in our lives. Thereafter, we shall move towards the overflow.

This *Element of Prayer* makes plain the necessity for us to pray for directions as we pray for the blessings. The very fruitfulness of our lives depends on it. Just think about it. We would, and do destroy the store's packaged items when we do not pay attention to the directions that come along with them. There are many persons reading this document who can attest to improperly assembling a store bought item, because they refused to first read the directions. Tell the truth men. Similarly we destroy gifts from Heaven when we pay no attention to the Spirit from Heaven. This wisdom is not hard to digest. We need only have receptive spirits ready to be blessed with the overflow. "It is not in heaven, that thou shouldest say, Who shall go up for us to heaven, and bring it unto us, that we may hear it, and do it?" *(Deuteronomy 30:12)*. What shall we then say to the Spirit's calling; oh so pleasant, directing and kind? The Lord can do a lot more with a little than we can ever do with much on our own.

Submission is the Way

Praying for discernment increases our submission unto God. We must not only submit our ears unto the Lord, but we must submit our spirits unto Him, also. We can hear yet never receive if we do not submit our spirits unto the Lord. This is the plight of some, whereas they disobediently try to do things their own ways; never taking heed to the voice of God. Our Savior did not forsake wisdom during His earthly ministry; thus, neither should we. "And Jesus increased in wisdom and stature, and in favor with God and man" *(Luke 2:52)*. Do not think for a moment that our britches are too big to receive directions and guidance. It is in those same sorrowful britches that we find ourselves lacking and desolate.

The very act of praying to the Lord for an increase in discernment causes our spirits to become more submissive unto Him, which in turn grants us further access unto His voice's directions. In a sense we ignite greater submission within us by merely calling unto Him for an increase in wisdom. It is the Spirit's desire that we come to an understanding that we can do nothing without His first making provisions. He makes greater provisions for us, discernment in this case, after we seek Him. Solely listening is not the act needed at this point within prayer; for exclusive listening is reserved for the *Element of Meditation*. What is required of us here in this *Element #5* is to seek God for Him to bestow upon us a greater spirit of discernment and wisdom concerning the brevity of our prayer request.

It is one thing to gain overflow from God through meditation as in *Element of Prayer Progression*™ *#8*, but it is something altogether different to receive directions and greater understanding from God strictly through discernment.   This discernment gives us greater understanding of even the things we are currently requesting. Let it be known that more of our prayers would be viewed as successful if we simply had greater wisdom and discernment about what it is that we are praying. Much discouragement occurs in prayer as a result of our limited wisdom about why it is that we are making a request, what it is that we are requesting and why it is that God is giving a certain answer. Our ability to receive of God's discerning voice is increased by our submission unto Him while in prayer and thereafter. A submissive spirit is vital. We cannot receive if we are not heedful, and we will not be heedful without first being truly submissive.   More is spoken on submission in other sections of this document as it relates to different precepts.

Limited Sight

Discernment is crucial to our prayer's success since man has limited sight. Our physical limitations prevent us from seeing into the future and seeing our way through life. Frustrations about our prayers often arise from our attempts to use limited physical abilities to understand the spiritual form and the function of what it is we request. Over and over, we have gone wrong by taking things into our own hands. We get lost attempting to see things unseeable by the naked and natural eye. That is the point. Most things for which we pray are still so unseen that it is impossible to make sense of such things without a submissive and discerning spirit directed by an all seeing God. The Lord knows how incapable mere man is in finding his own way. The Lord sees it all in advance and He gives us glimpses through our spirits by way of discernment. The Lord Jesus said it this way unto Simon Barjona, "... for flesh and blood hath not revealed it unto thee, but my Father which is in heaven" *(Matthew 16:17)*. I beseech you therefore my brothers and sisters to turn your limited sight into something that is beyond telescopic sight by allowing the Holy Spirit to speak unto you through prayer.

The Lord can see things we will never see; past, present and future. It is behooving that we choose not to tap into His power to see, as we blindly wreck our todays and tomorrows. Our natural sight is of great value and irreplaceable, but a discerning spirit is priceless and fortifying. The Lord makes a window available to us for viewing things that are blind to the natural eye, if we would simply, "Be not wise in our own conceits" *(Romans 12:16c)*.

"... I was blind, know I see" *(John 9:25)*, is only rendered true when we allow the Lord's Spirit to reveal true life wisdom that outweighs our natural limited sight. In the story of the above verse, the man was given his natural and spiritual sight by the healing power of the Lord Jesus. We too can receive healing for our spiritual sight and for our holy wisdom if we would simply allow the Lord and His Spirit to enter our lives.

Believers know and trust, "(For we walk by faith and not by sight)" *(II Corinthians 5:7);* thus, the sight we speak of in the previous paragraph is the sight called discernment. A discerning spirit can see things that are vague, if not invisible to the natural eye. There are things we will never be able to see on our own, but God's Spirit will reveal them unto us if we are connected, sensitized and submissive.

Waiting

We must pray that God grant us the wisdom and wherewithal to wait patiently for that which we have requested. Jeremiah had to wait 10 days for an answer to one of his prayers, as written in Jeremiah 42:7, "And it came to pass after ten days, that the word of the Lord came unto Jeremiah." Job said it this way, "... all the days of my appointed time will I wait till my change come" *(Job 14:14).* The Lord our God, alone, is the change we so desire and can receive, if we would simply learn the essence of waiting. Some of us have so much difficulty in waiting. Isn't it true the Lord has been waiting mercifully for quite some time for us to get ourselves together? So, why do we find it difficult to wait on His answers to our prayers, which come a lot sooner than it ever took for any of us to get ourselves together? Isaiah 30:18 states, "And therefore will the Lord wait, that he may be gracious unto you, and therefore will he be exalted, that he may have mercy upon you: for the Lord is a God of judgment: blessed are all they that wait for him."

Quite sure Elizabeth, wife of Zachariah and mother of John, prayed most of her life while waiting to have a child; since a woman's worth in Biblical days was measured heavily by her ability to bear children. She faithfully waited, whereas many Christians fall out of love with God and lose faith after their requests go unanswered for a period of time. This portion of this *Element of Prayer* is alone worth the price of this document, and more. Here's the deliverance for many, and this is a *key* for us all. God sometimes desires us to grow or acquire other strengths previous to receiving that which we currently are requesting. He already knows we will destroy the blessing if we receive it too soon, or before we are prepared. But oh, what a blessing it truly is to us after we have grown a bit and maybe even matured a little. Otherwise, what God meant as a blessing for us may turn out to be a curse prompted by our inexperience and/or inabilities. As an example, God may not have granted you that contract for $70,000 because He knew you were not in a position to keep your money hungry friends at bay. God will bless you with that contract, and more, after He replaces those good for nothing friends with people who do not desire wealth and fame to the point of being destructive. God is in the blessing business, but at times you must wait, and wait discerningly, so He can bless you with a spirit prepared for blessings and prepared to glorify the Kingdom. It is in this spirited preparation that the Lord's hand will bless you, your living and all those around you.

For others, maybe the Lord had to replace an unhealthy addiction, of some sort, with a more wholesome longing and desire for His Son Jesus. Often the Lord must remove and replace some things in our lives so to best insure that the blessings He does provide unto us will not end up as dung and mess. "Give not that which is holy unto the dogs, neither cast ye your pearls before swine, lest they trample them under their feet, and turn again and rend you" *(Matthew 7:6)*. God surely knows what we need and what it is we can currently handle. He also knows when we will use the blessing to glorify the Kingdom and when we will attempt to glorify ourselves. Are we as swine or as good stewards?

Prepared but Spiritually Disconnected

Some people are so absolutely emotionally wanting to receive a blessing, but are not in a prepared spiritual position to use that very blessing to glorify the name of the Lord. Someone reading these pages truly understands exactly what is being said here. That person knows in their heart the minute they receive of their requested blessing they will run out in the streets among the heathen and destroy it. Someone reading these pages knows what's being said because they have messed over a thing or two in the past. They lost everything they had as quickly, if not faster, than the time it took to receive it. Afterwards, they turned back to God asking for the same thing they just so childishly destroyed. Yes, we are still making reference to Matthew 7:6!

We should be more like Solomon. Solomon asked for wisdom to be able to discern to do the will of the Lord. He had carte blanche to ask for anything of the Lord and he chose discernment and wisdom. The amazing thing is he illustrated some form of discernment to even ask such a thing. "And Solomon said, Thou hast shewed unto thy servant David my father great mercy, according as he walked before thee in truth, and in righteousness, and in uprightness of heart with thee; and thou hast kept for him this great kindness, that thou hast given him a son to sit on his throne, as it is this day. And now, O Lord my God, thou hast made thy servant king instead of David my father: and I am but a little child: I know not how to go out or come in. And thy servant is in the midst of thy people which thou hast chosen, a great people, that cannot be numbered nor counted for multitude. Give therefore thy servant an understanding heart to judge thy people, that I may discern between good and bad: for who is able to judge this thy so great a people" *(I Kings 3:6-9).*

God was so pleased with this request that He blessed Solomon with greater wisdom than any person had ever seen, and blessed his living to a point of overflow so all the world stood as witness. Now that is the way to be blessed. We can say, that is being blessed beyond measure. So, how much more should we follow this great example of not only receiving of God, but also how to be obedient unto Him thereafter?

Preparation Through Growth

Sometimes we must grow in some area before God blesses us with what it is He has already set aside for us. The blessings and God are just waiting on us to gain more wisdom, gain more staying power, increase in resolve, or simply, change our attitudes; to name a few. God knows what is best, so we must pray that God's perfect will and power work in our lives to prepare us for great blessings. We truly should know we must be prepared to receive blessings from God.

The Lord our God does not play around when it comes to blessings. God is waiting for us to be prepared, so He can bless us like never before. For this reason I believe in praying for something only once. First of all, God knows our prayers before we pray them. Second, we tend to spend more time praying for the same item, when the Lord may want us to spend that time growing in an area which will prepare us to receive the blessing, thereafter. This is a *key* for us all. Be discerning and mindful to expend more energy maturing spiritually rather than duplicating so many prayers. Let me repeat, take some of that energy that it takes to duplicate prayers to now concentrate on growing and maturing till the Lord sees fit to bless our preparedness. Pray to God that He will reveal unto us the area in which we need to mature. Best believe He will reveal it unto us. Most of us need to grow and grow up a little more in order to receive what God has to offer. God is poised to bless us with more increase than we could ever imagine, but we must be readied through growth and maturity.

As an example, the woman and her child were blessed by the Lord through Elisha. There was a famine in the land yet she and her neighbors did not have enough pots/vessels to receive all that God had to give. "Then he said, Go, borrow thee vessels abroad of all thy neighbours, even empty vessels; borrow not a few ... And it came to pass, when the vessels were full, that she said unto her son, Bring me yet a vessel. And

He said unto her, There is not a vessel more. And the oil stayed" *(II Kings 4:3-6)*. She had more than enough at the end of the day, but what if she and her neighbors had been more prepared with more vessels? This is a lesson for us to know that God has the ability and resources to bless us, our families, our neighbors and our community, beyond that which we can imagine and beyond the size of our individual vessels. Our objective then is to allow our growth through the processes God prescribes and presents unto us.

We must not shy away from the process, the preparation and the growth; for in them we multiply our number of pots available for the abundance of blessings God is about to pour. We minimize our pots and vessels when we choose to forsake our growth. The very maturity we forsake today is the very territory increase we forsake for tomorrow. As in this Biblical story, God will not stop pouring the blessings until we stop growing and preparing. Preparation and growth begins with and continues through our receiving proper discernment from God. Our number of vessels will not run out, nor will the oil stop flowing if we gladly continue to receive discernment and wisdom from the Spirit of God. Oh taste and see!

How much more will God pour into our lives if, and when, we are more prepared to receive of it? "His lord said unto him, Well done, thou good and faithful servant: thou hast been faithful over a few things, I will make thee ruler over many things: enter thou into the joy of thy Lord" *(Matthew 25:21)*. Let's make this clearer. If we cannot be faithful over our character by continuing to have wicked attitudes, why would we think God will bless us with increase just so we can have wicked attitudes more places? Many of us who have bad attitudes want to continue to pray the prayer of Jabaaz, not realizing God does not desire us to spread our bad character in places where He wants us to spread His joy.

Many of us are void of increase, because God is waiting for us to develop new attitudes. Someone else may need to change a behavior before God blesses them. Others may need to change the company they keep or the places they frequent. Let it be known here today, God desires to bless us all. These blessings will be given unto us as soon as we receive of the greater blessing through the process of our change. God doesn't desire to make us doctors, as much as He desires to make us followers of Christ. His will is not so much for us to become wealthy, but to become more of His Spirit. As well, He doesn't even desire to make ministers as much as He wants us all to become more obedient unto His discerning Spirit. Our spirits must digest the fact that it is greater for us to mature than for us to acquire most things we pray to receive. Most of the things we pray to receive may satisfy us for a short moment, but our change and maturity will bless us for a lifetime and may help grant us added crowns in glory.

Action Packed Prayers and Living

Being a true prayer warrior is about putting our prayers into action, also. (34) This is a *key*. Far too many of us are still on our knees waiting for deliverance when God has already made provisions for us in accord with His will. Often our blessings are waiting for us to put into action that which we prayed to receive. How many of us truly realize sometimes we must walk in our blessing? That is a part of *Thanksgiving/Prepraise* which shall be further discussed in *Element #7*.

Let me further illustrate, if we pray for obedience than it is high time we put obedience into action in our lives. Stop waiting for the miraculous, when the miraculous has already occurred. God is a prayer answering God. It's just that most often He does not send us messages as inter-departmental sticky pad notes to tell us how and when the blessing had already been provided. Let it be our faith which realizes the Lord has already shown up and delivered. Let it be our faith which prompts us to realize He showed up the moment we began to pray. Let us even have greater faith to believe that God is so great that He made provisions before we kneeled to pray; for He already knows our thoughts and all of which we stand in need. Walk into deliverance this day!

At times the change we need is to act as if we have already been delivered. At times we need to walk as if we are blessed. At times we need to act as if we are healed. Many people testify of how the doctor gave them a negative report only to later find themselves completely healed with no trace of infirmity. The healing came about through their faith to walk as if they were already healed. Our spirits must discern when to wait on our change and when to walk in our change. Job said he was going to wait on his change to come *(Job 14:14)*, but the man of palsy took up his bed and walked *(Mark 2:12)*. In what way is the Spirit directing you?

Let us take this key a little further. It renders God a liar if we neglect to institute obedience into action in our lives after praying for such a thing. We claim God a liar and our relationship with Him to be fraudulent when we do not walk within the blessing which we prayed to receive. Do not make our God a liar! Or maybe you do not serve the same God I serve? Often God does grant us the desires of our hearts, but we must then walk in the way of victory. Many say their prayers have not been answered, when in fact, the prayers were answered but they refuse to act as though their prayers had been answered. If we pray to God for power, then we should act as though we have that very power. Am I talking to anyone who desires to be strong in prayer? If so, act as though you are a prayer warrior by living in the strength of this *Element of Prayer Progression.*™

These words emit of boldness. As prayer warriors we must walk in a measure of boldness which is produced by heightened discernment unto the Lord's voice. It is next to impossible to have the truthful boldness Paul spoke of in Ephesians 6:19-20 without a great discerning spirit, fully locked into the Spirit's directing. This boldness comes from having faith to know our steps are definitely ordered by the Lord. It is a boldness of faith which discerns God has already shown up, and we must walk and live in the victory. This is when our faith becomes impregnated by the power of our walk. Fact is, there is nothing more sorrowful than a Christian who claims faith and boldness, yet walks in defeat. How is your walk? How is your boldness? Are the answers to those questions driven by the faith in your level of discernment?

Faith to Discern

An issue arises when we attempt to have undo faith in ourselves, instead of discerning that nothing can be accomplished on our own strength nor abilities. We must put our faith in God. "Believe in the Lord your God, so shall ye be established; believe his prophets, so shall ye prosper" _(II Chronicles 20:20)_. The Lord Jesus asked His disciples while on a boat riding through a storm, "... Why are ye so fearful? How is it that ye have no faith?" _(Mark 4:40)_. The same is true for us in this modern day. We have spent so much time with the Lord and we have witnessed His great power, yet we still doubt the resolution of our prayers in His hands. Matthew 8:26 is written this way, "... O ye of little faith?" The fact is, many of us are fearful to walk in our blessings, while others are fearful of failing in the blessings provided. Faithless folk!

For all who know their faith is lacking, I urge you this very moment to ask the Lord for an increase of faith, as the disciples asked in Luke 17:5. It shall be given unto thee. We should not walk in a life filled with lacking faith when we have a Lord and God so powerful and faithful unto us. It makes no sense and it can be classified as down right sinful to have so little faith in such an enormous God. Yes, each of us has been given our own measure of faith, as written in Romans 12:3, but I am faithful enough to believe God would not leave any of His children short on faith in Him. For the Word tells us, "For God hath not given us the spirit of fear; but of power, and of love, and of a sound mind" _(II Timothy 1:7)_. That being the case, the Lord has granted us all a measure of faith at least high enough to believe on Him and to not fear walking in our blessings. I do pray you receive the deliverance through these words pertaining to discernment.

Eliminate Foolishness

It is a sad detail that there are those who pray foolishness, exclaiming words and statements without direction nor care. Praying in such an unexplainable and spiritless fashion destroys the possibility of our request being blessed. This foolishness we speak of here is not just as the foolishness spoken of in the earlier section entitled "What to do with It." Rather, this foolishness is more so in regards to our not being <u>wise</u> altogether. Foolishness is described in the Bible as an antonym to that of wisdom, as exclaimed in Proverbs 10:14, "Wise men lay up knowledge: but the mouth of the foolish is near destruction." Applying discernment in prayer has a way of eliminating this foolishness as we pray and as we live thereafter. I'm sure most of us are highly interested in our request being blessed by God rather than ruined by us, so let's go a bit deeper in this matter.

Praying for something does not guarantee it will bless our lives upon receiving it; especially in the manner we may think. Joseph said to his brothers, "... But as for you, ye thought evil against me; but God meant it unto good, to bring to pass, as it is this day, to save much people alive ...." *(Genesis 50:15-21);* for truly the brother's prayer was not their desires in earlier days. Truth be told this is the opposite of many of our life stories. Let me explain. God means for all of us to be tremendously blessed. He blesses us over and over again, often without our realizing it. Yet, in our foolishness we take God's good and turn it into curses due to our lack of wisdom. Proverbs 16:22 says, "Understanding is a wellspring of life unto him that hath it: but the instruction of fools is folly."

There are persons who can admit to being foolish and are now asking how might they change. I direct them to the power of James 1:5, "If any of you lack in wisdom, let him ask of God, that giveth to all men liberally, and upbraideth not; and it shall be given him." It can be said we all have done some foolish things during the course of our lives; if not, just keep living. This document's motivation is that we all shore up our prayers and living with success driven by discernment. Again, we may receive blessings through our prayers on a daily basis but never see the fruit thereof because wisdom was steadily lacking in our decision making.

Foolish ways shall reign in all who avert wisdom's calling. The Bible is so exact to say, "Be not wise in thine own eyes ..." *(Proverbs 3:7).* This speaks volumes for prayer warriors, as they must have wisdom to know several things: what to pray; what to do with the prayer's answers; how to respond to God's answers to prayers; and what is God's desire for their lives and prayers.

A person who prays and lacks wisdom surely isn't a prayer warrior. Some of us are endowed with some knowledge, but we all must seek the Lord's wisdom for the discernment necessary to have power in prayer. Most of us have the ordinary tendency to pray for more blessings (things) rather than to request that God grant us more wisdom to better work with what we already possess and what we shall soon receive. Answered prayers without the benefit of having wisdom can be more of a burden and curse than most of us can imagine. Not many would refute we live in times when much prayer is needed. The Lord just placed upon my spirit that there are many who are quite prayerful, but their prayers are often made ineffective by their lack of wisdom and discernment; creating foolishness.

Prayer warriors must be prudent during and after prayer; brought about by discerning spirits. Blessings come into fruition through discernment. What saith the Lord is better understood through discernment. What is most important in prayer is made the focus through discernment. All of which is impossible without wisdom's manifestation within our spirits. Let it be that all prayer warriors pray for more wisdom instead of requesting more things. Fact is wisdom can and will bless our lives more than the things we most often pray to receive. Wisdom is a great blessing. A great blessing we can ill afford not to obtain and properly utilize.

The proper utilization of knowledge is just as imperative as acquiring it. Not utilizing knowledge to the effect of it becoming wisdom tends to lead to the very foolishness we should avoid at all cost. Let us not be like some Biblical characters who received knowledge, but did not move in a discerning fashion and paid dearly for their foolishness, subsequently.

King Ahab was strictly told by God and the prophets not to marry the pagan neighbors; just as all God's children had been told. The King ignored this knowledge and command, led God's people into pagan worship, and died as a result. Throughout his reign he ignored proper advice, not discerning the source of the knowledge nor contemplating the repercussions. Samson rejected the proper advice from his parents not to seek women amongst the uncircumcised. In doing so he violated God's laws on many occasions and later came to a violent death at his own hands; a death shared by a band of Philistines. He survived four attempts on his life by Delilah and the Philistines, of which could have been totally thwarted from the beginning had he used discernment. How many similarly dangerous situations must we go through before we take heed to discern? Knowledge can be as foolishness to us all until we convert it to wisdom by taking discerning actions. Samson's life could have been marked with many great accomplishments by the power vested in him by God. Nonetheless, he is well known more for his bodily strength, than he is for the deliverance of his people or some other great call from God. What feats have we foolishly plundered due to our neglect to discern?

Some of our foolishness comes about due to our making repetitious request; which is spoken of in other portions of this document. These paragraphs to follow will site several reasons why praying repetitious prayers may create foolishness in our prayers and in our lives. First and foremost, God already knows what we stand in need; thus it may be futile to continue to ask. We all remember as infants how we use to call out, "Ma can I have it? Ma can I have it? Ma can I have it?" Ten minutes later — "Ma can I have it?" She surely heard our request, and her silence recorded her answer. Our asking the same thing ten times over did not change her mind nor her approach, for she knew the requested item was of no good to us, nor for us. She had lived long enough and had seen enough in order to have discernment concerning the requested item. Likewise, God listens to our cries as children, but sometimes does not change His approach; similar to Jesus in His moment of humanity when in Gethsemane He prayed that the cup be removed, but the Father did not change His approach nor will *(Matthew 26:36-42)*. He knows everything about our hearts, our propensities and the concerns of the requested item.

Second, repeatedly requesting things begins to fester in our spirits due to the request going unanswered. This magnifies the requested item within our hearts, minds and spirits. The item becomes our focus as we then take our eyes off God as Lord. After times of requesting the same thing, we begin to idolize the item and minimize God to the status of a bank machine or a mere blessing mechanism. This is *key* for us to remember, although many will try to attest that they would never purposely reduce God to such a stature. The point is our minds sometimes take us places often not purposed initially, just as psychologist and philosophers will proclaim. Repetition of the wrong things have ways of festering in our spirits, sometimes to the tune of foolishness. It is foolish to believe we know better than God. Above all, we cannot allow any item to make us take our main focus off God. God alone is the greatest blessing we will ever have; as has been mentioned previously within this document.

Third, God knows whether the requested item is good for us at that time or even at any time. God knows best and we should trust that. I declare to you this very day to not only be mindful of that which you pray to receive, but be careful not to pester the Lord, either. The fact is He just may grant the thing unto you merely to prove to you how much you should not have it. Many would rather see a thing with their natural eyes versus initially believing in God through their spiritual senses. We say we have faith in God yet we push Him to a point where he teaches us through the pains of experience. Far too many of us choose experience over faith and trust in God. It can mean one of three things when we do not receive an answer to our prayers: wait, no, or further prepare the soil to receive. This is the point where discernment becomes so vital; along with having a spirit sensitized to the voice of the Lord and His Word. Oh what pains we bear, not just because we do not carry everything to the Lord in prayer, but sometimes from our pestering the Lord to the point of our learning a lesson through experience. I urge us all to allow discernment to take root within our spirits so we may fortify our prayers success and minimize life's pains. Serving God is a joy, but painful enough in some respects that we need not compound the strife by foolishly nagging the Lord to do what He would lovingly prefer not to do.

Overall, let us seek to have more discernment so we may reap blessings of overflow and victory in all our prayers. Seek discernment with great zeal, after which, seek it all the more. Our spirits can never be too sensitized unto the Spirit's voice, so never think its quest to be complete. The very fruitfulness of our prayers depends upon our ability to discern.

A Biblical Illustration of Discernment

What greater Biblical example to give on how to pray for discernment and wisdom than that of Solomon. He prayed for the ability to lead God's people, "Give therefore thy servant an understanding heart to judge thy people, that I may discern between good and bad: for who is able to judge this thy so great a people? And the speech pleased the Lord, that Solomon had asked this thing" *(I Kings 3:9-10).* Solomon was of the Spirit enough to know not many things in life can fortify our living like that of wisdom and discernment. He exuded a wherewithal to know building a successful future called for great understanding of things, such as: how to acquire things needed; what to do with blessings received; and how to continue to receive directions from on high.

This story is such a great illustration of submission unto the Lord; so much that we should duplicate Solomon's spirit of communion. It is in this spirit that we allow God access into our prayers and into our living. It is in this very spirit that God makes ways out of no way. If we look closely into this story we can see how Solomon sought instructions, submitted unto the Lord and admitted to his limited ability to see. The sad part, but true, is in Solomon's later years he also became a prime example of how foolishness seeps into our lives when we no longer move with a discerning spirit unto God. Let us allow Solomon's living to stand as an example of how discernment, and the lack thereof, can mold our lives positively or negatively.

DISCERNMENT – *Progression of Prayer Element #5*

Exercises

INSTRUCTIONAL

1. Write a paragraph as to why the Lord prefers us to grow and mature more than He desires us to receive other blessings from our prayer request?

BENEFIT:
To transition our spirits to receive of the greater power in prayer. We will be blessed all the more when our focus becomes more connected with God's desires and His Spirit.

PERSONAL

1. On a sheet of paper write the blessing which seems to be eluding you.

   Now write a short statement about the area of your life in which you think God desires you to mature before receiving the above   blessing.

BENEFIT:
There are two major benefits. One, honest acknowledgment of the area in need of growth must occur before you can go about maturing in the said area. Two, you can now use the precepts within this chapter to discern how to handle God's answers to prayers.

DISCERNMENT — *Progression of Prayer Element #5*

General Questions

1. What is more important than receiving a yes or no answer to our prayers? Why?

2. What is the definition of discernment?

3. From where do we receive instructions for our prayer's blessings?

   Why do we often fumble blessings?

4. What happens when we misapply blessings?

5. What may God desire we do instead of duplicating prayers?

6. Besides maturing, what is something we must do after praying?

   What is one scripture within this chapter which gives support?

7. Based on scriptures, who should discern?

8. What must we do after making a request unto God?

9. How can we heighten our spirit's sensitivity?

10. What are two requirements for abundant living?

DISCERNMENT – *Progression of Prayer Element #5*

Advanced Questions

1. What are two causes for foolishness in our prayer lives?

   Where else, besides our prayer lives, does foolishness cause our blessings to become as curses? And how?

2. What are 3 reasons we should be submissive unto the Lord's sight and discernment rather than relying on our own sight?

3. Why may God not provide written directions to our blessings?

Sign

Pray this prayer with me:
A Prayer for Sign

"Father of all creation. Maker of my spirit and soul. Awesome are Thy ways and gracious is Your Son. Your power is infinite and Your Spirit is so dear. I worship Your divine power in all its splendor. Thank You for giving me an ear attuned with Your Spirit's voice; for without it I would be lost in my limited sight, downtrodden in my spirit and overcome by the enemy's attacks. So blessed are Thou for being so mindful of this Your servant and child that You would provide, protect and guide. I now pray You guide me so I can best receive of Your signs and principles. Let this chapter be of guidance and strength so I may be more assured to walk according to Your will. Your Word says if we ask we shall receive; so, I ask for power to receive signs from You that my ways shall be aligned with Your Spirit. By no other means may I be blessed than by Your blessing me Father. Bless me, oh bless me. Let Your blessings unto me be glory unto You. This I submit unto You in the blessed joy of Jesus, Your only begotten Son who died that I may have life and that I may pray in His name — Jesus, Jesus - Amen."

This section is to better enhance our understanding of the Biblical reasons for who should receive signs, how should we receive signs, why should we receive signs, what should we receive as signs, where should we receive signs and when should we receive signs. Our study of signs will be further enhanced if these verses are read previous to moving onto the chapter material; as this format will indeed better prepare our spirits to receive of the chapter material.

1) WHO should receive signs?
- Exodus 31:13 — The children of Israel
- Judges 6:17 — Those who have favour
- I Kings 13:5 — The man of God
- Isaiah 44:26 — His servants
- Matthew 16:4 — Not the wicked nor adulterous
- Mark 16:14-20 — Disciples; with those who proclaim the Word
- John 20:13 — Jesus
- II Corinthians 2:7 — Those who forgive and those who comfort
- Philippians 1:7 — Partakers of grace
- Hebrews 6:16 — Heirs of promise

2) HOW should we receive signs?
- Exodus 13:9 — With a strong hand
- Exodus 31:13 — By keeping the Sabbath
- Deuteronomy 6:8 — Bind them upon your hand
- Deuteronomy 6:9 — Write them upon the posts of your house and on your gates
- Judges 6:17 — The Lord talking to you
- I Kings 13:3 — Spoken by the Lord
- Isaiah 7:11 — Asking
- Mark 8:11 — Not tempting as Pharisee
- Mark 16:20 — With signs following; the Lord working with you; from the right hand of the Father
- I Corinthians 1:7 — Waiting
- I Corinthians 1:22-23 — Not as a requirement, but by the Word and faith in Christ crucified
- Hebrews 6:17 — By an oath; willingly more abundantly
- Revelation 15:1 — By the Angels

3) WHY should we receive signs?
- Genesis 9:15 — God will remember His covenant
- Exodus 13:9 — So the Lord's law may be in thy mouth
- I Chronicles 14:2 — To be lifted up on high
- Isaiah 19:20 — For a witness unto the Lord in Egypt; and a pillar

3) WHY should we receive signs? *(Continued)*
- Jeremiah 44:29 – To know that God's words shall stand
- Ezekiel 14:8 – To know that He is the Lord
- Ezekiel 20:12 – That they might know He is the Lord that sanctifies them
- Daniel 9:27 – To confirm covenant
- Mark 16:20 – To confirm the Word
- John 20:31 – That you might have life through His name
- Acts 14:22 – Exhorting to continue in faith and the going through tribulations
- Romans 15:8 – To confirm promises made
- I Corinthians 1:8 – To confirm you unto the end that you may be blameless in the day of our Lord
- Hebrews 6:16 – To shew unto the heirs of promise

4) WHAT should we receive as signs?
- Genesis 9:12 – Token of the covenant; bow in the cloud
- Exodus 13:9 – As a memorial between your eyes
- Exodus 31:13; Ezekiel 20:12 – Covenant between you and God
- I Kings 13:3 – Spoken by the Lord
- Isaiah 19:20 – For a witness unto the Lord
- Isaiah 39:22 – What to do; when to go
- Isaiah 44:26 – Confirm the word of His servant
- Ezekiel 12:11 – God is your sign
- Ezekiel 24:24 – The prophet of God
- Matthew 16:1 – From Heaven
- Matthew 24:3 - 25:46 – The coming of the Lord; the end of the world; no man knoweth but a sign will appear
- Matthew 24:30 – The coming of the Son of Man
- John 20:30 – Which are not written in the book
- John 20:31 – Those which are written
- Acts 14:22 – Souls
- Romans 4:11 – Seal of righteousness (circumcision); of faith
- I Corinthians 1:6 – The testimony of Christ
- I Corinthians 14:2 – Position
- I Corinthians 14:22 – Tongues for unbelievers; preached word for believers
- II Corinthians 2:8 – Love
- Philippians 1:7 – Defense of the Gospel
- Hebrews 6:16 – An oath
- Revelation 15:1 – End times

5) WHERE should we receive signs?
- Deuteronomy 6:8-9 — Upon thy hand, on the posts of your house
                                and on your gates
- Joshua 4:6 — Among you
- Isaiah 7:11 — Either in depth, or in the height above
- Isaiah 19:20 — In Egypt and at the border
- Isaiah 20:3 — Upon Egypt and upon Ethiopia
- Mark 16:20 — Everywhere; going forth
- Revelation 15:1 — In Heaven

6) WHEN should we receive signs?
- Exodus 8:23 — Tomorrow
- Exodus 13:10 — In his season from year to year
- Exodus 13:13 — Throughout your generations
- Exodus 13:16-17 — Forever; perpetual covenant; throughout their
                                generations
- I Kings 13:3 — The same day
- Isaiah 55:13 — Everlasting
- Ezekiel 24:27 — In that day
- Daniel 9:27 — A week
- John 20:30 — In the presence of the disciples
- I Corinthians 1:8 — In the day of our Lord Jesus Christ

> *"Ask thee a sign of the Lord thy God; ask it either in the depth, or in the height above."*   **Isaiah 7:11**

Sign (a mark or gesture that is meant to convey or make known information, proof, or a command; a discernable indication of what is not itself directly perceptible) is important for direction, correction, understanding and in keeping us in check or keeping us on the straight and narrow. It is on the straight and narrow where believers should desire to walk. Under perfect conditions it seems quite easy and doable, but the Gospel truth of the matter is, "... the spirit indeed is willing, but the flesh is weak" *(Matthew 26:41)*. Many philosophers and psychologist confer that people naturally desire to do right, but we surely know, "For all have sinned, and come short of the glory of God" *(Romans 3:23)*. We all need something greater than ourselves in order to walk the good walk of faith. A sign from the Lord our God is that something we need!

Remove Flesh and be Clothed in Spirit

Prayer is not just about our attempt to have God perform something for us. A greater portion of our prayer lives involves our being directed by the Lord, which is in constant conflicted with our natural and sinful propensities to move upon our fleshy desires. It is fact that many people claim to hear from the Lord yet they continue to move in directions not sanctioned by God simply due to their actually listening to the vanity of their own spirits. The vanity and desires of our own spirits will rise at times, but they must be drowned out by our attentiveness unto signs given by God, lest we verge off the straight and the narrow.

Believers must diligently try to keep in step with the Spirit of God and His will for their lives. As most believers know, this is not an easy task and can be most daunting at best; thus, reason we need as much help as we can get. The scriptures and God's wisdom poured into us are our help. The Lord has provided us with His Word in order for us to sustain, grow and walk in faith while faced with good times and trying times. Yes, we need to be directed by the Lord in good times also. Truth is our flesh rises up more than we would like during the good times, causing us to relinquish the power vested unto us through God's Word and His wisdom. Most of us begin our days with good intentions of walking in the correct direction, but it is made so difficult by the evil one and even by our own fleshy natures. Believers must always keep in mind, "... because greater is he that is in you, than he that is in the world" *(I John 4:4)*. He is great, especially in our weakest hours. He is greater than any other power in Heaven or on Earth, and He's able to direct us if we are attuned.

Directions not Doubt

The Lord is our master plan and Master Planner. Many of our chosen paths are not sanctioned by the Master Planner; thus we often wobble off the straight and narrow. Listening to ourselves and/or other meager beings can be dangerous at best; therefore we are in great need to receive signs and directions from our Almighty God. Some say we ought not look for signs from the Lord, but I declare to all this very day we must seek signs from the Lord and we must be mindful of why we seek them. Some claim we should not ask for signs because of I Corinthians 1:22-23 which says, "For the Jews require a sign and the Greeks seek after wisdom: But we preach Christ crucified, unto the Jews a stumblingblock, and unto the Greeks foolishness." These verses speak of sign in the Greek as "semeion" which is defined as indication, miracle, token, and wonder; especially pertaining to the supernatural. The Book of Joel speaks of these types of signs, as did our Lord Jesus. This is *key*, and the teaching is as follows. We ought not look for miracles nor indications to prove the Lord's power and divinity. We can look for signs for direction, but we surely sin if we look for indications of His providence or sovereignty. Looking for signs to prove His deity is a form of tempting. Our Lord and Saviour quoted Deuteronomy 6:16 when He was being tempted by satan. "Jesus said unto him, it is written again, Thou shalt not tempt the Lord thy God" *(Matthew 4:7)*. Many of us have tempted the Lord in the same vein as the devil, and it is high time we cease.

Always remember Jesus ministered in regards to the spirit of the matter, so it is imperative that we are directed by His Spirit in our prayers and in our general living. We should not be overly astonished that He can perform miracles, nor should we be in need of being convinced of who He is by the signs He provides. The New Testament gives examples of how Jesus most often performed miracles to indicate His divinity, while there were times He performed miracles solely through His compassion. Yes, our Lord is full of compassion, but fewer miracles were performed solely through His compassion for the participants. Those times of compassion were most often marked by the Lord's stating to the participants things such as, "The time is not yet" or "Do not tell anyone."

In Matthew 12:22-45 Jesus answered the scribes on this very topic. The Lord knew their intent was to know if He actually had the power and authority to perform such miracles. Their intentions were to know if Jesus was who He claimed to be and it had nothing to do with their wanting to be directed by Him. Hear me on this. Our asking for a sign is not to justify His authority, for we already claim Him as Creator of all things good; unlike the Pharisees and Scribes who were motivated by doubt and deceit. Instead, we ask not for a miracle, but <u>we ask for an indication how to move in the perfect will of the Father.</u> Big difference!

Matthew 16:1 again illustrates the Pharisee's intents of tempting the Lord to disprove His divinity. We, in asking for a sign, are in no uncertain terms doubting His position nor His power. We are simply attempting to operate and live more fully in the great will of the Creator. Many of us truly fall short in our endeavors due to our living outside of His will. Things we do outside the desires of God may seem successful for the moment, but in the grander scheme it still remains to be outside of God's desires. Have you ever performed something and all was well while doing it and it seemed to be of great success, even? All you were doing at the time seemed to click and work out, only to later find it was all either a waste of time or it ultimately added nothing to your life. Maybe after awhile it even set you back more than you were in the first place. This happens when we work outside the will of God. Quite similar to sinning, where all things seem ok at first, but the reaping surely comes.

The success of our prayers is not predicated upon our receiving deliverance, blessings nor easy living. The success of our prayers can only be marked by our being directed by God and subsequently doing as He desires. That is true success and that is *key* for us all. People often view success through a lens of prosperity rather than through the view of God's Spirit. Fact is God's will is sometimes our immediate pain, but His ultimate glory. To remember Jesus is our prosperity is something that may help us better understand; as this is another key.

There are not many things greater in this spiritual walk than to know for sure we are walking, running and working in the will of God. Let me say this — God's will in our lives is not always the rosiest, smoothest, trouble free route. This is a *key* for our prayer lives and living. We often pray to travel upon the shortest distances between our current locations and our destinations, and we want to be sent on the easiest paths. The sometimes painful truth is the easy routes are not always what God desires for us.

It is greatly God's desire that His children grow closer to Him, and sometimes that growth entails some trials and tribulations. "My brethren, count it all joy when you fall into divers temptations; Knowing this, that the trying of your faith worketh patience. But let patience have her perfect work, that ye may be perfect and entire, wanting nothing" *(James 1:2-3)*. Also, "There hath no temptation taken you but such as is common to man: but God is faithful, who will not suffer you to be tempted above that ye are able; but will with the temptation also make a way to escape, that ye may be able to bear it" *(I Corinthians 10:13)*. Also, how may we best know the ways out of tough situations if we do not adhere to signs given us by God? Often the resolutions to our trials and temptations reach beyond our abilities to rationalize anything lest our own fleshy desires and meager knowledge; thus, our need to pray for signs from the Lord.

Word, Signs and Mysteries are not Always so Literal

Be mindful of the underlying spiritual essence of many Biblical writings, such as the parables spoken by the Lord Jesus; since not all of the Bible is literal. There are so many underlying truths and mysteries in the scriptures, and our ability to receive of them depends on our first accepting and digesting greater spiritual increase through the attributes of God. It is necessary that we all diligently study the Chapter on the *Attributes, Character and Nature of God.* We would do ourselves and our fellow congregants much good if we would remember not all the Bible is to be taken so literally. Biblical and Seminary students, alike, learn this fact, yet still have difficulty in the recognition of deeper mysteries within scriptures due to their mentally disqualifying God's character and nature during their studies and devotionals. Many will change from this day on.

Those Greeks of us who tend to take all things so literally miss out on much of the teachings of our Lord and Savior. All of Jesus' teachings spoke to the spirit of the matter. Jesus exposed the motives of the religious leaders and fulfilled Old Testament scriptures by ministering in regards to the Spirit. Not only did the Lord fulfill Old Testament scripture by teaching the spirit of the Law versus the letter of the Law, but He ministered in a posture to prepare those who would follow Him in the coming Spirit Age, also. Writings in the Book of Joel shout of this Age.

Here is the blessing for us. We could never keep the letter of the law, but we are blessed to live within the Spirit of the law. Yes, we are under grace, Jesus Christ, but we should truly live in accord with the Lord's teachings of the Spirit of matters. Fact is most of the Lord's answers to questions were postured upon the Spirit of the matters. We must be aware the Bible includes figures of speech; like simile, metaphor, hyperbole, humanization, euphemism, irony, metonymy and others. The usage of figures of speech and the true meaning behind them will be lost and unappreciated if we are not of the Spirit and unaware of God's character. The Bible is to be handled in literature form, but we must be connected and directed by the Spirit in order to refrain from handling it as just another composite of writings. Again, if we do not receive the spiritual in verse but rather digest it all as literal, we have and we will truly miss out on some of the greatest blessings of Jesus when reading the Gospels.

What is Our Motivation: Reverence or Proof?

Jesus' first words in Luke 11:29 began with, "This is an evil generation..."
We should realize we are of a wicked era, but believers are set apart from
this world. If we truly know in our hearts, minds and faith that God hath
raised Jesus from the dead, we can truly ask for a sign from Him while
remaining, both, in the spirit of His fellowship and in the greatness of His
will. What is our motivation for receiving a sign? We are truly barking
up the wrong proverbial tree in asking for a sign if we are seeking further
endorsements that He is God. We must have faith that He shall provide a
sign and bless our living all the more, if we seek to stay in His good and
perfect will. This shows true due to our spirit's desire to abide in Him
rather than confirm Him. The Lord knows our hearts either way, just as
He knew the motives of the keepers of the Law and other Biblical
characters throughout His earthly ministry.

Understand the Lord will take care of us and provide us with signs if our
hearts are in the right spirit. Again, we surely do not need further
confirmations to know He is the Great I Am. We strive to live in accord
with His will due to our belief in His being the Great I Am. That is the
great motivation behind all we desire and why we ask for signs or
directions. It is no miracle that God would touch our spirits in such a
way to give us direction on which ways to go throughout our days. For
some of us it may seem a miracle or wonder that He cares enough to
speak to us and direct us, but that is of His grace and mercy. The wonder
is that we would be sensitized enough to hear His directions then move in
accord with His will and ways. Truly understand the difference between
a sign and a miracle. For the most part we are to seek a sign, a touch, a
sound, or something else that God would use to direct us.

To desire a miracle in the true sense of the word is to not have faith in the
Lord's divinity and power. We should have faith to believe, not only that
the Lord can make a way, but that He has the power to direct us in that
very path, as well. God has surely made a way for us all, but far too
many of us listen to directions given us from many sources other than
God. Always remember, "For my thoughts are not your thoughts, neither
are your ways my ways, saith the Lord" *(Isaiah 55:8)*. For that very reason
we must desire to hear from the Lord so to best insure we are traveling
down the right roads and on the correct paths.

Signs were requested and given throughout the Bible. Some were
requested out of disbelief in the Lord's power, while others were
requested out of reverence for the Almighty. We must live in reverence

for the Lord. Undoubtedly, many reading this document have never really witnessed the power of God through prayer; regardless of what they try to claim. So, I say unto those who do not live to give Him reverence, be weary and mindful of asking for a sign to confirm He has the power to answer prayers. This is a major *key* for most of us. "But without faith it is impossible to please him: for he that cometh to God must believe that he is ..." *(Hebrews 11:6)*. If we do not believe He is, we should not go to Him in prayer in the first place. Why pray to someone whom you do not believe? Our minds must already be set in belief that He is able to do all things but fail before we take posture to pray. Here in the *Sign Element of the Prayer Progression* we are merely confirming our walk within His will; not questioning His power. The Lord knows our levels of faith and He knows our heart's motives and desires. Let our moderations be about doing the Lord's will, then our steps shall be blessed by His directing and guiding. "Order my steps dear Lord," are the words of a favorite song. How might He order our steps lest He gives us signs along the way and lest we are sensitized to read and receive those signs? A sad shame that some of us go as far as to actually read the signs, but do nothing to implement the directions within our lives; thus falling short of the glory of God over and over again.

A Sensitized spirit

Here we speak of being sensitized to receive of God. We live in a day and age when some folk say God is no longer talking to His people and children. I beg to differ and say we are surrounded by so many distractions which diminish our heavenly antennae. The Spirit of God directs, moves and convicts, yet in all His directing we still must be sensitized to hear. Our spiritual hearing is rendered inept because we are so conformed to the world. Make no mistake about it, God is still showing us signs even today through nature, other individuals, events and many other ways. In addition, it can be said some of us are simply not expecting to hear from God, while others have been taught incorrect truths about signs. The later is often the case where we mix up the essence of signs as directions with that of miracles and wonders. Again, miracles were to prove the Lord's divinity, and we are in no way in need of that type of a sign. We are merely in need of His directions. He is already King of our lives. We just need the King to keep us on the right path. He is already Savior of our living. We just need the Great Shepherd to lead us along the straight path and the still waters.

I truly hope we understand the difference so to increase our fellowship with God and to increase our power to transition prayers into positive living. Let us all allow this document to foster that power and transition.

In this way we are active participants in our prayer lives and our faith walks. Fault is partially credited to our never being taught to receive God's voice. Some teachers, themselves, have been taught this principle, but lack the mental ability and are void of the spiritual vernacular necessary to convey it to others. This can be taught only, as I now teach, through the power of the Holy Spirit and by the directions of Christ Jesus.

We must truly believe without the Lord's directions we will be lost and traveling down all the wrong roads in life. The wisdom given unto us through the mere reading of His Word is a great provider of directions, whereas His Spirit's directions unto us, through us, in us and around us can enhance and strengthen our abilities to walk in the straight and narrow. Some folk falsely allege the Spirit's movement upon them as they claim every and anything as a sign from God. This fact manifest itself in, both, persons who are only out to affirm their own desires and in persons who attempt to overtly prove God's presence in their lives. Truth is, some of us are more concerned with appearance than we are with truth.

Far too many of us run around claiming, "God said this," and "The Lord showed me that." "Oh! A woman said this to me today and it confirms what I was thinking God wanted me to do." How many folk have heard these stories? Of course we all have heard them. We must be mindful and careful of what we claim as a sign from God, because the devil will pick up on it. The devil will use our ambitions against us. The devil will use our incorrect application against us. The devil will even use the Word of God against us. Best believe this to be true. He tried to use the Word against Jesus in the wilderness, so how much more should we think he will not hesitate to use it, and more, against you and I. "The thief cometh not, but for to steal, and to kill, and to destroy: I am come that they might have life, and that they might have it more abundantly" *(John 10:10)*. A personal and strong relationship with God is not to be pillaged nor on display to others as a show of spirituality. In such a show the robber shall find their spirits and hearts jailed in eternal damnation.

Much of what we call miracles are actually God's providence upon our lives: the divine power sustaining and guiding human destiny. The Lord has such a great care and concern for His children that He provides for us and covers us in ways we think to be miracles. It is a miracle, in the connotative sense, that God still cares so deeply for us after all the sin we have committed, but it is not within the denotative sense and deeper spiritual essence of the word. Miracles, signs and wonders performed by God, the Lord Jesus and God's servants in biblical days were acts that imposed Heavenly will upon Earthly elements that altered natural laws;

i.e. Jesus raising Lazarus from the dead, and His giving sight to the blind. These acts changed the natural course and pattern of nature, whereas no natural laws were broken to provide meal on our tables when we were hungry. No act upon nature was performed to cover us from that car accident, unless our cars were suddenly raised in the air permitting the offending car to pass underneath; or something of that sort. It may have more so been God's providence that delayed our travel so we did not reach that intersection at the time the major six car collision occurred.

We shall continue to live powerlessly until we assume the truth of scripture and religion. For this reason many of us who shout falsely about miracles and other spiritual matters remain so powerless against the wiles of the devil and his imp's trappings. The devil knows of our weaknesses through our shouting and praying untruths; thus he scoffs at us and attacks us all the more. Be empowered this day by moving forward in faith, knowing the difference between miracles and providence.

Directed and Guided

God can use anything He wants in order to direct our paths. Not only is He self-existent but He is also inscrutable, infinite and omnipotent. Who can know His ways? "O the depth of the riches both of the wisdom and knowledge of God! how unsearchable are his judgments, and his ways past finding out! For who hath known the mind of the Lord? or who hath been his counsellor?" *(Romans 11:33-34)*. We are not required to figure out the ways of the Lord, yet we are simply called to follow His ways, His directions and His will for our lives. For thousands of years the Lord Jesus has been simply saying, "Follow Me!" We must act as did Levi, the son of Alphaeus *(Mark 2:14)*, Philip *(John 1:43)*, Simon and Andrew *(Mark 1:17-18)* and James and John *(Mark 1:19-20)*; who all moved accordingly without question.

The Lord gave additional indications of what it is to follow Him: "And he said to them all, If any man will come after me, let him deny himself, and take up his cross daily, and follow me" *(Luke 9:23)*; "... I am the light of the world: he that followeth me shall not walk in darkness, but shall have the light of life" *(John 8:12)*; "My sheep hear my voice, and I know them, and they follow me" *(John 10:27)*; "But Jesus said unto him, Follow me; and let the dead bury their dead" *(Matthew 8:22)*; "Follow me, and I will make you fishers of men" *(Matthew 4:19)*.

(40) On the contrary, far too many of us have been and continue to be directed by the wrong things and often the wrong people. Make note to attend unto this *key*. We often accept word and direction from not only the

strangest sources and places, but far too often we follow the most ungodly sources. Sad to say, even sources inside the church who claim to be so saved can at times be poor sources for receiving proper directions. That is why it is so essential for us to have strong sensitized personal relationships with the Lord. There is no greater source to receive direction than receiving direction from God Himself. Although it is wise to stay close to people with great knowledge, as the Bible instructs, greater is it to get directions through a strong direct vertical connection with the Almighty; for He alone can confirm all directions.

I seek great counsel as I make it known that I endear to receive wise words from wise people. Albeit, I make no bones about telling folk my greatest source of help, strength and direction comes from my Father above. Yes, God will send people into my life to speak, both, over situations and into my living, yet He will not hesitate to speak directly unto my spirit without intervention. The choice is His as to how He relays directions unto me. I've grown to not mind where, what, nor whom He speaks through, as long as I get a word from Him. Oh, to hear a word from Heaven; but I am ever so mindful and guarded. We are responsible to guard our spirits. This _Element_, in and of itself, is a wise word unto someone; saying as the Bible proclaims, "Trust in the Lord with all thine heart; and lean not unto thine own understanding" _(Proverbs 3:5)_.

The fact is, many of us listen to God, but too many of us keep leaning. Picture what I'm saying! We get in the presence of God but our torsos and heads are leaning slightly away from Him. This we do as we adhere to our own understanding; thus, not fully trusting in Him. He can see us leaning. He knows our hearts and our desires. He can see us leaning. This is what minimizes our sensitivity to His voice. He can see us leaning. This is why the fullness of blessings continue to elude our lives. He can surely see us leaning! So, why don't we stop leaning and start fully trusting in Him, so He can guide and direct us. "In all thy ways acknowledge him, and he shall direct thy paths" _(Proverbs 3:6)_.

Word was given to Ahab after he sought God's directions _(II Chronicles 18)_. Yet, Ahab did not heed the message from God through Micaiah and Jehoshaphat, but chose to listen to all the other sources of information that best suited his own desires. We must not only pray to the Lord for answers, but we must heed to His answers; no matter how they may be wrapped or delivered. Makes no sense to pray to God for direction yet refuse to receive it once its given. Signs may even come through the most unlikely and/or most disliked sources. We must know and believe God is in full control and can use whom and what He pleases, when and where He pleases. The _key_ here is to discern and be aware.

Commitment is a Must

The inability to hear from God normally results from non-commitment. "A man's heart deviseth his way: but the Lord directeth his steps" *(Proverbs 16:9)*. A way to help our commitment to keeping our ears harkened unto God begins with making a change in our hearts, minds and spirits. This change emanates from our seeking God with truth in our hearts, while neither being tentative in our minds nor wavering in our spirits. Prayer warriors must be earnest to hear from God and truly willing to be directed by Him. Our having commitment to hear from the Lord is a tremendous must, since a non-commited heart or spirit will vacillate, waver and lean. As we all know, "No man can serve two master: for either he will hate the one, and love the other; or else he will hold to the one, and despise the other. Ye cannot serve God and mammon" *(Matthew 6:24)*. We cannot serve God and ourselves. Our heart's commitment is bound upon our spirit's willingness. These two go hand in hand more than one can imagine. Simply put, if our heart's commitment is torn, then so will our spirit's willingness be torn. All of this affects our spiritual hearing. Who is able to listen to the fullness of the Lord with half an ear? It is difficult enough to pay attention to God with two whole ears, let alone trying to do so as with partial appendages.

Matthew 11:15 says, "He that hath ears to hear, let him hear." It does not say, "He who has some attention," nor does it say, "He who has a portion of interest." The verse even goes as far to say we should harken both ears unto the Lord; not just one or the other. So, do not misunderstand how important it is to be fully committed and willing to listen for directions from God. There are so many distractions in our world today, external and self imposed, which can easily distract us from God's voice. We must make a concerted effort to diligently hear His voice's directions. This is what makes this *Sign Element* so important. Through it all we must still be directed by Him and not motivated by our own desires nor external forces that are not of God. "Know ye that the Lord he is God: it is he that hath made us, and not we ourselves; we are his people, and the sheep of his pasture" *(Psalm 100:3)*. If we are of God how much more ought we recognize that we must be committed to receiving directions from Him?

Listening to the Wrong Things

We listen to just about everything in order to try to make sense of our living. We listen to love songs to get directions on how to please our mates. We listen to the weather station to know how to dress the next day. We listen to our stomachs growl in order to recognize it's beyond time to eat. So, how much more should we listen to God's directions for all our living? He created us and He created this earth, so He knows how everything intertwines. We listen to the Federal Regulators to know what's bad to eat. We listen to the television stars to know the hottest trends in clothing. We listen to so many sources to get supposed understanding on how our lives should play out, yet all these things pail in comparison to the signs and directions given us by God.

The fashion guru's can tell us what is hot and approved to wear for the summer, but God gives direction on what is suitable and profitable in His eyes. Be mindful, for this is a *key.* Man can tell us of temporal things, whereas God gives directions for things eternal. Which will we desire? It may be alright to be fashionable for mere man, but we should desire to be forever in the grace of God. Make no mistake about it, we must listen to He who gives us fruit that is guaranteed not to fade. "For bodily exercise profiteth little: but godliness is profitable unto all things, having promise of the life that now is, and of that which is to come" *(I Timothy 4:8).* "For what is a man profited, if he shall gain the whole world, and lose his own soul? or what shall a man give in exchange for his soul?" *(Matthew 16:26).*

The Lord will grant us increase and directions if we faithfully desire to hear His voice for signs. Again, we do not seek His signs to acknowledge His deity, rather to acknowledge His will for our lives. As well, this is less a new teaching and more having been a misapplied and misunderstood application; for reason most of us have sought signs even from a variety of places other than at the Thrown of Grace and God's voice.

We must develop strong prayer lives and faithful devotionals with the Lord in order to rectify all the noise we listen to on a daily basis. The plethora of noises will drown out the voice of God if we do not diligently mark most of our time with dire attempts to hear from Him. Reverse the old pattern so the voice of God speaking unto us blocks out, or drowns out the worldly edits. It is a given that one of the two sounds will win over the other. Which will it be for us? Will the Lord's voice direct us by way of signs through our prayer lives, or will the world's causes command our steps? Woefully, some of us swear by the world's standards before even considering what saith the Lord; partly due to what we've been improperly taught and partly due to our lack of Christ Spirit within. Both these reasons are attended to within this document, through which it is the Spirit's desire that we gain proper focus.

Our Way of Living Affects our Hearing

The way we live may or may not render our prayers mute unto God, for the choice is His; but sinful living will drown His voice, assuredly. God still answers our prayers, favorably or unfavorably, no matter our living habits, yet the noise caused by the way we live renders our hearing insensitive to His voice and directions. Listen, we will almost always have grand difficulty hearing God's answers to our prayers if the way we live is greatly apposed and obtuse to His character. It can be likened to that of walking pass a construction site in a major city. If too close to the actual construction, the noise can be so boisterous that the warning siren of a fire truck may be drowned. The same is with God trying to speak unto us when we are too close to worldly activities. Our living unto this world (sin) may be so raucous that the Lord's signs are rendered mute.

If we get overly close to the world's way, God will strike some dramatic occurrences in our lives in order to get our attention; instead of turning us over to a reprobate mind, maybe. These dramatic occurrences can include, but are not limited to: losing things that are important to us; the Lord's covering being removed from over us, allowing the wiles of the devil to frustrate our living; the Lord's hand making difficult the things which are normal and easy. The Bible tells us, "But God hath chosen the foolish things of the world to confound the wise; and God hath chosen the weak things of the world to confound the things which are mighty; And base things of the world, and things which are despised, hath God chosen, yea, and things which are not, to bring to nought things that are: That no flesh should glory in his presence" *(I Corinthians 1:27-29).*

It is important to keep our ears sensitized to the Lord's speaking while steering clear of the world's distractions and it's metaphorical construction sites. Living unto the world's ways and standards will pierce our prayers and undercut our faithfulness unto God. How many times have we missed hearing the Lord's voice and directions due to leaning our ears towards the world's noises? It probably can be easily counted by remembering all the times we found ourselves in trouble and in distress. More than likely the Lord tried to warn us before each of those times we fell for the tricks of the devil. It was at each of those moments when the activities in our lives were so deafening that the voice of God could not be heard, nor could His signs be distinguished. I submit on this day we illustrate to God how important to us is our connection with Him by minimizing the noise which surrounds us and which may abound in our spirits. The abounding portion I speak of is the evil, wickedness, sin and plain old fleshy desires that continue to permeate our living.

It is not enough to just have a relationship with the Lord, for all of us surely have some type of relationship with Him, whether it be near or distant. For example, there are those of us who have earthly relationships in which we do not listen to a word the other person says. Most of us have been guilty of that fact at one time or another, if we were to be honest. Technically speaking they are relationships just the same. That is the point. We must grow and develop beyond where we presently reside with God to another level of relationship and communion with Him.

We must go to a level which keeps us sensitized to His voice and directions. A level which empowers our knowledge to wisdom's activity. A level that helps us move along the straight and narrow, dodging the arrows which pierce our faithfulness unto God. A level which says, "God I love You and I will follow You." "Now therefore, if ye will obey my voice indeed, and keep my covenant, then ye shall be a peculiar treasure unto me above all people: for all the earth is mine" *(Exodus 19:5)*.

It is a peculiar people who listen to the voice of God and shun the world's knowledge and standards. It is not popular to follow the voice of God, but it is eternally profitable. Most of us desire to walk in profitable ways. These profitable ways begin and end with our seeking signs from the Lord, while at the same time avoiding the great stumbling block of ages, called "ourselves." We must be mindful that our ways of living can be the very obstacles that prevent us from receiving signs and directions from Heaven. We tend to blame the devil and everyone else, but often it is ourselves who make the choices which then allow distractions to drown out signs from the Almighty. These very choices affect our living and our prayers.

Dialogue

The *Sign Element of the Prayer Progression* can also be stated as a portion of our dialogue with the Lord. Not only is prayer about God hearing from us in acknowledgment, adoration, thanksgiving, praise and worship, but a huge portion of prayer is about us hearing from Him in sign and meditation. Everyone who prays should have a great desire to hear back from the Lord, realizing monologue is not advantageous in our prayer lives. We all must seek to dialogue with the Lord, and to be totally on point, it is better to hear from the Lord than for Him to hear from us. For the Word tells us He already knows what we stand in need even before we pray. "Be not ye therefore like unto them: for your Father knoweth what things ye have need of, before ye ask him" *(Matthew 6:8)*.

This lends us to understand a main importance of prayer is, "How might we hear from Heaven?" This *Element* may be the toughest portion of prayer for many of us to actualize; for it takes a sensitized spirit to recognize a sign and direction from the Lord. Most of us have heard from God through His chastening us, but few of us are in tuned with Him enough to hear His voice and directions outside of mere conviction. Receiving a sign, for many, can be as farfetched as seeing a pot of gold at the end of a rainbow. The inability to fathom a sign from God is mere indication of some folks' lack of faith in God's great power. Let us not be of they who's prayers collapse and fail due to disbelief.

One of the Greatest Signs Given

For two reasons Jesus, in the Olivet Discourse, gave answer to the disciple's request to be given a sign of things to come: first, the disciple's spirits were just; second, He wanted them to be prepared. The Lord desires us, His children, to be of that same just spirit and preparedness. The Lord will surely give us signs if our spirits are just in asking, so we may best understand our surroundings and better understand how to walk in His ways. The disciples were not looking for a miracle to signify Jesus' divinity. On the contrary, they were truly eager to receive understanding from Him. That is to be our position in prayer, as well. This is a _key_.

This discourse is the very scriptural writing which many of us saved folk continue to lean on as understanding that we are now nearing the days of the Lord's return. For years and generations these stated natural disasters and occurrences have increased in number and increased in devastation. These occurrences continue to make us mindful of the end days which are sure to come. This discourse further illustrates our need to ask for and receive signs from on High, and it refutes any statements from they who may claim we are not to ask for signs. Make no mistake of our need to get signs from God in order that we may refrain from leaning on our own fleshy understandings. It is our very fleshy and twisted understandings which continue to get us into trouble on a daily and seem to capture us into a heap of mess on a regular basis. The Bible is quite specific in telling us, "Be not wise in your own conceits" _(Romons 12:16c)._

Truthful Claims of Scripture vs Cliche Artist

Some of the best verses to include in our prayers are those which state things such as; "I will lead thee," "I will direct thee," "The Lord will show thee," "God will make your path," and so on. In the _Request Element_ we spoke of these types of verses in addition to God's promises. There are not many things more potent for our spirit's increase than to know our steps are truly, I say truly, ordered by the Lord and are in accord with His Word. Many of us say, "My steps have been ordered by the Lord," but fact remains we often recite those words only as etiquette, cliche or tradition. There remains such a small number of believers who are truly moved and directed by God, while the larger number of us continue to make false claims of the words. I do declare this very moment, the sooner we truly get on board with the Lord's directing our paths through His signs, the sooner we will be strengthened in our spirits and emboldened as prayer warriors. "Divers weights are an abomination unto the Lord; and a false balance is not good. Man's goings are of the Lord; how can a man then understand his own way?" *(Proverbs 20:23-24).*

Many are called hypocrites due to their out-of-context use of words and scripture, and due to their laying claim to verses that do not reflect in their living. Many of these faithless cry tear at the first and second hint of trouble; trouble originally caused by their faith being rendered useless because of their misuse and abuse of God's Word. The Word of God can empower anyone if it is received in context of what the original writers were given by God, and if the Word is received with faith in God's power to fulfill it. Many are the successes of devils who refuse to empower folk, as they refuse to teach how important it is to truthfully allow the Lord to direct. Many are the sore and unhealed afflictions of they who are bound unto making their own ways through the trials and turmoils of life. "O Lord, I know that the way of man is not of himself: it is not in man that walketh to direct his steps" *(Jeremiah 10:23).*

One of our main deliverances in life occurs when we go beyond simply seeking the Lord. This deliverance I speak of is our submitting to the Lord's directions. A person can seek the Lord all day and all night, but never adhere to His directions upon finding Him; thus much searching is negated. What a shame it is for someone to spend so much time and effort seeking the Lord, only to ignore His directions once they are found of Him. Believers must tap into one of our greatest blessings; being directed by God. "The steps of a good man are ordered by the Lord: and he delighteth in his way" *(Psalm 37:23).*

Often the Lord gives us wisdom for living through His Word, such as written in Psalm 119:133, "Order my steps in thy word: and let not any iniquity have dominion over me." It must be reiterated, in order to be directed and convicted by the Word we must first be attuned with His Spirit. "If we live in the Spirit, let us also walk in the Spirit" *(Galatians 5:25).* How else might we best walk in the Spirit then by the act of being directed by the Spirit and receiving signs? We must be led by the Spirit in order to best ensure we are on the right course. How else might we have strong faith lest we are certain our steps are being directed by the Lord?

Many people, especially the secular, claim their conscious told them which ways to go in life. This type of secular thinking has tainted our minds and diminished the power of our being led by the Holy Spirit.

True believers know this voice to be the Spirit of the Living God and not just any internal sound. It is the Spirit's directing which sends us to blessings and diverts us from trouble. This directing is often achieved through signs given unto folk who are sensitized. We must be sensitized!

Signs may come to us as loud, obvious and overtly noticeable, or they may come to us as faint indications of wisdom through the Word of God; to name just a few ways. The true blessing resides in our having the ability to be directed by the Lord in many forms, fashions and ways. But, some folk go to the extreme by falsely claiming some actions as movements of God in their lives; partly caused by their overzealous hearts. It is overzealousness that carries a many folk into a realm of false prophesy, misguided prophecy, and cliche type claims.

We must be mindful of God's directing hand so not to be misguided nor overzealous about unfruitful personal impulses. So many folk retract their steps after first claiming God to have ordered those very steps; in a sense claiming the Lord a liar through their own fickle evil. These types of superficial professors may never tell the truth that they have never heard God's directions and that they are listening to their own cliche'd claims, only. These false witnesses testify against themselves. I urge us all to be leery of persons who first claim to be directed by God, only to move in a different direction shortly thereafter, deserting the very word they first claimed as being from God. The Lord's directing is perfect and is not to be abandoned nor forsaken; even when He leads us into trials.

Staying the Course

As true believers we should be very mindful not to abandon the word and directions given by God. This is a *key*. If we pray to God and receive directions from Him, then stay the course and do not prove God a liar. What would have happened to a chosen people if Noah had abandoned God's directions after say ten years, thirty years, or even ninety years of building the Ark? Noah was steadfast for one hundred and twenty years unto God's directions pertaining to the Ark. What may have happened to a chosen people had Moses forsaken God's directions and returned to a plush living in Egypt after five, twenty or thirty years of living at the foot of the mountain? Likewise, Moses could have abandoned God's signs and directions after being in the wilderness for two, ten or even thirty-five years. It would have been humanly easy for Moses to stop following God's directions since the people had been unruly and since other nations were mocking them. Let me make this point and key a little more personal. There were many matriarchs, patriarchs and other Biblical characters who did not waver from God's directions and signs, but none more important than our Lord and Saviour Jesus. What if our Lord had abandoned the Father's directions when doubted by His earthly family? What would have become of you and I had the Lord said, "Forget it, I'm done with this" and turned tail when the keepers of the Law sought to disprove His deity? Where would we be if the Lord had decided to come down from the cross, thinking the Father was wrong in His directing?

It was not always easy for those chosen vessels, and at times the very results of God's directing may not have been very clear to them. Through it all they remained faithful unto the words and directions God placed upon their spirits. It is truly a wicked and disobedient person who claims God's directions to have come to them, only to turn wayward from that direction when things do not seem to add up perfectly according to human reasoning. Always remember, God's ways are not our ways. Let us all be willing vessels, sensitized to the Lord's directions and signs. Let us all be committed and convinced that the Lord's directions are perfect.

King David said this strongly,
"For I have kept the ways of the Lord, and have not wickedly departed from my God. For all his judgments were before me: and as for his statues, I did not depart from them. I was also upright before him, and have kept myself from mine iniquity. Therefore the Lord hath recompensed me according to my righteousness; according to my cleanness in his eye sight. With the merciful thou wilt shew thyself merciful, and with the upright man thou wilt shew thyself upright. With the pure thou wilt shew thyself pure; and with the froward thou wilt shew thyself unsavoury. And the afflicted people thou wilt save: but thine eyes are upon the haughty, that thou mayest bring them down. For thou art my lamp, O Lord: and the Lord will lighten my darkness. For by thee I have run through a troop: by my God have I leaped over a wall. As for God, his way is perfect; the word of the Lord is tried: he is a buckler to all them that trust in him. For who is God, save the Lord? and who is a rock, save our God? God is my strength and power: and he maketh my way perfect" (II Samuel 22:22-33).

To What Are You Listening?

Yes, the Lord speaks to our spirits on a daily, and more often than one might imagine. The fact is, far too many folk speak so loudly to themselves that they lack the ability to hear God's signs; especially when the signs are given in a soft voice or a subtle movement. We must realize the difference between being directed by our souls' desires and that of being ordered by the Lord's Spirit.

Truth is many folk claim, "The Lord confirmed my direction by this sign" or "Today the Lord sent this woman to tell me such and such, which confirms that I should do a certain thing." Most often, God will not first send others to give us signs for our life's movements. Do not get me wrong, God will send directions and signs through others, as happened on many occasions with Biblical characters; such as, with the prophets and kings, Ananias and Paul, John the Baptist and Jesus, and others. Even so I say again, <u>most often</u> the Lord will not first send such signs and directions through others instead of through our individual spirits, for two reasons. First, God desires that we individually stand extremely close to Him, as He desires us to be highly sensitized to His Spirit. Most often He chooses not to yell directions so loudly that we would be comfortably confident in hearing and believing, nor does He choose for us to rely heavily on hearing His directions from anyone other than Himself. More will be spoken on these precepts in just a moment. Both of the above modes of communication indicate a distance or a barrier between God and us, whereas, God does not desire to speak to us from a distance nor does He desire to have anything impede the connection between He and us. He will give us signs through others if need be, of course, but His grand desire is for us all to be closer than close to Him in spirit. Make every effort to digest this wisdom.

Second, God desires we move upon His signs with faith in His power. Best believe His signs most often will not be distinguished with one hundred percent confirmations. Let me make this clearer. The Lord will surely give us signs for directions, but He does not want us to worship the signs nor does He desire that we wholeheartedly rely on the sign; void Him. Rather, He wants us to have faith in His hands. This is the place where our sensitivity to the Spirit is so essential. Listening to our neighbor's intermediate voices and the loudness of our own flesh can cause difficulties and eventual pains. Understand, our neighbor's voices can even be directed by the devil in an attempt to move us in the wrong directions and appose the will of God. Sensitivity to God's Spirit weighs heavily on our knowing God's nature and character. Yes, the Lord's ways are most often mysterious, but He is plain and concrete in His nature and attributes. We can be greatly sensitized to the Lord's voice and signs if we would gain more knowledge of His attributes; which are spoken of at greater length in the chapter on *Attributes, Character and Nature of God.*

We can gain further sensitivity to the Lord's voice by spending more quality time with Him, as well. Some of us simply do not spend enough time with Him to be able to recognize His voice nor His ways. "Jesus answered them, I told you, and ye believed not: the works that I do in my Father's name, they bear witness of me. But ye believe not, because ye are not of my sheep, as I said unto you. My sheep hear my voice, and I know them, and they follow me" *(John 10:25-27).* "He that is of God heareth God's words: ye therefore hear them not, because ye are not of

God" *(John 8:47)*. "And when he putteth forth his own sheep, he goeth before them, and the sheep follow him: for they know his voice" *(John 10:4)*. This is a simple principle that is rarely taught with power sustaining: the sheep know the shepherd's voice and ways, because they spend most of their day in his presence. Let me repeat that - the sheep spend most of their day's hours in the presence of the shepherd. This is the greatest manner in which we will be empowered to recognize the Lord's voice's directions and signs. When was the last time you meditated on the Lord for fifteen hours out of a twenty-four hour day?

I often cringe when someone says how crystal clear God's signs have been given them. This I say, because most of us in this modern day are not close enough to the Lord to know anything definite about Him nor His ways. As well, the Lord would not remove from our midst that very thing which He most desires of us; our faith in Him. Listen, by making some things crystal there is a removal of a large portion of faith's illustration, thereafter. I will say this much, often God strongly confirms our movement only after we have taken a step of faith to move upon His giving us an initial faint sign. This is a *key* for us all to understand.

For most of us who are attuned with what's being said here, the next question becomes, "So Reverend your telling us signs are few and far between?" The answer is this — the Lord's signs and directions are numerous and of many facets and ways, but they are most often more faint than we think; earshot that we can still hear, but faint enough that we must get closer to Him in order to discern and understand. Also, signs are often faint enough that after we receive them we must walk by faith in He who sent the sign rather than lean wholeheartedly on the sign itself. This may seem deep for the unengaged spirit, but as we grow in this document we will grow in His Spirit, as well. "For in Him we live, and move, and have our being ..." *(Acts 17:28)*. Let us not be eager to receive signs in our own conceits, but truly seek them in the Spirit of Christ. This I say, since not one of us has ever found the Lord; for He is the One whom found us. The Lord makes Himself, His wisdom and His signs known in tremendous ways once we begin to seek Him in truth.

God's Directions

Being directed by God should be our spirits' and hearts' sole desire in prayer. We most often worship the Lord for the things He does for us, but very seldom are we rejoicing to be His servants; directed by His voice, signs and will. Even the most devout Christians are often less celebratory when it comes to being directed by God's great will. Our shouts of hallelujah often begin and end with, "How great Thou art unto me," and

"How glorious are Your great blessings." Our hearts should feel that one of the greatest blessings that can be bestowed unto us is for the Lord to use us in His great work of redemption. How full would our joy be if we would only submit to His directions and guidance? Our serving Him strongly begins by our first receiving His directions. Let it be known, God can direct us through speaking to our spirits and giving us physical signs, if we desire and seek to be used by Him.

Prayers should be filled with request that our spirits be made more receptive to God's voice and signs. Let us transition our spirits from always needing to pray for incidental blessings, asked through our immature spirits, to that of our desiring to pray with an eternal purpose driven by an understanding of what true blessings include.

Traditionally, we are taught to serve God through reading and adhering to His Word; the Bible. Far too few teachers go to the further extent to guide believers to truthfully seek to hear God's voice and to attentively watch for His signs. As believers, we miss out on a major aspect of our relationships with God when we forsake His signs. The written Word surely convicts us, directs our morality, and molds our desires through covenants; whereas, God's voice and signs increase our abilities to be used by Him in complement to the Bible. "For the eyes of the Lord run to and fro throughout the whole earth, to shew himself strong in the behalf of them whose heart is perfect toward him..." *(II Chronicles 16:9a)*.

David was directed by God and faithfully leaned on the Lord's directions as he wrote, "Even there shall thy hand lead me, and thy right hand shall hold me" *(Psalm 139:10)*. Gideon sought a sign from the Lord, although his asking for direction bordered on asking for a confirmational miracle to solidify his faith in God's ability. We must be mindful, as previously mentioned, not to need confirmation that God is the great I Am. Chapter 6 of Judges is filled with a conversation between God and Gideon illustrating how we must be sure that our actions are directed by the Lord. Gideon personally had some issues with his own abilities and strength of character; which can be viewed either as his being weak and incapable, or conversely it can be seen as his having faith in the victory that could be had through his being obedient unto God's directions, only. Believers are often looked upon as weak when we move upon the Lord's directions. Fact is, we should consider ourselves as finite beings in need of the Lord's directions. Obedience unto the Father's voice often begins with our ability to recognize who we are not and with our acknowledging our dependence on Him. Gideon can be seen as doing these very acts. We, like Gideon, face major enemies, so we too must remain determined not to move without certainty of our being led by God. Many of our failures in life have come by way of our acting without God's ordained hand. Receiving signs of direction from the Lord can better ensure our victory over any enemy or foe. "For thou art my rock and my fortress; therefore for thy name's sake lead me, and guide me" _(Psalm 31:3)._

So many of us talk and even sing songs about the Lord's leading us, but few of us energetically and truthfully try to hear from Him for direction and guidance. On the one hand, many of us secretly love the sinful and misguided ways we live, which is confirmed by our unwillingness to seek God's directions in the first place. It is simple to equate that whosoever truly desires to succeed in their being changed will assuredly seek God's directions. On the other hand, others of us think hearing from God is so "Woo;" thus we keep an arm's length distance from Him. Such a shame we live in a time and age when people believe in werewolves and vampires, but refuse to believe in the Creator of Heaven and Earth. To that I say, "Wow!" Two of the devil's tricks are to, one, make us disbelieve he and God even exist, and two, make us ashamed to know the Lord personally. Any of us can become stronger in our hearing from God, if we can get beyond those two wicked tactics used by the devil. To enhance our abilities to hear from God we must first believe He exist, and second, not be ashamed to claim Him. Then, and only then, will our ears, eyes and spirits begin to gain sensitivity to the Lord's voice and signs.

The majority of us live in the world of denial, saying, "I don't want others to think I'm out of my wits by claiming to have heard from God." I declare this very day, "Get over it, and enjoy a fruitful and blessed relationship that can be had only with the Lord our God." This is a _key_ for us all to hurdle. Some of us come out of the runner's starter blocks with a blast, yet refuse to jump over this first hurdle. The Lord Jesus proclaimed, "Whosoever therefore shall be ashamed of me and of my words in this adulterous and sinful generation; of him also shall the Son of man be ashamed, when he cometh in the glory of his Father with the holy angels" _(Mark 8:38)._

It is a reality that the Lord still speaks to us all the time through signs. It can be said that we refuse to hear from God, pray tell, all the time. Prayer warriors must seek to receive signs from the Lord, which can come by way of many means and vehicles. "For as many as are led by the Spirit of God, they are the sons of God" _(Romans 8:14)._ Let us truly understand there are dangers to not listening to the directions of God. There is no gray area. Either we are listening to the Lord and walking in accord with His directions and signs, or we are heeding the ways of a sinful world while walking in step with wayward thoughts and fleshy desires. No ifs, ands, nor buts about it. Lightheartedly, I can imagine the Lord saying,

"Either you is or you ain't my baby!" But, we do know the Lord's chastening can be more harsh than that. Let us be found seeking His directions before He decides to chasten us in order to get our greater attention.

"Let wisdom be our guide," shouts many lessons throughout the Bible; most of which are written within the great Books of Poetry. So, what is it we ought do when our flesh gets the best of our rationale? There are those who deny we battle our flesh minute by minute and on a daily basis. Yet, the fact remains we are condemned to our flesh until the Lord returns to escort us to glory. We must lean on the Lord's directions every minute of every day, in order to best secure victory over sin, and to best do His will. Our prayer lives must not be void of our concentrating on the Lord's directions. Our most fruitful prayers are those which center heavy attention on our hearing from God instead of our pouring our souls out to Him in dire hopes of receiving a gift or some other general blessing. This is a *key.* Throughout our communing with God we should continuously focus on hearing from Him. Our posture of seeking His voice in the *Elements of Sign and Meditation* should reflect our very desire to be directed by Him.

Remaining focused on the Lord can be difficult at times. Let us be mindful that even when it is not our own flesh which wars against us and causes us to take our focus off God, there are greater enemies which lurk around the corner trying their best to disrupt our spiritual connection with Him. We must become more spiritually trained for all the battles within and without. "For we wrestle not against flesh and blood, but against principalities, against powers, against the rulers of darkness of this world, against spiritual wickedness in high places" *(Ephesians 6:12).* The subsequent verses proceed to tell us of the importance of being girded up with the full armour of God and they commence by telling us of the necessity for prayer and supplication. I say this day, a major part of prayer is to hear from God more so than to speak to Him. The Word tells us the Lord already knows our hearts and of what we stand in need before we pray. Therefore, we must complete the circle of fellowship by taking time to listen for His responses and directions, and we must disallow distractions to rise as road blocks to that hearing. Far too few of us wait in meditation for God's directions <u>after</u> praying, and even fewer folk attempt to pay attention to the signs God may give us <u>throughout</u> our time of prayer. Needless to say how little we seek to hear from him throughout the balance of our day.

(48) Also, I believe in my spirit God so desires us to have victory, so much that He's mindful to send us signs, directions and convictions more readily when our wisdom and faith are failing. Take heed for this is a *key.*

We all can testify of those moments when we are at our weakest and most worldly. It is in those moments when we attempt to lean on prayer, scripture and even the words of other believers. It is natural for believers to make those attempts. And, let it be known it is very essential to be able to lean on those supports so to best ensure our success during this walk of faith. It can be said many of us try to lean on God and the scriptures only in times of need, but let it be understood we must diligently seek the Lord's voice and signs during good times, also. In both instances He knows we lack the ability to make it through on our own wisdom. It is in those very moments when the Lord faithfully attempts to move us and direct us unto victory. "... for when I am weak, then am I strong" (*II Corinthians 12:10*). The Lord knows how difficult it may be for us to hear His voice at times; especially when the noises around us desensitize our spiritual hearing. It is a sad scenario that we often allow those distractions to block our abilities to take advantage of some of the greatest gifts God provides unto us. Those gifts are the Lord's directions by way of His Spirit, voice and signs. Surely, it is not the case that the Lord is not speaking to us. It is often the case that we stop listening as the distractions, in good times and in bad times, are allowed to overbear our spiritual hearing.

As believers we should truly have faith in God's undying attempts to ward us from dangers and to direct us into His will. It is just as important, if not more important, for us to be directed in His will as it is for us to be directed out of perils. We have free will, but the Word and faith also tell us His hand strongly urges us in the path of righteousness. He loves us that much! He even went to the extent of giving us His Son Jesus.

The Bible says;
"And you hath he quickened, who were dead in trespasses and sins; Wherein in time past ye walked according to the course of this world, according to the prince of the power of the air, the spirit that now worketh in the children of disobedience: Among whom also we all had our conversation in times past in the lusts of our flesh, fulfilling the desires of the flesh and of the mind; and were by nature the children of wrath, even as others. But God, who is rich in mercy, for his great love wherewith he loved us, Even when we were dead in sins, hath quickened us together with Christ, (by grace ye are saved;) And hath raised us up together, and made us sit together in heavenly places in Christ Jesus: That in the ages to come he might shew the exceeding riches of his grace in his kindness toward us through Christ Jesus. For by grace are ye saved through faith; and that not of yourselves: it is the gift of God: Not of works, lest any man should boast. For we are his workmanship, created in Christ Jesus unto good works, which God hath before ordained that we should walk in them" (Ephesians 2:1-10).

Make or Break

For two reasons a sign is make or break for us all. First, a sign from the Lord can give us the confidence and reassurance needed to make difficult decisions, and it can encourage us to hang in there when times get tough. It is an unbeatable assurance to know the Lord is directing our paths. This assurance is possible only if we first trust in Him, His signs and His directions. There is no assurance if there is no trust. It is an unbeatable combination and a great uplift to our faith when we trust in Him and allow Him to direct us by way of signs. It is an unbeatable and awesome life we live when we live by faith in the Lord and His signs.

Many mountains have been moved in many of our lives simply by the faith we have had in our Lord and Savior. On the contrary, many of us continue to falter and stumble through life's twist and turns due to our disbelief in God and our disconnect from His Son. "And Jesus said unto them, Because of your unbelief: for verily I say unto you, If ye have faith as a grain of mustard seed, ye shall say unto this mountain, Remove hence to yonder place; and it shall remove; and nothing shall be impossible unto you" *(Matthew 17:20)*. I'm sure we all have some mountains we would like to move out of our lives. Best believe we will have the ability to move those mountains if the Lord proclaimed it possible. If we are incapable of moving mole hills or mountains, it may be that we lack the necessary faith in His signs and directions. How magnificent is our God to give us the *key* to victory! Follow His lead and follow His signs; in faith.

Feeling alone is an emotion that rocks everyone's faith at one point or another. Fact is, everything may seem ok in life until there is a feeling of being alone. The ultimate cure for that feeling is to receive signs and directions from God; indicating at that moment we are not alone. Often, all we need to make it through to another day is to be assured that God is with us and directing our steps. I personally feel empowered when I feel the presence of the Lord directing my life. I can surely shout the scripture that tells, "With man it is impossible, but with God all things are possible" *(Matthew 19:26)*. Prayer warriors can move mountains with God's signs!

A feeling of "possibility" is made evident through the presence of the Lord by way of His sign's directions. What better way to live an empowered life than by living with God's hand directing our steps? This is made manifest when we pray for God's signs, then move upon them with faith and power knowing He is in full control and fully able. I am most encouraged and empowered when I can feel the presence of the Lord upon me. I know someone else can testify of that truth, as well. No greater time is His hand upon my being than when He gives me a sign to direct my ways. It is the Lord's will that we walk into our destinies; thus He sends us signs to best assure the path of our steps. Walk in!

It is the Lord's will for us to walk into victory, yet we act as if we do not want victory. I say this because we pay so little attention to the very signs He sends us; the very signs which are intended to deliver us into our destinies. It is hoped someone is being helped within these pages, for these words are written to bring forth deliverance and blessedness. The very blessedness of God. Let me take this point just a little further. We cannot walk boldly, as we should, unless we are assured of our steps. It is a simple concept and a basic truth that we walk lightly in those areas we are most tentative. If we are confident we are walking with the Lord, we will have no reservations and no hesitations about the steps we take and the directions we are headed. We will feel empowered and walk more boldly as long as we believe we are walking according to the steps He has laid. Thus, it would behoove us to receive signs from God.

In His leading we can be assured of where it is we are going. This is true solely because of who is leading. There it is! We must be led by the Lord. Many a ill-gotten path are laid forth by the wickedness of men. "Many sorrows shall be the wicked: but he that trusteth in the Lord, mercy shall compass him about" *(Psalm 32:10)*. A favorite hymn is "Blessed Assurance," especially because of the first few words. "Blessed assurance Jesus is mine." Oh, that in itself is enough to get me over. I love the entire song, but it begins right where our spirits ought reside. Jesus Himself makes this point even clearer, "I am the vine, ye are the branches: He that abideth in me, and I in him, the same bringeth forth much fruit: for without me ye can do nothing" *(John 15:5)*. Our faith should rest on the fact that we can do absolutely nothing without the directions and provisions of the Lord through His signs.

Having assurance, or not, can be make or break for our faith. No assurance, no faith. Fact is we will pray with little faith if there is no assurance in He unto whom we pray. It is that simple to understand. It is easy to shout, "Jesus is my assurance," but what happens to our boats built of wood once the stormy sea billows roll? What is it we do when the turmoil and the strife erupts in the midst of our day? "I stand and still stand," is the cry of they who have faith and assurance that the Lord is directing their steps through signs; although the way may seem bumpy and shaky. We can and will stand through the storms when we are assured that the Lord is, not only, in our lives, but that He is directing our lives, as well. We can go with boldness if we know it is the Lord who is leading us — because we first trust in Him. If we trust in the Lord, our assurance shall rise as His signs move us with their intended power and purpose. Otherwise, we will continue to be broken by life's ups and downs, as the devil continues to plot against our success.

The second reason signs from the Lord are make it or break it for us all is simply that the presence of God's signs can give us victory while the lack thereof can cause us to travel wrong roads in life. Sounds simple; as it is. Yet, often we must hear wisdom before we move upon wisdom. Oh, the stony roads we have traveled in darkness on account that those roads were not first ordained by God. It is an impossibility for us to go wrong if we keep walking in the direction and ways God points out through His signs. That has been and will always be make it or break it for us. Seek the Lord's signs and we will be victorious! Go without the Lord's directions and, sooner or later, we will surely be broken. Our ways may seem ok to a point, but rest assured the devil is busy; although he is a liar and is without truth. The devil's ploy is to pleasantly lure us in another direction only to later break us and kill all that we are. Are we being directed by God's signs, or are the devil's ploys luring us? We must ask ourselves which side of that simple question and equation do we reside? At this point, I would've loved to have inserted fifty blank pages so readers could get the full effect of that last statement. Instead, I submit this question unto all — To whom are you listening and unto what signs are you moving?

Some of our lives continue to be broken for our neglect to move in accord with the Lord's signs. God can make a way out of our no way simply by our following His signs. It is hoped that everyone understands how blessed our lives will be once we truly tap into walking in the directions God set forth for our lives by signs. Our prayer lives will be blessed and our spiritual lives will blossom if we would ever connect to His signs. If it is a desire to make the devil mad, simply begin to follow God's signs and ignore the enemy's wicked wiles. Just get connected then watch the devil go nuts! Many of us are so broken in our lives because we are so disconnected from receiving the Lord's signs and directions; making the devil happy. These facts are true also: many of us have lives unhindered by the devil's wiles because we already are not living in line with God's signs; just as there are those of us who's lives are wrecked with strife caused by a devil who's mad that we are following God's signs versus following his evil ways. Which is your case?

50 Here is a *key* for us all. Many of our prayers have been answered by God, but we never received the blessing because we missed the signs He provided in response to our prayers. Let me say it this way. Many of us have been successful in prayer by means of getting God's attention and getting Him to respond, yet, we ultimately failed due to our neglect to connect with His response which came by means of signs.

Many of us are lost and broken because we are not being led by the Lord. Oh, I say that with much power, strength, conviction and love. Be aware that we also can be broken in what appears as success. The brokenness in our lives can be mended by our following that which the Lord tells us through His signs. He is giving someone a sign right now, but that person refuses to take heed; thus, he or she will continue to live in brokenness. Weighing in the balance of our true success is our ability to, first, seek signs from the most High God through prayer, then second, act upon those signs with the assurance that He alone is faithful unto His directing us. The fact is, we can correctly speak and do many things in prayer, but ultimately render our prayer fruitless by failing to heed to God and His directing response. The fruit comes by way of our prayers being answered and by our lives being changed as we move upon God's signs.

It is truly hoped that this document press upon our spirits how our prayers are blessed and empowered when we merely receive of the Lord Himself. Let it be that we truthfully seek signs in prayer, yet let our ultimate goal be to receive Him. This is a major point for us to remember, since many of our prayers are answered indirectly through our living unto Christ. Our faith, living and prayers will be blessed tremendously if we would only receive of this *key*.

It is prayer's ultimate goal for it to be heard of and answered by God. Yes, it is a great blessing to receive increase in our lives through prayer, but our intentions in prayer should be to get a favorable answer from God, which does not always involve the comfortable increase we tend to desire; as proclaimed in the Chapter of *Discernment*. Also, it is hoped this document press upon our spirits the importance of how we are to solidify our prayers by our actually adhering to God's directing answers. It is a shame to cry out to God in a monologue fashion, refusing to acknowledge the fact that prayer and relationship with God is a two-way street or dialogue. I say "is," for prayer is a larger basis of the relationship. If prayer is ever to be a monologue, let it be God speaking and not us; for He has so much more to say than we ever could say in a million years.

Live a life directed by God's signs and Word, and live a life full of the goodness of Christ Jesus. That is all we really need in our prayers - His goodness. It is truth that we do not have the capacity to receive all His goodness, so what more might we need? Let me tell it! In His goodness we have His grace and His mercy. In His goodness we have His ever loving kindness. In His goodness we have joy and peace. We will find ourselves greatly blessed if we could, and would, just receive of His goodness. Be led and be blessed! Be leery and be broken.

A Biblical Illustration of Sign

The story of Gideon's fleece of wool is a Biblical illustration of how servants of the Lord, including we modern-day saints, are to operate within signs provided by God. Judges Chapter 6 tells us how Gideon wanted to be assured that God wanted him to go into battle. The story is filled with great illustrations of Gideon's communal relationship with God: he was sensitized to hear the Lord's voice *(vv11-17, 21-23, 34)*; he was strengthened by his willingness to praise and honour the Lord *(vv19, 24, 26)*; he was thankful to do the Lord's will *(vv17, 19-20, 34)*; and he was willing to wait on the Lord's directions while he stayed the course *(v18)*.

This story is a great testimony since Gideon, like many of us, was slightly tentative in his abilities. He loved and worshiped the Lord, but he was not always so sure in his faith walk. A number of us who have tremendous calls on our lives can testify that the magnitude of our God appointed and God gifted assignments can be a tad bit frightening, yet exciting. Gideon felt this pressure and it drove him to eagerly be assured of the direction God was sending him; thus he was moved to get a sign through the dew and fleece of wool. Verse 39 tells us one of two things, or both: first, Gideon was aware that he should have followed the first sign given by God and not possibly angered God by asking for a second sign; second, Gideon had a dire eagerness to be fully assured to move in the direction God was setting forth. Some may go as far to view him as being weak as a believer, yet we shall believe at that juncture in his faith walk with God it was his reverence for God which drove his tentative behavior. We too must be sensitized, committed and eager to move according to God's will for our lives. Gideon's motivation to receive a sign was to ensure to do God's will and not to prove God's deity. Through it all Gideon did as the Lord said; although it went against popular belief and, supposed, better human judgment. Let us be mindful and bold in humility to ask for signs from God then move powerfully upon His directions. Not only will we be blessed by walking in the will of God, but those around us shall ultimately be blessed as well.

SIGN — *Progression of Prayer Element #6*

Exercises

INSTRUCTIONAL

1. Read the definitions of the words dialogue and monologue in the dictionary. Write a short paragraph using at least three words from the definitions as the theme of your writing. Indicate within the paragraph the reason dialogue in prayer is so very important.

BENEFIT:
To stress the importance of our need to have dialogue with God in prayer; making transition from monologues of tear sessions only.

PERSONAL

1. Pray these items unto God each day this week upon waking in the morning and before going to bed at night: Pray that He bless you with a spirit that is receptive of His voice's directions and thank Him in advance for all the signs He shall give unto you in the day to come. Be mindful to include mention that you shall praise His name all the days.

BENEFIT:
To create a covenant with God in regards to His blessing your spiritual ears, your spiritual sensitivity and your willingness to glorify His name. As well, the daily prayer of this matter should remind us that nothing is done in our lives unless God blesses it to be so.

SIGN — *Progression of Prayer Element #6*

General Questions

1. With what does our faithfulness in prayer begin?

2. What is the main importance of prayer?

   Why?

3. Our inability to fathom receiving a sign from God can be an indication of what?

4. Why did Jesus proclaim no sign would be given to this wicked generation?

5. What is the definition of sign?

6. What are two main reasons signs were requested during Jesus' earthly ministry?

7. What can we do in order to discern the Lord's voice and signs amidst all the distractions which surround us?

8. What do we mistakenly call miracles in this modern day?

9. Why was Ahab unsuccessful even though he sought God's directions?

10. What should we pray to receive instead of requesting incidentals and possessions?

SIGN – Progression of Prayer Element #6

Advanced Questions

1. What is another term which can describe the *Sign Element of the Progression of Prayer?*

   Write a short paragraph as to why this is one of the main importance' of prayer?

2. Choose a scripture from the "Why" section at the beginning of this chapter. Write a short paragraph as to the effect of this scripture if we neglect to have dialogue with the Lord?

3. With what does one of our main deliverance' begin? After which, to what must we commit?

   How are these two acts reflected in Galatians 5:25?

Pre-Praise Thanksgiving

Pray this prayer with me:
A Prayer for Pre-Praise Thanksgiving

"Everlasting, always available Lord. You are the joy in my spirit, the blessedness in my living, the sun in my day and the smile upon my heart. For all this and more, I simply must praise You. Glory! I have great thanks in my spirit for all You've done for this Your servant, yet I get so extremely excited to give You pre-praise thanksgiving for all You are about to accomplish in me, through me and for Your kingdom's sake. I am sold out to know You are a game changer who can right every wrong ship and turn around any situation. At this moment, it is hoped You will grant me additional increase by the reading of this *Chapter on Pre-Praise Thanksgiving*. Grant unto me the blessed increase needed to glorify Your Holy name in advance of Your showing any of Your power in my situations and circumstances. Let it be a testimony of faith that Your name shall be praised all the more for things unseen and things yet to happen. Increase in me. Oh, increase in me. This I pray with praise in the glorious and matchless name of the Son Jesus — Amen."

This section is to better enhance our understanding of the Biblical reasons for who should give pre-praise, how should pre-praise be given, why should pre-praise be given, what should be given pre-praise, where should pre-praise be given and when should pre-praise be given. Our study of pre-praise thanksgiving will be further enhanced if these verses are read previous to moving onto the chapter material; as this format will indeed better prepare our spirits to receive of the chapter material.

1) WHO should give pre-praise?
   - I Chronicles 16:8-11 — hose who seek the Lord
   - II Chronicles 29:31 — The congregation
   - John 12:27-28 — The Lord Jesus
   - I Corinthians 15:57-58 — Us; the brethren

2) HOW should pre-praise be given?
   - I Chronicles 16:10 — With the heart and rejoicing
   - I Chronicles 23:30 — As commanded
   - II Chronicles 29:31 — With a free heart
   - Luke 18:38-39 — With a repented heart; loudly and unashamedly
   - Philippians 4:6 — Make it know unto God
   - Philemon 4 — Making mention always in prayers

3) WHY should pre-praise be given?
   - I Chronicles 29:14 — Because all things come from God
   - II Chronicles 20:22 — So the Lord will fight your battles
   - II Chronicles 29:31 — For consecration and submission unto
           God's will
   - II Chronicles 33:16 — In serving the Lord
   - Psalm 50:23 — To glorify God
   - Psalm 86:6-10 — Because the Lord will answer
   - John 12:27-28 — Pre-ordained by God
   - I Corinthians 15:57 — Because we will have the victory
   - I Corinthians 15:58 — So we may be stedfast, unmovable and
           always abounding in the work of the Lord
   - I Thessalonians 5:18 — It is the will of God

4) WHAT should be given pre-praise?
   - II Chronicles 29:13 — His glorious name and God Himself
   - I Corinthians 15:57 — To God

5) WHERE should pre-praise be given?
- I Chronicles 16:8-11 — Among the people
- II Chronicles 29:31 — In the house of the Lord; Near
- John 12:27-29 — In the presence of others
- Philippians 4:6 — In everything
- I Thessalonians 5:18 — In everything
- II Thessalonians 1:3 — In the sight of God our Father

6) WHEN should pre-praise be given?
- I Chronicles 16:8-11 — While seeking the Lord; When calling upon His name
- I Chronicles 23:30 — In the morning, evening, Sabbaths, New Moons, Feast, continually
- Psalm 86:6-10 — When praying
- John 12:27-28 — When your soul is troubled
- Philippians 4:6 — When praying and making supplication; in everything (previous to receiving)
- I Thessalonians 5:18 — In everything

Glory Unto His Holy Name!

"Be careful for nothing; but in every thing by prayer and supplication
with thanksgiving let your requests be made known unto God. "
Philippians 4:6

Pre-praise thanksgiving is advance celebration in the form of thanks, for blessings and victories unseen, yet soon to come. "Now faith is the substance of things hoped for and the evidence of things not seen" *(Hebrews 11:1)*. It is not something conjured with the hope that something wished may occur. Pre-praise is a testimony of faith that is empowered by, both, a belief in God's power and His willingness to show up to provide in His own way, and a belief that we shall be made better because of it. It is this assurance and confidence which spurs believers to give God praise and thanks far in advance of the realization of any blessing or any deliverance. Through the *Prayer Progression* believers' spirits are heightened in the Lord in order that they may speak things which be not as though they were *(Romans 4:17)*. Pre-praise thanksgiving is an act of faith and a tribute unto God that gives Him the glory and the honour for the things that shall soon come to pass. These acts of faith are bound in two truths that are set in the spirits of believers while in prayer: the fact that God is in full control; and He can do all things, but fail.

Honour and Glory are God's

Giving God pre-praise in the presence of other people acts as a public acknowledgment and testimony of God's deity and power. The fact is, God will get the greatest honor and glory when we are delivered, if we do two things: announce in advance that our situations are in His hands; and proclaim His soon to come victory over the said situations. Many of us are still in dire and tough situations simply because we have yet to give the Lord pre-praise thanksgiving. Some of us refuse to put faith in the Lord's delivering power, while others flat out refuse to give Him the honour once they are delivered out of trials. The Lord knows we have the propensity to toot our own horns once we are blessed, when we neglect to give Him praise in advance. You know who you are! This is a *key* to great prayer power. Yes, some of us forget to give the Lord thanks and honour once we are blessed. Oh, you Israelite of old! But, let a problem arise again and there you go running to the Lord for help, unashamedly.

A way of receiving unfavorable answers to prayers is to refuse to give God honour through pre-praise. This wisdom is supported by facts and scriptures throughout this chapter. For instance, we all should be aware of the fact that God is a jealous God and desires all the glory. Blessings are not of our own doings, but by the will of God we are healed, covered, given increase or decrease, strengthened, protected, etc.

We must not get so full of ourselves to think anything to be accomplished in our lives will be done by our power. We are highly favored as His children, but we are not the Most High. Do not think for one moment we have any ability to do anything outside of failing when we operate on our own. God is fully aware He has all power in Heaven and Earth, but I am sure it is good to His hearing when we acknowledge His greatness by faith through pre-praise. He is God and God alone whether you and I acknowledge Him as such, or not. We all know how good our hearts feel when someone acknowledges we are able to succeed in a task. We tend to not want to disappoint those who show trust in our abilities, while at the same time we are further encouraged by their words. Remember as children how our parents proclaimed, "You can do it!" What joy it gave us to be so encouraged. Sometimes that was the added push that granted us the power for victory. How much more should we grant honour and acknowledgment unto the Lord? In no way are we attempting to grease-the-wheel, if you may. We must truthfully acknowledge that God is great and greatly to be praised for all He is about to accomplish in our lives.

Some of us lack God's favor in our lives because we lack His pre-praise thanksgiving on our lips. How can we say we are blessed and highly favored when we lack His pre-praise thanksgiving on our lips? How can we be highly favored when we cannot highly exalt His name in faith of knowing He will deliver us? Please don't forget how Jesus blessed many upon their strong faith and pre-praise. "And behold, they brought him a man sick of the palsy, lying on a bed: and Jesus seeing their faith said unto the sick of the palsy; Son, be of good cheer; thy sins be forgiven thee" _(Matthew 9:2)_. The subsequent verses illustrate how Jesus healed the man of the palsy; as their act of faith acknowledged that He had the power to do all things but fail. It takes great faith to give the Lord pre-praise for future blessings, and best believe faith and trust are the base of our ability to give pre-praise thanksgiving. Those of little faith tend to forsake giving God pre-praise; for doubt. We cannot live in the power of God with doubt in our spirits. "And when he came into the house, the blind men came to him: and Jesus saith unto them, Believe ye that I am able to do this? They said unto him, Ye, Lord. Then touched he their eyes, saying, According to your faith be it unto you" _(Matthew 9:28-29)_. Those verses also tell us little will be done for us, if we have little faith. Pre-praise is a testimony of our faith! And there it is. Matthew 13:53-58 illustrates how folk of Jesus' country didn't have faith in Him; thus, He didn't perform many mighty works there. Let it not be our country nor lives that share in such a plight by having so little faith. Let us be found shouting pre-praise victory long before He blesses us. Show faith in Him and He will bless us. Have doubt in Him and He may go to a neighboring country to perform great works for others who have more faith.

Higher Level of Faith

Pre-praise thanksgiving is the time in prayer and in worship when we can illustrate our faith in the Lord. We truly have an opportunity in this *Element*, even more so than in all the other *Elements*, to say to the Lord, "I trust and believe in Your abilities and power." We should already possess a certain level of faith in order to go to the Lord in prayer in the first place. It is amazing how some of us can doubt His power, yet still get on our knees. Pre-praise thanksgiving is faith displayed on an entirely higher level than where most of us currently dwell. It is the duty of this document to change that circumstance and deliver power to 100,000 prayer warriors equipped with new faith in the Lord's great abilities. Truthful pre-praise is like faith on steroids, or like faith to the 10th power. Pre-praise is not a going-out-on-the-limb kind of thinking; as if to say, "I'm gonna go-out-on-a-limb and say God will." No baby! Pre-praise thanksgiving is having an assurance deep in our spirits previous to praying. An assurance so deep and powerful that we know at the end of the day we shall be blessed and God will be glorified! It takes someone to be sold-out for Jesus in order to truly give Him praises and thanks in advance of receiving any hint of a blessing.

Some folk will claim to give the Lord pre-praise only in hopes of conjuring up a deliverance. Pre-praise is not a feeble attempt to make our deliverance come into fruition through a patsy type relationship nor a fake illustration of hope. Make no mistake pre-praise is a convicted act of knowing God will or already has made a way. At this point in prayer, the milk fed believers may make attempts to convince themselves that a deliverance can happen. We all know the type of person who claims to believe it is so, but is always seeking a surface value reassurance that there is an inkling of a possibility of something coming to pass. Being a prayer warrior is not for the faint of heart nor the slight in faith. In being a prayer warrior we must first be sound in our belief in God's Word and God's faithfulness, no matter how the situation looks to the human eye. Hebrews 11:1 must permeate our spirits during this *Element of Prayer Progression*. Pre-praise thanksgiving is built upon the premise that it is a done deal! If God is in it, we are going to win! Our faith then takes us to the level of believing we have already won!

Sold-out

In order for our hearts and spirits to be sold-out on the Lord's power to deliver, we must first believe everything will greatly work out on our behalf no matter how the Lord answers our prayers. This is a major *key* for us all; such that it is mentioned in several portions of this document.

It will bless our spirits and our spiritual living if we can settle in our minds and hearts that God's way is the best way. "There is a way which seemeth right unto a man, but the end thereof are the ways of death" *(Proverbs 14:12).* "All the ways of a man are clean in his own eyes; but the Lord weigheth the spirits. Commit thy works unto the Lord, and thy thoughts shall be established" *(Proverbs 16:2-3).* Give heed to know the Lord is perfect in all His ways, lest we fall by our own desires and ways. Settle our hearts unto God's ways then we shall settle into prosperity and power. As I always proclaim, "True prosperity is in Jesus Christ!"

Accept the fact that we all have messed up a lot of things by the very workings of our own hands and by the jumbled thoughts in our own minds; if we accept nothing else. In accepting that truth, we can then begin to accept being sold-out for the perfect will and ways of God. I do declare this very day, we cannot give God truthful pre-praise thanksgiving until we are sold-out for the way He will provide. Say and live, "Not my way Lord, but Your way!" "Thy kingdom come. Thy will be done in earth, as it is in heaven" *(Matthew 6:10).* Be sold-out to believe the Lord is perfect in all His ways, if we must be sold-out for anything. We might as well say it right now! Say, "I'm sold-out in believing the Lord is perfect in all His ways." Go ahead and say it out loud. Get practice saying it now so our prayers can be blessed later. A multitude of us are sold-out for so many other things worldly, but wince at the thought of being sold-out for Jesus. Some of us are sold-out for fame, positions, money and honey, while our spirits are crumbling at the cores, all along. Become sold-out for the Lord and witness prayers being blessed in great fashions.

Our being sold-out for the Lord also means our being faithful to shout His pre-praise during all situations, all adversities and in advance of all victories. In other words, we must not be ashamed to give the Lord His glory in advance of our victory no matter who else does not think it to be fashionable. Let us settle in our spirits at this very moment, that the unknowing and the dis-spirited have never found it to be fashionable to have faith crazy enough and bold enough to believe the Lord is going to powerfully show up in our situations. Luke 18:35-43 tells of how the disciples urged a blind man to stop shouting about the Lord. The man continued to exult in the Lord because he had faith bold enough to believe everything would change in his favor as long as Jesus was in the picture. Many of us have yet to receive our deliverance' because we are ashamed to shout out the Lord's victory in advance and in the face of others.

I do declare our healing is not far away when Jesus is near. Our deliverance is soon on its way when the Lord is in the picture. Our blessings are often at hand, yet we tend not to act as though the Lord is near and able. We may not see how the victory will come about, just as the blind man could not see, but we too must have a sort of blind faith in order to praise the Lord in advance of our deliverance. One part of the definition of the word "advance" speaks of onrush, march, flow, stride, leap, jump and momentum. If we truly believe God is about to show up, we should give Him praise that jumps and leaps. If we undoubtedly know a thing is going to work out in our favor, we should get so excited that we jump out of our shoes due to giving the Lord so much pre-praise.

Spectacular, Providence, Mercy or Miracle

The Lord is still in the miracle working business, but we should start looking for Him to do the spectacular. Hear me. Miracles are acts performed by God and Heavenly bodies working upon creation with the breaking of natural laws. (i.e. Jesus turning water into wine and the man born blind given sight). Most of the miracles Jesus performed were to illustrate and proclaim His deity to a disbelieving people. We are not as disbelievers in Christ, thus we should look for the spectacular versus the miraculous. Many of us confuse God's providence upon our lives with that of the Lord's performing miracles. The Lord's providence upon my life had me to leave work a little late so I was fortunate not to have been in that fatal car accident down the street − not a miracle. The Lord's providence or covering upon your life ended that harsh relationship before someone got hurt − not a miracle. God performs the spectacular with use of His eminent and transcendent powers. He performs things through our lives that we never thought possible in a million years. God will blow our minds performing the spectacular if we simply would take our hands off situations and trust in His ways. God will do the spectacular, if we simply would stop trying to box Him in. Don't we realize how small are our boxes compared to the spectacular ways of God? Oh, we must know and accept God as great and spectacular.

It was not a miracle that some stopped smoking before their lungs turned char-black and they passed away; for there were no changes in the laws of nature. We can say it was greatly spectacular how God's mercy saw fit to give us another living day on this side of six feet deep. Yes indeed, we also falsely claim some things as miracles that are simply, but greatly, God's mercies upon our lives. "Miracle" sounds so much greater, so we tend to blurt it out every chance we get. Saying the word miracle seems to make us appear to be more sanctified. Let it be understood the devil plays on our ignorance, and we often cause him to attack us simply by our walking in the cliches of faith, rather than walking in the power of the truth, spirit and context of God's Word. Let us not be law-keepers (as Pharisees and such), but let us not be spiritual law-breakers, either.

It is *key* that we live upon the true context of God's Word and not fall into the trap of living religiously fake lives based in cliches which tend to weaken our spirituality. We appear to be oh so religious by shouting cliches, not realizing its damaging affect upon our spiritual connections with God. The Bible clearly says, "God is a Spirit: and they that worship him must worship him in spirit and in truth" *(John 4:24)*. A portion of that truth is the context of what God meant for the writers to convey.

Seeing Pass the Pain

The most difficult times to give God pre-praise thanksgiving is in those times of pain and despair. Dismal moments make most things difficult. We may be able to cry out to God for help in times of pain and struggles, yet pre-praise during those moments may seem to be the furthest thing from our hearts and spirits. The devil can jump on our backs at times and make us feel there is no way out of our circumstances. But, the devil is a liar and the truth is not in him; as proclaimed in John 8:44. It is especially in those despairing moments that we must muster faith in the Lord's power and willingness to deliver us out of darkness; so to give way to the light of victory. "But thanks be to God, which giveth us the victory through our Lord Jesus Christ" *(1 Corinthians 15:57)*. We begin to gain power to praise God during the pain when we realize and believe our deliverance is not in consideration of any works in which we have done, but it is only by our faith in the Redeemer's blood.

The devil wants us to feel alone and helpless so we will give up hope and give up the fight. He really works on us after he has succeeded in isolating us from others and from God. He then begins to make us think we are lower than a foot print and are incapable of prospering in anything. But, again and again, the devil is a liar. God will always show up on His children's behalf and has already provided us with a way out of our situations. He alone is able, as confirmed previously with Matthew 9:28. We must muster the faith and praise in knowing the Lord is able to do the impossible even when the possible does not seem anywhere near. Our prayer lives depend on it! We must truly know and believe what Jesus told the disciples, "... With men this is impossible; but with God all things are possible" *(Matthew 19:26)*. We will give God joyful pre-praise after we have first secured and anchored the belief in our hearts that He can do the impossible to deliver us, heal us and bless us. In other words, we must look pass the pains of our situations and look unto the power of God.

Tough times are opportunities for us to show our faith in the Lord. Tough times are great opportunities to please the Lord; as we should be eager to please Him at all times. The Bible tells us, "But without faith it is impossible to please him..." *(Hebrews 11:6).* How then might our God deliver us if He is not pleased with us? Let me say it another way. If we do not have faith in God's ability to deliver us and bless us, what gives Him the pleasure of granting our actual deliverance? Sometimes He allows us to be placed in tough situations just so we can show ourselves faithful unto Him. Pre-praise thanksgiving is the embodiment of faithfulness which tells the world and the devil, "God is" and "God will!" Not sure if I'm writing to any "God will" folk right now, but I will give the Lord thanks for all He is about to perform in my life. How about you?

As mentioned, before we even settle down to pray, we ought have settled in our minds that God is able. As a matter of fact, we should recite those very words before we begin to pray. "He is able! He is able!" No matter how situations may appear it does not change the fact that He is able. A lot of things may change in our lifetimes, but the Lord will continue to remain "able." His abilities are not dependant on the severity of our situations. Through it all He is still able. He was able before creation and He will remain able throughout eternity. Fixing this fact in our spirits will have us to automatically shout out God's pre-praise thanksgiving. We will not be able to hold back thanksgiving unto Him when we have fixed in our hearts that He is in full control and He is fully able to do all things — but fail. When I think about His goodness and all He's able to do, my soul cries out — Hallelujah! My soul cries out — I shall have victory!

Pre-praise thanksgiving can be mustered in three basic ways: by remembering past victories granted by the hand of God; by having sheer faith in who God is; and by having faith in God's promises given unto us in His Word. Let's venture a little deeper into each of these ways as we examine how they strengthen our abilities to give God pre-praise.

Praise Him for What He's Done

First, the *Elements of Prayer Progression*™ up to this point (1-6) should have given us great increase in our spirits through the remembrance of victories God has provided unto us in the past. Sparks should begin to fly in our spirits and pre-praise should naturally follow any remembrance of the things the Lord has done for us: blessings, coverings, etc. Thereafter we should have faith believing, "Jesus Christ the same yesterday, and today, and for ever" *(Hebrews 13:8).* By this time an excitement should grow within us having anticipation of what's to come while claiming things like: "If He did it yesterday, He will surely do it today;" "There are great things to come in the future;" and "We can rely on the Lord, for He was able then and He is able now." Pre-praise will flow from a spirit that has truthful faith in an immutable and able God.

It is difficult to see light at the end of our circumstances when clouds are overhead, thus it may be easier to set our hearts on remembering when the Lord delivered us in times past. Each of us should be able to recall times when the Lord had shown His delivering power. The more beaten and lowly our days, the more we must recall how He delivered us in the past. David declared, "Give thanks unto the Lord, call upon his name, make known his deeds among the people. Sing unto him, sing psalms unto him, talk ye of all his wondrous works. Glory ye in his holy name: let the heart of them rejoice that seek the Lord. Seek the Lord and his strength, seek his face continually. Remember his marvelous works that he hath done, his wonders, and the judgments of his mouth" _(I Chronicles 16:8-12)._

Simply counting our blessings is ok for _Thanksgiving #3_, but this _Pre-Praise #7_ goes to another level in thanks Pre-praise thanksgiving demands more of our faith to be activated. It takes faith to claim victory where defeat is all that is in sight. It takes faith to announce success where failure seems imminent. Pre-praise is more than just giving God thanks. It is giving Him thanks built upon faith in knowing He is able, all powerful and willing to care for all our needs. That is a huge distinction between _Element #3_ and _Element #7_. It does not take great faith to thank God for what has already occurred, but hefty and lofty faith is needed to thank Him for the things unseen, as proclaimed in Hebrews 11:1. We all could use a larger dose of "unseen" faith. "Unseen" faith prompts us to thank God for His seeing, moving and positioning unseen dangers and blessings in and out of our futures. "Unseen" faith need not wait till the deliverance or blessing arrives before thanking God. "Unseen" faith courageously stands amidst trials while thanking God for the unseen victory. In context "now" is as "moreover" in Greek; not a type of faith.

Our excitement to give God pre-praise comes from our expectancy of hearing from Him and seeing Him do great things on our behalf and in accord with His will. Many folk say, "We ought have an audacity of hope." This audacity anchors our faith and empowers us to give God pre-praise. "Which hope we have as an anchor of the soul, both sure and stedfast, and which entereth into that within the veil" _(Hebrews 6:19)._ Within hope there resides a certain level of expectancy and confidence. The more certain we are that the Lord is going to show up on our behalf the more we will give Him pre-praise. No expectancy, no pre-praise.

Praise Him for Who He Is

The second way to muster pre-praise thanksgiving is by having sheer faith in who God is. This calls for us to be, both, familiar with His attributes and believe in them. There surely will be a praise upon our hearts and our lips if we believe in His attributes. This belief strengthens our faith to trust that our prayers will soon be answered. For example, there is no doubt we will give God pre-praise in every situation if we believe He is omnipotent (all powerful). To believe He is all powerful is to know He can do all things but fail. Quite similar is the pre-praise that's generated within us when we believe in God's providence (divine guidance), which can assuredly place a shout of praise on our mouths even when the road is rocky. "And the Lord shall guide thee continually, and satisfy thy soul in drought, and make fat thy bones: and thou shalt be like a watered garden, and like a spring of water, whose waters fail not" _(Isaiah 58:11)._

Each of God's attributes, character and nature should give us great energy to shout His pre-praise thanksgiving, yet there are two which should give more oomph to our praise unto Him. First, there is something extremely spirited in knowing and believing God to be faithful. Oh, He is faithful! There are not many people in our lives who we can dub as faithful, and there are none faithful like our great God. There should be an excited praise for things to come when our faith proclaims the Lord will not forsake us. There is someone we can count on if no one else has our backs, just as there is a great friend who will forever be in our corners even when others forsake us. His name is Jesus, our Lord and Saviour.

Second, God's attribute of love _(1 John 4:16)_ is the rock which powers most things on this earth. Faith that God is love will promote pre-praise in our hearts beyond compare. Anyone who loves us will not allow us to go without, nor will that person allow harm to overtake us. Love is what causes a mother to nurse and protect her children throughout the child's life. I declare, God's love is greater than the love of our mothers; if that can be imagined. We will give the Lord pre-praise for His willingness to do everything a loving Father would do for His children, if we first would settle in our spirits the fact that God is love. The Bible tells us charity/love is the greatest gift and attribute anyone can have. That's because God is love. See the Chapter on _Attributes, Character and Nature of God_ for increased understanding of how to better praise God for who He is.

Praise Him for His Promises Made

The third way to muster pre-praise thanksgiving is to have faith in the promises God made unto us in His Word. Those who have faith and trust in the Lord's Word will give Him pre-praise. Little faith, little pre-praise. If we have faith and trust in God then we should excitedly trust in the promises made in His Word. Jesus Himself referenced Deuteronomy 8:3 when He said, "... It is written, Man shall not live by bread alone, but by every word that proceedeth out of the mouth of God" *(Matthew 4:4)*. Live we must, on the promises of the Everlasting Father. To trust in the Lord's Word is to live. Dead are they who do not trust in the Word. Dead are they who have the Word, read the Word and profess the Word, but do not have faith in the Word. There even are many who proclaim God's Word every Sunday but fail to give Him pre-praise because they don't have true faith and trust in the very Word they proclaim. There is great power in trusting God's Word. Truthful trust and truthful faith in His Word will automatically translate into pre-praise unto the Author of the Word.

No better time to say this than now — truthful faith in His Word transforms into great hope, which enables believers to walk in the blessings of the scriptures. Some things are provided unto us directly by God, whereas other things He has set in such a way that we must activate the power of faith to unlock the promises in His Word. For example, "... they that wait on the Lord shall renew their strength ..." *(Isaiah 40:31)*. The act of waiting takes active faith in He whom we wait upon. We must have some hope and faith to promote the patience to wait. Too often we are told to wait on the Lord without indication of what it actually takes to wait. No greater way to muster the active faith it takes to wait than through our trusting in the promises made in His Word. Scripture begins to take on power and life within our prayers when we have active faith in the assurances (promises) He made in scripture. The following verses are empowering: "... weeping may endure for a night, but joy cometh in the morning" *(Psalm 30:5)* — an assurance; "For with God nothing shall be impossible" *(Luke 1:37)* — an assurance; and "... no good thing will He withhold from them that walketh uprightly" *(Psalm 84:11)* — an assurance. The infallible Word of God written of man divinely inspired by God. The Word awaits each of us to grab hold with both reigns to show proof in our lives. Many of us have faith like stallions waiting to be unleashed through our willingness to activate our trust, faith and pre-praise thanksgiving.

Unleash the Power

Unleash the power. Unleash the greatness which is in Christ Jesus and then, and only then, will we give the Lord the pre-praise He deserves. The Lord truly deserves our pre-praise, for He will surely show up in our situations. We ought get excited to know the Lord will show up. A setback is just a set-up for the Lord to show-off. Surely we all cry at the onset of a trial, but after a moment we ought remember who we serve and how great is He. There ought come a moment during trials when we begin to get excited and give the Lord pre-praise, recognizing He is about to show His face in a mighty way. His Word tells us this very thing, "Now therefore stand and see this great thing, which the Lord will do before your eyes" _(I Samuel 12:16)._ "For the eyes of the Lord run to and fro throughout the whole earth, to shew himself strong in the behalf of them whose heart is perfect toward him" _(II Chronicles 16:9a)._ Are you one for whom the Lord can show Himself strong? Prayer warriors must strive to be in that number. It all begins with faith that His Word is true and that His power supports His Word. <u>God's Word and our faith in that Word serve as conduits for His power.</u> That power is made manifest to us and apparent to others when we show faith in His Word by giving Him pre-praise thanksgiving. Pre-praise should fill our prayers and our open proclamations. Let it be known unto man and unto God how much faith we have in His soon to come appearance in our situations.

There should never be a lack of pre-praise within true believers, since their faith is stabilized through their trust in God's power and Word. When we know and truly believe He will never leave us comfortless _(John 14:18)_, showering pre-praise in our prayers becomes automatic. When we are convinced the Lord will fight for us _(Nehemiah 4:20)_, it will not take much for us to shout God's pre-praise each time our enemies come against us. This is where and when the power of God's Word becomes our source of strength _(Exodus 15:2; Psalm 18:1, 28:7, 73:26)._ Not only must we remember He has made assurances and promises, but we must remember He's a promise keeping God, also. Not too many things worse than a person who makes a lot of promises they cannot keep. But, we serve a Lord who will fulfill every promise He has made. He does not keep just one promise, nor does He keep just some promises. The Lord will make fruit of every promise He's made. The Bible tells us, "So shall my word be that goeth forth out of my mouth: it shall not return unto me void, but it shall accomplish that which I please, and it shall prosper in the thing whereto I sent it" _(Isaiah 55:11)._ That is a fact we should already have settled in our hearts, minds, spirits and souls before, during and after our prayers. There should be no doubt in our minds the Lord shall perform each of His promises; past, present and future. If there is nothing else we can trust, our hearts should be confident we can lean on God's Word.

Many people may remember the promises made in His Word, but they lack the power to give Him pre-praise because they lack belief that He's a promise keeper. To remember and even recite His promises is one thing, but to have faith He will keep those very promises is another story, all together. This is a _key._ The culminated power is in the faith to believe God can do just what He said He would do. There is a culminating affect to believe He has made promises, but the culmination of power shows fruit in our believing He will surely do as He said. Our prayer lives gain in strength when we make this fruitful connection in our belief. More is spoken of God's promises in the writings within the _Request Element._

The Word of God should be the first and last thing in which we trust. In this way our minds will be settled on the fact that God is a rock in a weary land. King David said it this way, "My soul, wait thou only upon God; for my expectation is from him. He only is my rock and my salvation: he is my defence; I shall not be moved. In God is my salvation and my glory: the rock of my strength, and my refuge, is in God. Trust in him at all times; ye people, pour out your heart before him: God is a refuge for us. Selah" *(Psalm 62:5-8)*. Many of the Psalm writers illustrated how their lives were blessed because God was their rock, fortress and strength. Our lives likewise can be blessed, if only we would stand in faith believing His Word to be true and worthy to be trusted.

The Lord must be glorified no matter our spirit's choices on how to generate or muster pre-praise. Prayer warriors and strong Christians alike do not have the option of whether or not to give God pre-praise. The only choice is how we generate the pre-praise. Having a strong relationship with the Lord involves knowing how to enter into His presence and how to generate pre-praise unto Him. Yes, we must learn how best to generate pre-praise, for there are times we may not necessarily feel like praising Him. Make no mistake, not feeling like praising Him does not eliminate our need to praise Him. Do not allow difficulties to dictate pre-praise.

"And he said unto me, My grace is sufficient for thee: for my strength is made perfect in weakness. Most gladly therefore will I rather glory in my infirmities, that the power of Christ may rest upon me. Therefore I take pleasure in infirmities, in reproaches, in necessities, in persecutions, in distresses for Christ's sake: for when I am weak, then am I strong" *(II Corinthians 12:9-10)*. Here are two applications of this verse: first, we should praise the Lord knowing how our infirmities give us increase and growth; and second, we should have faith to praise the Lord knowing He is in full control and He has a covering of protection over His children.

The Lord is our strength and power, thus we should find it in our spirits to give Him pre-praise thanksgiving even through our trials and tough times. Do not neglect the One who can and will provide a breakthrough no matter how the situation may first appear. The Lord will show up in our despairing moments even when others forsake us. There are no hopeless moments for they who wait upon the Lord nor for they who live within His victory previous to its actualization.

The Larger the Issue the Larger the Thanks

There are no bad moments to give God pre-praise. As a matter of fact, the worse the situation appears the more pre-praise we should give unto the

Lord. The larger the issue, the larger the deliverance. Let our pre-praise match and supercede the ensuing deliverance and breakthrough. Those situations which seem impossible must be interrupted with impossible pre-praise; knowing the Lord is about to show up and make a way. Likewise, when there seems to be no way out of a trial, give the Lord no-way-out pre-praise to celebrate the Lord's soon to come victory. Let us all spiritually practice that the larger the trial, the larger the pre-praise.

Do we not realize the Lord our God can never fail? Why don't we greatly celebrate in advance of His showing up if we so believe He can never fail? If we are sure in our faith God will not and cannot fail, there should be no hesitation to give Him thanks in advance. To understand this document is to understand our pre-praise will never be in vain.

Let me ask the question — why should our God do anything for us if we do not believe in Him? Jesus' earthly ministry was flooded with times He blessed, healed and delivered those who first had faith in Him and in the Father. On the other hand, how disappointing could it have been, and is, to want to bless someone, yet that very person have no faith? There is an annoying tone to disbelief which can be seen in our neglect to give the Lord pre-praise. Not all of us are blessed to be, or even desire to be deep thinkers; nevertheless, we all must take the time to think of the consequences of our actions or non-actions, just the same.

A Change is Going to Come

To not give God pre-praise can equate to not believing He is able nor willing to work things out on our behalf. Not giving God pre-praise sets ourselves up for doubt to settle into our minds and spirits; rendering our prayers ineffective. I say again, realize today that some of our prayers have yet to be answered favorably because we have yet to give God pre-praise thanksgiving. Giving the Lord praise in advance illustrates faith in His power and willingness. Pre-praise solidifies our initial faith. Much of our change and deliverance must begin with our change in belief, after which our advance praise unto God will come forth. This is a *key*.

Naturally and often, each of us looks for a change in our station in life, our financial condition, our health and/or some other similar components, which have little to do with becoming the salt of the Earth. Whereas, if we would seek a change in our belief, our spirits then would be helped and we would have a different outlook on all the above mentioned items, as well. This is when our prayers begin to take on new life, new direction and new determination. A change in our belief and in our outlook will promote great pre-praise in our subsequent prayers. We can safely say

Job spoke of this when he declared, "If a man die, shall he live again? all the days of my appointed time will I wait, till my change come" _(Job 14:14)_. Job and his friends first needed a change in their belief in order to be empowered to then wait on the change for the components within Job's life. Job seemed to have had some form of belief throughout, vacillating or not, but the change in his strength of faith was truly made evident towards the end of his story.

Oh, this is a simple formula we tend to overlook, since we have all been taught that everything will be ok as long as we merely bow on our knees and make our supplications known unto the Lord. No! Everything will not always be fine, and it often takes more effort than merely bowing on our knees to get a favorable answer from God . All faithful Christians and truthful prayer warriors come to a point in their Christian development where they begin to pay more attention to the details needed to abide in God's presence and get a prayer through. It is upon this recognition Christians become birthed into a newness of living with Christ Jesus. This is a newness of living that propels them into a realm of power beyond anything they had previously imagined. There is a great abiding which begins with a change in belief.

Far be it for us to think we can go to great lengths and different levels in our spirituality without a change. No change — No growth. No growth — No next levels with God. "Levels" is plural, for we continue to grow in grace till the Lord's return. "But grow in grace, and in the knowledge of our Lord and Savior Jesus Christ" _(II Peter 3:18a)_. Growth is surely what we all desire, but proper growth is what we will lack if we are void of the faith and belief it takes to give the Lord pre-praise thanksgiving.

Growth and Change, or Name it and Claim it?

Mind you, pre-praise thanksgiving is not "Naming it and claiming it," "Tagging it and bagging it," theology, for there are some things which are not for us to have; period. Let us be mindful that some things are good to the flesh, but not profitable unto the spirit. We take unto the body for gain, yet it defiles the spirit. Yes, it is true that God quickens the dead and calls those things which be not as though they were, as He had done with Abraham and with Sarah; referenced in Romans Chapter 4 _(especially vv13-25)_. Yet, here we speak of a blessing which is often greater than the things in which we pray to receive.

Let's view it from this angle. What the Spirit has for us to claim is the Lord's victory within us. This victory may or may not include that which we pray to receive, directly. Most often the victory over which the Spirit wants us to shout pre-praise is that of our change which takes place in the midst of our prayers and our heightened communal connection with the Father. This is a brunt of this document. We will become spiritually strengthened and changed through the studying and implementing of these *8 Elements of Prayer Progression.*™ Most often and unfortunately, the change within ourselves is not the change we first seek through prayers. Today is the time for us to change our perspective about prayer and communion with God! More of our prayers will be answered on our behalf once we change in our belief of what prayer is all about.

Many of us believers become discouraged when prayers seem to go unanswered, not realizing we first sought the wrong changes. We must come to realize God's will for our lives sometimes does not include the very thing for which we pray. Some things we pray to have may even take us down some good roads, but those roads just may not be the roads the Lord wills for us to travel. This is a *key* for us all to remember in order to remain faithful unto the Lord; even when He denies or delays some of our prayer request. These *Elements of Prayer Progression*™ are designed to increase the propensity for us to get a prayer through, as well as reduce, if not eliminate, our becoming discouraged over denied prayers or our becoming frustrated by the length of time it may take for God to respond. Often times our change is our increase!

Here is another *key* to encourage us. We are not to give the Lord just any type of pre-praise and thanks. We give Him pre-praise thanksgiving for knowing He will provide in His own way, and we shall be taken care of no matter how He provides. That is putting faith in Him alone, and not putting all our hopes in the receiving of what it is we request. Hear me and digest this! As prayer warriors, our focus should begin to switch from the very thing which we request through prayer to that of the perfections of He who provides blessings in His own way. Our focus should begin to shift from having both eyes on the prize, as we always say, to the realization He who provides the prize is the true prize. This is a new direction for many today. Keep our eyes on the true prize − Jesus.

Let me say this, I have come to a level of faithfulness to believe I just need Jesus. I do not necessarily need all those other things I ask of in prayer, but I truly need Jesus. I have more than all the world can offer if I have Jesus. Just give me Jesus! You can have all of what you prayed to acquire, but give me the Lord. Fact is, if I have Jesus I have all I will ever need, and more! I need to let this point go, cause I could stay here and bless His holy and righteous name through the next fifty pages; for He is sovereign and good, and He has been oh so good to me. In saying that, we must be careful that we not ask for too many things outside of asking for our Lord. Let us not be as the Israelites who asked to be like their neighbors who had kings ruling over them. This is a *key* which can help us refrain from making frivolous requests. Remember, He may very well give us that which we request and we may not like it. So let our pre-praise be focused on the Giver instead of focusing solely on what we pray to be given. That is when the oil starts to pour!

Let me tell you, I am thankful even for the things the Lord has not bestowed upon me. Often, I have subsequently realized I would have messed up all of what God intended as a blessing had I gotten my hands on it at a time He had not ordained. We all can attest to have received something before our time and ended up destroying the very thing God intended as a blessing. Sometimes we are not prepared to receive of the blessing and other times the thing is just not in God's plans nor in His will for our lives. So, I declare today we thankfully and patiently wait on the Lord's perfect timing and appreciate His perfect answers.

There are many a faithful, even, who have died with hearts angry at God because of prayers they thought to have gone unanswered. The true underlying anger was with the fact that God answers prayers His way and in His time. Some folk have lived for nineteen years after praying for something only to come to the twentieth year to finally realize God had actually answered the request two years after they made the request. The quandary came about from God answering the prayer in a way which may have been unexpected and undetected. Just maybe their spirit had not grown enough at that time in order to spiritually detect that the prayer had been answered. Let me make it just a little more plain. Some of us have prayed to meet a man or a woman who will be for us, "The best thing since sliced bread." Some of us have never gotten married because the Lord answered our prayers with someone who did not appear as we were expecting, so we did not walk into the blessing. Had we been spiritually mature enough to discern God's answer we would have realized that the unsuspected person was the epitome of that sliced bread. Others have gotten married but kept praying that same prayer, only to realize years later that their spouse was and is that very God send.

Listen, we will never understand all of God and His ways, for He is surely incomprehensible and inscrutable, but we can surely help our situations by having faith in His showing up on our behalf. Jesus tells us, "Be not ye therefore like unto them: for your Father knoweth what things ye have need of, before ye ask him" *(Matthew 6:8)*.

Be Not Discouraged

Emphasis

Asaph, a leader in King David's choir, thought enough about giving thanksgiving unto the Lord that he repeated it twice in verse. "Unto thee, O God do we give thanks. Unto thee do we give thanks ..." *(Psalm 75:1).* Repetitions in the Bible declare greater emphasis, of course. Let us be mindful and take heed of God's Word, especially the iterated verses. How much more should we give the Lord thanksgiving if it has been repeated in the same verse? Not many Biblical verses have been repeated in this fashion, thus our spiritual antennas should be on full alert and respond in resemblance.

We, the children of God, are called to give Him great praise, which declares our emphasis of love and trust unto Him. This emphasis must be illustrated within our prayer lives, as well. What greater way to show our trust in the Lord while praying than to give Him pre-praise thanksgiving? There is a great emphasis on trust when it comes to giving God praise in advance. *Element #3 of the Prayer Progression*™ *– Thanksgiving,* emphasizes things past and things present, while *Element #7 of Pre-Praise Thanksgiving* emphasizes trust and faith in God for things to come. Spiritual emphasis of faith and trust do not come easily, but the fruit thereof is glorious. We cannot give God thankful pre-praise without openly showing an emphasis of faith and trust in His power and love. As mentioned before, pre-praise thanksgiving is like having faith on steroids. In this day and age we surely need such empowered faith.

Fact is, at this point of prayer there will surely be an emphasis made by us all, one way or another. Either there will be an emphasis of strong faith and trust, or we will emphasize how little faith we have in He who is trustworthy. Make no mistake the standard for our prayers will be set and established by our level of faith in the Almighty. Being a prayer warrior takes great and emphasized faith that goes beyond meager knowledge of God's blessed hands. Let us illustrate to the world and to our God that we come forth in supplication with an emphasis of great faith and trust in He who has all power to do all things – all things great. So, what will be your emphasis this day?

Where Did All The Thanks Go?

It can be said that there are folk who are not thankful for anything nor anyone. We all may even know a person or two who seems to never be thankful for anything. They are always on the edge of take, take, take, but never bending in one iota of thanks. As mentioned previously in this document, I am a firm believer that our horizontal relationships are reflective of our vertical relationships with God. It can be believed that people who are not thankful amongst the brethren are just as unthankful in the face of God. When we are a thankful people we are just that — thankful. Thankfulness comes from a spirit and a heart of appreciation. This can be said of our appreciation of things to come, as well.

Unappreciative people tend not to give thanks to others for what they are about to do for them. These types of people can witness everything others may be doing for them, yet refuse to give them thanks. Sorrowful to say they treat the Lord in the same manner. Some folk find it so difficult to exalt others for matters concerning themselves. It is a painful sight to see someone have so much pride it causes them to omit edifying others for what those persons are about to do for them. These persons tend to want to take self-credit for everything that will happen in their lives. This is the wrong road to travel, since we can do nothing without God. He unquestionably deserves all the credit and all the pre-praise.

Some unthankful people even see what the Lord is about to bless unto their lives yet they refuse to give Him pre-praise, thinking it is a given that He should automatically bless them because He is God. Only a sorrowful and demented people would think He's obligated to do anything for us. The Lord has no obligations other than to Himself, His Word, His character, nature and will. The finite beings of this earth are not on that list, but are as recipients, only, of that list. Therefore, each of us should be ever so thankful; even with free will.

Misdirected Thanks

It can be said, for the most part, we are generally thankful for what we have and for what we have received. Albeit, the fact remains far too many of us who are thankful give thanks to the wrong things or the wrong persons and for the wrong reasons. We give thanks to our neighbor for their help yet neglect to give thanks to the God who sent the neighbor our way to give the help. One thing that would help us all in our attempts to be thankful is to remember nothing happens by chance. If we are true believers, we know He has already mapped out our victory and existence.

Faith that God is in full control should steer us to rejoice in all situations; fully aware we already have the victory. If we are to be strong in faith, we must believe all blessings come from the great providing hand of God. "Every good and perfect gift is from above, and cometh down from the Father of lights, with whom is no variableness, neither shadow of turning" *(James 1:17)*. We ought give God thanks always if we truly believe in that verse and if we have faith in the power that is behind it.

It is good to thank our fellow man for things done on our behalf, but we must never forsake giving the ultimate thanks unto God. He alone is the root of all our blessings and deliverance'. It is God who is sending that doctor to perform the operation that will be a success. Give Him pre-praise thanks. It is God who is giving us the blessing of children who will take care of us in our old age. Give Him pre-praise thanks. It is God who is about to give us that job which will pay our bills and put food on our tables. Give Him pre-praise thanks. It is God who did it in the past and it will be God who will do it all in the future. Give Him pre-praise thanks. Do not thank just the doctor, but turn and thank God in advance of Him sending the doctor. Do not thank just the boss for that promotion, but turn and thank God in advance of His pricking the spirit of the boss to give the promotion. Do not squelch blessings by misdirecting pre-praise.

Most of us have heard the term "misappropriation of funds" and how it is unlawful and corrupt to conduct such transactions. Well, how much more sinful and wicked is it to misappropriate our thanks? The Lord deserves all of our pre-praise thanks. Let us be mindful and never forget He is a jealous God and He wants all the glory, honour and praise. God does want us to encourage one another, as we have been called to show the love of Christ, but He wants to be extolled and exalted above all things. He desires to be recognized for things past, things present and surely for things to come in the future. Yes, it is great to thank others for what they are intending to do for us, but do not forsake giving God the ultimate praise in advance. It is sad to imagine some of us are lacking in future blessings merely due to our giving thanks to the wrong persons or wrong objects. If we neglect to give God pre-praise, He just may neglect to bless our living. It is His choice and we should not be taking such chances. Our prayers are too important to be taking any chances.

It is here where we make the connection of pre-praise and exorbitant faith. It is in excessive faith where we have the ability to thank Him in advance. The "now" kind of faith that some folk want to proclaim of Hebrews 11:1 is exclaimed here as the type of faith we must possess in order to praise and thank the Lord in advance. We must first unequivocally believe God is in full control in order to muster the faith required to give Him pre-praise thanksgiving for the success of future events. It is by our faith that we are healed. It is by our faith that we are delivered. As well, it is by our faith that we open our mouths to thank the Lord for future successes and blessings. Thanks be unto God for the things He is about to do. Will you show forth exorbitant faith in God's power and ability to bless you?

God Will !

The Holy Spirit's Activation

We must reside in the realm of strong faith and trust in order to give God thanksgiving in advance; similar to that of working in our gifts. We must have an "over-the-top" kind of faith in order to honestly and powerfully give God thanks for the unseen. Our faith must be bolstered by great power from on High before pre-praise thanksgiving will go forth honestly. It is the power of the Holy Spirit residing in us who gives us that faith large enough to have pre-praise thanks on our lips in prayer even before the blessing has been actualized. The immense power of the Holy Spirit is rendered able in our prayers by our first having faith and trust that God is in full control. The Holy Spirit's power is more strongly activated in and through believers who trustingly have it set in their hearts that God is who He said He is and that He is able to do all things, but fail. The Lord Jesus answered the disciples saying, "... Verily I say unto you, If ye have faith, and doubt not, ye shall not only do this which is done to the fig tree, but also if ye shall say unto this mountain, Be thou removed, and be thou cast into the sea; it shall be done. And all things, whatsoever ye shall ask in prayer, believing, ye shall receive" *(Matthew 21:21-22).*

It is safe to say those who lack the ability to give God pre-praise thanksgiving also lack the faith needed to activate the power of the Holy Spirit. We should ask ourselves the question, "Is the power of the Holy Spirit strongly activated in my life?" One may be able to tell how much the Spirit has been activated in our lives by the amount of truthful thanksgiving we render unto God in advance of receiving a blessing. It is simple to say much of our pre-praise is connected to our level of faith and to the amount of the Holy Spirit's power that has been energized in our lives. For those of us who lack pre-praise on our lips, let us pray to the Father, Son and Holy Spirit for the Spirit's activation in our trust through repentance and faith. Anyone can simply thank God, but it is only the faithful and trusting who can give Him truthful pre-praise-thanksgiving.

Our Humility, His Credit

Giving the Lord praise before the results appear helps to ensure we will not take credit. Many of us are famous for grabbing unmerited credit. We pray unto the Lord for things to occur in our lives, then once the blessing arrives we do not hesitate to shout how we have done such great things. The Spirit of God is a discerner of hearts and He sees how we often conjure imaginations of what we will do once our blessings arrive; like, how we will tell the world of our strengths when we give our acceptance speech, as if we have won an award on Broadway. This type of posture gives rise to egos that tend to boastfully take credit for victory.

This is the way the devil seeps into our spirits, attempting to steal the Lord's glory and honour. This reason alone makes giving the Lord pre-praise thanksgiving an imperative act. We must give the Lord praise even before the blessings arrive so that we may keep the real reason for our successes foremost in our hearts. God is the reason we have anything at any time. Our humility about all that occurs in our lives is highly important for the continuation of our success. Pre-praise reduces the temptation to take credit for what is to come.

Pre-praise sets the foundation of our testimonies and future praise. In most things this is the foundation that carries us through unto our victories. In most things starting on the wrong foot (foundation) will often land us in the wrong places, and no different is our praise unto the Lord. His praise must permeate our spirits from the outset, not only to announce to ourselves who is responsible for the victory, but to announce our humility and submission unto God, as well. Ultimately, this makes known unto the Lord just how our spirits are prepared to receive of the blessings He has stored for us. The Bible tells us, "God is jealous ..." *(Nahum 1:2);* and we surely want no parts of His jealous rage.

The fact is, many of us miss out on our blessings because the Lord knows we will try to take the credit for the work of His hands; whether done purposefully or not. It is reckless and sinful how we have the nerve to attempt to steal what is due unto the Lord. He will not bless us until we change our spirits to desire for Him to receive all honour, glory and credit. The Bible, in II Chronicles 20:22, gives illustration of how God blessed Judah by setting ambushments against their enemies; only after they began to praise Him.

One of the remaining concerns is how the thievery of God's credit has been made easier by the culture of this western society. Lifting the chin and broadening the shoulders are viewed as par for the course of successful people. Humility has been ruled out and shunned in a society bent on reality TV. This has resulted in our inability and unwillingness to submit unto God in prayer, and has caused us to forsake giving Him praise, honour and glory for what He is about to do on our behalf. Prayer warriors must not fall into this trap set by the devil and perpetuated by societal ills of all types. Much of our prayer's successes will rely upon our humility, reinforced through our giving Him pre-praise and credit.

Giving the Lord pre-praise thanksgiving keeps us humble in knowing He is the great Provider; Jehovah Jireh. It has a way of reminding us there's no one like Him in all of life. Our giving God praise for what is about to occur minimizes, if not eliminates, our puffing out our own chest. This

Prayer Progression will, in effect, place us in a powerful mode of having a purpose to please God. Isn't that our ultimate desire? We all should joyfully agree that our greatest desire is to please the Lord. By the end of this document we shall come into a greater understanding that our prayers are most effective when our hearts and spirits are devoted to satisfying the Lord. We shall then proclaim as Paul testified in I Corinthians 15:10, "But by the grace of God I am what I am: and his grace which was bestowed upon me was not in vain; but I laboured more abundantly than they all: yet not I, but the grace of God which was with me."

A Story of Pre-Praise

Joshua Chapter 6 tells of a story of God directing the children of Israel to give pre-praise in advance of the victory over Jericho. Attention must be given to the word use: verse 5 — blast; verses 3, 4, and 7 — compass the city; and verse 5 — great shout. These words express actions of pre-praise in faith. How many of us show such faith in the face of our trials? "Give Him pre-praise" were the Lord's instructions to His people then, and He directs us to do the same today. Israel performed these acts of faith seven times, illustrating their complete faith of an ensuing victory. Why is it we Israelites of today refuse to give the Lord pre-praise merely once?

This was a great victory over a city who's walls were fortified and unscalable. How many of our life's situations seem as difficult and tumultuous? Yet, we forsake the faith it takes to bring about the victory through pre-praise in prayer. We all have some Jericho's in our lives, thus we must show our faith in an able God who will bring down the walls that keep us out of our promised lands.

Verses 10 and 20 of this chapter illustrate how the Israelites gave the pre-praise before the breakthrough and previous to their beginning to fight. Let this be example to us today how we should stop being so quick to fight before we celebrate the Lord's victory. Woefully, there are those of us who are always amped to fight, in essence thinking we have any real say in the victory. We must begin to show less confidence in our abilities and show more faith in God's power. Pre-praise is a demonstration of great faith. Please understand this _key_. Let us not be so quick to arms when God is calling us to first edify Him through pre-praise. Just like Jericho, our greatest victories will be those battles that are preceded by our giving God great thanks for the victory unseen. There are great victories for us all, but the Lord requires each of us to shake our tambourines, lift our voices, do our dance, clap our hands and sing His praises — in advance.

PRE-PRAISE THANKSGIVING – *Progression of Prayer Element #7*

Exercises

INSTRUCTIONAL

1. Choose one verse from the Why, How or What sections of this chapter and write a short paragraph as to how that verse relates to one of the sections within the written body portion of this chapter.

BENEFIT:
To sharpen your ability to choose wisdom within these *Elements of Prayer Progression*,™ then comprehend and apply them to your living.

PERSONAL

1. Select one of the three basic ways to muster pre-praise thanksgiving. Announce your choice to a friend who will act as a check to ensure you will practice how to muster pre-praise. At the end of the week testify to that same friend how the exercise has benefitted your pre-praise.

BENEFIT:
There should be a couple of benefits. First, your sensitivity to give God praise should be heightened. Second, your testimony to your friend should give them a willingness to learn how to enhance their ability to give the Lord pre-praise.

PRE-PRAISE THANKSGIVING — Progression of Prayer Element #7

General Questions

1. Over all the other *Elements* within the *Prayer Progression*, *Pre-Praise Thanksgiving* is the *Element* where we can most illustrate what unto the Lord?

2. What are three basic ways to muster pre-praise?

   Which is dependent upon scripture?
   Which is dependent upon God's character, nature and attributes?
   Which is dependent upon our history with God?

3. Much of our change and deliverance begins how?

4. List four things pre-praise thanksgiving is likened unto within this chapter?

   How do we obtain this type of faith needed for pre-praise?

5. What must we remember in order to see beyond the pains of our situations?

6. How can we refrain from making frivolous request?

7. Where should we direct our pre-praise thanksgiving?

8. Is there a way to tell how much the Holy Spirit's power has been activated in our lives? If so, how?

9. Give two reasons why some people get angry at God when their prayers seem to go unanswered?

10. What are two reasons we should not become discouraged by seemingly unanswered prayers?

PRE-PRAISE THANKSGIVING — Progression of Prayer Element #7

Advanced Questions

1. Is it enough to believe God has made promises in His Word?

   If so, why?
   If not, what else must we do? And why?

2. For generations we have entered prayer with our focus on the item we are requesting to receive. What should we now have as our focus in order that we may best receive change?
   And why?

3. Write a short paragraph illustrating the difference between *Thanksgiving Element #3* and *Pre-Praise Thanksgiving Element #7?*

Meditation

Pray this prayer with me:
A Prayer for Meditation

"Victorious Father. Victorious Lord. Victorious Spirit. You alone are victory. There is victory in Your presence. Victory in Your Word. Victory in Your name. Hallelujah! I thank You for all You have done, and I now praise You for the victory which is meditation. The victory of my prayer is to hear from You Father, so I bless Your Holy name for permitting me to meditate upon You. Speak to me Father as I focus on Your voice's directions and Your Spirit's movement. My prayers are not complete lest I hear from You. You already know my every need before I utter the first word, thus I recognize prayer is about getting an answer from You, rather than just getting a prayer through to You. Tell me of Your directions and of Your will even through the precepts of this document. Blessed God teach me how to hear from Heaven and I shall lift the name of Jesus with all of my being. I have tried things my way, now permit me to go Your way. Speak to me. Direct me. Navigate me. It is Your ways that I seek to follow above all else. Your Word declares You shall be found if I seek, so empower me with an ear to hear from Heaven. It is written that only by faith may You be pleased, so I do pray that my increased faith and ability to hear from You is pleasing unto Your sight. If I am to hear from anyone, let it be that I hear from You, blessed God. I shout glory and I pray in the name of Your victorious Son Jesus, who sits at Your right hand making intercessions for this Your child — Amen."

This section is to better enhance our understanding of the Biblical reasons for who should meditate, how we should meditate, why we should meditate, what we should meditate, where we should meditate and when we should meditate. Our study of meditation will be further enhanced if these verses are read previous to moving onto the chapter material; as this format will indeed better prepare our spirits to receive of the chapter material.

1) WHO should meditate?
- Psalm 1:2 — The godly and the blessed
- Psalm 41:1 — The blessed
- Psalm 64:9 — All men
- Proverbs 29:7 — The righteous

2) HOW we should meditate?
- Genesis 24:63 — Lift up your eyes and see
- Deuteronomy 4:39 — In your heart
- Deuteronomy 32:7 — Asking the Father
- Deuteronomy 32:29 — Be wise
- Joshua 1:7 — Not turning to the left nor right from the law
- Joshua 1:8 — Not departing out of your mouth
- Job 37:14 — Stand still
- Psalm 1:2 — With delight
- Psalm 5:1 — Consider
- Psalm 19:14 — With the heart; acceptable unto God
- Psalm 64:9 — With fear and declaring
- Psalm 104:34 — Sweetly and gladly
- Psalm 119:15 — With respect
- Psalm 119:97 — With love
- Psalm 119:148 — By the eyes preventing the night watches
- Luke 21:14 — With a settled heart
- I Timothy 4:15 — Give thyself wholly

3) WHY we should meditate?
- Deuteronomy 4:39 — Because the Lord is God in Heaven above and Earth below; there is none else
- Deuteronomy 32:7 — The Father will show you
- Joshua 1:8 — So you may observe to do according to all that is written in the Book of Law; so your ways will prosper
- Psalm 1:1-2 — To be blessed
- Psalm 19:14 — To be acceptable in God's sight
- Psalm 41:1-3 — The Lord will deliver you in time of trouble; as well as preserve, keep and strengthen

3) WHY we should meditate? *(Continued)*
- Psalm 63:6-7 — Because He has been your help
- Isaiah 43:18 — The Lord will do a new thing; it shall spring forth
- Matthew 6:28 — You will be provided for
- Luke 21:14-15 — The Lord will give you a mouth and wisdom;
- I Timothy 4:15 — That your profiting may appear to all

4) WHAT we should meditate?
- Deuteronomy 4:39 — That the Lord is God
- Deuteronomy 8:5 — That the Lord chasteneth
- Deuteronomy 32:7 — The days of old, the years and generations
- Deuteronomy 32:29 — The latter end
- Joshua 1:8 — The Book of the Law
- Job 37:14 — The wondrous works of God
- Psalm 1:2 — The Law of the Lord
- Psalm 5:1 — The Lord to give ear
- Psalm 8:3 — God's Heavens, the work of God's fingers
- Psalm 48:9 — His loving kindness
- Psalm 49:3 — Shall be of understanding
- Psalm 64:9 — His doing
- Psalm 77:12 — All His work and doings
- Psalm 104:34 — Of the Lord
- Psalm 119:15 — In His precepts and His ways
- Psalm 119:97 — His Law
- Psalm 119:99 — His testimonies
- Psalm 119:148 — In His Word
- Ecclesiastes 7:13 — The work of God
- Isaiah 43:18 — Not the former things, nor things of old
- Matthew 6:28 — Not for raiment

5) WHERE we should meditate?
- Genesis 24:63 — In the field
- Psalm 48:9 — In the midst of His temple
- Psalm 63:6 — Upon your bed

6) WHEN we should meditate?
- Deuteronomy 4:39 — This day
- Joshua 1:8; Psalm 1:2 — Day and night
- Psalm 63:6 — In the night watches; when you remember Him
- Psalm 119:97 — All the day
  Haggai 2:15 — From this day and upward
- Luke 21:14 — Not before you answer

"But his delight is in the law of the Lord; and in his law doth he meditate day and night." Psalm 1:2

So few of us actually listen while conversing with others, and far fewer listen to God when we pray. It is amazing that we pray to God for answers to our concerns, yet forsake listening to Him so He may impart wisdom and direction unto us. It is hoped we come to realize meditation (to engage in a mental and spiritual exercise for the purpose of reaching a heightened level of spiritual awareness) is one of the most important steps in prayer. The truth of the matter is a warrior is quite enthusiastic and eager to hear a word from God after becoming greatly attune with His Spirit through exercising the previous seven *Prayer Elements*.

The whole of prayer is to get a response from God. The responses we seek range from things such as direction and healing, encouragement and peace, to that of deliverance and blessings, comfort and forgiveness. No matter the case, we are motivated to hear from God in some form or fashion. Our lives should be patterned after the Lord, thus we should at least feel a need to be directed by the Lord. How might we know His Spirit's directing if we are not listening and seeking?

Prayer is not a monologue. Truthfully and sort of conversely, prayer should be less than a dialogue, given our humanly minuscule contributions. There are some who talk entirely too much, saying entirely too little of any importance. Someone just laughed and others gave a giggle knowing good and well they talk entirely too much and listen far too little. At the least we all know someone who's talkative. It is truth we spend so little time listening, for reason we have so much to say; so we think. The Lord is omniscient and is aware of everything in which we stand in need. The Bible tells us, "But when ye pray, use not vain repetitions, as the heathen do: for they think that they shall be heard for their much speaking. Be not ye therefore like unto them: for your Father knoweth what things ye have need of, before ye ask him" *(Matthew 6:7-8)*.

In believing God already has knowledge of our needs, why, oh why, wouldn't we spend more time and energy getting into the spirit of listening versus running our vocal cords? A part of getting into the spirit is listening to the Spirit. This is a *key* that seems so mundane that we tend to overlook it; thus faltering in our prayers. This is two part. First, we must listen to the Spirit in order to enter into the spirit realm. Contrary to common belief, we cannot enter into the spirit unless we are ushered in by the Lord's Spirit. It is not something we fleshy beings can do on our own. Second, we are able to listen to the Spirit after being ushered into the spirit; and no time sooner. Our spirits cannot be steeped in the flesh to constantly hear crucial and sometimes faint directions from the Spirit. Make no mistake about the importance of this key. Forsaking this key will potentially cause the demise of our prayers. It is truth we all want to hear a word from Heaven, so why not listen to He who is the Creator of Heaven?

Our hearts and minds should truly be more sensitized to God's Spirit by the time we have reached this point in the *Prayer Progression*. Here is where many folk falter in becoming prayer warriors. Most folk think prayer is thirty seconds of "Hello God," thirty-five seconds of "Here I come to You again Lord," and forty seconds of "This is what I need You to do Lord." All who think of prayer in this form and fashion are sadly mistaken and are often left with empty prayers. It is a sad mistake to think we have done enough to motivate our spirits to hear from Heaven after praying such abbreviated prayers. A world-class runner takes up to two hours preparing their mind and body for an upcoming race. Similarly, a tour bike rider will take up to an hour spinning just before beginning major races. An opera singer may take a variety of moments preparing their voice through drills of different types in order to ready themselves for a concert. They all prepare in order to get into the spirit and body of their sport or craft. Likewise, those who pray are made to be warriors through progression, which ultimately equates to their period of spiritual preparation.

Spirited Energy

We can truly say truthful prayer is not a simple drill, but an exercise or activity wherein energy is exerted. We must exert energy in order to get into a high spirited mode with the Almighty. There are no exceptions. This exertion of energy is not as much bodily as it is spiritual. As athletes become attune with their bodies and surroundings, Christians too ought become attune with their source of power. That source of power is the Spirit of God. A power source so mighty and strong, and truly worthy of our attention and devotion. Giving the Lord attention demands we minimize the output of our speaking and relinquish unto His Spirit's input. This takes a spirited effort.

For many of us it would take a miracle to get us to stand still for a moment, not to mention how much more it would take to get us actually to listen. Today there is a truth that ADHD (Attention Deficit Hyperactivity Disorder) does exist, but far too many have inappropriately begun to claim it as more of a crutch than as an actual condition. There may even be a chance of increasing our listening skills amongst our friends (horizontally), if we would only sharpen our skills of listening to

God (vertically). As mentioned previously, our horizontal relationships with others are truly reflective of our vertical relationship with God. To make it plain, it is difficult to listen to others if we have never made an effort to listen to God. Listening involves relinquishing self, an effort of which many of us refuse to engage. This very refusal renders far too many of us weak and unable. There is no need to complain that our prayers are not being answered if we first refuse to submit self unto the very Spirit who answers prayers. Our submission engages our listening.

Denied Access

Meditation involves more than just sitting quietly in the center of an empty room staring up at the ceiling in bewilderment. Meditation's strength comes from our sensitivity to God's voice and from our willingness to hear that very same voice. Some of us claim God, but are not truly willing to hear from Him. We, in our spirits, deny Him access for several reasons: we are afraid of His sanctifying power that will clean up our lives; some folk are merely going through the motions of religion; some do not truly believe God actually exist or that He has all power to do all things good; we have succumbed to the will of this world and find it difficult, at best, to now submit to God's will; most of us are fearful of the persecution from others and how they will view our sanctity; some are only concerned that God grant what they ask and are not interested to hear Him speak; and mostly, we simply have not been taught how to harken unto His voice. Which is your poison? Recognize your state and endeavor to change it. Each of these will be discussed now in short.

First, fearing God's sanctifying power is something we sometimes do unconsciously. We say we want our lives cleaned up, but we secretly enjoy our sinful states. The Bible tells us, "No man can serve two masters: for either he will hate the one, and love the other; or else he will hold to the one, and despise the other. Ye cannot serve God and mam'mon" *(Matthew 6:24)*. Yet we try anyhow; as fickle as we are. This effects the way we pray in that we tend not to be truthful about our desire to hear from God. In this we tend not to enter into prayer with conviction, confidence and power. We are at a loss from the beginning when we are betwixt in our desire to hear from God, and when we enter prayer not fully committed unto God. Fact is, some of us would propose to die while in our flesh rather than to change our ways and kill the flesh.

Second, going through the motions of religion is a disease that has befallen far too much of the Church membership. In such, we enter into prayer half heartedly and without real purpose. Playing church has rolled over into many of our adult relationships with the Lord, causing us to not take seriously our need to pray and to desire to hear from Him. God knows we are just going through the motions so He denies us the spiritual access required to hear His voice; just as we first denied Him access into our spirits. Denied access is something we cannot sustain spiritually.

Third, sorrowfully many of us simply do not have faith that God exist and that He has all power to do all things good. I truly wonder if such persons really recognize the pain caused by such a lack of faith and a lack of spiritual communion with God? "The fool hath said in his heart, There is no God" *(Psalm 53:1a)*. Lacking in faith guarantees our denying the Lord; both, in spiritual access and in having an ear poised to listen. Hebrews 11:6 tells us, "... for he that cometh to God must believe that he is, and that he is a rewarder of them that diligently seek him." Without such acceptance and belief, we surely will not desire to hear anything He has to say, nor will we desire to make the effort needed to enter into His presence to pray functionally.

Fourth, the ways of the world have become so ingrained in many of our lives, making it difficult to submit to God's will through our prayers. We may love God and even believe He is real, yet we enjoy entertaining the ways of the world which then cause a disconnect in our communing with Him. The Lord Jesus simply said it this way, "If ye love me, keep my commandments" *(John 14:15)*. Wow! He made that rather plain without elongating His words. Subsequent verses indicate a couple of the benefits of our loving God; such as, our being loved of God and our having the Comforter abide with us for ever. Some of us have a difficult time letting go of some things we enjoy of this world, to a point where it renders difficult our abilities to give God access into our proverbial closets. "Lord change that, but still allow me to do this," can be heard in the spiritless background of many of our prayers. The Lord Jesus said, "For what is a man profited, if he shall gain the whole world, and lose his own soul? or what shall a man give in exchange for his soul?" *(Matthew 16:26)*.

Fifth, most of us are fearful of the persecutions we will receive from others if we enter into the so called "sanctified spirit realm;" which is necessary to be a true prayer warrior. Let me help by saying, this so called realm is not so much an outward show as it is an inward manifestation. Jesus told us in John 14:21 He will manifest Himself to us if we love Him and keep His commandments. It is my spiritual guess not many of us love the Lord enough to allow access for His manifestation to dwell within. It takes a sincere and strong love for the Lord to allow Him access without care nor concern of the persecutions and snares from others. I dare us this day to trust that God can sustain us through all the snares, and believe He will bless us in spite of the persecutions.

Sixth, a basket of us are only concerned that the Lord fulfill our request, and are less interested in hearing His voice. "Just grant me this Lord" is prayed by many of us on a regular basis without any interest in our granting Him access into our spirits. Few times do we ask for the Lord's presence and voice in our situations. That is too complicated for most of us who are void of an ongoing relationship with the Lord. An ongoing relationship empowers us to know there is no deliverance nor blessing greater than His presence. An ongoing relationship with God tells us in faith that in His presence there is deliverance, healing, blessing, power and joy. Fact is, we often need to hear His voice and have His presence in our lives in order to fulfill our prayers, thereafter. God's ways are best and sometimes those ways are made evident through our hearing His voice rather than Him snapping His finger or wiggling His nose to fix our situations.

Seventh, the brunt of us simply have not been taught how to harken unto God's voice. The sad reality is often our teachers did not know how to hear from Heaven themselves. This is often the case since there are generations of people who continue to fall to the wayside spiritually; due to them following the teachings of immature and worldly Christians. It is one thing to follow the teachings of someone who claims to have been in church all their lives versus being taught by someone who is actually filled with the Spirit of Christ and directed by the Father's voice. We were taught as infants to harken to the voices of our parents in order to survive. So, why do we, as Christ' children, find it so difficult to bend our ears towards Heaven with the distinct purpose of granting the Lord access into our spirits? There are not many powers granted to humans that are greater than the power to hear the voice of our God, the Creator. This is a power which enhances and transforms our prayers into vehicles for successful living. How better can we ever survive? Today we will change the pattern of our prayers from being fruitless in spiritual deafness, to that of being fruitful in our willingness to hear His voice.

Meditation is the Fullness of Monologue

As briefly mentioned, meditation, like the *Prayer Element Sign,* is dependent on our realizing and accepting that prayer is not a monologue. For this very reason, many who tend to talk too much or shut others down while in conversations have a difficult time rendering their own prayers successful. Speaking to the Lord is not the gist of prayer. Many whom are unsuccessful in prayer think prayer involves telling the Lord what is on their hearts, only. Nothing could be further from the truth. The crux of our seeking the Lord is to get a response or answer from Him.

Definitions of monologue entail the following: sketches performed by one actor or person; one sided conversation; exchange which is less than that; and, talk monopolized by one person. Any monopolization should be left to the Lord. He has a lot more to say than we ever will. Let us not think so highly of ourselves that we think we have any pertinent information to add to the help of our situations, reaching beyond the wisdom of God. In this portion of prayer we must more so exhibit humility and submission. It is a humbled heart that realizes its ineptness and its inability to do the necessary. Only God has all the answers, thus submitting our ears unto His voice is imperative to the success of our prayers.

As our parents used to tell us when we were young, "Boy you never listen," or "Girl you never stand still for a moment to hear a word I say." Sure that sounds familiar to most, but it is sad to know that the Lord our Father is still saying those very words to many grown adults and to many who claim to be grown Christians. It is only those who listen for God's voice who are grown in Christ Jesus. We must seek that level of maturity which urges Christians to hear from God, above all cost. Mature Christians have a dire need and grand desire to hear from the Lord. In some respects meditation and listening are similar to, and connected with, the *Prayer Element of Sign.* Depending on our level of Christian maturity we may not receive a sign from the Lord until we first meditate.

This document lists *Meditation* last in the *8 Elements of Prayer Progression*™ so prayer warriors will sit to listen to God in a step uninterrupted by any desire to speak another word. It is *key* that we not be so eager to speak during meditation; but listen. We must develop a skill for listening in order to become strong prayer warriors and strong spiritual beings.

Overflow and Meditation

We must not be eager to talk during meditation, yet there will be times when we may revert back into any of the previous *Elements* of prayer; especially when we are ushered into the Lord's overflow. Overflow is a place where the Holy Spirit takes over our spirits and leads us as He may. At that time all bets are off as to what may take place, but surely know additional answers and signs do flow through these added moments of spiritual pouring. Christ' Spirit's manifestation abides in the overflow as our ability to hear His voice is increased through our heightened awareness. Albeit, here is an essential *key* for us all. In that time of overflow we must be mindful to listen and not just shout. Hear me on this. Far too many born again Christians get their shout-on through the overflow manifestation and totally miss the sound of God's voice. Overflow is not just a point to praise excitingly, but a point where He most readily speaks.

Again, prayer is a dialogue throughout, even in parts of meditation. Our
(64) partaking in the dialogue within meditation is to actively listen for His
voice. "Actively" listen is *key* here. Shouting His glory during the
Element of Meditation may revert our prayers back into the *Element of
Praise* with worship. This may hinder the fruitfulness of our meditation,
disallowing us to hear God's answers to our prayers. Hearing His answers
is paramount to the fruitfulness of the *Element of Meditation*. As well,
praise in the overflow of meditation could even transform the prayer into
a session of monologue, whereas we are then the ones who are most
prominently speaking rather than God. Of course, it is great to praise the
Lord vehemently, but there comes a time in prayer when our part in the
realm of participation resides in our actively listening for His speaking;
during which we ponder all that was previously prayed, as well.

Let me reiterate, overflow is the place we all should desire to dwell
during worship and prayer. It is in the overflow that God pours His
power, His Spirit and His oil. We must allow Him to transition us into
the overflow as much as possible. Far too few believers' spirits have
been elevated simply due to their reluctance to allow the Lord to
transition them into His overflow. Oh, the abundance that is in the
overflow! Overflow can be likened unto walking into a room and
flicking on the lights. So much in the room becomes visible and clear.
We are trans-formed into high praisers and fruitful believers when the
Lord's Spirit rest upon us in His fullness. Many do not become fruitful in
Christ Spirit until they have first enjoyed His fullness. We may know His
Word from Genesis to Revelation and we may know all the external
writings we can find, but we will never, ever, know the power of the
Lord's manifestation in us until we meet up with Him in the overflow.
Oh, I can go there right now just by talking about it! It is that place
where His joy rest upon our cares. It is that place where His loving hand
touches our hearts. It is that place where we realize He is all we need. I
get excited when I think of, speak of and enter into His presence by way
of the overflow.

Through it all, we must remember for what reason we have come unto
the Lord in prayer. It is a fine line to be able to walk closely with the
Lord in the high spirit of overflow during meditation at the same time of
actively listening without transitioning back to high praise and worship.
We must contain ourselves without shutting down the Holy Spirit's
movement. Fine line! I Thessalonians 5:19 says, "Do not quench the
Spirit." This is with a capital 'S' indicating the Spirit of God. Quench
translates into extinguish. The fine line also comes about when we grow
to realize living a religious life is not about praise and worship, only.
There is a brain function which must occur for us to receive of the Lord's
directions. It cannot be all praise and worship, while it cannot be all
brains, either.

Don't Block Your Blessing!

It is imperative and urgent that we actively listen for what saith the Lord. What saith the Lord can make or break our very being and existence. Dare I not say some folk are so accustomed to shouting God's glory, but fail to come into the spirit realm of His glory due to their inability to hear His voice amidst all their own shouting. Oh, do not get me wrong. Anyone who knows me will tell you I love to get my praise and shout on. Yes! I love to give Him praise for who He is and for all He's done for me. Yet, the fact remains we will be lost in our praise and lost in our prayers if we do not take the time to listen to what the Lord has to say. I must reiterate, it is not as important for us to tell God what we need or want, as it is important for us to hear His response and answer. The Bible resound-ingly tells us God already knows all of which we stand in need, but there is no scripture which says we already unequivocally know what He wants us to do and in which direction He wants us to travel. It is that simple to understand how imperative it is for us to hear Him versus Him to hear us. Mind you, we had all the opportunity to plead our cases in the *Elements of Prayer Progression*™ that led up to this point. So now, take the time to open the tent door and hear what saith the Lord in meditation.

We often hear folk shout out cliches like, "Don't block your blessing." In the case above, it is not merely a cliche to say we block our own blessings, the hearing of the voice of God, when we shout and praise overtop our listening. Here again, we are not to quench the Spirit of God speaking unto us. This is a time in our prayers when we must recognize where the Spirit is leading. He may be leading us back to another *Element of Prayer* or He may be leading us to intently listen to Him. Here is when it pays to have a strong relationship with the Lord in order to best discern His leading, and in order that we not miss the boat and be left at the shore through another moon or storm. I firmly believe, "What God has for each of us is for each of us," but we must be led in order to receive Him and receive of Him.

Becoming More of a Listener

Those who love dialogue often fare better in their prayer lives, for they naturally seek to hear from the other person with whom they converse. As Christians we must grow to a higher level of dialogue in order to increase our victories through prayer. A dialogue is defined as an exchange in a conversation of opinions, ideas or resolves. Conflict is imminent where and when dialogue does not exist. Some psychologist and philosophers, alike, strongly suggest conflict is the beginning of every good resolution. They will incur it is the conflict which brings about healthy and prosperous resolution. Although true in some instances, I declare today that conflict in any sense of the word, or anyone's definition, will render prayer ineffective. Let me say it this way, it is conflict which disallows many of our relationships to be fruitful. In what greater sense will conflict negatively affect our communicating with the Lord? The Bible says, "Again I say unto you, That if two of you shall agree on earth as touching any thing that they shall ask, it shall be done for them of my Father which is in heaven" *(Matthew 18:19)*, and "Can two walk together, except they be agreed?" *(Amos 3:3)*. I don't know about you, but I will stick with what scripture says about spiritual matters. So, how much more should we be in agreement with the One who answers our prayers? Our coming into agreement with "what saith the Lord" more so happens through our connecting with His Spirit by way of our becoming better listeners in our prayers.

In Agreement Through Submission and Dialogue

Agreement in prayer demands several things, but we will mention two here. First, this agreement involves a uniting of our submission unto God with our acceptance of who He is. Submission and acceptance work closely together to bring prayer warriors into spirited harmony with the Spirit of God, just as they are both essential parts within the first seven *Elements in the Prayer Progression.*™ There can be no agreement if there is no harmony. It is the striving towards, both, the optimum level of submission and the greatest degree of accepting God which powers warriors into a blessed state of agreement with Him.

Second, this agreement involves a great level of dialogue. Again, we speak of harmony and union. Dialogue is a union amongst parties that centers on success and not selfishness. Sad to say many of us attempt to individually win in our horizontal conversations, but at least let it not be so in the vertical with God. In accord with the *Elements of Prayer Progression,*™ we have presented our side of the dialogue as we progressed from acknowledgment and recognition to pre-praise thanksgiving. Now it is time and place for the most important portion of the agreement or dialogue − hearing from God. Here we take time to hear from God through meditation and listening, since there can be no dialogue if we refuse to listen. As mentioned previously, the majority of us make request unto the Lord and fail to take even a moment to hear back from Him. It is a sad commentary to pour out our all unto a faithfully listening God, only to jump up from prayer before He has any opportunity to give His answer. It can be highly declared that this is when and where many of our prayers collapse and falter.

Solitude vs Noise

It is important to understand the necessity to have isolated quiet time with God in order to hear His speaking, most often. Our Lord Jesus would even depart from others in order to speak unto the Father, so how much more should we take heed to do the same? "And in the morning, rising up a great while before day, he went out, and departed into a solitary place, and there prayed" *(Mark 1:35)*. "And when he had sent the multitudes away, he went up into a mountain apart to pray: and when the evening was come, he was there alone" *(Matthew 14:23)*. "And it came to pass in those days, that he went out into a mountain to pray, and continued all night in prayer to God" *(Luke 6:12)*. "And he went a little farther, and fell on his face, and prayed ..." *(Matthew 26:39)*. "He went away again the second time, and prayed ..." *(Matthew 26:42)*. "And he left them, and went away again, and prayed the third time ..." *(Matthew 26:44)*. In Matthew 6:6 the Lord spoke specifically about solitude and prayer, "But thou, when thou prayest, enter into thy closet, and when thou hast shut thy door, pray to the Father which is in secret; and thy Father which seeth in secret shall reward thee openly." Let it be our duty to make time for prayer unto the Lord in solitude.

A *key* to hearing from the Lord is to block out the noise of this world and of ourselves. Yes! We, ourselves, sometimes make just as much noise as the world. At times, it is not even enough for us to get away from just the distractions that the world so easily offers. Most times we must also remove the noise of ourselves so the voice of God may be heard more clearly and distinctly. Some of the noise or conflict arises when we think we have all the answers to our concerns. The Lord desires we lean on Him for all the answers, and in doing so, we must first listen. The Word says, "Trust in the Lord with all thine heart; and lean not unto thine own understanding. In all thy ways acknowledge him, and he shall direct thy paths. Be not wise in thine own eyes ..." *(Proverbs 3:5-7)*.

It is in the time of quiet, listening and submission when our spirits are best receptive unto the Holy Spirit's speaking. The Lord can speak and does speak through anything and at anytime, but we must take time to quiet our surroundings and quiet our own speaking if we truly desire to increase the probability of our being blessed to hear His voice, directions and signs. There are not many things worse than some interruption that comes just as God is about to give us a word of deliverance and direction. Many of us are still in our same sinking boats due to our inability or unwillingness to isolate attention unto the Lord's voice.

66 The *Element of Meditation,* in itself, is a *key* to our having a successful prayer life. Even the success of our natural living depends on our hearing from the Lord. Each of this document's *Elements of Prayer Progression*™ are keys to a strong prayer life and fruitful living, but hearing from the Lord is the ultimate goal of our communicating with Him.

Do not take lightly the act of listening for God's answers. For two reasons too many of us underestimate this importance. First, we are taught to speak to God more so than we are instructed to listen to God. Improper and milk-like teachings come from those who, themselves, are actually weak in prayer. Those very same persons whom neglect to teach of truthful listening to the Lord often have issues overwhelmingly unresolved in their own living, spawned from their own spiritual immaturity. This I say in love and out of the fact that our prayer lives can regulate our natural living. Our natural living will exhibit more spiritual living when we commit to listening for God's answers and directions. I firmly believe each of us desires to live more fruitful lives; thus I say, it is a huge beginning for us all to not underestimate our need to listen for God's voice through meditation.

Second, others of us do not think it to be worth all the effort it takes to actually hear from God. We illustrate how much we underestimate the act of hearing from God by our unwillingness to commit the necessary time. It is true that developing the sensitivity to hear the voice and directions of God does not happen over night, and it takes a bit longer when we are not accustomed to His presence in the first place. Being able to discern God's directions may take some time and some doing over a period of strengthening our relationships with Him. Make no mistake about it, it takes effort and time to be granted the great gift of hearing God's voice. But oh yes, it is one of the greatest gifts we can ever receive.

Also, make no mistake in knowing it is well worth all the effort and all the time it may take to hear from the Lord. We should have a mind-set of determination bent on hearing from the Lord no matter how long it takes and no matter the effort needed to make it happen. Let me say it this way, many of our concerns and trials have come about because we chose to go about things without first knowing what saith the Lord. This alone makes it all worth the effort and time it takes to be directed by God. He can make the crooked places straight and the rugged places smooth, if we would seek His voice and desire His directions above all else. "Every valley shall be exalted, and every mountain and hill shall be made low: and the crooked shall be made straight, and the rough places plain" *(Isaiah 40:4).* On the contrary, at times we've chosen the simpler paths not knowing that the Lord desired us to go the tougher routes, afforded with

His covering and ultimately receiving a greater blessing at its conclusion. The major point here is how might we know the directions we should take lest we hear from Heaven? That question's answer is well worth all the time and effort, no matter how much time and no matter how much effort it may take. Our being able to avoid the unnecessary pitfalls and receive all the blessings set aside for us in this life makes minute the effort it takes to be directed by God. Are big blessings awaiting your listening?

This is the very posture and place God desires and demands us to reside. A place where we abide in Him as He abides in us. This is the same place where we listen intently for His voice. No greater place to be than at the foot of our Lord, adhering to His voice. According to scripture, Luke 8:41, Jarius fell at the feet of Jesus and besought Him to come into his house. The man delivered from demon possession in Luke 8:35 sat at the feet of Jesus clothed and in his right mind. If I were to preach this right now, I would mention that we all come to the understanding that we ought to be at the feet of Jesus after we come to our senses and right minds. The question begs to be asked, "Are you yet in your right mind?" I say "yet" for every knee shall bow and every tongue shall confess that Jesus is Lord, eventually. Let your "yet" be today instead of when the Lord returns.

In Luke 10:38-42 Martha and Mary sat at the feet of Jesus; as verse 39 says, "also." Of course, Martha became upset at Mary's neglect to work, as Mary took additional liberties to stay at the Lord's feet. Mary fell to the feet of Jesus as written in John 11:32, in regards to Lazarus' dying. In Revelation 1:17 we see the Apostle John fell to the feet of the Holy One. All these believers sat at, or fell to the feet of the Lord for guidance, worship and reverence. We too must sit at the feet of the Lord during our meditation periods in order to receive directions. It is imperative that we assume the spiritual and humbled posture that shall usher us into victory and into the Lord's presence. Get to the feet of the Lord and get answers to prayers. Meditating and listening should replicate bowing to the feet of the Lord our Savior. Bow and be blessed. Meditate and see victory.

We have two additional difficulties with our attempting to be successful in meditation: taking the time to create an atmosphere of solitude; and avoiding falling to sleep. First, creating the atmosphere that is most conducive to hearing from the Lord is difficult at times; especially for the parents of small children. A one-year old child does not yet know to respect our personal time spent with the Lord. Those of us who are quite busy have the same difficulty of creating the atmosphere for meditation and prayer. Our clients, bosses and general environments are more concerned about increase in areas not necessarily in the scope of religion.

Second, falling asleep during prayer is a common ill that many have confessed to battle. It is easy to first be motivated to speak to the Lord in prayer, yet find ourselves unintentionally dosing off to sleep, thereafter. The common cure for dosing off in prayer is time. We will develop the stamina and wherewithal to stay awake over a period of time and sessions spent in meditations with the Lord. We must be consistent and persistent with our prayer times in order to develop this stamina. It may even help if we keep in mind great spiritual fruit comes about in prayer after we make our meditation time consistent and persistent.

The fact is, the Lord will create the opportunities if we are persistent and consistent in seeking Him through prayer and meditation. We can be living witnesses unto others if we diligently seek the Lord through prayer while in tough atmospheres that would normally deny such activity. The Lord allows tough situations just so we can show others how faithful we are unto Him. Faithfulness cannot truly be exhibited in perfect circumstances. Today, let us commit to show others our faithfulness unto the Lord by carving out the time for prayer and meditation. Carve-out time is the *key* here! Accept the fact that neither the times nor the opportunities will easily present themselves. We must take the time and create the atmosphere, just as Mary did in Luke 10:38-42. Mary may have understood this key as she may have realized the work and chores will always be present. Likewise, we must be forward and bold to make the time and make the environment for dialogue with the Lord. Prayer warriors know how essential it is to create the time and not allow their present atmospheres nor the apparent distractions to dictate otherwise. Our success in prayer depends on the radiance of this key in our lives.

Hearing from God is the Essence of Prayer

For many it may seem meditation is something in addition to prayer. On the contrary, we must wrap around our faith the fact that hearing from God is prayer. It is not that meditation is just within the activity of prayer. Please understand, the goal of prayer is to hear from the Lord, which most often occurs during meditation. As we exercise this fact in our prayers we will not only be amazed at the things God reveals unto us, but we will begin to realize a more dynamic and fruitful living, also. There is nothing more important in our prayers than to hear from Heaven! Sorely we concentrate on getting a prayer through more than we will to hear of God.

"Hear, O my people, and I will speak ..." *(Psalm 50:7).* This verse gives us more indication of how the Lord will speak if we would simply adhere to His voice. We are all familiar with how our elders turned from us in disgust because we would not listen at times. They wanted to impart wisdom unto us to help us along our way, but we chose not to listen; thus they became frustrated with our ignorant ears and disobedient postures. How much more will God turn from us if we so obstinately choose not to listen? Some of us have yet to hear from the Lord because we have chosen not to listen. He is constantly speaking to us, so why do we refuse to listen? For some of us, God's permissive will is allowing the consequences of our disobedience to fester in our lives. All of us should recognize just how attentive to God's voice we truly are or are not. We should now turn unto God with keenly alerted ears, seeking His guidance, if we lack in attentiveness unto His voice. Let it not be said of us that God sought to speak to us, yet we chose not to listen. If we choose Him as our God then choose to listen to Him, as well. It is even commanded that we listen to God, so why do we still choose not to listen nor adhere? The Lord truly chose us first. Let us now receive of His voice's calling and directions, since it is for us to accept. He will not press the issue, unless any of us are as Jonahs, set to do His work in obviously great manners. We must keep in mind free will is not always so free; as Jonah soon came to realize. Jonah paid the fare to get on the boat traveling opposite God's directions, yet he later paid another price for his disobedience. If we do not oppose God, He will not oppose us.

Let us go a step beyond just the hearing. Psalm 39:12 exclaims, "Hear my prayer O Lord ..." The Lord surely hears us and sees all we are going through. The concern in our prayers is not that the Lord does not hear us, and sometimes it is not that we, in turn, do not hear Him. Often the issue becomes that we refuse to do as He says; especially when the task in itself is problematic. We are fearful of the unknown while other times we are fearful of the grief we may receive from they who become upset with us for doing as God says versus doing as they say. All in all, disobedience unto God is just as harmful to us as not listening to Him in the first place. Let me make it clear, there are those of us who do acknowledge hearing from the Lord, but just choose not to do as He tells us. Some of us do listen to God, but in our childish wickedness we choose to disobey. We desire things of this earth more than we desire to be obedient unto God. We desire our lustful meditations more than we desire to surrender to His perfections. We desire to do what our neighbors tell us rather than having a desire to yield to the leading of our all-knowing and all-powerful God. The game of tennis gives a good illustration of how we must "consolidate the break." The players make every effort to win the game which their opponent is serving; called "breaking." The consolidation comes about when the player then holds his or her own serve the game after breaking their opponent. The prayer application is this — it takes much effort to hear from the Lord, but the break, or breakthrough, bears fruit when we actually do as He says (the consolidation). Amen!

Defiance Negates Trust

We are a defiant and perverse people who are truly undeserving of goodness and mercy. Let's be honest, so to receive the breakthrough. This I say today — take heed to listen to the Lord and do as He says so we may glorify Him and magnify His Spirit. Blessed is the light that shines from obedience. Executing the very things God asks or commands shows our trust and faith in Him. Defiance illustrates distrust! The trust must foreshadow the obedience. Learn to truthfully trust Him and the obedience will naturally follow. Teachers most often illustrate obedience as an isolated event in our spirituality. In the same standard, teachers fail to pattern obedience after trust; as if with disdain. Obedience can be taught all year long without effect if believers are not first taught to trust. It is natural that we follow those things we have first come to trust. Backward minds do otherwise, but the spirited effort is to first develop trust. The hymn writer simply says, "Trust and obey" in that order. "For there's no other way to be happy in Jesus, but to trust and obey."

Better Listeners

Being a good speaker may ensure our being heard by all who are truly listening, but on the contrary, prayer requires that we become better listeners. Let me say that this way. A person can be the greatest speaker who ever lived and still not be heard if no one is listening. That said, God is the greatest speaker past, present and future, but He is still not heard by they who refuse to listen. This remains the issue, or might I say, road-block, which prevents our deliverance through prayer. We tend to pray to God for deliverance, then not listen to Him for directions on that very deliverance. How woeful! Do we not know how to spiritually listen? Have we not been taught to listen? Do we not exercise our abilities to listen? Or, do we not care to listen? What ever the case we must now mature in our abilities to listen while praying. We live in a time when listening to the Lord's speaking is imperative to our very success and existence in the midst of a wicked world that grows colder each day. We, as believers, must eliminate the term "monologue" from our vocabulary, and we should actually cease speaking when we should be listening. The strength of our prayers depends on it. The success of our living relies on it. Our victories in the midst of a decrepit world rest upon it.

You Talk Too Much

Listening is something most of us are not accustomed to doing; especially that of listening intently and passionately. Our society is built upon the thinking that those who have something to say actually have something to say. The fact is we must understand where wisdom confronts eagerness, or shall I say, where wisdom contest aggression. Aggressive folk in our society are thought to be intelligent and smart. On the contrary, aggression in itself often hinders high level thinking and impedes heightened spiritual awareness. Here we can equate having a monologue mentality as being aggressive. Oh, best believe there is a large number of Christians who have monologue mentalities. This mentality not only must be altered, but it must be totally changed. Those of us who like to talk too much have the farthest way to go in changing this monologue mentality; but be encouraged, "I can do all things through Christ which strengtheneth me" *(Philippians 4:13).* Like most things difficult, this change will take Christ' working in us and through us. Let us begin to overcome this daunting task by saying to ourselves, "I can and I will do this — through Christ Jesus."

One statement can be made to help us best understand how essential listening is to the success of our prayers. One statement to effect our listening in our prayers is simply this, "If we are not listening we are not receiving." The simplicity of that statement may cause some of us to miss its essence. The statement pleads how essential it is that we listen while in prayer, instead of speaking, in a sense attempting to receive something other than God's voice. A conflict arises when we speak in prayer at times when we should be listening; caused by a thought that we know of what we stand in need. As long as we think we already know that which we need, we shall never empower our listening skills to reach a height-ened spiritual level needed to truthfully hear from Heaven. Most Biblical and Seminary students are told they must drop their presuppositions in order to receive of the true context of Biblical writings. I hereby exclaim the same in regards to our prayers, whereas, before we kneel we must first drop our presuppositions of what we think we need, so to best receive of God's directions. This is especially true for when we enter meditation. In this way we shall empower our spirits to freely receive of God's answers. This is a *key* which we all must assume in our prayer lives.

The Need to Receive

Listening is the beginning of receiving in prayer, and in the case of prayer it is better to receive than to give. I know you and I have been taught "It is more blessed to give than to receive" *(Acts 20:35),* so let me make it crystal clear I am not opposing scripture. What I am saying is prayer warriors give strong attention to hearing and receiving the Lord's voice and directions. Being attentive is the emphasis of a prayer warrior. They settle into prayer with strict expectation of receiving word from Heaven, notwithstanding all the praise, worship and thanksgiving.

Fact is, we surely cannot give God anything in prayer that will give Him increase; for He's already self-sufficient as the beginning and the ending of all increase. We can surely give Him praise in _Prayer Elements #1, #2, #3 and #7,_ but we assuredly cannot give Him a tittle of a word pertaining to that which we stand in need. He alone has all the answers and every direction for anything we may need. If we are to give God anything in prayer, let us give Him our spiritual ears, our obedience and our trust.

He Already Knows, so We Might as well Listen

Far too many of us think we know it all and so we talk too much. Some of us talk right through our breakthroughs and through our deliverances. We all know folk who just want someone else to think they are smart about a subject, thus they talk all the time. All the time! Did I say, all the time? As mentioned, we cannot fake the fact that what we do in the face of our fellow man we most often replicate with the Lord. This is where talkers have the difficulty of being blessed by the Lord in and through prayer. This is a big _key_ for many of us. Do not think for one moment we can turn off our need to talk too much now that we are speaking unto the Lord in prayer. It does not happen that easily.

I proclaim this very moment, what you see folk doing amidst the brethren they also perform in prayer and in living unto the Lord. For of that truth, activities with our fellow man should be as practice for times we spend with the Lord. It takes both an heedful heart and an attentive spirit to listen to others in the first place. Whereas, we must even go to another level in spirit in order to receive of the Spirit's directions. I charge us all this day to begin to develop a level of spirit, eager to listen and receive directions from the Lord.

If we truly believe in God's power and His Word, we will keep in mind He already knows that which we stand in need even before we pray. The Word tells us to make our petitions and supplications known unto the Lord _(Acts 1:14; Philippians 4:6),_ and to pray without ceasing _(Acts 12:5; Romans 1:9; I Thessalonians 5:17)._ Let us now realize that none of the above scripture verses say anything about talking too much, nor do they direct believers to neglect listening to God. The Lord already knows what we needed before we settled down to pray, and He is waiting for us to come to Him to receive directions and deliverance. Let me ask, "Is God still waiting on you to stop talking and to do more listening so He can bless you?

Listen to Receive

Training to Listen

The major way to train our listening is through our exercising our listening. There are not many fix it diagrams or methods which can help increase our skills to listen more intently in prayer like that of simply closing our mouths and directing our thoughts on what saith the Lord. We live in such a modern era when quick fixes are the norm. Well, my brothers and my sisters the basics are what's needed in the case of our listening in prayer. The basic in this case is to be quiet and listen for the Lord's voice. It is high time we start listening in our prayers, thereby reducing and eliminating our need to try to talk through our situations.

"Fake it till you make it," is still a big mantra for the masses. We humans at every turn attempt to reduce the embarrassment of our ignorance. In doing so we miss opportunities to grow and move in the proper directions. Blessings are made and broken at the very juncture of "fake it" and that of "be honest." Trying to talk our way through in prayer tends to put us in that fake it mode, to whatever extent; as we try to think we know the answers. In training our listening skills we must be more apt to turn things over to God, then listen for His answers; rather than try to figure things out by rambling. Those who do play the fruitless game of over-talking in prayer end up missing God's voice and missing the blessing. Contrarily, they who take the posture of listener receive increase and direction beyond measure. It all begins with exercising our hearing or putting into use our listening. Take the time to exercise listening instead of talking. What will it take to get us to listen? For some it comes by way of pain and suffering.

I declare many will begin their change by the words, "We must listen to receive." The Bible says, "The secret things belong unto the Lord our God: but those things which are revealed belong unto us and to our children for ever, that we may do all the words of this law" _(Deuteronomy 29:29)_. Do not be mistaken to think we cannot receive the Lord's speaking unto us. We should not only train-up our children in the ways they should go _(Proverbs 22:6)_, but we should transform and train-up ourselves in our listening and living unto God, as directed in Romans 12:2. How else may we know God's will for our lives lest we listen to Him? He will grant us answers if we seek Him in truth and if we are sensitized to receive.

Relationships and Listening

Let us speak for a moment on relationships — the horizontal and the vertical. We will surely be blessed in our vertical relationships with the Lord if we would learn how to better listen to Him. In turn, our increased listening in our vertical relationships will show fruit in our horizontal relationships. We will become better communicators with our fellow man, if we learn the art and importance of listening to God. It is in our vertical relationships with the Lord where we learn how to be better saints among the brethren. To learn how to be a better friend to our neighbor we must begin by being a better friend to God. To learn how to love our brothers and sisters we must begin with showing better and truthful love to the Lord Jesus. To learn the essence of listening we must begin by taking time to listen to the Lord. It will fare us greatly to increase with our Father in Heaven so we may in turn do the same here on earth.

Something to remember when it comes to listening and our relationships is that we will surely be attentive to those things which interest us. The more a thing interest us the more attentive we will be to that very thing. Our attentiveness is in parallel with our willingness to listen. Let us be forward to admit we spend time with and listen unto people who peak our interest. Most of us can attest there were persons we chose not to listen unto because we felt they had nothing to say or they never peaked our interest from the beginning. Let me make this point very clear and close. This is no way to treat our God. Believe it or not, we indirectly tell God He is of no interest to us when we refuse to listen to Him. It is a crying shame how some of us treat our God. When was the last time you truly and eagerly sought to hear a word directly from God? We should answer that question, at worst, by saying, "This morning." Unfortunately that is something to which most of us cannot attest. This is a great *key* for us all in our quest to become strong prayer warriors.

I do not apologize for opening your eyes to see this shortcoming, for I am called to minister the word in season and out of season; as proclaimed in II Timothy 4:2. It is through the opening of our eyes that we will bring forth 100,000 true prayer warriors, prepared for times at hand and times to come. I send forth this charge this day for all to illustrate to God and this world how much God is of interest to us by strongly seeking to listen to Him. There are not many ways greater to show someone disrespect than to not listen to them. Woe unto us if we choose not to listen to the Lord after today. A prayer warrior is a believer who is close to God and is one who shows Him great respect by constantly seeking to hear His voice's directions. Purchasing and reading this document was the beginning of your showing desire to be strong in prayer. Now you must go forth with these precepts at hand and with a heart seeking His voice.

This is such needed wisdom, albeit some of us will still fail to recognize how the Lord blesses us through our relationships with Him. His blessing us is not always as direct nor plain as we would like. We often pray that the Lord bless things like our homes and families. Fact is He may fulfill the blessing through us if we would listen to His teachings in our prayers. He even may teach us to respect our soon to come home in Glory, which in turn will give us indications how to respect our earthly homes now. These and other blessings He may fulfill in our lives, if only we first would get closer to Him by listening. Receive and be blessed.

It is simple to understand many of us fail to listen to our wives, husbands, sisters, brothers and neighbors simply because we never take the time to listen to our Lord; who teaches us how to listen to our fellow man. Our vertical and horizontal relationships match and mirror one another more than most will admit. Some will vehemently claim they treat the Lord well while they dog their brethren saying, "I love God more than my brethren." This somehow may be true in our minds, but the actual truth of how we care for the Lord comes to light in our actions towards others. As explained before, we are liars if we claim to be able to turn on the love dial for God and turn it off for our neighbors. The Bible says, "If a man say, I love God, and hateth his brother, he is a liar: for he that loveth not his brother whom he hath seen, how can he love God whom he hath not seen? And this commandment have we from him, That he who loveth God love his brother also" *(1 John 4:20-21).* It is a simple but Biblical truth.

Our characters do not have some type of easy switch that can be turned off and on to the tune of our likes and dislikes. For the most part, our character remains fairly consistent in all we do. In other cases we try to fool people just as we try to fool the Lord, but He knows how we truly despise Him in our hearts just as we despise our neighbors. Our mouths may say one thing, but our hearts testify against us. We, your brethren, cannot see just how you treat the Lord, but He can see your heart and motives. You may be able to fake out mere man, but there is no fooling God. You are only fooling yourself if you think any differently. "... for the Lord seeth not as man seeth; for man looketh on the outward appearance, but the Lord looketh on the heart" *(1 Samuel 16:7).*

Having a Thirst

We must have a thirst to hear from the Lord in order to truly be fruitful vessels available to be used of Him. That thirst will demand we take the time not only to talk to Him, but more importantly take the time to listen for His voice. A thirst for the Lord's voice takes us to another level of worship unto Him. A thirst is a proverbial, "Laying it all on the line." Thirst occurs when submission meets desire, and desire then meets attentiveness. We cannot just want to hear from the Lord, but we must have a strong desire to receive of Him. There is an unquenchable fire that burns in our spirits when we have a desire for the Almighty's voice and directions. For true believers, hearing of His voice any one time even does not extinguish their desire to further constantly hear from Him. This is a desire that says, "I must dwell in the presence of the Lord, always." I personally have never had an addiction other than that of a healthy and strong desire to hear from Heaven, but I imagine an addicts desire for drugs, alcohol, sex and other things drives him or her to great lengths to satisfy that fix. Well I declare this very day, we must have that same, if not stronger, desire for God's voice. If I could minister directly to someone here by saying, know ye that any addiction can be replaced by having a strong and healthy thirst to hear the voice of God. If we must be addicts at all, let us get fixed on hearing the voice of the Lord. The Bible declares it this way, "O taste and see that the Lord is good: blessed is the man that trusteth in him" *(Psalm 34:8)*. "How sweet are thy words unto my taste! yea, sweeter than honey to my mouth" *(Psalm 119:103)*. You have tasted everything else, why not truly taste of Jesus? If I can have anything, give me word from on High, then I will stay fixed on it.

Some who are unknowing or unsympathetic may criticize the analogy of an addict, but it is used to fully stress the fact that many, who are called believers, do not thirst for God's voice. A great number of believers are far too lukewarm about their relationships with God. The example also serves as strength for they who truly know that bad habits must be replaced with good practices in order for a person to move into victory.

Having a lack of thirst for God's voice may be the reason many have not heard from the Lord. This may be the very reason many have had little success in their living. Maybe, just maybe, we ought check our spiritual desire gauges. This is what the scriptures speak of "seeking." Seeking is more action packed than any normal verb, since it has thirst as a major component. How can one truly seek if there is no thirst? How can a person thirst, but not truly seek?

We can liken some people seeking after God's voice to that of a light jog rather than of an all out sprint. These light joggers make feeble attempts to secure temporary relationships of listening to God just to receive from their prayers, whereas, prayer warriors develop a true thirst for the Lord's voice to effect change through their prayers. The Bible is rather explicit in its referencing seeking, so let us be just as clear in our desire to listen for His voice. "One thing have I desired of the Lord, that will I seek after; that I may dwell in the house of the Lord all the days of my life, to behold the beauty of the Lord, and to enquire in his temple" *(Psalm 27:4)*. Then shall you cry out like Asaph saying, "Whom have I in Heaven but thee? and there is none upon earth that I desire beside thee" *(Psalm 73:25)*.

It is God's desire that we are intently driven to listen for His voice. The intents of our hearts will be evident by the truth of our thirst for His voice. Our hearts cannot lie and they will surely expose our level of faith and belief in God. It is a key for us to show great increase in this area of our faith. We must develop an unquenchable thirst that keeps us striving to seek that which provides us with power, direction and strength — the voice of God. This is a *key* for not only our prayer lives, but for our living a strong life of faith unto God, as well. We all can fare well by developing more thirst for the Lord and His voice.

Not Just Hear, But Answer

It can be said that meditation is all of prayer. That is meant to say meditation is about hearing a word, answer or direction from the Lord. I do thank God for blessing me by listening to my cries, but I bless His name all the more for bestowing upon me answers to those cries: an answer for my prayer; a direction for my ways; a light unto my darkness; a covering for my territory; a joy for my sorrows; a calm for my concerns. A word from God can and will make everything alright.

We must transition from just wanting God to hear our prayers to wanting God to answer our prayers. Many have yet to see the fruit of their prayers and have yet to evolve into prayer warriors, because they are idle at wanting God to simply hear their cries. I don't know about you, but I want the power of Jesus working through me as the Father answers my prayers. Fact is, not only has our Father heard our every cry but He sees all that is happening in our lives before we ever speak the first word in prayer. He is ever present and all knowing. Now is the time for us to grow up and grow into having strong desires for God to actually answer our prayers. Sad to say a number of us do not listen for His answers, for reason that we never expect Him to answer in the first place. If the truth were told, we often enter prayer with the sole objective to cry out to God. That is a little simple minded when you think about it; especially when we should realize we serve a prayer answering God. We often shout that He is a prayer answering God, but we do not live like we know it, nor do we pray like we believe it.

Prayer warriors are at another level of communion with God where they are expecting Him to answer their every prayer. We are conscious in knowing He may not answer every prayer as we so want, but we are respectfully expecting an answer, nonetheless. That is the hope and the faith within those who are called prayer warriors. One hundred thousand new prayer warriors will gain strength from this *key* and show power in a world needing help from the Lord our God.

King David was a prayer warrior who knew it was not enough to want the Lord to hear his cries, only. If David was not fighting a battle, chances were he was either praising God or praying; chiefly so In his prayers he could be found asking the Lord for an answer. Such was the case in Psalm 138:3, "In the day when I cried thou answeredst me, and strengthenedst me with strength in my soul." We can receive comfort by knowing someone simply hears our cries, but strength and power are obtained when we additionally receive answers and directions from them. At times it is important to receive comfort through our prayers in order to mentally and physically survive till our breakthrough occurs, but prayer, for the most part, is about receiving a word from the Lord. There are times we merely must cry out to the Lord, just as the psalmist illustrated in 130:1-2, "Out of the depths have I cried unto thee, O Lord. Lord, hear my voice: let thine ears be attentive to the voice of my supplications." Let it be known that it is good that someone will listen to our cries, but the *Element of Meditation* is for hearing a word from the Lord. Do not forsake this and you shall be blessed.

This *Prayer Progression* gets to the nuts and bolts of prayer. For example, it is all cute to hear someone shout, "The Lord heard my cry!" Tell you what you do the next time someone says those very words. Turn and ask them, "What did He say?" Like I tell persons in business, "Cute does not sell nor does it get it done." I want to know what He said to do. Being a prayer warrior is not about being cute, it's about getting answers. "I thank You for listening Lord, but tell me what to do in my situation!" Psalm 118:5-6 says it this way, "I called upon the Lord in distress: the Lord answered me, and set me in a large place. The Lord is on my side; I will not fear: what can man do unto me?" An empowering light grows inside me when the Lord gives me answers. What can man say, or do, when an all-knowing and all-powerful God gives answer to prayer?

Psalm 27:7 says, "Hear, O Lord, when I cry with my voice: have mercy also upon me, and answer me." It is a loving and merciful God who will give answer to our prayers. Be the prayer warrior you are called to be by not ending prayer without earnestly asking for an answer from the Lord. Lamentations 3:22 declares, "It is of the Lord's mercies that we are not consumed, because his compassions fail not." Far too many of us continue to get swallowed by our trials, simply due to our neglect to get answers and directions from the Lord. Some of us, a long time ago, should have gotten tired of being overwhelmed by our situations. A wise man once said, "A man will not change his situation until he is fed up." How many of us are fed up with our trials lingering and causing so much pain? The time has come, and is, when we change our situations by receiving pertinent answers from God.

Chapter 42 of Jeremiah speaks heavily on the point of hearing an answer from the Lord through prayer. This chapter is not only a good example of how we are to seek the Lord's answers, but it tells of how we are to, thereafter, respect and obey the answers given. It is our choice to either receive the Lord's mercy by seeking and following His directions, or become consumed by our trials through disobedience and disregard.

Our Hearts Desires

Hearing from the Lord was the greatest desire for most of the faithfuls throughout history, as it should be the greatest desire of Christ's children today. The milk fed should strongly desire to get closer to Him in order to recognize His voice, and those on meat should have full blown appetites to hear from Heaven on a more regular basis. In either category of believer the fullness of Christ' manifestation within is made evident by their desire to be near Him and to receive His voice's directions. In both categories of believers there must develop a strong desire to transition from merely needing to speak to the Lord to that of needing to hear from the Lord. The churched often cry out "I need to have a little talk with Jesus," and there are hymns and spiritual songs that reflect the same message. Yet, I declare this day we must grow a generation who's heart's desires are to hear God's voice more than speak to Him. As humans, we often have the grave issue of not only having twisted desires, but we then teach the same things to others. We have far too many teachers who will fight everyone in the church for the opportunity to teach; sold-out on being seen and void of a desire to truly move people closer to the Lord. Always needing to be heard and seen is an issue that permeates several generations; especially in this western world.

Oh yeah, it is great to talk to the Lord, but hearing from Him is of greater importance. Many Christians spend a lot of time talking to the Lord and are still idling in pain, despair, destruction and desolation. I can boldly say their conditions often persist primarily due to them talking to Him, but not hearing back from Him. It can be said that we do not hear back from Him for two natural reasons. First, we often have a need to always be heard in prayer instead of having a desire to listen while in prayer. Second, we lack passion and thirst to trust that the Lord will actually speak to us and speak to our situations through our prayers.

Listen ~ Hear

His greatest will is for us all to be saved, but He also desires us to prosper — in Him. Here is a turning point and *key* for us all. Sorrowfully, our prayers are spawned by our desire to prosper in some area other than in God, Christ and the Holy Spirit. Oh, let's be honest. We pray to have homes. We pray to be healed. We pray to find mates. We pray for food on our tables. We pray for a good job with great pay and benefits. We pray that our children grow trouble free. We pray for so much prosperity in so many areas other than the area of our being in Christ Jesus. The Bible says, "But seek ye first the kingdom of God, and his righteousness; and all these things shall be added unto you" *(Matthew 6:33)*. The Bible also tells us in Matthew 10:31 and Luke 12:7 how the Lord provides for the sparrow and that we are of more value to Him than they. Yet, we still tend to display this great need to ask the Lord for so much increase in areas outside of Him. As I've said before, it is not the goal of this document to have us to stop praying for things, but it is the Lord's will that we desire Him, above all else. In doing so, we shall be blessed with all we need and even some of what we desired in the first place.

In addition, it is truly ok to desire prosperity, but how about desiring the Lord Jesus! This paragraph and the previous paragraph are borderline *Request Element* points, yet they fair stronger here in the *Element of Meditation*. These words are so tailored for meditation because it is in meditation when we not only ponder over all we have prayed, but when we more strongly seek His voice upon our situations, as well. It is great to have our prayers answered, but we will find God's presence to be the true answer to our prayers. Hear me! Yes, it is great to have the Lord direct us on how to walk, how to talk and how to live, but a truly spirited blessing occurs before all that comes into fruition. This does not negate the fact that throughout all of prayer we should seek a word from God.

There is an awareness in the forefront of the minds and spirits of all the faithful Christians who love God for who He is rather than just for what He provides. This is an awareness which strongly acknowledges that God's presence is the very blessing and answer that they so seek. Do not get me wrong, for I am no different than anyone else, but let me testify. I like having things, but what I like having most is the great feeling that comes over my spirit when I am in His presence. That is my heart's greatest desire. At that point everything else takes second fiddle. At that time all time stands still. At that very moment of being in His presence, there is no greater blessing that can be had. All who have truly been blessed by His presence and His voice can truly say, "Just to be in Your presence O' Lord." Grant me that, Father! That is a part of that peace that passes all understanding proclaimed in Philippians 4:6-7. Of course, prayer and supplication are a part of that scripture, as well.

Be Careful for What You Pray

I Samuel 8:7-22 illustrates how the people Israel asked for a king. God granted them a king, but they were given their request just to show how they, and we, must be mindful of what is asked; especially in asking for something other than God Himself. The Israelites were persistent in their desiring and asking for something other than God; similar to the contents of our prayers today. Yes, this hits home for most of us. For this reason I explain to folk how they must be mindful of their application of the verse which says, "Pray without ceasing" *(I Thessalonians 5:17)*. This Word tells us to constantly stay in communion with God, more so than to continue to pray for the same thing over and over. The Bible also declares, "... no good thing will he withhold ...." *(Psalm 84:11)*. Understand, He knows what's good and what's not good for us. Believe that truth and be blessed.

God does not give us all we desire and ask, for He knows what is profitable and not profitable for us. Nonetheless, if we persist in asking for the very things of which we are not ready to receive, the Lord may grant our request just to prove the point. He may grant our persistent request for things that are flat out not good for us, in order to grow us out of our immaturity in prayer; allowing the anguish of the unfruitful request. Our continuing to pray for the same thing over and again may be viewed as our having disbelief of God's being in full control. Woe unto all who do not believe God is omnipotent and omniscient. The Lord Jesus declared in Matthew 6:7-8, "But when ye pray, use not vain repetitions, as the heathen do: for they think that they shall be heard for their much speaking. Be not ye therefore like unto them: for your Father knoweth what things ye have need of, before ye ask him."

It is a shame that some of us need to see the devastating and destructive results of our repetitiously praying for things that are not ours to possess. We should rather listen to and willfully accept His answer of "No;" which sometimes comes by way of His not responding at all. In this way we can save ourselves and those around us a lot of unnecessary pain and anguish. We must mature to be more apt to pray, "Remove far from me vanity and lies: give me neither poverty nor riches; feed me with food convenient for me: Lest I be full, and deny thee, and say, Who is the Lord? or lest I be poor, and steal, and take the name of my God in vain" *(Proverbs 30:8-9)*. He may cover us from total devastation, but who wants to go through any unnecessary trials, no matter the extent? Yet, we bring the unnecessary upon ourselves by persisting on receiving that which we should not possess, cannot handle or may not be of Christ. It has been illustrated in previous *Elements* and is proclaimed in the Word of God, "... for we know not what we should pray for as we ought," *(Romans 8.26)*.

Nevertheless, I do thank the Holy Spirit for illuminating unto me the fact that we should know for what to pray once we mature in Christ. Once we transition from milk to meat we should have already come to grips that we are to pray for God's presence in our lives, first and foremost. That should be our desire above all else. "Be ye ever present in our lives, Oh Lord. Don't just protect us, but fill us. Don't just provide for us, but dwell in us. Don't just increase our territory, but give us an overflow of Your Spirit. Don't just make a way for us, but speak unto us the way in which we ought travel." Oh, how much more could anyone be blessed? Not just that the Lord made a way, but He told us through meditation which way would result in our being blessed. Is anyone being stretched this very moment? Thank God for the stretching. Stretch me Lord!

As babes in Christ He had to gingerly lead us by the hand along the way. As matured Christians we have become able to follow His voice's directions. I thank God for leading me by the hand, but I shout His glory that I am mature enough in Him that my spiritual ears are sensitized to receive His voice's directions. Those who receive of this wisdom shall be blessed. "For the preaching of the cross is to them that perish foolishness; but unto us which are saved it is the power of God" *(I Corinthians 1:18).* Prayer warriors have matured spirits and are called by God to discern His voice's directions. "That thou mayest love the Lord thy God, and that thou mayest obey his voice, and that thou mayest cleave unto him: for he is thy life, and the length of thy days: that thou mayest dwell in the land which the Lord swore unto thy fathers, to Abraham, to Isaac, and to Jacob, to give them" *(Deuteronomy 30:20).*

Babes in Christ often pray that the Lord make a way for them, while matured prayer warriors come to realize He has already made a way; thus, they ask for the spirit to discern. When in the midst of a trial, those who live according to the flesh and those who live with wavering faith think in terms that the way shall be provided some day. Whereas, mature Christians stand in faith of the Word knowing God has not forsaken them. The Bible says, "There hath no temptation taken you but such as is common to man: but God is faithful, who will not suffer you to be tempted above that ye are able; but will with the temptation also make a way to escape, that ye may be able to bear it" *(I Corinthians 10:13).* This verse tells the mature in Christ a way of deliverance has already been provided. The verse says, "... with the temptation ....," therefore, it is merely up to us to discern the Lord's voice as to the path to travel for the victory. The mature Christian is aware that we have free will, yet they have faith that God knows the end before it ever begins.

The mature in Christ can be found saying, "I know it may seem like I am in deep trouble, but there is something within this trial the Lord wants me to learn." They do not cry, "Help me Lord," most often. They have faith to know their help is already at hand and they must spend more time discerning the way to go, rather than spending precious moments crying overflowing rivers of "Help me." In no way am I saying we are not to cry, for there are times when it's healthy to release some pain through our tear ducts. What I am saying is that as prayer warriors we have a deep responsibility to mature to a level of faith set forth by the very Word of God. Many of our successes and our neighbor's victories are dependent upon the prayer warrior knowing what saith the Lord of our faith fathers.

Sounding Board?

If our goal in prayer is to hear from Heaven, why do we so often use the Lord as a sounding board, only? The Lord says, "I am bigger than that!" Our friends and family can be used as just sounding boards, for they may not possess the ability to help us with our concerns. This may be the truthful realization and testimony of many who have yet to seek God's directions, and of many who continue to reduce God to the status of sounding board. Could it be there are those who just need a friend to hear their cries? Could it be there are those who believe He is a friend who sticks closer than a brother *(Proverbs 18:24)*, but lack the faith to know He will answer their prayers and deliver them *(Psalm 118:5)*? Could it be there are those who believe the Lord will hear and listen *(Psalm 120:1)*, but lack the spiritual maturity to believe He has all power in heaven and in earth *(Matthew 28:18)*?

Whatever the case, it is time — I repeat — it is time for us to mature to the level of claiming our rightful place in the spirit, so we may show forth the Lord's power within. In doing so, we must initially lift God to a position higher than sounding board. He is available for more than simply bouncing tears and ideas. He is the great "I Am" *(Exodus 3:14)*, and He is able to do all things but fail. But God! But God! He has all power to do all things but fail. Not only does He have the ability to help us with our concerns, but He possesses the will to take care of our concerns, also. So, let it be known this very moment God is larger than some ordinary sounding board, just waiting to hear of our tears and pains. He is a Way Maker who is ready, willing and able to hear our cry and answer by and by. We've heard it before, now let us live within its power.

King David often asked the Lord to hear his prayer, asking things like, "Hear the right, O Lord, attend unto my cry, give ear unto my prayer, that goeth not out of feigned lips" *(Psalm 17:1)*. David also knew to pray for an answer from God, "Hear my prayer, O Lord, and let my cry come unto thee. Hide not thy face from me in the day when I am in trouble; incline thine ear unto me: in the day when I call answer me speedily" *(Psalm 102:1-2).* Let us be mindful of the example of David and not call on God just for Him to hear, but for us, in turn, to hear His voice through meditation and all of prayer. Psalm 20:1, 4 reiterate this point, as verse 1 calls on the Lord to hear, while verse 4 entreats the Lord to answer.

Do Not Be Afraid of Success

Entering into prayer is an indication that we are anticipating the success of our request; or is it? Faith says the very act of settling down to pray is a testimony that we expect victory and fruitfulness to be the outcome; or does it? The point is, far too many of us enter prayer half-heartedly and partially doubtful that our prayers will be answered by God. This is not due to our disbelief in God, per se, but can be attributed to our disillusionment and fear of success. Someone now may be saying, "How can a person be afraid of success?" Well, best believe it to be true. We can partly credit it to our never being groomed to admire and embrace the success of our prayers in the first place. As we mature into prayer warriors, we now must carry a posture that says, "Our being a Christian is success in itself." It should be natural for us to expect success through our prayers after such an awareness of our inheritance.

If you are not afraid of success, then ask the Lord to answer you! We are not to be afraid of the success that awaits our prayers. Jesus is our success and we will always be victorious as long as we are in His presence and hearkening unto His voice. See, many of us have been so deep in despair in our own shortcomings that we find it difficult, at best, to imagine we can have such great success with and through an unseen God. Success in itself, first, is a matter of having faith in an unseen God. Truth be told, the faithful can see God because He dwells with them and in them. "And I will pray the Father, and he shall give you another Comforter, that he may abide with you for ever; Even the Spirit of Truth; whom the world cannot receive, because it seeth him not, neither knoweth him: but ye know him, for he dwelleth with you, and shall be in you" *(John 14:16-17).* Please receive of this power, for this document is to open the scriptures unto us.

We are already successful in that we even are able to enter into prayer. It is success to have the awareness to pray to God, and it is victory to know we have a Lord who is available. We are clothed in success and perfumed in the victory of Jesus, as we are chosen by God and have an inheritance with the Son. We should have that same expectation of success through meditation. To meditate is to anticipate the success of hearing directions from the Father. There is a rock of power which rises within the faith of prayer warriors; breathing of success. This expectation is as riding a rushing wind stabilized by faith in the Word that declares, "And all things, whatsoever ye shall ask in prayer, believing, ye shall receive" _(Matthew 21:22)_, and "I can do all things through Christ which strengtheneth me" _(Philippians 4:13)_. Spirited expectation involves a certain level of faith in ensuing success. As prayer warriors we are clothed in this faith, so we enter meditation expecting to hear from on High.

These words I write, revealed, may seem as nonsense to the stony at heart and to the unaware, but to them who believe it is power — oh power. Take, receive and utilize this power granted unto you by the power vested in me. The power is Jesus the Christ our Savior who has all power to answer all our prayers.

Convinced in Advance

Before entering prayer we must already be convinced we are about to hear from the Lord. "When I call, He will answer; somehow," should be our belief prior to getting on our knees. Best believe His answer is sufficient. Why else would we pray to Him? Why pray unto Him if we are not truly convinced in hearing from Him? It is my hope all of us speak over ourselves before entering into prayer saying, "I'm about to hear from Heaven!" What power! This is a _key_ for us all.

Enter ye into prayer with a heart and spirit convinced that in a moment ye are about to hear from the Lord. That moment can happen throughout prayer, but will often occur during meditation. Do not forsake the _Element of Meditation_ and thereby not forsake hearing from the Lord. We can and will hear from the Lord if our hearts are willing and if we take the time to allow Him to open our spirits, hearts and minds. He is not going to force us to listen to Him, most often; but He surely is available.

We should believe in our spirits God is available even before sitting down to pray. Oh, He is available! As a matter of fact, we ought say it a few times right now — "He is available! He is available! He is available!" Try Him and witness His power and greatness. That is what this document is all about — empowering us with the tools God has prescribed unto us, both, to get into the fullness of His presence and to hear directions from on High. It is my prayer that I have best submitted unto His using me, saturated in that said power so to best convey His word through this document and unto His people.

One hundred thousand new and strong prayer warriors shall be brought forth if we allow the Lord to empower us through these keys and precepts. The devil may try to tell us it is not possible, but the devil is a liar; as proclaimed in John 8:44. The Lord has sent forth His word and has laid out His plan. No devil in hell nor imps on this green earth can lay to rest that which God has ordained!

Importance: Cry or Listen

It is of greater importance to hear from the Lord than it is to tell Him all our concerns; as mentioned previously. Some of us, many of us, well quite frankly most of us like to complain and cry more than we desire to produce progressive results. Oh, I know I am right about it. More folk would be more silent in prayer if it were not so; direly attempting to hear from God. If it were not so, folk would not be so eager to jump up from prayer after they have poured out their heart unto the Lord. If it were not so, more of us would be waiting for the Lord's voice in meditation, thereafter.

As mentioned and proclaimed in verse, the Lord already knows what we stand in need before we pray. The missing part is our knowing "What saith the Lord" in regards to that which we stand in need. The answers to our prayers are in His voice's directions, and not in our crying out to Him. As a people made by God, we have the propensity to feel better momentarily after unloading the thing, concern or issue off our chest. We just want someone to listen to all of what we are going through, after which we seem to feel somewhat delivered. "Help us God to transition our thinking and living!"

We must transition our mode of thinking and living from being mere criers to being great listeners. Take time to listen for a word from Heaven. King David exemplifies this point in Psalm 5:3, as he gave prayer unto the Lord, then waited in expectation for His voice. We too must become a people seeking to hear from God in our prayers, rather than seeking to be heard of by God, only. Some of us are just so bent on being heard. Life stops for so many of us until we feel our pleas have been heard. No matter how the crowd may move, we must seek to hear from Heaven; thus we must meditate in our prayers, giving God the time and opportunity to speak to us. "Give us a word, O' God!" This is one of the biggest areas of change for the large majority of us. Let us make the commitment to begin this very day!

A Change

In religion preachers and laypersons, alike, have all been filled with much Word and wisdom to a point where we feel a need to tell something to someone. Not that we feel we know it all, but that we have a desire to share. Let it be known that prayer time is no time to feel like flexing our wisdom and knowledge, nor is it time to demonstrate all of our highfalutin abilities to express our trials and concerns. Prayer is a time bent on doing all the things necessary to hear a word from Heaven. Preachers, leaders, and laypersons must change our thought patterns in order to become more successful in prayer, shepherding and spiritual living. As we have read, it takes more than just being able to verbalize scripture and "woe is me's" in order to get a prayer through to God. So, understand how much more it takes even to then get an answer from Him.

Success in prayer takes a receiving spirit and a listening heart, convinced that God knows best. Our focus must be on hearing the voice of God rather than sharing our voice with Him; thus, our need for meditation. He already knows how our voices sound. Prayer is not even a time for voice try-outs nor complaining rehearsals. Our every attempt in prayer is to get an answer from God, not to take part in the next season's film production nor cd release entitled, "What I cried unto the Lord." As a matter of fact, more than half of our attention should be bent towards hearing the voice of God throughout all of praying. It is going to take practice and a willing spirit to be able to speak and listen at alternating moments. This is prime reason this meditation is so important to have at the end of prayer. Let me say it this way, the *Meditation Element* is situated at the end of prayer and as a solo event for the sake of importance and isolated concentration. We must listen for the voice of God throughout prayer, for God only knows when He will choose to speak. Yet ending with meditation can best ensure our hearing from the Lord if our spirits were not quite sensitized during the previous seven *Elements*. It is often more functional to listen or speak separately, although the power of His Spirit is most potent in our listening during periods of heightened spirituality within praise and worship. Through practice and getting closer to the Lord we shall become mature in our abilities to hear His voice and directions. Listen and be blessed.

Not a Substitute for Prayer

Many of us think of meditation as a substitute for prayer. We tend to say, "I didn't pray today, but I did meditate." Beginning now, we must think of meditation as a supplement or *Element* of prayer. Strong prayer does not exist without sensitized listening to the Almighty; thereby, the crux of

75 meditation. This is a *key* for us all to progress as prayer warriors and as strong Christians. Far be it we use meditation as just another vehicle to talk to God versus taking the time to submit unto His ministering and speaking. Who does not want to be ministered unto, especially by God Himself? We all need ministering; thus, we should be excited to go into meditation, using the time wisely and productively as a period of listening for the greatest voice of all.

A prayer warrior's mindset is different than most others; as is the strong Christian's mindset. At a certain level of Christian development there comes the understanding that we are all accountable to someone; or we should be accountable to someone. Ministering to others and praying for others demands us to first be accountable unto God for our directions. This directing will not occur with the best precision unless we are first listening to God. In such, meditation becomes our fueling method. Without spiritual fuel (directions) our prayers and Christ centered living chug along at the brink of stalling.

Psalm 119:97, "O how I love thy law! it is my mediation all the day." Here, meditation (siychah) is defined as reflection, devotion and prayer. Within this portion of this document we speak of the *Meditation Element in the Prayer Progression* likened to Psalm 39:3 as (hagiyg), which illustrates musing as an adjunct to prayer: something that adds to the performance of a main piece. This verse tells of how David first gave careful thought of God and the things which were at hand, seperate, but in concert with his speaking. Again, we can meditate without praying, but truly understand it is not a straight substitute for prayer in the *Prayer Progression*. In Psalm 1:2, a favorite for most of us, meditation (hagah) is defined as murmur, ponder, imagine, mourn, mutter or roar, but here as well, there is no mention that it is as prayer in and of itself.

As a personal testimony, much of my personal time as a youth and adolescent was spent on my knees in prayer. It was truly what got me through it all. As I grew in my personal relationship with Christ I found meditation to be powerful and quite useful in times when I could not still away to actually get on my knees for needed prayer. Learning of meditation was one of the greatest powers vested upon my spirit, but at the same time in my innocence it became a kinda bump in the middle of my road of spiritedness. I say this because I came to use meditation as a substitute for prayer, rather than an incorporated part of prayer. During my college days, I meditated and contemplated on God more than I prayed unto Him. That was the bump. Those days would not have been marked with so many poor decisions, including the letting go of "A rose in a watered glass," had I been on my knees in prayer more often.

You can be a good person with a good heart and still make poor decisions if you are not in prayer unto God. Life is far too difficult not to be in direct communication with God; especially if you too are progressive and highly favored. Great gifts can be directed by a great God, only! Do you have great gifts?

It was not until three years after graduating from college that I came to the reality of how harmful my incorrect application of meditation had taken its toll on my life. Meditation had almost totally substituted my prayer life. Understand, my life has been anything but perfect, yet since adolescent age my life has been marked with thinking of God at least a few times per day, truthfully. Very few days since then have I gone without meditating on God at least several times within each day. Albeit, I became presumptuous to think my connection with the Lord was strong enough that I did not have to continue to nourish the relationship through consistent and regular prayer. My misguided thinking was fostered by a brazen comfort of having began a personal prayer life with the Lord at the mere age of eight. This was my costly mistake that should be your learning illustration. Prayer turned into meditation which began to linger into thinking and pondering; thus, all of the actual prayer time (communion) with God had all but been replaced. It was at that juncture I realized, both, meditation's proper place and the need for full consistent prayer.

I speak these words unto you this day in hopes that you do not go days, months, or even years, as I, making pour decisions simply because of working outside of the confines of true prayer. There is no substitute for a strong prayer life with the Lord. You can love Him, think of Him and meditate upon His Word, but none of that substitutes for the formation of life that proceeds faithful prayer unto Him. Prayer is your soul's vessel for direction; no if's, no and's nor but's about it. Meditation is quint-essentially important in prayer, but it is not prayer in nor of itself. Meditate within prayer and be blessed beyond measure.

MEDITATION — Progression of Prayer Element #8

Exercises

INSTRUCTIONAL

1. Scriptures proclaim several reasons why we should meditate unto the Lord in prayer. List four of those reasons, along with scripture support. Also, write one short prayer for each which incorporates the scripture and the reason.

   BENEFIT:
   To increase our awareness as to why we should meditate, and to increase our abilities to incorporate scriptures into our prayers.

PERSONAL

1. Choose one of the seven ways we deny God access unto our spirits which best depicts your prayer life. Pray for five minutes each day for a week, asking Him to grant you a renewed spirit and living to help overcome your present spirit of denying Him access.

   BENEFIT:
   Pray believing and it shall be done unto you. The success of this exercise will grant you a closer relationship with God, able to better hear his voice through prayers. You will have a renewed and empowered spirit in prayer.

2. On Monday meditate these words slowly for two minutes, "Speak to me Lord. Give me direction." On Tuesday meditate those same words for four minutes. Then each day thereafter, increase the time by two minutes, so to reach fourteen minutes on Sunday.

   BENEFIT:
   To increase our stamina to stay awake and alert during extended periods of meditation; allowing for the time it may take to hear from God. Also, to increase our spiritual awareness and focus on God's voice, ultimately training our listening.

MEDITATION — *Progression of Prayer Element #8*

General Questions

1. How are we ushered into the spirit? What may happen if we are not ushered into the spirit?

2. What is one thing that engages our listening to God? Why is it difficult to listen to God and to others?

3. Shouting God's glory or not actively listening for God's voice within meditation may revert us back to what? Why may this be to our disadvantage?

4. What are two reasons we tend to underestimate the importance of hearing the voice and directions of God? What should be our mind-set about hearing from God?

5. What do we render God as when we only expect Him to hear our cries rather than give answer to our prayers?

6. What scripture does this chapter reference which indicates God has already provided us with a way of deliverance? What must we then do in order to travel the path of deliverance?

7. Thirsting for God's voice is a major part of what? And what does it involve in addition to our simply hearing God's voice?

8. What could be the concern that prevents us from totally capturing the very essence of prayer even if God is listening to us and we are listening unto Him?

9. What occurs when submission meets desire and desire then meets attentiveness?

10. How can our horizontal relationships benefit from our becoming proficient in meditation?

MEDITATION — *Progression of Prayer Element #8*

Advanced Questions

1. What are the seven ways we deny the Lord access into our spirits during prayer?

2. Write a brief sentence as to your theological position on I Thessalonians 5:17.

   This chapter gives examples of why it may be detrimental to continue to pray for the same thing over and again. What is one example?

3. Write a short paragraph on the difference between *Meditation* as an *Element* in contrast to that of prayer as an exercise. Include a brief portion on the dangers of not recognizing the difference.

Attributes/Character/Nature of God.
His Essence

Pray this prayer with me:
A Prayer for Attributes

"Timeless, eternal and all-knowing Father. You alone are to be praised, and magnified. There is no one greater. There is no love greater. There is no power greater. I bless You God. I do bless You God. To know more of You is my greatest passion. I can know how to live and how to pray by knowing Your character, attributes and nature. So, bless my spirit now to learn more of You through the reading of this chapter's writings. Help me Lord to absorb all which is of You, then I shall glorify Your name from the mountain tops to the valley lows. Oh, to know more of who You are! I am excited to enter this next chapter with the understanding I shall finish its reading with a spirit increase established upon Your character and attributes. My change is on the way! Bless Your name God. Glory! Manifest Your attributes in my character, and bring me Your grace and Your mercy. Through it all, let someone else witness the greatness of Your character working through me; giving them a renewed desire to seek You. They and I shall enter Your presence with more power sustained by increased knowledge of You. These words I submit in prayer by the power of the Holy Spirit, the love of You and the name of Jesus Christ my Lord and Saviour — Amen."

An essential part of becoming a prayer warrior is to know God's attributes, nature and character. Therefore, it is a must that we live and pray in accord with them. <u>It is not enough to simply know how to pray.</u> <u>We must know the very essence of who we pray unto.</u> This is a *key* for all who endeavor to gain strength in prayer and in spiritual living.

Let us use reading a book as an analogy to make this point. There are many who read a book yet never take time to know the author. Similar to our elementary school days when the instructor would give extra credit for knowing the author of the book we studied. Sorrowfully, there were many who did not get the extra points. It is essential that believers know the Author of the Book we profess as our life source.

Many ask the question, "How can I know the Author by means other than reading the Book?" Well, I am glad the question has been asked. The answer is this — we must spend time with the Author along with reading what was written by the Author. It is imperative we not only read the Words written, but we must commune with the Author of the written Word, also. I submit this for our hearing this day. Let us take a view from the reverse. <u>If we know the Author we will gain a better understanding of the Word He wrote</u>. It is true we can know the Word without getting to know the author, but then we could be classified with mere heathen and carnal Christians. As a matter of fact, there are a lot of devils who can quote scripture to no end. Some will quote twenty-five scriptures in ten minutes of ministering in every attempt to fool listeners into thinking they know the Author; only to fool themselves.

If we know the Author, He will give us the spirit to receive the Words He wrote, just as He will reveal the Word's mysteries unto us. We will be as mere keepers of the Law if we do not get to know the Author outside of simply reading about Him. As mere readers of His Word we strain to be religious, and we more often miss the mark. We must spend time with the Author who wrote the Word we believe to be truth. I ask the question, "How can we know the Word to be truth, if we do not truly know the Author to be truth?" This thinking may seem to be as reverse to many; for we humans tend to do things in backward fashion, unbeknownst.

The nature and attributes of God can be described as the essence, spirit and substance of what constitutes His inherent being. It is a blessing to know God will not and cannot contradict His own nature, character, attributes and will. That alone bears reason enough for prayer warriors to diligently attempt to deluge and immerse themselves with every tittle of His every essence. I proclaim it is through the knowledge and application of God's attributes that this world and Heaven shall see 100,000 strong prayer warriors emerge and go forth to perform great works through prayer and living. Read forward, digest and be blessed.

Pray to Whom You Know

It is so imperative that we know the God unto whom we actually pray. The Bible declares, "How then shall they call on him in whom they have not believed? and how shall they believe in him whom they have not heard? and how shall they hear without a preacher?" *(Romans 10:14).* Many of us start off on the wrong foot with regards to prayer by not even knowing the nature and attributes of our God. Our prayers are misdirected and they meander along, due partly to our being unaware of God's make-up and how His attributes affect our prayers. This entire *Chapter of Attributes, Character and Nature of God* is a *key* for us all. It is guesstimated that ninety percent of us have never truthfully contemplated a need to be familiar with God's attributes. Likewise, many of us have not given ample thought to how our prayers' successes and failures are dependant upon how much we pray in accord with His character and attributes. This entire document illustrates how we are to learn of God by way of His Word and by way of our communing with Him.

It is shameful, but true, we do not know the Lord as well as we should. Just as shameful is how we pray to an Almighty God in neglect and disregard of who He is and His attributes. Please hear me in saying this. Our prayers will have purposed vision and holy direction when we learn to speak to the Lord in accord with His attributes and character. As a simple example, the blessing you prayed to receive last week never came into fruition because it was against God's character to provide such a thing. Need a second example? Here it is — Praying for someone to die (not imagining that anyone would pray such a prayer) will not be granted by God since it is His will that we all live; as He is good in character. Good in regards to God's character and attributes is that He is inclined to bestow blessedness and He takes holy pleasure in the happiness of His people. In the same case, praying that someone's life be taken, in effect, goes against God's character of merciful (withheld merited punishment). Instead of praying that someone die, we should resort to pray in accord with another attribute of God — Just (having moral equity). In this example we should be able to at least partially see how we would resort to pray that God would be just in dealing with the person rather than our requesting God to step out of His character of being merciful.

Unjustifiable Claims

Let us make it a little closer to home for some of us. We may be of they who surely pray, but we are not truthful prayer warriors if we do not pray in accord with God's nature and attributes. Yes, we may pray, but being a prayer warrior takes knowing the Lord, versus just being able to do the proverbial, "get a prayer through." Of course, I am not judge nor jury, but it is a simple fact many folk claim themselves as prayer warriors and yet they ask the Lord for some things which are so outlandish and opposite to His will, nature and character. Don't be mad at me, for I am merely unwrapping the message sent by God. First, it is the duty of us all to accept where we are spiritually so the Spirit then can deliver us into another level of victory. It is now our individual responsibilities to accept what is and what is not truth of us, then move forward into the power which can surely be ours.

Let me give further examples. Athletes know in order to succeed in their chosen sport they must play and compete in accord with the rules and directions of the game itself. Penalties and losses occur when players, willfully or otherwise, offend these very directions. Our legal system is set-up on the same premise. Breaking the laws or rules of the land will affect the offender to pay the penalty or do the time. Likewise, our Christian living and our prayers are regulated by the rules or sovereignty that is God's nature, attributes and will. Penalties are paid and victories are won depending on a person's regard for God's nature. Let us truly understand, we cannot expect success in our living nor in our prayers when either are effected outside of God's nature and attributes. This we must fully absorb in our spirits in order to come forth as prayer warriors.

Beyond Doing the Right Thing

(78) Here is a deliverance and *key* for us all. We all have been taught from childhood to follow God's commands, and that is it. We have been taught to follow His laws or we will pay the price. This is true indeed, but let us examine this point from another angle. Let us understand we render all our prayer attempts fruitless when we disregard God's attributes. Just the same, many of our prayers became a waste of time when we prayed for things which were of good intentions, but apposed the Lord's will. The road to hell is said to be paved with good intentions. Good intentions and simply doing the right thing can both fall short of being in accord with the Lord's attributes. "There is a way which seemeth right unto man, but the end thereof are the ways of death" *(Proverbs 14:12).* It is a sin to not know our God and it is a sin to live opposite His nature, character, attributes and will.

Beyond Good Intentions

It is not by accident that God has inspired the writings within the pages of the Bible so to give us an understanding of who He is by way of His nature, attributes and character. In this way He designed numerous verses to help us gain victory through our learning of Him. Sad to say, we have incurred many failures and distresses in living and in prayer, because we have resided outside of His attributes, character and will. Even many good people with good intentions have failed in much of life because they were not taught to live and pray in accord with God's nature and attributes. To some, this business about God's character, attributes and nature may sound mundane and rudimentary, but make no mistake that it is essential to our success in living and in prayer. There are not many things that are as essential as praying in accord with God's attributes. Let it be from this point forward we all commit to become more familiar with God's attributes and begin to apply those character traits unto ourselves, our living and our prayers; where applicable and possible.

Guidelines

The Lord desires we live in Him and move in Him so we may be in accord with His attributes, which are the very guidelines for our victory. "That they should seek the Lord, if haply they might feel after him and find him, though he be not far from everyone of us: For in him we live, and move, and have our being; as certain also of your own poets have said, For we are also his offspring" *(Acts 17:27-28)*. How else might Christ be made manifest in us lest we live and pray in accord with His attributes? "... and I will love him, and will manifest myself to him" *(John 14:21)*. Having the manifestation of Christ within should be an ultimate goal for any child of the Most High God, yet we constantly ask for things other than His presence in our lives. How many of us can truly say His manifestation is at the foremost part of our thoughts, desires and prayers?

The Bible simply, but profoundly, gives us guidelines according to God's character, as in I Peter 1:15-16, "But as he which hath called you is holy, so be ye holy in all manner of conversation: Because it is written, Be ye holy; for I am holy;" referencing Old Testament law in Leviticus 11:44. II Peter 1:3-4 says it this way, "According as his divine power hath given unto us all things that pertain unto life and godliness, through the knowledge of him that hath called us to glory and virtue. Whereby are given unto us exceeding great and precious promises: that by these ye might be partakers of the divine nature, having escaped the corruption that is the world through lust." John 4:24 is another strong example of how the Bible expresses God's attributes as guidelines for our living and worship, as it proclaims, "God is a Spirit, and they that worship him must worship him in spirit and in truth." How much simpler could it be expressed and commanded of how we are to live and pray?

Further explanation is given within this document of how believers must incorporate God's attributes into our mode of prayer in order to best usher in the presence of the Almighty and in order to best increase the chances of victory in our prayers. I reiterate, praying indifferent to God's attributes may render our prayers bankrupt and fruitless. I then ask, why pray if we are not going to best purpose and position ourselves for victory? The Lord desires us to operate in spirit and in faith unto Him. Yet, we seem to always want to do things our own ways, fruitlessly expecting the best results. Many parents have exclaimed to their children, "It is my way or the highway." We serve a merciful God, but woe unto them who continue to muddle through worship experiences in ways non-prescribed and opposed by His Word. Why else have many of our prayers gone unanswered? Why else do we continue to fumble the baton of faith passed to us by our devoted Savior? Why else does a world, so sick in sin, continue in impenitence and disbelief? We should allow this document to enlighten our ways in the path of God's nature, attributes, character and will. In doing so, our prayer lives shall flourish and prosper.

Attributes Begin to Manifest

There is a blessedness about getting to know the nature and attributes of God. After instituting His attributes into our prayers, those same attributes begin to take hold of our living, as well. I repeat, the very attributes we truthfully apply in our prayers shall begin to manifest themselves in our living, thereafter. "Now thanks be unto God, which always causeth us to triumph in Christ, and maketh manifest the savour of his knowledge by us in every place. For we are unto God a sweet savour of Christ, in them that are saved, and in them that perish. To the one we are the savour of death unto death; and to the other the savour of life unto life. And who is sufficient for these things" *(II Corinthians 2:14-16)*. Then, what a blessed joy to begin to see and understand the indwelling of Christ, in truth. There are many people who simply should not be so bold to proclaim the Lord's working in their lives. Let me say it this way. It is great to give God credit and honor for what is happening in our lives, but the truth is some of us lack the knowledge of His attributes that would in turn give the truthful awareness of His working power. Plainly said, some of us do not know enough about God's character, nature and how He works, to be able to claim His working in our lives. Many of us have heard others talk about God, yet we have never taken it upon ourselves to know Him for ourselves; in truth. We shall see the prosperity through the truthful pain.

Few of us can express any attributes of God beyond the Fruit of the Spirit. Shameful to say many of us are not even aware of the Fruit of the Spirit written in Galatians 5:22-23. Woe unto a people who call themselves children of God, but do not even know their Father's nature and character. A blessing truly comes over a believer's living when he or she applies God's characteristic to their prayers. It takes effort to institute God's attributes and character into our prayers, but it is such a blessing when the fruit is revealed in both our prayers and our living. Exercising His attributes in our prayers stretches our hearts to adopt those same attributes into our general living. As our sensitivity unto the Lord begins to increase through the application of His attributes in our prayers, we begin to realize the need to incorporate His attributes into our living, also. In this way, we seek to make Christ manifest in our living as we witness the success of the use of God's attributes in our prayers. Jesus, Himself, spoke of prayer and manifestation in John 14:16-21, so why should we consider them any less important and still think success will be ours?

Oh, the Change!

Our entire living can be transformed through our praying in accord with God's attributes. It is truly a life changing experience to go to such a level of awareness in our prayers. This very awareness has no choice but to elevate our general living through our use and application of these precepts. There are many attributes of God, and it is urged that we study them all and study them constantly. We will not cover all of God's attributes within this document, but it is the duty of this document to shed light on how God's attributes affect our prayers and living. For one thing, praying in accord with God's attributes and character help to eliminate babbling in our prayers; as His very attributes stand as guides. They also serve as power unto us in prayer because God is a promise keeper. The Lord made promises and covenants through His Word directed by His nature, character and attributes. Praying in concert with them grants us more victories and less heartaches.

Also, God's attributes give us a glimpse at who He really is, while at the same time they provide focal points for our prayers. Our prayers must have direction that comes from something greater than our desires, wants and natural tendencies. Most of us can be deemed as babblers in prayer since our mere requests are normally our most prominent guidelines. Woeful! Let it not be so after the reading of this document. Our prayers' directions must come from the very essence of God. Prayers that are void of the essence of God begin and often end in failure. In addition, it gives God great glory and honour when His essence, or attributes, are used as the focal points of our prayers. This indirectly removes selfishness and childishness from our prayers, as well. It is essential that prayer warriors grow to understand the importance of how our living and our prayers extend beyond ourselves. For this reason, using God's attributes as focal points provides us with every opportunity to honour and glorify Him.

It is the intent of God's attributes to bring our prayers unto the focus they truly ought to center — on God. Yes it is true, we need deliverance, healing and blessings, but our primary focus in prayer, as well as in living, must be on the Lord. Honour Him and He will honour us. Honour is one of those things we cannot receive unless we give it. We can give love and not get it in return, and the same goes for money. Honour on the other hand will never come our way unless we are honourable unto others. I once ministered unto a Christian that he should do more honouring of the people rather than ruling over them, but he never could grasp the principle; thus the people never accepted him. The same is true for our honouring God. Likewise, those who honour God's people normally honour God, as well.

The attributes and character of God are so essential to our prayers that to neglect them is to forsake the very essence of God's Spirit. To forsake God's attributes in prayer can be likened unto babbling and gibberish. Much of our living goes likewise as we neglect to embrace His character. Therefore, if we allow this section to resonate in our spiritual lives, fruit unparalleled and savory shall come forth as we proclaim, "Oh taste and see that the Lord He is good: blessed is the man that trusteth in him" *(Psalm 34:8).* The Lord already knows us, the question is do we know Him? Let us now explore the following three reasons it is imperative to know the Lord's attributes: in order to best commune with Him with power; in order to know what He expects of His children; and in order for His children to know what to expect from Him. These three reasons do not follow in order, for they are intertwined in their association.

Many of us fall out of relationship with the Lord cause we do not know what to expect from Him. Milk fed Christians tend to depend heavily upon receiving blessings from God in order to substantiate their faith. On one hand, immature Christians do not realize nor do they want to accept God's attributes like that of "just," but they may always be found pleading for Him to show forth His attribute of "mercy." Many of us want to grow in Christ, but still want to have a blind eye in regards to God's attributes that do not seem to fit our fleshy desires. This ignorance, denotatively speaking, renders our spirits incapable of discerning what to expect God to accomplish at different times. In the same way we do not know what is expected of us as His children, since we do not accept nor emulate His attributes. Some of us do not live according to His attributes cause we were not taught that we too are to maintain those attributes. We live and pray in any old fashion, for the most part, due to our ignorance of God's nature and our ignorance of what it means to us. As examples the Bible tells us, "... ye shall be holy; for I am holy ...." *(Leviticus 11:44);* "And we have known and believed the love that God hath to us. God is love; and he that dwelleth in love dwelleth in God, and God in him" *(I John 4:16).*

Whenever we are confronted with God's chastening judgment, we have a grave tendency to shut down any communion with Him; although He remains faithful and true. We are always expecting His mercy and grace, which is naturally more digestible than His chastening and His wrath. When it comes to our faith, we are similar to running water, whereas we constantly seek the path of least resistance and minimal difficulty. We would know how to live and we would know what to expect of God if we simply learned of His character, then accepted it in its entirety. We must move beyond sifting through His attributes, as if to ignore the ones we do not prefer; whether consciously or unconsciously. If we are to prefer God at all, we must prefer all of who He is! No sifting.

Untold numbers of so called believers falter in living and in prayers simply because there has never been a sweltering need within us to be like Christ; as the Word commands. Our entire living begins to blossom and mature once we begin to accept and take upon ourselves the very attributes of God. This is what is expected of us. Be ye like Christ. We forever fall short when we forsake God's attributes, as the controversies of spirit continue to mount and separate us from fruitful communion with Him. Maybe we do not assimilate more of His character and attributes because we really do not like Him that much. We want what He possesses but we do not want who He is. That is a huge "mmmmm" moment! We would make much more effort to accept and to assimilate His character if we truly endeared Him the way we profess. Or maybe we envy Him like some of us envy our neighbors. Fact is, our spiritual relationships with God would function a lot more smoothly if there were not so many contradictions between His character and ours. The duty of this document is to clear up the contradictions. Oh, what a glorious time warriors will have in the Lord once we are on the same page with Him!

In addition, possessing knowledge of what to expect of God in reaction to our living and prayers minimizes our frustrations and maximizes our power. Knowledge is power, and an ultimate power is having knowledge of God's nature and character. This leads us to think how could we ever have communion with someone we do not truly know? Our communal relationships with the Lord are frail, at best, when we are unaware of or do not accept His attributes. The Bible says, "Can two walk together, except they be agreed?" *(Amos 3:3)*. Many of us agree to walk with God only when it suits our natural side. This tells us we must become more spiritual in order to accept more, if not all, of God's character.

We surely cannot know it all — thank God. Yet, we do need to know as much as we can in a spiritual sense, in order to best know, both, our role in faith and God's position as Lord, Father, Creator, Sustainer, etc. This is reason for this document's inclusion of God's attributes and how they relate to how we pray. Maximum effect will come about in prayers by our diligence to digest His attributes. Do not forsake them and they shall not forsake us. Every relationship is strengthened by the partners having more knowledge of each other's characters. God already knows us; for He created us. It is beyond time we knew more about God! Amen! To follow are a few of God's attributes, character and nature. Learn them. Digest them. Live and pray in accord with them. Be blessed by them.

The Attributes of God and our Prayers

Love (I John 4:16) — nature of His person and an attribute

Prayer warriors who know and trust that God is Love (unselfish concern about another's welfare) are given blessed power in prayer, as we pray with that same loving spirit. A loving spirit is a blessed joy unto a prayer warrior and all parties involved. It is a loving spirit that commands a person to pray for the highest good of another person. It is a loving spirit that encourages a person to pray with other's best interest at heart. Likewise, we should be mindful of who we ask to pray for us, since some persons are undercover about not having our best interest at heart. Fact is, a loving spirit prays for others without selfish motives nor ill-intents.

Prayer warriors have loving spirits in prayer, which is a blessing unto themselves, those around them and the Kingdom. It is a loving heart which prays peace, joy, kindness and the other Fruit of the Spirit *(Galatians 5:22-23)*. A great way we can love one another as we are commanded in John 15:12, is through a loving spirit in prayer. How else might one pray for their enemies lest he or she is truthfully of the loving Spirit of Christ? Paul said it this way, "And this I pray, that your love may abound yet more and more in knowledge and in all judgment" *(Philippians 1:9)*.

It is love which will set our spirits free to pray powerful prayers that yield results even on the behalf of our enemies. "Bless them that curse you, and pray for them which despitefully use you" *(Luke 6:28)*. That scripture is much more difficult, if not impossible, to live within when we are void of love. A loving spirit will pray that their enemies come into a saving knowledge of Jesus the Christ, rather than pray that they be crushed like road-kill on the interstate; as discussed in the *Element of Request*. It is truly a grown spirit in Christ that can pray lovingly for enemies; even while they are being persecuted and pained by that very enemy. If it is true, and it surely is true, "... charity shall cover the multitude of sins" *(I Peter 4:8)*, then that same love can yield fervent prayers that direct blessings of change unto the most wicked sinner on earth. How else might Jesus pray intercessory prayers for such a sinful and wicked people; such as us? His love truly abounds toward us and we must abound in that same love in order to become effective prayer warriors.

Our spirits are granted access unto prayers of blessedness when our hearts are first wrapped in love. There are prayers that cannot be prayed by persons who's spirits are not set upon the love of God. "Access Denied" registers on the prayer's scale for many of us due to our refusal to operate our prayer lives on the basis of God's love. For too many of us our selfish motives abound more than our loving kindness. All the attributes of God are truly important for us to acknowledge and pray in accord unto, but love sets the table for many of the other attribute's involvement in our prayers and in our living. Grace cannot abound where love does not first have anchor; likewise for the characteristics of mercy, faithful and others.

We all probably can name a few people we may deem unworthy of love. But the fact remains, none of us are deserving of the love God grants unto us, still He commanded His love toward us in that while we were yet sinners Christ died for the ungodly, as written in Romans 5:1-11. "But after that the kindness and love of God our Savior toward man appeared" *(Titus 3:4)*. Let those of us who desire to be prayer warriors incorporate the great love of God into our lives and prayers, so our fruit may be plentiful and continuously ripe.

I must warn everyone, be prepared for more attacks from the devil and his imps as love takes stronger hold of our prayers and our living. The devil hates those who show love; especially when conventional wisdom says to do otherwise. How dare we love those who aim to kill us and how dare we pray for those who plot evil traps to snare and destroy us? Well, we dare! So, it is on! The Lord reports, "These things I command you, that ye love one another. If the world hate you, ye know that it hated me before it hated you. If ye were of the world, the world would love his own: but because ye are not of the world, but I have chosen you out of the world, therefore the world hateth you. Remember the word that I said unto you, The servant is not greater than his lord. If they have persecuted me, they will also persecute you; if they have kept my saying, they will keep yours also. But all these things will they do unto you for my name's sake, because they know not him that sent me. If I had not come and spoken unto them, they had not had sin: but now they have no cloak for their sin. He that hateth me hateth my Father also" *(John 15:17-23).*

Jealous (Exodus 20:5)

One of the greatest blessings in prayer is to believe and accept that God is Jealous (not accepting rivalry nor unfaithfulness). The Bible says, "... for I the Lord thy God am a jealous God...." *(Exodus 20:5).* Without a doubt we will truly be mindful of the things for which we pray when we acknowledge the Lord's jealous character. As an example, praying for things which will ultimately replace God in our lives is an absolute no-no. The fact is, the Lord knows our hearts and refuses to grant us some of our request because He knows those very things would end up separating us from Him. You and I may not realize that fact while we pray, but God knows all things past, present and to come. To make it very clear, it is pleasing unto the Lord when while praying we acknowledge there is no greater need for us than the Lord Himself.

Believers who accept God as jealous are granted access into a higher place of spirit for having respect for God. A place many others surely do not reside. If we were to truly think about it, we would realize how disrespectful of God we have been for praying for certain things we humanly call blessings. Let me make it a little clearer. The Israelites were greatly disrespectful to pray and ask to have a king in place of God's direct touch in their lives. "But the thing displeased Samuel, when they said, Give us a king to judge us. And Samuel prayed unto the Lord. And the Lord said unto Samuel, Hearken unto the voice of the people in all that they say unto thee: for they have not rejected thee, but they have rejected me, that I should not reign over them" *(I Samuel 8:6-7).* God so loved His people that He granted their request, but in His jealousy He appointed them a king whom was to be unjust and a thorn in their side.

It is bad enough to have a prayer go unanswered or answered unfavorably, but worse is to turn the very jealous wrath of God against ourselves. This case shows us how important it is for the Spirit and Christ to make intercessions for us. The Bible declares, "Likewise the Spirit also helpeth our infirmities: for we know not what we should pray for as we ought: but the Spirit itself maketh intercession for us with groanings which cannot be uttered. And he that searcheth the hearts knoweth what is the mind of the Spirit, because he maketh intercession for the saints according to the will of God" *(Romans 8:26-27).* "Who is he that condemneth? It is Christ that died, yea rather, that is risen again, who is even at the right hand of God, who also maketh intercession for us" *(Romans 8:34).*

Let us not be like-minded as the Israelites in the above example, causing the Lord to place His jealous wrath upon us. Let us be mindful in our prayers of not requesting of God those very things which disrespect our Father-child relationships. As prayer warriors, you and I must first and foremost decide to be respectful of who God is in our lives. This respectfulness will in turn be a guideline for our prayer requests. Both Exodus 20:3 and Deuteronomy 5:7 shine brightly in our prayers when we truthfully choose to respect God's rightful position in our lives. I have personally lived to witness God's jealous hand, as confessed in regards to having had a broken leg that jarred a sports career. Make no mistake that God desires to be first in our hearts, minds and lives. In fact, He will fight tooth and nail to illustrate to us His desire to be number one in our lives. Not only will God fight, but His point will be made above all else.

The prophet and writer Nahum was so moved by God's jealous character that he began the Bible book by writing this in a repetitive and vehement approach, "God is jealous, and the Lord revengeth; the Lord revengeth, and is furious; the Lord will take vengeance on his adversaries, and he reserveth wrath for his enemies" *(Nahum 1:2)*. How important must be this point for it to be stated at the beginning and so strongly?

We ought make it our business to not fight such a battle against God. Our arms are entirely too short to box with an all-powerful God, and it is such a pleasure and blessing to accept Him as number one in our lives in the first place. He will surely give us most of the desires of our hearts if we would simply count Him as Numero Uno in our lives. His jealousy fuels a lot of the anger He has towards us. Choose not to fuel that flame, for that flame has a tendency to burn brighter than a mid-summer's sun in the midst of the desert.

Understand this with power, as a *key.* The extent of our spiritual abilities and our potential as prayer warriors relies on our capacity to make God number one in our prayers and in our living. First, to the extent that we make the Lord number one in our prayers is the height of how our prayers line up with His will. God will automatically become the focal point of our prayers once we truthfully decide to make Him number one. Sounds mundane, but it is often overlooked as we attempt to focus so much on our request, instead of focusing on how our request' align with the nature, character and will of God.

Not sure how many of us have been in a relationship where the partner was, or is, jealous. You cannot imagine the full extent of what I am saying if you have never personally been there. But those of us who have experienced such jealousy know how important it is to keep that person as the number one priority. Otherwise, the world would turn upside down, the cock would crow, the wolves would howl at the moon and sun, the outer banks would wash away, the dogs would bark all night long, and the very jealous wrath of that partner would surely be felt. Greater, if you can imagine, is the jealous rage of our God. Make Him number one, make Him happy and be blessed. Otherwise, like the old folk used to say, "If Moma's not happy in the house, there better not be anyone else happy in the house, either." Just the same, the children of God would be wise not to be happy until we have made God happy and honoured.

Second, the Bible declares if we, "... seek ye first the kingdom of God, and his righteousness; and all these things shall be added unto you" *(Matthew 6:33).* Simply put, the key then is to put God in place as number one in our lives. We must do those things which position our prayers for success in order to have the best chance of getting our prayers favorably answered. No sense in praying if we do not figure to start with the mind set of positioning ourselves and our prayers for the best possible results. This positioning begins and ends with us putting God as number one. It is not a matter of appeasing God in order to get what we want, but it is simply a fact that His rightful place is as number one, and we become all the more blessed in response to us putting Him there.

Inscrutable (Romans 11:33)

It is tough, if not difficult, for us humans to accept the inscrutable (inexplicable and mysterious ways) attribute of God. It is tough enough for most of us to follow a God we cannot visibly see, let alone trust in His mysterious workings. Our faith in His inscrutability comes by way of our submission unto Him, and through our past experiences with Him. Many of us can testify of at least one time the Lord has mysteriously delivered us out of an impossible situation, but even with that knowledge only a few of us have fully submitted unto Him. We do submit to the fact that we have no clue on how the Lord will work things out, but we still tend to have difficulty going to the next level of faithfully trusting in Him. Zophar said it this way, "Canst thou by searching find out God? canst thou find out the Almighty unto perfection? It is as high as heaven; what canst thou do? deeper than hell; what canst thou know?" *(Job 11:7-8).*

Faith in God's inscrutability increases our prayer power as we relinquish, to Him, control over the "what" and the "how" things will be worked-out on our behalf. Prayer warriors do not enter into prayer with an expectation of how a thing will be done, yet we have confidence in knowing it shall be done. Putting God in a box of our finite expectations will only lead us to a minimized belief in His actual capabilities. Let it be known many of our circumstances are in need of the mysterious to occur. The ordinary never worked in many of our cases past, just as the ordinary may never work in cases to come. We ought get excited to pray about some things that appear so very difficult, simply in believing that God is about to do the extra ordinary.

It is hard to think of anything being entertaining while going through tough times, but it can be empowering to begin to imagine the entertaining show or display of power God is poised to shower upon our situations. Fireworks, if we can imagine. The main event, if we can picture. The spectacular, if we can have faith. We truly do serve a spectacular God who's eyes roam the earth to see for whom He can show Himself strong *(II Chronicles 16:9)*. Besides the Book of Job, where may we find these words, "I would seek unto God, and unto God would I commit my cause; Which doeth great things and unsearchable; marvelous things without number?" *(Job, 5:8-9)*. Who else other than Job has seen such great calamity, and such great miracle working power? Can we be found with that high level of faith in God's inexplicable ways?

Self-Existent (Exodus 3:14)

Prayer warriors who trust that God is self-existent (not dependant upon anything nor anyone) are strengthened in faith to realize that God is the only and final source for answering prayers. In life we often spend so much of our time contemplating to whom we must speak in order to get to the person who has the authority and power to actually help our situations: the manager, supervisor, CEO, owner, or some other person in charge. We constantly try to position ourselves in the face of the person who can make the final decision. During our trials we spend much of our time trying to figure out who is the decision maker and who has the pen or the power to turn around a bleak situation. Maybe something went wrong with a product we purchased. Maybe our mortgage payments or rental payments were misapplied by the company. Maybe we received the wrong grade from a class. Whatever the scenario we have spent much time speaking to different folk in all attempts to get to the person who had the power to set things right.

Well, believers who know God is in full control and needs no one else to confirm His decisions and actions (self-existent) are given power to pray with conviction and confidence. The confidence that we are talking to the right one in order to get the needed action for our concerns. It is great and of great power to know in our spirits we are in the right department to have something done on our behalf. He is God all by Himself, and is not dependent on anyone else to make decisions and to make things happen.

Omnipotent (Revelation 19:6)

Similar to self-existent, there is a power that is bestowed unto warriors who believe God to be omnipotent (all-powerful). There should be a great confidence that builds within us when we believe God has all the power to handle all our needs and concerns. Not too many things worse than to speak to persons till our faces turn black and blue, only to later realize they did not possess the power to be able to help. A sad scenario to go through half a day speaking to a plethora of persons who had no real power to help our cause. So sad, so painful. Real power is the *key* here.

Some folk have some power, but not everyone has real power. Real power is that power to do all things at all times; no matter the situation. Real power is sustaining power that is able to endure throughout a given task and objective. Real power is omnipotent power, and there is only one with such power − He is God. Jeremiah 32:17 says, "Ah, Lord God! behold, thou hast made the heaven and the earth by thy great power and stretched out arm, and there is nothing too hard for thee." The Lord Himself asked the rhetorical question of Abraham, "Is anything too hard for the Lord?" *(Genesis 18:14a).*

What a blessed assurance to know that the God we serve is capable of handling all our prayer requests and all our needs. There is a great confidence that builds from the awareness that He is all powerful over all things. There is no time that needs to be wasted in filtering through handfuls of folk who are incapable and/or unauthorized. Our God not only has the power, but He is authorized to utilize His power, for He alone is the authority. He is El Shaddai − God almighty and all powerful. God Himself proclaimed to Abraham, while still Abram, "I am the Almighty God..." *(Genesis 17:1).* Take heed of God's power, then receive of the blessedness and faith which come from that knowledge and acceptance.

Omniscient (I John 3:20)

Believers who know God is omniscient (all-knowing and all-seeing) are empowered in prayer by the fact that He already knows of what we stand in need before we settle down to pray. The Bible says, "The Lord looketh from heaven; he beholdeth all the sons of men. From the place of his habitation he looketh upon all the inhabitants of the earth. He fashioneth their hearts alike; he considereth all their works" *(Psalm 33:13-15).* Prayer warriors truly believe God is omniscient as they are energized to seek His directions in the *Element of Meditation,* more so, than they are eager to bleed their hearts unto Him in the *Element of Request.* It is not that we should not desire to make request of God. Rather so, the prayer warrior has faith in God's ability to see and know everything before it ever happens; thus, the prayer warrior spends more time trying to receive an answer instead of taking valuable moments attempting to tell God the details of everything He already knows.

True believers in God's omniscience understand and rely on the fact that God knew their need before the need ever arose. They have faith built upon God's having already made a way, and it is their objective to hear directions for that provision. Their objective in prayer is no longer so much about speaking to the Lord, as it is about hearing a word from Him. "I know the Lord sees what I am about to go through, so let me hear from Heaven," is the mind-set of they who believe in God's omniscient power.

Omnipresent (Psalm 139:7-10)

Prayer warriors who believe God to be omnipresent (present everywhere at the same time) have prayers empowered in ways unseen. There are several ways God's attribute of omnipresent gives prayer warriors power. First, this power comes by way of knowing we can pray for someone who resides on the other side of the planet and faithfully believe God will be here to listen to the request and He will be overseas to fulfill it. Not believing He is everywhere at all times minimizes our faith in His abilities; thus, places God in a box. His abilities are larger than any box we can ever create. The Bible declares, "The eyes of the Lord are in every place, beholding the evil and the good" *(Proverbs 15:3)*.

It is fact that our lack of faith in God's attributes cripples the success of our prayers. We must have faith that our God is everywhere at the same time, if we believe He is actually God. Many of us think it not possible for Him to be omnipresent due to our finite and humanistic minds. Some of us tend to place the Lord in a box which is labeled, "I cannot visualize this happening." This is the same box where we reside because we sadly live by sight and not by faith. We must be empowered to have more faith in God. It is appropriate to say at this point, God is almighty and ever so qualified with all divine characteristics and attributes; whether we believe it or not. If we have less faith in God, it does not make Him any less God. He was God before we existed and shall be God forever more.

It is truly empowering to believe God can answer all prayers whether the recipients are near or far. How dwarfing would it be if we could pray only for those in our small neighborhoods and/or while God was visiting said neighborhood? Faith must tell us God personally visits every neighborhood at all times. He is available to help all those persons and things for which we pray; no matter where they may reside.

Second, God's omnipresence allows us to pray for several things and places at once with faith that He can answer them all at the same time. We do not have to wait for our first prayer to be answered nor confirmed before requesting something else. How hindering would it be if God was limited to answering only one prayer at a time? Our God is much bigger than that. King David concluded there was no place he could run to be out of the presence of God. "Wither shall I go from thy spirit? or whither shall I flee from thy presence? If I ascend up into heaven, thou art there: if I make my bed in hell, behold, thou art there. If I take the wings of the morning, and dwell in the uttermost parts of the sea; Even there shall thy hand lead me, and thy right hand shall hold me" *(Psalm 139:7-10).*

Third, it is empowering to know the Lord does not have to forsake our prayers just to answer the prayers sent forth by our neighbors. We need not be jealous of God answering someone else's prayers, since we understand He can bless all our prayers at the same time and with the same attentiveness to each. The Lord is still with me although He traveled with you to a remote area. A prayer warrior is not betwixt to think God may or may not be available to answer his or her prayers. Our faith tells us He is everywhere, yet He is always available to come see about each of our needs. There is no need for us to covet our neighbors answered prayers if we believe God is omnipresent. Sad to say, they who covet have no belief in His ability to be everywhere at the same time. What also is sad is that many of us have felt the jealousy and envy of persons, even in the church, who have immaturely imagined our anointing and favor had any affect on their favor or the lack there of. An envious person is one who does not believe God to be omnipresent.

(81) This is a *key* to deliverance for all those who find themselves jealous of others being blessed by God. We must have faith that God can bless everyone, everywhere, and at the same time, so we need not become jealous of others receiving blessings. A humanly jealous spirit is a spirit lacking in strong faith. Make no mistake about it. A prayer warrior rejoices with those who's prayers are answered for they know that God is in the business of blessing all His children and blessing them at the same time, if necessary. How depressing it would be to have to wait for God to go through a backlog of prayer request before getting to our individual prayers? In that case, it may be too late by the time He got to us; notwithstanding, we serve an on-time-God whose not immobile. I would guess an immobile god would appropriate only one prayer per person per week at the time of such a backlog of prayers, so to minimize added backlog. We are to be thankful that our God handles all our prayer requests at their appointed times. Thanks be to God who does not have to divvy answered prayers; nor does He divvy His presence, for that matter.

Immutable (Malachi 3:6; Hebrews 13:8)

Prayer warriors who have faith that God is immutable (never changing, constant and never differs from Himself) are given confidence to believe the Lord will neither switch up nor change. Let me make it plain. The Lord will not change His character, the game, nor the playing field, in the midst of our prayers. Another great assurance is knowing God will not even change His ways from the last time we prayed. What can be a worser blow to our confidence in prayer than to try to rely on someone who continues to change each time we speak to them?

The Lord our God can be counted upon to never change. He will surely remain the same God tomorrow as He was yesterday and is today. It is great to know some things will never change in an ever changing world. "For I am the Lord, I change not; therefore ye sons of Jacob are not consumed" *(Malachi 3:6)*. We all can surely attest to a time when someone told us one thing at one particular time, only to later rescind those very words. Some people and some things will change up without a flinch of an eye. Others will change but openly lie and swear they never said certain things nor acted any differently than before. Simply wicked! Nonetheless, it is so assuring to know our God will not and cannot vary.

The Lord's being constant bodes well in our getting to know His attributes and character. It is not as though we are trying to pin down a moving (changing) target. Prayer warriors know God will not change, as they make it their purpose to know His very character. Prayer warriors know they have power in His attributes. Praying in accord with God's attributes is a great source of power for prayer warriors; thus it is reassuring that those very attributes do not change from day to day, Sunday to Sunday, or even year to year. We should submit to the fact that we can pray confidently in accord with His attributes and character, since He does not change and His power is great.

Let it be known our success in prayer is not majorly due to our having the mental or spiritual ability to get a prayer through to God, per se. I sort of wince when people say, "I know how to get a prayer through to God." Reason being, our prayers are successful because they are aligned with the very will of God as they align with His attributes; having less to do with our abilities. Please do not miss this *key!* Our success as persons who pray has less to do with our capabilities, and more to do with God's unchanging ways; as our requests align with His will for our lives. Those who trust and believe this key are well on their way to becoming strong warriors on the battle field for the Lord. Those who do not believe in His immutable attribute most often have issues with their being submissive.

This extent of belief calls for great submission unto the Lord's will and it calls for us to let go of our own desires. That is not something most of us are ready nor willing to do. Pray for it and the Lord shall provide. The Lord Jesus declared, "... My doctrine is not mine, but his that sent me. If any man will do his will, he shall know of the doctrine, whether it be of God, or whether I speak of myself. He that speaketh of himself seeketh his own glory: but he that seeketh his glory that sent him, the same is true, and no unrighteousness is in him" *(John 7:16-18).* Our prayers become as similar as they align unto God's will and, more so, become His proclamation void of our simple desires. This is at the embodiment or quintessence of prayer as the manifestation of Christ within us, along side the usage of the attributes of God, begin to reveal that which is to be prayed. So, there we have the success of it all.

Faithful (Deuteronomy 7:9)

The Lord's attribute of immutable goes hand-in-hand with His attribute of faithful (cannot change nor fail to perform His promises). "Know therefore that the Lord thy God, he is God, the faithful God, which keepeth covenant and mercy with them that love him and keep his commandments to a thousand generations" *(Deuteronomy 7:9).* "If He said it, I believe it," is the motto of the prayer warrior. A portion of having trust in God is built upon His faithfulness unto His Word and promises. Prayer warriors who believe in God's faithfulness have driven confidence to give higher levels of pre-praise thanksgiving. Pre-praise thanksgiving is built upon faith that proclaims victory is already won because the promise was already made by God. The prayer warrior already knows a thing is done even as he or she speaks it out of their mouths in prayer. "God made the promise and He will keep the promise" is the empowered mentality of a true believer and prayer warrior.

Our God is a keeper of promises and covenants; of this we can be assured. How can a person doubt when the promise has already been made? I'll tell you how. It happens because some folk do not first believe the Lord is faithful. Many of us have been burned in life by others who are disloyal and unfaithful; thus we tend to be gun-shy in our belief and trust. Some others of us have a difficulty in trusting in God's faithfulness because we are unfaithful ourselves. Most often our distrust in others comes from our projecting our own attributes onto others and even onto God. God's faithfulness is incomparable.

There is no one as faithful as our God. No one! He is what faithful is! He is the standard of all His attributes, but we must truly digest the fact that He greatly is the benchmark of faithfulness. We can depend on God.

It is essential that we not only have trust in His faithfulness, but it is imperative that we learn of His promises made. We must gain awareness of His promises and pray according to them in order to witness great victories through our prayers. This is a *key* for us all. Many of us fail in prayer because we omit to pray in accord with His faithfulness of promises made. This attribute empowers us as prayer warriors by the mere fact of knowing God is faithful unto His children. Great strength for prayers comes from our belief that God will not forsake His children in whom He created and in whom His Son is made manifest. In many portions of the Bible it is declared, "God will never leave you nor forsake you" *(Deuteronomy 31:6,8; Joshua 1:5; I Samuel 12:22; Psalm 94:14; II Corinthians 4:8-9; Hebrews 13:5).* We can move mountains when this belief is seared in our spirits, and best believe we all have some mountains to move.

The Bible says, "Thy faithfulness is unto all generations: thou hast established the earth, and it abideth. They continue this day according to thine ordinances: for all are thy servants" *(Psalm 119:90-91).* There is a great amount of assurance that builds within our living and prayers once we realize God will be faithful even when we are not so faithful, at times. All of us continue to live less than perfect lives, yet we can go into prayer with an assurance that our imperfections do not thwart God's faithfulness unto us and our prayers. Although true, prayer warriors do not lean on the cross without making every attempt to give back. The Lord knows of our short comings and He makes up for the difference, but above that, He is a God who loves to reciprocate. "Therefore the Lord hath recompensed me according to my righteousness; according to my cleanness in his eye sight. With the merciful thou wilt shew thyself merciful, and with the upright man thou wilt shew thyself upright. With the pure thou wilt shew thyself pure; and with the froward thou wilt shew thyself unsavoury" *(II Samuel 22:25-27).* The same is with His faithfulness and His other attributes. How much are our lives and our prayers additionally blessed when we are faithful unto God? The greater blessing then occurs as we commit to being faithful in our living, as well. The faithfulness of God must be allowed, not only, to bless our prayers, but it must be allowed to permeate in our every commitment to be faithful in our living.

Faithful parameters

As prayer warriors our faithfulness must go beyond the general parameters of our simply being faithful in our living. We must expand those parameters to that of our being faithful unto that which we have prayed unto God. Let me put it another way. We must do as we have prayed. If we pray that the Lord bless our finances to pay off debts, by all means we must not go out and buy a new vehicle when the Lord grants the increase. In this case, paying off the debts with the increase God provides is to be faithful unto what is prayed. We must show ourselves faithful just as the Lord has been faithful to favorably answer our prayers.

Our prayers are as covenants with God. Refrain from deviating from covenants prayed. The Lord will subsequently answer our prayers favorably if we are faithful to adhere to the covenant of our prayers. Let us take faithfulness another step further. Our faithfulness to our last prayer will sometimes affect God's faithfulness unto our subsequent prayers. This is not in contradiction to our stating that God is faithful even when we are not faithful. On the contrary, this expands the parameters of faithfulness unto a broader aspect of covenant keeping. We are able to affect greater expanses in our prayers once we have positively established a heightened level of covenant keeping with God. Immature Christians are immature about keeping covenants; whereas, true prayer warriors have the power to faithfully request the fruitful desires of their hearts. Proverbs 20:25 tells us to keep our vows declaring, "It is a snare to the man who devoureth that which is holy, and after vows to make enquiry." Romans 1:18-32 makes additional emphasis by declaring those who do not keep covenant shall be turned over unto a reprobate mind and are worthy of death. Have you kept your covenants prayed?

Think of our answered prayers as God giving His good stamp of approval. We should be extra mindful to remain faithful unto what God stamps with a yes. For example, business owners are familiar with the fact that banks expect them to do exactly what they proposed to do with the monies the bank lends them. The bank's stamp of approval is an act of agreeing that all the business owner has proposed is a good idea and worthy of support. Likewise, when God approves our good ideas or covenants, He too expects us to do as we proposed to do with the blessings He bestows upon us. We would fare well to give unto the homeless, if we prayed to God to receive blessings specific for the homeless. So, not only are we to be faithful unto God's word, but we must be faithful to our own words in covenants of prayers. "If a man vow a vow unto the Lord, or swear an oath to bind his soul with a bond; he shall not break his word, he shall do according to all that proceedeth out of his mouth" *(Numbers 30:2)*. Deuteronomy 23:21-23 exclaims it this way, "When thou shalt vow a vow unto the Lord thy God, thou shalt not slack to pay it: for the Lord thy God will surely require it of thee; and it would be sin in thee. But if thou shalt forbear to vow, it shall be no sin in thee. That which is gone out of thy lips thou shalt keep and perform; even a freewill offering, according as thou hast vowed unto the Lord thy God, which thou hast promised with thy mouth." Scripture makes it rather clear we are to keep covenants!

Let me shed more light on the subject matter and on Matthew 25:21. The Word says, "His lord said unto him, Well done, thou good and faithful servant: thou hast been faithful over a few things, I will make thee ruler over many things: enter thou into the joy of thy lord." This is a *key* for us all. The Father our God will not hesitate to bless our prayers if we develop a track record of being faithful to our own request. Many of us do not live in the joy of the Lord simply because we cannot be trusted to do what we prayed we would do once we received the requested blessings from God. If we are faithful, we shall find ourselves blessed of God. Let me say that again. Let us be faithful unto that which we pray and we assuredly will find ourselves continuously blessed by God. It may sink in further this way — God is greatly mindful of covenants, and the keeping thereof. Faithfully join into covenant prayers with the Lord, and our lives and others around us shall reap of plenteous blessings. We cannot beat God giving unto His faithfulness, nor can we be anything other than faithful if we are to become prayer warriors; as God is faithful.

A final word on faithfulness. Just as God is faithful unto us and our prayers, we must be faithful in our entering into prayer with Him. We must do more than vacillate in our praying unto God. Faithful prayer warriors have regular, consistent and diligent prayer lives; marked by spiritual increase, great successes and blessed victories. Any portion of our faithfulness in prayer is begun by faithfully praying. It is that simple. A foundation for successful prayer lives begins by being faithful to enter into prayer. Be consistent and diligent, and be blessed.

Righteous and Just (Ezra 9:15)

The Bible declares, "As it is written, There is none righteous, no, not one" *(Romans 3:10);* nonetheless, our prayers should be guided and blessed by God's character of righteous and just (having moral equity). God is the only judge and He is the only one who is righteous, yet prayer warriors must allow this character of God to reign eminent in prayer and in living.

A portion of our prayers which is directed and blessed by this attribute is how we realize we cannot pray for things that are unreasonable in nature. As an old adage says, "The punishment must fit the crime." The Old Testament calls it, "... life shall go for life, eye for eye, tooth for a tooth, hand for hand, foot for foot" *(Deuteronomy 19.21).* We are now under grace, the Lord Jesus Christ, and no longer bound by the law, yet we can apply a principle of this verse unto our prayers and our living. The principle here tells us we should steer clear of excesses. As well, we are not judges nor jury; thus again, we should remain clear of excesses and we shouldn't be eager to punish. As example, we do not pray to receive 30 million dollars when our needs are far less. We do not pray that someone receive a Bentley when it is not feasible within their lifestyle and when simple travel means will provide the need. We do not pray that someone would die because they simply threw some foul language at us. "He is the Rock, His work is perfect: for all his ways are judgment: a God of truth and without iniquity, just and right is he" *(Deuteronomy 32:4).*

Another part of this attribute which blesses our prayers is that God will repay all who do wrong. "Seeing it is a righteous thing with God to recompense tribulation to them that trouble you" *(II Thessalonians 1:6).* In accord with such, we tailor our prayers to involve the Lord being just upon our enemies versus our praying a particular judgment upon them. It is the Lord who shall ultimately choose the justice or punishment. The Bible tells us "Not rendering evil for evil, or railing for railing: but contrariwise blessing; knowing that ye are thereunto called, that ye should inherit a blessing" *(I Peter 3:9).* The Lord Himself says, "To me belongeth vengeance and recompence ..." *(Deuteronomy 32:35).* As we can see our prayers are guided by His very attributes. Tailoring our request within His nature and character lends for the greatest success for our prayers.

In that same mode, prayer warriors have faith that the Lord is just, so they lean not unto their own spitefulness during prayer. Know that He is just. It is this very just attribute, along with other aspects of His character, such as love and faithfulness, that drives the Lord to avenge the wrongs done unto His children. Let us simply be vigilant to pray in accord with God's attributes as we stay out of His way so He may do His job without our unwarranted interference.

Let me drop a couple of bits of spiritual wisdom and mystery of God's power. First, we all feel compelled to pay evil for evil done unto us, but the Bible proclaims vengeance is the Lord's. We can be the most punishing to our enemies by allowing God to exact His vengeance and wrath upon them. Let's take a few moments to make this quite clear. Our punishment upon our enemies will never be exact, which will then cause the Lord to give them some form of additional mercy. Mercy is probably the last thing we want for our enemies when they have wronged us; let's be honest. So, knowing that our punishment will never, I say never, duplicate the punishment God will give, then why would we do anything that will prompt more of God's mercy unto our enemies? The Bible gives us an example of how God used the Assyrians to punish His people Israel, Isaiah chapter 10, but their punishment and arrogance was excessive; thus God's anger subsided towards Israel. Point is, allow God to exact His punishment upon our enemies the way He desires, if it is our desire to truly "get them back;"in a proverbial sense.

The second point on this bit of spiritual wisdom is this: our mishandling punishment upon others may cause God to then punish us. The Biblical example given above is a prime illustration. God turned and punished the Assyrians. I say this day, let it go and let God. We shall be witnesses of His power and wrath upon the evil who come against us. God's wrath and hand upon them shall be more entertaining than any of our favorite television shows; or theirs.

Having this sort of morality and reasonableness in prayer takes tremendous humbleness and diligence, but there are great blessings awaiting all who pray in such ways. First, the person for whom we pray receives the blessing of the answered prayer, if it is God's will. Second, we receive a great spirit increase when we pray with morality. There is a blessed joy which manifest within us when we remove evil plots and fancies of excess from our hearts, thoughts and prayers. It is the evil and the judgmental who die slow and definite deaths within their spirits. The Lord desires that we live life with joy; thus, He reserves the judging process for Himself. We cannot handle thoughts of judging others nor can we handle humanistic wicked imaginations, and still spiritually live. Repaying is an imagination and wickedness, and in doing so we will rot our spirits' inner core. So, be blessed by praying in reasonable fashion. The Lord our God is Qedosh Yisreal (morally perfect) and He alone is Yahweh Tsidkenu (our righteousness and standard for right behavior).

Forgiving (I John 1:9)

To believe that God is just, is to believe He is forgiving (to cease to be angry toward another). "For his anger endureth but a moment; in His favour is life ..." *(Psalm 30:5)*. Prayer warriors who have faith that God is forgiving exhibit confidence to still go to Him in prayer although sins were committed in the past. This is so essential for many of us who still hold ourselves miserably unworthy and incapable, due to our past sins. In this we have the assurance to still be able to reach out to Him in prayer and communion.

The Bible tells us, "If we confess our sins he is faithful and just to forgive us our sins, and to cleanse us from all unrighteousness" *(I John 1:9)*. This cleansing and sanctifying is a life long process during which time we must not forsake going to Him in prayer. We would never go to the Lord in prayer if we always held ourselves to the iron for our sins of omission and commission. It is even through our prayers and communion with the Lord that we continue to ask for and receive forgiveness. "To the Lord our God belong mercies and forgiveness, though we have rebelled against him" *(Daniel 9:9)*.

Believers who know God is forgiving have more vigor and dedication in prayer, as well. The strength and conviction of our prayers should be elevated once we truly have faith in His forgiving character. It should bless and empower our spirits to call upon Him all the more. Don't allow the devil to persuade us that we are not entitled to go to God in prayer. It is because of our lack in all things that we indeed need to stay in prayer with our forgiving God, who stands near and available at all times.

God's forgiving attribute places parameters on our request of Him, also. We must pray in the same forgiving spirit as the Lord's character. We should not pray to have our enemies struck down like gnats with a swatter. We must pray as Jesus prayed, "And forgive us our debts, as we forgive our debtors" *(Matthew 6:12)*. The Bible also says, "But if ye do not forgive, neither will your Father which is in heaven forgive your trespasses" *(Mark 11:26)*. This is reiterated and commanded of us in Luke 6:37 and Ephesians 4:32. Let's face it, we can surely muster the strength and spirit to forgive our brethren and enemies for their small violations against us, if Joseph could forgive his brothers for such a heinous act as throwing him into a pit and selling him off *(Genesis 50:17)*.

The parameters of our prayers are set by God's very nature and attributes. This is a *key* to remember and practice. His forgiveness is no different in this respect, and all the more important to the control of our prayers. One great thing to remember about praying strong and successful prayers is we must remove and eliminate any evil spirit within us so the Spirit of Christ may reign to bring forth the fruit of supplication.

We must relinquish our spirits to accept that being a prayer warrior is to have a spirituality above the norm. A healthy and hearty communion with God which bears success requires a spirit greater than most are willing to obtain and sustain. It is such a spirit that Christ dwells in richly and is made manifest. That is the Spirit Christ speaks of in John 14:9-21. Let it be known today a spirit of unforgivingness ruins any chance of our having power to pray unto God for the bearing of fruit. I need not repeat that last sentence for I am sure we all shall read it again.

It is those of us who have clean hearts who can even venture to be prayer warriors. Let me make this a little more plain. There are many a people who can mouth some of the most vibrant prayers, yet they fall short of the thrown of God's grace simply due to their having spirits scorched in turmoil and strife, first apprehended by unforgivingness. God knows this is important for our power in Him, thus He implores us to forgive others, religiously. Not just for the sake of those we forgive. No, my brother and sister. No matter how evil and unrepented the other person, <u>forgiveness is</u>

essential for the sustaining of our own abilities to commune with the Lord at great heights.

Forgiving others is a great benefit unto ourselves. For a moment, think not of the effect it has on the forgiven. Oh, please receive this. Think of our own empowerment unto God when we are forgiving others. Yes, there is a slight selfish motive, but true to heart is our need to sustain our right spirit for communion with God. Fact is, you and I can forgive others all day and they still not be forgiven of God, anyhow. See II Kings 24:4. He is the final say on forgiveness. I am concerned that a person receives God's forgiveness when I speak it unto them, but after I have forgiven them, I switch my focus to my soul's condition in apprehending Christ Jesus; which will not fully occur till His return. In the meanwhile, it is my duty to keep my spirit's condition right, both, for sound communion and living with the Lord, and for powerful prayer unto Him.

This approach does not minimize our concern for those who are to be forgiven by us, yet a better mind set is achieved by our accepting our own soul's condition in light of forgiving them. Some folk will unintentionally drain us of our communal spirit by having us become evil unto unforgivingness. The devil knows this, as he will intentionally attempt to make us feel unforgiving towards others and towards ourselves. His main goal is to disrupt and ruin our spiritual relationships with God. Do not allow the devil and his imps to succeed in their God condemned jobs.

The Lord says now an unforgiving heart has no eternal glory. An unforgiving spirit is as an hardened heart and of the branch cast into the fire; of which Jesus spoke in John 15:1-9. Hence, the root of many of our angers derive from unforgiving spirits. It is urged that we not permit others to condemn our spirits to that of a spiritual jail where we are unable to benefit from a life of power and strength.

Alright! Those previous paragraphs were engrossed in the "us." Let us again get back to those for whom we pray. We are of no great benefit to sinners, hence us all, if we are not willing to pray forgiveness of sins. We often look upon the sins of outsiders as pitiful and disgusting. We frown upon folk who are caught up in sinfulness, and we dub them as pariah or persons to be outcast and shunned; especially when we feel as though we are above that particular sin. In other words, we think ourselves as Holier-than-thou now that we have been saved by Christ. We pre-judge others as unworthy of this salvation we have been saved unto; as if we were truly ever worthy. But, thanks to His forgiveness and mercy (of which we will speak of in a moment) that all the repented in heart, who claim Him as Lord, shall receive of this salvation.

A prayer warrior must have a heart, not just lips, bent on forgiving others. We must forgive even those whom we do not know. Question is, how can we truthfully forgive those who we do not know if we cannot forgive those in whom we presume to love and see each day? Only a twisted mind can make such a thing work psychologically. The Lord knows it all to be different. The heart steers our emotions and actions. Once the heart becomes set in one direction it becomes difficult, at best, to turn the other way. Some of our most helpful prayers as warriors will be to pray for the forgiveness of sins of others. "To open their eyes, and to turn them from darkness to light, and from the power of satan unto God, that they may receive forgiveness of sins, and inheritance among them which are sanctified by faith that is in me," as spoken by Jesus in Acts 26:18. Jesus also made point that it is more important to heal person's relationships with the Father by forgiving sins, rather than to heal the body *(Mark 2:3-12)*. Forgiveness becomes power gained by all parties involved, so let us pray unto God that He forgive their sins and ours.

Merciful (Psalm 103:8)

Prayer warriors who believe God to be merciful (compassionate treatment towards others, especially towards those who are undeserving; withheld merited punishment) have confidence that we can go to the Lord in prayer even though our pasts are deluged with sinfulness, unfaithfulness and even disobedience; somewhat similar to that of the attribute of forgiving. "Go and proclaim these words toward the north, and say, Return, thou backsliding Israel, saith the Lord; and I will not cause mine anger to fall upon you: for I am merciful, saith the Lord, and I will not keep anger for ever" *(Jeremiah 3:12)*. That is good news for us all since, "For all have sinned, and come short of the glory of God" *(Romans 3:23)*. We all surely do not receive what we deserve.

Many of us know we have done some things worthy of our destruction. Great lengths are taken by many, even believers, to stay clear of talking to the Lord, at times, because we have yet to make things right with Him in some matters of old. We convince ourselves that we are not worthy to go to the Lord because of our old natures, or things past. So, we become weary and disbelieve in God's merciful kindness. We become so weary and disbelieving, at times, that we ask the same question Asaph had asked, "Has God forgotten to be gracious? hath he in anger shut up his tender mercies?"*(Psalm 77:9)*. The response and answer to all who utter that question is provided by God in Isaiah 49:14-15, "But Zion said, The Lord hath forsaken me, and my Lord hath forgotten me. Can a woman forget her sucking child, that she should not have compassion on the son of her womb? yea, they may forget, yet will I not forget thee." Only God has greater love for a child than that of a mother.

We must fully believe and trust God and His Word, "If we confess our sins, he is faithful and just to forgive us our sins ..." *(1 John 1:9)*. So I declare this day, let us go to the Lord in confession and repentance, then be empowered to go to Him in prayer with hearts convinced that our God is merciful. Pray believing the Lord is merciful, and pray that He will hear and answer our prayers.

Chapters 29 and 30 of the Book of Deuteronomy give us illustrations of how we shall be blessed of God and rejoice in His prosperity after we turn unto Him. "And it shall come to pass, when all these things are come upon thee, the blessing and the curse, which I have set before thee, and thou shalt call them to mind among all the nations, whither the Lord thy God hath driven thee, And shalt return unto the Lord thy God, and shalt obey his voice according to all that I command thee this day, thou and thy children, with all thine heart, and with all thy soul; That then the Lord thy God will turn thy captivity, and have compassion upon thee, and will return and gather thee from all the nations, whither the Lord thy God hath scattered thee. If any of thine be driven out unto the outmost parts of heaven, from thence will the Lord thy God gather thee, and from thence will He fetch thee" *(Deuteronomy 30:1-4)*. These and the other verses within the two chapters give strong indication and assurance of how merciful is our God. Again, it is in these assurances that prayer warriors can confidently reach out to the Lord with truthful heartfelt repentance.

Our Lord's mercies outweigh all the sins we have committed; even sins we have committed which are of lesser or greater human degree than those sins committed by the Biblical Israelites. I Peter 4:8 says, "... charity covers the multitude of sins." Charity is love, of course; and God is love. This I say today, what greater love is there than the Lord Himself; thus, He alone covers that which we have done wrong. He alone is love enough to grant mercy for all we have done in the past and all that we will do in the future. Mere man would condemn us all to eternal damnation, "But thou, O Lord, art a God full of compassion, and gracious, longsuffering, and plenteous in mercy and truth" *(Psalms 86:15)*. "It is of the Lord's mercies that we are not consumed, because his compassions fail not" *(Lamentations 3:22)*. Guilt alone would kill our every desire to commune with God, therefore it is the duty of this document to empower believers to a heightened level of assurance in God's being merciful.

There are those of us who have not yet gone to God in prayer since we last sinned, because we are trying to build up enough works of good graces to make up for all we have done wrong. Let it be known this very moment there are no works we can perform to gain the mercies of God. "Not by works of righteousness which we have done, but according to his mercy he saved us, by the washing of regeneration, and renewing of the Holy Ghost; Which he shed on us abundantly through Jesus Christ our Saviour" *(Titus 3:5-6)*. It should bless our spirits to know we do not have to perform any works for His mercy. Repentance and faith are all that is required of us. Our faith in His mercy should encourage us to confidently go to Him in prayer although we have previously sinned. We would never go to Him in prayer if we did not believe in His mercies; for we shall be guilty of some sin, either by omission or commission, and we will not be made perfect until the Lord returns. "As it is written, There is none righteous, no, not one" *(Romans 3:10)*.

In addition, the Lord's attribute of mercy should be unto us as another blessed parameter for our prayers. The Lord says, "Be ye therefore merciful, as your Father also is merciful" *(Luke 6:36)*. We ought not pray certain things if we believe God to be merciful. These certain things include not being quick to pray vengeance upon others. Praying vengeance does not illustrate mercy; thus retaliation should be far from our lips. How much greater retaliation could come upon our enemies than for us to pray their deliverance unto kindness; or better yet, unto salvation. In accord with mercy, our prayers should not be positioned in hostility, either. Hostility is one factor which can truly render our prayers ineffective unto God. Hostility kills the spirit. It kills the spirit within us and it kills our spirit's connection with the Spirit of God. There is absolutely no mercy in hostility. We all must, and I do say must, remove all hostility in our hearts for the sake of our living and our prayers, alike. It is through our love and our mercy that many of our prayers will be answered of God. The Bible declares in Ephesians 4:26 we should not go to sleep on our anger nor our wrath. If we allow anger to linger in our hearts, it will fester into hostility within our spirits.

Vindictiveness should be far from our lips in prayer when we are joined unto God's Spirit in mercy. A vindictive heart cannot pray with a spirit of Christ. What might have happened to all the keepers of the law had Jesus been vindictive? Woe unto us, even. As well, a heart of mercy must refrain from bitterness in prayers for three reasons: a bitter heart results in cracked prayers and dried up living; it is impossible to pray for an enemy while having bitterness in the spirit, which then eliminates half the power a prayer warrior possesses; a bitter heart beats to a drum distant from the very mercy that can cure the world's sicknesses and diseases. In the same manner, mercy will restrain us from being cruel, grudging, and spiteful. Let us be merciful unto others in prayer just as the Lord has shed His merciful kindness toward us. Bear ye the fruit of mercy so the Lord our God may be glorified in the fulfillment of our prayers.

The Lord's attribute of mercy is one of the greatest parameters for our prayer lives. It is through His mercy that He forgave us. It is through His mercy and love that He sent His only begotten Son as a living sacrifice to pay our sin debts. It is His very mercy which keeps us from being fully consumed in the fire of our sinfulness. Let it be this same mercy that guides our prayers unto fruitfulness, as we demonstrate to the Lord how His sanctifying power continues to profitably mold and direct our lives. Having nothing else, we should have love coupled with mercy to carry us far along the way.

In addition to mercy guiding our prayers, it is a merciful heart that gives blessed increase to the soul of the person who is praying. Here are two illustrations of how this happens. First, the increase occurs because thoughts of mercy put a person's mind in a spirit of compassion. It is all but impossible to have success in our prayers without first having compassion. Compassion is having a feeling of sympathy or sorrow for others. Compassion is the base of the "effectual fervent" spoken of in James 5:16. We ought pray for ourselves to have more compassion lest we become quite ineffective in living and in prayer. It was the compassion of our mother's prayers that got us through much of our messes. It is the same compassion within our prayers that covers our children in these trying days and times. As prayer warriors, we must check our compassion levels before entering prayer, so to best produce successful results. I repeat, there will be little capability of producing success in prayers without compassion within our hearts and spirits. The truth is many of our yesterday's prayers proved to be ineffective because we truthfully lacked compassion when we entered prayer. Following this document's *Prayer Progression* will help to increase our compassion to levels capable of bearing great fruit and capable of mountain moving victories. Realize God is compassion.

The second way a merciful heart gives blessed increase to the soul is, our mercy reduces and eliminates our own selfishness, which in turn adds selflessness unto our soul's. Great increase in life occurs when we become selfless. It is in the spirit of selflessness that we, both, desire to help others, and we go great lengths to figure ways to give increase unto others. This is a *key* for us all, so let me make it a little clearer. The Lord seeks to bless those who's hearts are full of compassion in order to bless others who are in need. Many are the philanthropist who began meagerly giving to others through the compassion on their hearts, only to later find their vats blessed all the more; even to overflow. God blesses our compassion. Let me say that again — God blesses our compassion.

Thinking of the needs of others will prompt God to bless us all the more. God knows our compassion and He knows the needs of others; thus, He will provide overflow so to fulfill our compassion and the needs of others, at the same time. I've often told my nephews, "If you want to be successful and blessed, spend most of your time caring for the needs of others." God desires to bless those in need and He is looking for compassionate hearts in order to fulfill those very needs. Let us become compassionate through mercy, then watch how our spirits and our living increase beyond measure. Who can measure the increase God gives?

Good (Romans 2:4)

Believers who have faith that God is good (takes holy pleasure in blessing those who believe in Him) are encouraged to pray unto Him with confidence in the results. It is truly encouraging to know God is in the business of blessing His children. We surely do not look unto God as a bank machine nor blessing machine, but it does bless the soul to understand that He truly stands ready, willing and able to bless us. What could excite us more than to know the Lord takes great pleasure in pouring out blessings; so much that we cannot receive of them all? Malachi 3:10 tells us, "... if I will not open you the windows of heaven, and pour you out a blessing, that there shall not be room enough to receive it." Oh, that is being blessed. So, who's ready to be poured unto?

It is amazing how many people do not go to the Lord in prayer. If they only knew and believed He takes so much great pleasure in making His followers happy. Our Lord and Savior declared it this way, "... If thou knewest the gift of God, and who it is that saith to thee, Give me to drink; thou wouldest have asked of him, and he would have given thee living water" *(John 4:10)*. That's a good Lord. Countless people are without happiness and blessings in their lives, because they continue to seek joy and happiness amongst things and people whom do not have their best interest at heart. The Lord desires to bless His children, whereas many others are out to take from us rather than give unto us. If those others were to give anything to us, it would be drama; if anything at all. Let them keep the drama and let us seek the goodness of God.

The things, places and people with whom we seek to gain happiness and spend large amounts of time are sometimes the very things, places and people who continue to drain us of our last bit of happiness. The Bible declares in Proverbs 11:28, "He that trusteth in his riches shall fall; but the righteous shall flourish as a branch." They will drip us dry of our joy and happiness if we are not careful and protective. On the other hand, the Lord pours into us and is a giver of good things. The Bible tells of this in no uncertain terms in these two verses: "... no good thing will he withhold from them that walk uprightly" *(Psalm 84:11);* "Every good gift and every perfect gift is from above, and cometh down from the Father of lights, with whom is no variableness, neither shadow of turning" *(James 1:17).*

God desires to pour into our living the blessings and happiness we so seek. The shame is we keep looking in directions opposite of a God who is in the blessing business. No one can bestow happiness upon us like that of the Lord our God. We should get excited not for reason that He will always bless us, but for fact that He is eager and able to bless us. "I will still be excited to pray to a good God even if He does not bless me with that which I stand requesting," are the resounding words of they who believe in the goodness of a great God. We ought take example of Daniel 3:17-18 which speaks of three Hebrew boys who faithfully realized the power of believing God to be good and able.

It's exciting to be on the winning team with the winningest Captain — God. In my adolescence I played on an undefeated basketball team for the two years our age group was together. Week after week, it was greatly exciting to be on a team that brought happiness upon the faces of all those involved. Success and winning are infectious. God's goodness grants unto us that same kind of infectiousness that gives power to our prayers. We ought know in our hearts and spirits He is the winning God who blesses, both, those who seek Him and those who believe in His Son. We are not only on the team where our Captain, God, is in the business of blessing us, but He is in the business of giving double portions, as well. "Let the elders that rule well be counted worthy of double honour, especially they who labour in the word and doctrine" *(I Timothy 5:17).*

There are some attributes, like sovereign, which God alone stands as, yet most of God's attributes are to be incorporated into the lives of believers. The Bible says, "... there is none that doeth good, no, not one" *(Romans 3:12).* Although true, we are not excused from making every full attempt at becoming good; similar to our respectfully striving to become holy and other attributes only God is able to truly stand as. It is impossible for us to have some of the nature and attributes of God due to our being condemned to our flesh until the Lord returns and due to God being deity. That does not mean we are to abdicate unto evil. Prayer warriors give great effort to allow the Spirit's sanctifying power to work within them. That said, wholly endear God's goodness then witness the fruit thereof.

Gracious *(Romans 5:20-21; II Corinthians 12:9)*

Prayer warriors who trust that God is full of grace (giver of things we do not deserve; unmerited favor) are empowered in their prayer lives and find relief in their general living. The relief comes in knowing the Lord will bless us although we are surely undeserving. Any sensible person would realize none of us are perfect and none of us have yet to do what God requires of us. Undeserving is an understatement for most of us, yet God is still gracious enough to bestow blessings upon our lives. Some of us were so unruly in the past that we now wonder why God even cared enough to bless us as He has. For others we may have never thought we could have inherited so much favor after all the ungodly places we visited throughout each of our lifetimes.

God's grace gives us optimism to enter into prayer. This is an optimism which empowers us to move confidently in prayer, asking our hearts desires, full of hope to receive that which we do not deserve. Persons unfamiliar with God's grace will wrongly predetermine their own prayers useless on account of their lasting guilt about the things they did in the past. Others, who do not know of God's grace, will predetermine the same judgment upon their prayers, but for reason they know they are not presently doing what is right in the sight of the Almighty. Either way we are mistaken to automatically cast such a judgment upon our prayers.

Our having knowledge and faith that God is full of grace does not give us carte blanche to be openly and wilfully unrighteous while still expecting God's grace to be bestowed upon us. "Shall we continue in sin, that grace may abound?" *(Romans 6:1)*. Many of us make the mistake to think God is required to give us grace. Huge mistake! This miscalculation often causes some of us to fall out of love with the Lord. Some of us have been told only half the story of His grace, therefore, when things seem not to go our way we become dissatisfied with faith and with God, altogether. Let it be known here today that God is not required to give His grace at any time, nor at any moment, nor for any particular reason.

It is our duty to attempt to live righteous lives while appreciating the grace God does provide unto us when we do fall short. "We then, as workers together with him, beseech you also that ye receive not the grace of God in vain" *(II Corinthians 6:1)*. The true in heart can confidently move into prayer knowing the Lord looks favorably upon their sincerity and may grant them grace. This confidence is generated by knowing grace is God's to give and He does desire to give grace unto they who are sincere in their hearts and in their living. Grace is a gift as declared in Ephesians 3:7. In other words, knowledge of God's grace gives stability in faith to enter into prayer unto the Lord, yet it is not to be taken for granted. "Let us therefore come boldly unto the throne of grace, that we may obtain mercy, and find grace to help in time of need" *(Hebrews 4:16)*.

Truth *(I Samuel 15:29; Titus 1:2)*

Believers who trust that God is truth (cannot lie and does not need to lie) are given great power and confidence in prayer. It is such a boost in confidence to know someone's word is their bond. That is the blessing of being a child of a God who stands behind the Word He has spoken. No greater truth has the world nor Heaven known. Mere man relies on the FDIC to secure their financials, yet no greater security can anyone have than to know they can trust in God's truth; and not for tender's reason.

Our trust often begins and ends where another persons truthfulness is manifested or lacking. It is simple to understand a person cannot be trusted if they renege or go back on their word. How did you feel when someone tricked you into believing they would perform a certain thing only to witness them later withdraw their words? How heavy was the weight of your heart's dismay when your so-called friend deceived you with words and promises they never had intentions of upholding in the first place? The Bible says, "They speak vanity every one with his neighbour: with flattering lips and with a double heart do they speak" *(Psalm 12:2)*. Unkept words create distrust and disharmony. The Bible is quite clear in what it says of they who do not keep their word — "Ye are of your father the devil, and the lusts of your father ye will do. He was a murderer from the beginning, and abode not in the truth, because there is no truth in him. When he speaketh a lie, he speaketh of his own: for he is a liar, and the father of it" *(John 8:44)*. On the contrary, prayer warriors must be about truth, just as God is truth.

God is a harmonious God and He desires we have trust in Him. He can be trusted because He keeps His Word, and He does not go against His character nor His nature. It is imperative to learn and digest the character and nature of God so we may live and pray within those parameters. You and I can rest assured He is unchanging (immutable), which should strengthen our awareness in the fact that He is the ultimate truth. "That by two immutable things, in which it was impossible for God to lie, we might have a strong consolation, who have fled for refuge to lay hold upon the hope set before us" *(Hebrews 6:18)*.

Belief that God is truth and trustworthy is a basic strength in our praying unto Him; after first believing He Is. A foundation of our ability to pray begins successfully with our abilities to, both, pray in accord with God's

Word in truth and leave prayers at the throne of grace in faith knowing He Is. For most of us, acquiring a great faith in God began by His first being truthful to His Word and promises. Psalm 100:5 and 117:2 proclaim His truth endureth to all generations and forever; respectfully. To become the warriors we desire, we must know God is full of truth; above any other truth known to man. "God is not a man, that he should lie ..." *(Numbers 23:19)*. A power in prayer comes about after believing in God's truthfulness. A lack of faith in God's truth minimizes prayer's successes. Faith in His truth builds great trust and it spiritually empowers believers, sizably.

The truth of God is as a parameter to our prayers, as well. We must pray in a truthful manner if we believe God Himself is truth. We deceive only ourselves if we are less than truthful unto God in our prayers. He knows our hearts and the intents thereof; so, we might as well be truthful. We can trust the Lord, but can He trust us? Do we pray in truth or do we make request with ill gotten motives? Are we sincere in speaking to the Lord or do we communicate with a tricky tongue? The success of our prayers weighs in the balance of our abilities to be truthful in prayer. "And they will deceive everyone his neighbour, and will not speak the truth: they have taught their tongue to speak lies, and weary themselves to commit iniquity. Thine habitation is in the midst of deceit; through deceit they refuse to know me, saith the Lord" *(Jeremiah 9:5-6)*. Prayer warriors and strong Christians, alike, cannot afford to be untruthful; for therein lies a difference between answered and unanswered prayers.

An example of how we humanistically and wickedly handle truthfulness in our prayers is we often pray to God saying things like, "I will come to Church every Sunday and I will never do that thing again, if you get me out of this one situation, O' God." All of those words become as mere rhetoric when we are delivered and thereafter stay home or go to the ball game on the day of worship. Too many of us walk down the very same paths we pledged not to return. We later have the nerve or audacity to ask God for something else, claiming yet another covenant promise. How might our spirit's have the boldness to do such a thing, and what would make us think God will honour another covenant request when we failed to keep to the one previous? Truth has much to do with being covenant keepers, and prayer warriors must emulate God as a covenant keeper.

Let us speak a little more on covenant; which is based heavily in truth. Make it a point to declare and keep covenants with God and with others, so to be found truthful. The Lord Jesus said it this way, "But let your communication be, Yea, yea; Nay, nay; for whatsoever is more than these cometh to evil" *(Matthew 5:37)*. I beseech us all to make covenant with the Lord this very moment to learn more of His attributes in truth and spirit.

Pray this prayer today:

"Lord I enter into covenant with You as I commit to learn more of Your attributes and nature, so I may be found worthy to be a prayer warrior and Your child. If it be thine will for this covenant, show Your character to reveal yourself unto me in ways untold, yet spirit withstanding. All the earth shall see Your greatness thereof and shout Your glory. Give me even the spirit to keep this covenant, that I may live in truth and in power. This I do pray with thanksgiving in my heart and in Jesus' name — Amen."

The Bible says, "... for them that honour me I will honour, and they that despise me shall be lightly esteemed" *(I Samuel 2:30)*. The Bible goes on to say in Romans 1:25-32, covenant breakers, among other unrighteous actors, are worthy of death. Death to our spirits. Death to our living. Death to our prayers. At some point in our lives, we all have mistakenly or aimlessly broken a covenant, or two; whereas for some it has become habitual and purposed. The later spiritual criminals are evil enough to say some things knowing full well they have no intentions of keeping that word or covenant. Today let us understand how vile of an act it is to break a covenant; therefore choose to follow in God's footsteps of truth. The Lord our God of ultimate truth looks angrily upon they who break covenants. <u>It can be said breaking a covenant is one of the worst moral untruths and immoral acts a person can commit.</u>

Decide this very moment to enter into covenants with the Lord and keep them, above all else. We serve a God of covenants. The Bible warns not to make a vow if you cannot keep it. The old folk use to say, "Don't make a promise you can't keep," while others have said, "Don't make a vow you do not intend on keeping." God knows the intents of our hearts. Therefore, I urge us to be excited to enter into covenants, but be just as delighted to keep them. "Now therefore, our God, the great, the mighty, and the terrible God, who keepest covenant and mercy, let not all the trouble seem little before thee, that hath come upon us, on our kings, on our princes, and on our priests, and on our prophets, and on our fathers, and on all thy people, since the time of the kings of Assyria unto this day. Howbeit thou art just in all that is brought upon us; for thou hast done right, but we have done wickedly" *(Nehemiah 9:32-33)*. In other words, we, the supposed believers are the one's who offend truth; not God.

The Lord will enormously bless us through covenants kept. A positive track record of keeping covenants with God and with others will render us blessed and prosperous beyond measure and compare. Pray in accord with truth, then watch the blessings flow in many directions. You will be joyfully amazed at how the Lord blesses all those who keep truth and covenant as fine garments; wrapped with the grace of our Almighty Lord.

Self-Sufficient (Psalm 50:12)

The faithful who believe our God is self-sufficient (not having a need outside of Himself) are given power to trust the God of our prayers can provide all our needs by Himself. In certain places of secular terms we find a need to get one person to help in one area, a second person to assist in another area and yet a third and a fourth persons to help in some other parts; all of which comes together to complete one act or one need. This is not the case with our self-sufficient God. He alone is Jehovah Jireh, or Provider. This is a name proclaimed by Abraham in Genesis 22:14 when he was about to sacrifice his son Isaac.

There is power gained in coming into the knowledge that God is our only need for all our provisions. It is the powerless in faith who have not yet rested upon the fact that God alone can provide every need. A prayer warrior goes into prayer having great confidence that once he or she finishes praying to Jehovah Jireh there is no need to consult help from any others. Abraham told Isaac with faith and confidence, "The Lord will provide." That is the same level of faith that resides within a true prayer warrior who invariably exclaims, "Once I pray unto the Lord there is no need to go to anyone else nor look unto anything else for provisions." That is the level of belief that gets results with the Lord! Would God have provided Abraham with a ram substitute for the sacrifice had he not proclaimed that God was the sole provider of his needs, or had he traveled with a third person for some sort of backup? We may never know, but faith tells us much of our spirits' help and power comes through having enormous faith in the providing power of the One True and Living God.

Fact is we must be connected to this God, our God, who does not need anything outside Himself. What greater source of power to bless and direct our prayers? Let me answer that by saying, there is no greater power! What is a greater assurance than to know our prayers shall reach a God who needs absolutely nothing lest Himself? Let me answer that question also — There is no greater assurance! The Bible makes it clear, "Neither is worshipped with men's hands, as though he needed any thing, seeing he giveth to all life, and breath, and all things" *(Acts 17:25)*.

In the *Element of Prayer Progression*™ *#8* we speak on the subject of our having faith in God in order to be successful in prayer. That faith is built upon our knowing and accepting God as our only provider. Overly trusting in things and people outside of God will render our faith minuscule and powerless; especially in prayer. As well, many of us try to accomplish things on our own simply because we never developed faith and trust that God is enough. Accepting the Lord our God as our sole provider will further transition our faith into knowing He is enough. It is great to enter prayer with a mind convinced that God is enough, followed by voicing the very words, "God is enough." Oh, we will not be full successes in prayer until we are truly convinced He alone is more than enough. We ought not enter into prayer without first being sold-out that God is more than enough for all our concerns and for all our living.

The truth is we should look back on all of our life and have true faith that it was only God who provided our every need. It was not Daddy, nor was it Momma who provided for us. Let us make it clear this moment that God provided the very things we needed by first providing it unto others as mere vessels. Mom and Dad, and who ever else for that matter, were only conduits through whom God made provisions unto us. That is the place or realm true prayer warriors reside. It is a place of strong faith in God as provider. A prayer warrior does not believe this through the unawares of cliche, but through a belief system mounted by faith and through a track record of personal testimonies. If we are truly blessed of God, He has given us some "only God" testimonies. Again, we are not speaking of cliche. We are talking about being witnesses to how God put people and things into our lives at just the right time and from worlds apart, even. By worlds apart it is meant that only God could have made certain paths cross through willing and obedient vessels. It is truly empowering unto our next prayer to have such powerful testimonies of God's making provisions in times past. Oh, I've got some testimonies to tell; just as we all should have. I feel pain and sympathy for all who do not have extreme and mysterious testimonies of God's power to provide.

Some people proclaim testimonies on small levels because their faith is akin. The larger scale workings of God are what I direct us to ponder this moment. Ponder the very scale of workings that usher us into strong faith believing no one but God provided and provides all our needs. Many of these types of workings come by way of great pain, which many of us are quick to evade. We must realize and accept there are some pains that are fruitful to our faith. This document is not advocating we seek pain in our lives, but it is suggested we not get in the way of God working His power when the pains and the sufferings do come our way. That is the time when our faith's increase truly begins. Far too many of us shout that God is our self-sufficient God, simply from the perspective that it is Christian fad to exclaim such statements. On the other hand, that proclamation is spiritually ingrained in the hearts of prayer warriors by way of their actually living under God's providing power. It is not enough to just shout it. The real power for they who pray comes about through a personal witness of God's ability to provide every need.

Folk who truthfully witness the power of God's providing hand, joyfully reach a point where they too can honestly proclaim, "I will lift up mine eyes unto the hills, from whence cometh my help. My help cometh from the Lord, which made heaven and earth. He will not suffer thy foot to be moved: he that keepeth thee will not slumber. Behold, he that keepeth Israel shall neither slumber nor sleep. The Lord is thy keeper: the Lord is thy shade upon thy right hand. The sun shall not smite thee by day, nor the moon by night. The Lord shall preserve thee from all evil: he shall preserve thy soul. The Lord shall preserve thy going out and thy coming in from this time forth, and even for evermore" *(Psalm 121)*. Someone once said, "I realized God was all I needed when I reached a point where He was all I had." This is that same point where we must have faith enough to believe He is self-sufficient and alone able to attend unto our every need. Superficial professors will claim it without truly living it, serving plate-fulls of lies worthy of hell's fire.

We ought truly know our help comes from the Lord, and the Lord alone. That is true prayer power! That is when "feet" are put on statements like, "Let go and let God." That is the way Abraham must have felt in his faith. I declare this very day, be obedient unto God and watch His will prevail in our favor. We cannot let go and let God, until we truly believe, and I mean truly believe, He is Jehovah Jireh.

Sovereign *(Isaiah 46:9)*

Prayer warriors who believe God is sovereign (the sole ruler of all things) are empowered to pray over all things with confidence. This confidence is first revealed through the believer's realization that God has all power over all creation. Confidence in His power and belief in His ultimate rule are quite essential, since both declare to believers that their prayers are reaching the One who has the final say over all movement in Heaven and Earth. Nothing happens unless God allows it; negative or positive. Praying to someone or something with less than ultimate power is fruitless and truly witless. A waste of time it would be to pray to God if He were, say, a manager, supervisor or someone else who had less than the final say. Do you truly believe God is the final say?

Prayer warriors pray unto God with confidence knowing the buck stops at Him. What God says goes, no matter what the enemies nor the devil may attempt or suggest. They may suggest that the drama upon our lives will be our final demise, but warriors in spirit know only God is sovereign and He alone has the final say. God alone controls all things at all times, no matter what our current situations, and no matter how persuasive our enemy's attacks. The Lord not only knows the ending befoe the beginning, but He has full control over both, as well. Let our spirits be encouraged and empowered by knowing nothing begins nor ends without God's permission. Understand the two essential points for which to confidently pray to God — permission and authorization. He alone is the authorization.

Satan even knows of God's ultimate power, as illustrated in the story of Job. Chapter 1 verse 10 tells how satan acknowledged nothing could come against what God has His hand upon. Chapter 2 verses 6 and 7 reiterate God's sovereign power as His permission is needed for satan to do any harm to Job. Knowledge of God's sovereignty is weakness unto satan, but it is power to the children of the Most High. "Na-Na-Na Na-Na" can be humorously sang by Christians in the face of the devil, while having full assurance that God is sovereign. It is not that pain and suffering will never knock at the door of God's children. Please do not be mistaken to think anything of that similarity. Troubles will come our way; even as prayer warriors. The sovereignty of God commands, "There hath no temptation taken you but such as is common to man: but God is faithful, who will not suffer you to be tempted above that ye are able; but will with the temptation also make a way to escape, that ye may be able to bear it" *(I Corinthians 10:13)*. The Bible also proclaims to us, "No weapon that is formed against thee shall prosper; and every tongue that shall rise against thee in judgment thou shalt condemn. This is the heritage of the servants of the Lord, and their righteousness is of me, saith the Lord" *(Isaiah 54:17)*. Only a sovereign God can do such a thing for you and I, at the same time of having all control over all things and over all creation. Anyone with less than all power cannot perform such things. "The Lord hath done great things for us; whereof we are glad" *(Psalm 126:3)*. Great things He has done, for He is sovereign.

God's sovereignty permeates our prayer lives with great power and confidence. Confidence that urges us to pray with great assurance and certainty that we serve a God who has the final signature on everything that happens with all creation. At this point of awareness of God's sovereignty some folk cry foul claiming, "How could He care if He allows such pain and misery in the lives of those He loves?" This is the same point in which our faith must resound in high esteem that God is perfect in all His ways; whether we understand them or not. Always let us remember God is perfecting us, even as He allows the enemy's tricks to inadvertently build us in spirit and in character. "And not only so, but we glory in tribulations also: knowing that tribulation worketh patience; And patience, experience; and experience, hope" *(Romans 5:3-4)*. Joseph said it best in response to his brothers' hateful acts, "But as for you, ye thought evil against me; but God meant it unto good, to bring to pass, as it is this day, to save much people alive" *(Genesis 50:20)*. So let not our hearts be troubled by the pains and strife that will come our way, surely; for God has a master plan and He is in full control.

We can surely pray to God with faith in knowing we have entered the right place to get all the right answers and actions. I have always said, "Either you are on the inside with all the information or you are on the outside with little information." We cannot be fully familiar of all things, because God is alone sovereign; but, we can certainly reside in the inner courts by praying in faith that He is in total control of all things made.

We enter prayer with great faith in God's sovereignty; believing He shall reveal His will and give glimpses of His workings. "But as it is written, Eye hath not seen, nor ear heard, neither have entered into the heart of man, the things which God hath prepared for them that love him. But God hath revealed them unto us by his Spirit: for the Spirit searcheth all things, yea, the deep things of God. For what man knoweth the things of a man, save the spirit of man which is in him? even so the things of God knoweth no man, but the Spirit of God. Now we have received, not the spirit of the world, but the spirit which is of God; that we might know the things that are freely given to us of God" *(I Corinthians 2:9-12)*.

We ought gain in strength when we believe our prayers are lifted to a God, not of weakness, but of sovereign power! Innumerable prayers ramble and fade as persons are unaware of the character of whom they go unto in prayer. Contrarily, boldness comes about in the prayers of they who are confidently aware of God's being the sole ruler and controller of all things. It is by this level of faith that our prayers will resound the glory of God, shouting, "Wherefore thou art great, O Lord God: for there is none like thee, neither is there any God beside thee ..." *(II Samuel 7:22)*.

Infinite (Psalm 147:5; Luke 21:33)

Believers who trust that God is infinite (having no limitations) have increased encouragement and power in, both, our lives and our prayers; especially when we recognize how we are naturally finite beings. Let's make this plain. <u>There is no limit as to what God can do!</u> Countless numbers of our situations appear to us as all but lost causes, but we can rejoice in prayer knowing His long arm of deliverance can reach atop the highest heights and beneath the deepest depths. No situation is too far gone nor too desolate for our limitless God. It is blessed assurance when we recognize we need not ever throw in the towel on our situations, having faith there is no thing too far gone for God's hand to reach. The Lord Himself rhetorically told Abraham, "Is anything too hard for the

the Lord?" *(Genesis 18:14a),* as Sarah jokingly listened, standing at the tent door in disbelief. Who can measure the greatness of God's reach? Can a rod be stretched to His expanse? Can silver be weighed to His breadth's equal? Can a volume be a degree to His immensity? I dare say not!

To be a strong prayer warrior we must have ingrained in our spirits and living the fact that God is limitless. We must believe his power is limitless in every way shape and form. There must be no doubting His blessings are inexhaustible today and forever. The expanse of His greatness is unmeasured. His ability to deliver is unbounded. His very faithfulness is endless. The very reach of His wings of protection are unrestricted. In all that we believe we must conclude that our God is the very definition of limitless.

Knowledge and belief in His limitlessness is a part of the prayer warrior's foundation of faith. This attribute of God is key to the release of powerful prayers that touch the ends of the earth while shaking loose the grips of weaknesses that surround many of God's children. The truth is our prayers' requests are all but limitless due to God being infinite Himself. The *key* for us is to believe God to be limitless, in order that we may have faith and spirit to pray prayers that are boundless. The only bounds for our prayers' requests are the very attributes, character, nature and will of God. God can and will give us the ends of the bounds of our prayers, if we trust and believe that He is. Our faith is defined in the ends or endlessness of our belief that God is infinite. "But will God indeed dwell on the earth? behold, the heaven and heaven of heavens cannot contain thee; how much less this house that I have builded?" *(I Kings 8:27).*

We unfaithfully place God's power inside the small boxes we constructed out of our own disbelief, skepticism and finite humanism. Shamefully an untold number of us can believe only to the extent of our own limited and finite abilities. We know our abilities are pint-sized, yet we seem to have a difficult time transitioning our trust to believing in a limitless God. What makes it so difficult for us to believe we are so weak and He is so strong? We are so short and He stands beyond the expanse of the universes? We know only that which we have previously encountered, whereas, God's knowledge began before time and will extend past the end of Earth's days? Our living and our prayers deserve more than what we alone can provide.

It behooves me that more of us do not make the effort to get more deeply connected with He who possess that which we will never possess — infiniteness. Instead, we continue to attempt to connect with millionaires, famous people, and others who are seemingly well to do. It is true we go to great lengths to meet humans who have what we do not currently possess. We diligently seek earthly powers, positions and possessions in attempts to become large and in charge; never realizing that we will never be fully in charge. Our God is and will always be in charge and in full control; for His very reign is infinite. Why is it we seek increase in the creation rather than in the Creator? That is a question that can be answered only by each individual. It stands to say, we shall never reach our potential in life nor in prayer until we believe in God's infinite abilities. It is His boundless power that works through our hall closets of abilities, delivering us unto unimaginable victories. The marvelous has yet to happen for us, because we have yet to believe in God's spectacular.

A sad scenario would be to pray to a god who's ability was limited. In similar fashion we should not rely so heavily on mere man for help in our situations. Mere man will let us down, as we all can attest. It is not that our fellow man always chooses to be unfaithful, but it is simply a matter of truth that man's abilities are limited from the start. It is nice and well when we do receive help from another man or woman, although it can be discouraging when they fail or forsake us. But God says, "... so I will be with thee; I will not fail thee, nor forsake thee" *(Joshua 1:5)*. His name is Jehovah! He is the only one with unlimited means, so there is never a situation nor circumstance which cannot be met by His great abilities.

All of God's nature, character and attributes are important, of course, yet this is one of those attributes in which prayer warriors must already have strong belief even before settling down to pray. How can we pray to someone we do not believe to be limitless? It is a fruitless endeavor from the start to not believe He is limitless. This is a "make it or break it" for our prayers to be able to leap out of the proverbial horse gate. There is no power in a prayer that is not built upon faith that God is infinite. There were many times Jesus proclaimed that it was by faith that persons received healings and blessings. Likewise, we are no different in this modern day, whereas, we too need to have faith in God's ability to perform what no one else can perform and in ways like no one else can perform them. It is in this type of faith where blessings are first formed. The Bible declares, "... for he that cometh to God must believe that he is ...." *(Hebrews 11:6)*. We often like to talk about the reward portion of this verse, but the foundation of it all is in our first believing that He is. We surely cannot believe He can, if we do not first believe that He is!

Countless numbers of us rightfully acknowledge our being finite and incapable. Some of us have gone overboard, even, in this acknowledging, to a point where we have rendered ourselves incapable of receiving God as infinite. This is a point of II Corinthians 12:10 which says, "... for when I am weak, then am I strong." We must first realize we have no power outside of the limitless power of the Almighty working in us, through us, and around us. Acknowledging our finite abilities must be matched with our relinquishing power over to a Father who is limitless and eminent, which then ignites power in our prayers.

Our prayers come to life at the moment we surrender all our minuscule power over to God's eminence. We may be able to accomplish some things ourselves, but God can do all things; and all things good. The heights of our prayers are reached as the greatness of God is permitted to workout all our concerns.

The major blessing that is spoken of here is not so much that He will bless us beyond measure, as much as it is about our having the faith that He can bless us beyond any limits and beyond our present circumstances. Greater is the faith than the visible result of the faith. Yes, there is a joy in knowing God will bless us immensely, but the joy and the blessing begins when we first believe He can; before, not after He blesses us. After believing He can, we are then able to accept the ways He blesses us even when those ways are not what we expected. Understand God's limitlessness also refers to His ability to bless us in ways unknown and untold; as in inscrutable. The strong prayer warrior then says, "I will be blessed however You bless me Lord." The ability to truthfully say those words comes from a belief that He is, rather than just that He will. Lets make it a little more plain. When we believe He will, only, we may get frustrated if we do not recognize the blessing. Whereas, we have faith to sustain in times God does not send a blessing we so expect, when we first believe He is not bound by anything other than His own character, nature and will. It is just as much, if not more, about our having the faith that He is infinite, than it is about our receiving anything tangible through His limitless power. We are well on our way to becoming prayer warriors armed for battle when we fully digest the point of God's limitlessness.

Incomprehensible (Isaiah 55:8)

Prayer warriors who believe in God's incomprehensible character (none other than God can understand Himself) are provided with great injections of submission unto our spirits and great increases of trust in God. This submission and trust enables our prayer lives to grow in great power. We must fully accept that we are unable to understand God and His many facets of workings. It can be said that faith is not needed where comprehension is present. Hebrews 11:1 proclaims that very fact. Our trust and faith in God must be wrapped around our acceptance of His being incomprehensible.

Our faith is not in full bloom if our spirits are not thrilled and overjoyed of being incapable of understanding God and His ways. The enormity of God and His ways are far too large for us to ever wrap our small minds around. It is in this acceptance that our faith begins to be greatly empowered to a level outreaching general belief. This thing called faith must be impregnated by our submission and acceptance of the greatness of our God, which is hugely exalted in His being incomprehensible. There are those of us, who are called believers, who say "He's a great God," but still cannot come to spiritual grips that He alone can understand His own workings. This is a *key* for us all. When we accept and submit to God's being incomprehensible, then and only then will we be able to accept how and when God chooses to work things out for us. Too large a multitude of us get frustrated with God and want to quit following Him because we never get to a point in our faith where we accept how God serves our plate of deliverance and/or blessing. This non-acceptance interferes with our abilities to pray with power.

Still, others of us choose not to wait on God because we don't understand what He's doing and why He's taking so long. They who accept God as incomprehensible do not have a problem waiting. Our posture should be to submit to watch and wait for as long as He takes. They who wait and truly believe God to be incomprehensible often can be heard speaking of a next level type of faith, saying, "God has already provided a way. I just have to discern the blessing and walk into it." For truly, there are times we are still waiting, sadly enough, because we have yet to recognize the blessing had been provided already. God declares, "For my thoughts are not your thoughts, neither are your ways my ways ..." *(Isaiah 55:8).*

Our greatly persecuted brother Job smartly said it this way, "I know it is so of a truth: but how should man be just with God? If he will contend with him, he cannot answer him one of a thousand. He is wise in heart, and mighty in strength: who hath hardened himself against him, and hath prospered? Which removeth the mountains, and they know not: which overturneth them in his anger. Which shaketh the earth out of her place, and the pillars thereof tremble. Which commandeth the sun, and it riseth not; and sealeth up the stars. Which alone spreadeth out the heavens, and treadeth upon the waves of the sea. Which maketh Arcturus, Orion, and Pleiades, and the chambers of the south. Which doeth great things past finding out; yea, and wonders without number. Lo, he goeth by me, and I see him not: he passeth on also, but I perceive him not. Behold, he taketh away, who can hinder him? who will say unto him, What doest thou?" *(Job 9:2-12).* We too must testify of the great things we can understand of God, but we must also shout glory in recognition that there are powers and ways of God we will never comprehend.

Leaning on our own understanding and taking things into our own hands is the very reason we have ended up in so much trouble and turmoil. Getting ahead of God was the root of our issues and will be the cause of our downfall in the future; all of which began by our not accepting God as incomprehensible in the first place. As prayer warriors we can avoid pitfalls and those supposed unanswered prayers by fully admiring and relishing God's incomprehensible character. Embracing this attribute of God will propel our prayers and communion with God to a level seen by far too few believers. Let us take time to joyfully wrap our hearts and spirits around this truth. This is more a truth and less of a concept than any can imagine.

Let us place our spiritual arms around God's incomprehensible character and hold to it with all our soul's strength. Let us willingly entwine our faith around God's perfect ways. Bind fast faith and secure belief unto the acceptance of how we will never fully comprehend the enormity of His ways. Gladly rejoice in anchoring faith's keystone upon the Father's ability to perform some things that will absolutely blow our minds. The scripture, "I can do all things through Christ which strengtheneth me" *(Philippians 4:13),* gains more power in our living when we accept and believe He can fulfill some activities within and through us that are far beyond our understanding and imagination. Truth be told, we don't even have imaginations creative enough to envision what God has in store for them who love and believe Him.

Before a true prayer warrior goes into prayer, he or she has already committed in their spirit that God's answers to their prayer will be nothing like what they thought in their wildest dreams. They know through experience and faith that God's answers never fully, nor in part, replicate their thoughts on the matter. He is perfect in all His ways whether we believe and accept it or not.

We should be thankful that we cannot fully understand how the Lord works, for our ignorance stands as testimony to His greatness; no matter how intelligent we are. Woe to us if we served a god who was not above our understanding; otherwise it would be as the blind leading the blind. "... Can the blind lead the blind? shall they not both fall into the ditch?" *(Luke 6:39).* Most of us have fallen into ditches after consulting our friends who had no more smarts nor power than us. So, I am truly thankful to be incapable of fully understanding God. Actually, let me say it this way; for the previous sentence almost suggest there could be they who can understand God. "I am truly thankful to serve a God who is incomprehensible to all but Himself." That is the truth and strength of what is being said here.

Let me repeat, it should excite us to <u>not</u> have the ability to understand God and His ways. Not only does it prove His greatness, but it demonstrates our need to submit unto Him and trust all He does. I indeed hope this document's portions on submission and trust help many who, like my sister at the Church, desire more command of these two areas.

I believe in God's being incomprehensible to the point where I get excited when some troubles come my way. No, it is not a masochistic standpoint. On the contrary, it is from a faith's perspective. I have witnessed God's showing up in some mighty ways when things appeared destitute. The fact is we must go through some very troubling times in order to truly see the Lord's great power and witness His incomprehensible ways. It is a blessing if any of us have never gone through anything needing of God's great delivering power; while on the other hand, there are those of us who have some non-conventional testimonies of how God appeared when things were all but said, done and over. "But we had the sentence of death in ourselves, that we should not trust in ourselves, but in God which raiseth the dead: Who delivered us from so great a death, and doth deliver: in whom we trust that he will yet deliver us" *(II Corinthians 1:9-10)*. At times, we should feel an excitement in our faith when circumstances get tough. Our faith should know we are being put on display for God's great power to be shown to the masses. Troubling times bring about situations when God shows up in ways incomprehensible.

There are three reasons all of us should relinquish to trust God to show up and show out in tough times. First, history has shown we made it through tough times past, even times we thought there was no way out. The question then becomes, "Why get distraught over today's drama when yesterday's trials did not destroy us?" Prayer warriors have faith that it was by God's incomprehensible power that we made it through on yesterday, and it will be that very same power that will get us through today. Believing and receiving God as incomprehensible gives us an increase in faith unparalleled by any concerns life may dish out. I've heard some people proclaim, "Trouble doesn't last always!"

Some folk wonder how I stay so calm in some of the storms they see me go through. They would be even more amazed at the calm, if they only knew the full extent of some of the envy and jealousy I've had to endure. Well, the calm comes about by having history with an incomprehensible God who showed up yesterday when I needed Him, and I have faith that He will show up again today if any troubles arise. We all should have some history with the Lord so to set our belief to higher heights of faith and trust.

Prayer warriors can pray with great power and conviction during trying times, yet remain as cool as a fall breeze. This act of faith is made possible due to their history of witnessing God's unfathomable works. "Then they cry unto the Lord in their trouble, and he bringeth them out of their distresses. He maketh the storm a calm, so that the waves thereof are still. Then are they glad because they be quiet; so he bringeth them unto their desired haven" *(Psalms 107:28-30)*. Fact is, a warrior can be found saying, "I don't know how He's going to do it," but in the excitement and depths of their faith they know they shall have victory. In this sense, true prayer warriors do not have ordinary history books with God. The prayer warrior's history book is not filled with defeats and let-downs, nor is it sprinkled with God's not appearing in times of need. On the contrary, the history books of strong warriors are bursting at the seams with at least one testimony of how the Lord showed up in turmoil and incomprehensibly turned what seemed to be a lost cause into a triumph.

It only takes one time for the Lord to show up and do some impossible things on our behalf for us to gain mighty faith in Him in the future. "And again, I will put my trust in him" *(Hebrews 2:13)*. Our history books do not have to be filled with numerous testimonies to constitute a bursting at the seams. I do declare this very day that one testimony of a divine incomprehensible act can joyfully burst the seams of anyone's history book. I do not wish trouble on anyone, but I do pray that all would truly accept God for who He is — incomprehensible.

The second reason we should be able to relinquish to trust God to show up in difficult times is that His Word tells us He will. "Hath he said, and shall he not do it? or hath he spoken, and shall he not make it good?" *(Numbers 23:19)*. Simply put, our God is a covenant keeper, and He desires we have faith and trust in Him. "If God said it I believe it," must be the motto of every prayer warrior. "... It is written, Man shall not live by bread alone, but by every word that proceedeth out of the mouth of God" *(Matthew 4:4; Deuteronomy 8:3)*. This level of faith in God will grant us a willingness to relinquish to trust in Him each and every time trouble knocks at our doors. This level of faith is not impossible, although it does take tremendous faith to constantly trust the Lord to show up when pain and difficulty both come ringing the doorbell at the same time.

Fact is, just because we do not answer the bell does not make pains nor difficulties go away. What we can do is rely on God's fulfilling His word instead of simply ignoring the troublesome ring at the door. Troubles will come! Oh, troubles will come! But, the prayer warrior leans on the Word of God with Kung Fu grip, reassured that the Lord is about to follow through on His Word. Just how good is your grip?

No trouble in hell nor on Earth can hold back the strength of a prayer warrior who truly believes in God's willfulness to fulfill His Word. One Psalm writer wrote it this way, "Let my supplication come before thee: deliver me according to thy word" *(Psalm 119:170).*

The Word is power unto itself, but it truly comes alive for the prayer warrior once he or she stands with faith's foot planted firmly on the fact that God's Word has the last say. "Verily I say unto you, This generation shall not pass, till all these things be fulfilled. Heaven and earth shall pass away, but my words shall not pass away" *(Matthew 24:34-35).* The prayer warrior knows not how God will fulfill His Word, yet he or she faithfully knows it shall be fulfilled just the same. "I cannot see how, but God has already seen the way," can be heard from the mouths of prayer warriors. Much of the Word will remain incomprehensible for most, if not for all of us, but we rest assured in our faith that God will deliver on His Word and His promises. "Trust in the Lord with all thine heart; and lean not unto thine own understanding. In all thy ways acknowledge him, and he shall direct thy paths" *(Proverbs 3:5-6).*

Relinquishing to trust God to show up is not always easy, however, it is made easier by having faith in the Word God laid forth. Yielding to His Word may prove easier than having unadulterated blind faith. The Word even tells us God understands everything, as written in Psalm 147:5, "Great is our Lord, and of great power: his understanding is infinite."

The third reason we should relinquish to trust God to show up is that He will actually "show-out." Let me explain further. It is exciting to know we are about to witness something amazing by the Hand of God. This knowledge can even calm our nerves while going through a storm. "His incomprehensible ways are about to do the miraculous in our situation," should be our testimony in times of need. Make no mistake about it, trouble is painful; but oh, the joy to see His hand in action. Our society has come to look for the unexpected and unusual, and so it has turned into a reality show society. We have cameras on just about every cell phone because we are looking to video the next amazing mishap. People can be found taking video of an abduction or offence instead of getting involved to help stop the offence. What is more sensibly amazing is to witness the incomprehensible power and ways of God. That, my brothers and sisters, is what's amazing to watch above all things to watch. Some may talk about the eight wonders of the world, but let me tell of how exciting it is to stand in witness of the great and incomprehensible power of God's hand. He works in such a way we could never fully understand, and oh how great it is to witness. Forth of July and New Years Eve fire works are not to be compared to the spectacular and incomprehensible works of our God. Fireworks! If you want to see fireworks, just stand in the presence of a true believer who is deep in the midst of a trial. God does not like to just show up. He is not like the philanthropist that shuns the recognition associated with giving. God wants and demands the glory for all He's done; so much that He will put the believer on display in a lowly place just to exalt him or her to a mountain top. I am sympathetic of those who have never had a valley low/mountain top experience, or at least witnessed one. Oh, the fireworks! I speak not of the fireworks that occurred as celebration after getting to the mountain top, but I shout glory of the fireworks which occur while the believer is being delivered by God. The incomprehensible can only create great fireworks. Something we never expect. Something we never imagine. Something we can never conjure in a million and two years.

Even if we have previously witnessed such great power of God, it is still beyond our comprehension as to how He will provide the next victory. That is the greatness of our Lord. We can stand in total view of Him working the unbelievable in our lives, yet we cannot understand how He's doing it. An unhindered front row view will still leave us baffled. We may very well be spiritual lost causes if those types of activities and powers do not excite us. I know it excites me, for I know in my time of need I am about to witness one of the greatest acts ever seen. At times the devil can present some deep troubles that require more than some holiday fireworks to get me through. Yet, if I really pay attention and do not close my eyes too tightly due to the pain of my troubles, I will witness the 9th, 10th and 11th wonders of the world performed by God, on my behalf.

This is the same fireworks and greatness that should excite us to relinquish to trust God to show up. Count it all joy in times of despair, cause God will explosively come see about His chosen. It is no minor thing of how God will provide for those who stand firm on faith in His great power. This is the same greatness that excites prayer warriors to pray to God with power and conviction.

It's difficult to relinquish unto God during tough times; especially when we do not understand what God is doing. Instead of simply relinquishing unto God we ask questions like, "Why does God allow some things to happen in our lives?" Relinquishing becomes easier if we would remember two simple facts: some things are allowed to occur for our general benefit and other things happen in order to increase our spirituality. Either way, prayer warriors must be comfortable with having faith at another level, proclaiming we will never have all the answers to why God allows certain things. Prayer warriors must trust His Lordship and trust that whatever He deems necessary is in our best interest.

From this point forward let it be that God's incomprehensible character stands as something our naked eyes view as positive. There are times God performs some things which cause us pain; consequently, we think it incomprehensible that He loves us as He sends us through. Fact is, God knows the grand scheme of it all so He plots courses that will benefit us best and give Him the greatest glory. I recall the old folks would say, "This behind beating is gonna hurt me more than it is gonna hurt you, but you will be better for it in days to come." Who can fathom any future benefit of a today's chastening or pain? The fact is, the benefits of the incomprehensible became apparent as the lessons learned of past chastenings kept us out of trouble's way in future travels. These lessons eventually led a path to the successes of our adulthoods.

The same type of chastenings that were given by our parents are similar to those given by God; yet sometimes His are much more painful. We most often cannot understand what God could be thinking with some of the things He does in our lives. Yet, hindsight proved how great He was, and is, for the way He incomprehensibly handles things. Some of us have even come to a point in our faith where we are thankful for God taking us through some things rather than taking us over or around them. We have realized that it was the very thing we had to go through, not around, that propelled us to the greatest heights in our lives. We must let go, let God and have faith that He knows the most profitable route for our successes and for His greatest glory. Even through the pain we must relinquish to say, "Father knows best." Point is our relinquishing unto God should not be predicated upon how things are going in our lives, nor upon what we can fully understand; but merely that He is God.

Now mind you, this relinquishing I speak of is not of weakness, but of power. It is through this submission that our faith is empowered enough that we then appropriately take our Kung Fu grip off matters and take hold of God, so His great power and direction can become prominent. Our power resides in our ability to excitedly expect and accept God's incomprehensible power. The ride is truly great if we would only sit back and enjoy. Put on the spiritual 3D glasses and watch God turn some confusion into joy. "Oh, I see now," will be our exclaims.

Attributes Over All

Becoming a prayer warrior is as much about learning and praying in accord with God's attributes, character and nature, as it is about knowing how to enter into His presence to submit a request. Strong prayer cannot exist without our first having strong command of the use of God's attributes, character and nature realized in our living. In such, our first order of business must be to digest them as best we can, along with the _8 Elements of Prayer Progression._™ Then, we must move on to incorporate the elements and God's attributes into our prayers.

We must testify of a God who is faithful to His attributes. Yes, He is faithful to His children, but that faithfulness comes by way of His faithfulness unto His character first and foremost. He was righteous before we were formed and He was just before the first sin was ever committed. Best believe He was faithful to His nature, attributes and character before all His creation was formed; for He has always been immutable. Thanks be to God we can save ourselves much suffering and have greater success in our prayers by gaining a better understanding of His attributes. He will always be faithful unto who He is.

This chapter list only nineteen of God's attributes and character, but we are all hereby charged with the duty of learning more of them, along with His nature. Do not take learning of them lightly, for they are a great source of power to our prayers. The studying of them will constitute as a fruitful way of seeking the Lord. It is every believers' responsibility to learn of Him in whom we pray unto. The fact is, our character will change for the better once we learn more of His character, and once it is revealed unto us what is expected of us in regards to His very character. One hundred thousand strong prayer warriors shall result from this charge and duty. Be one!

Attributes, Character and Nature of God — *Progression of Prayer*

Exercises

INSTRUCTIONAL

1. Research the definition of compassion. Write your own definition and give one Biblical example of how compassion was shown within the scriptures you chose.

BENEFIT:
To stress the importance of having compassion in our prayer lives, and to move us closer to being the most effective prayer warriors we can become.

PERSONAL

1. Select an attribute of God that you feel will be most beneficial to your prayers. Write a short paragraph as to why this attribute is so essential?

BENEFIT:
To impress upon our spirits how necessary it is for us to digest God's attributes, character and nature, then incorporate them into our lives and our prayers.

Attributes, Character and Nature of God — Progression of Prayer

General Questions

1. Upon successfully applying God's attributes into our prayers, what must we then do to enhance the manifestation of Christ within us?

2. How does praying in accord with God's attributes help our prayers; such as eliminating babbling?

3. In what do we have confidence if prayer warriors do not enter into prayer with expectations of how God will work things out?

4. What is a key to our prayers' successes if our prayers are not necessarily successful due to our having some great mental or spiritual abilities?

5. In being faithful in prayer, what is a foundation block for having a successful prayer life?

6. What is a base of covenant spoken of in this chapter?

7. In regards to God being infinite, what is more of a blessing than knowing He will bless us beyond measure?

8. What attributes of God listed within this chapter can we not emulate?

9. What could possibly stop the success of our prayers if we pray with good intentions?

10. What are three reasons we should relinquish to trust God to show up in difficult and tough times?

Attributes, Character and Nature of God — *Progression of Prayer*

Advanced Questions

1. What is the main reason God's attributes, character and nature proves to be so powerful in our prayers and in our living?

2. What are the three reasons it is imperative to know the Lord's attributes, character and nature?

3. Write a short paragraph as to what is the embodiment or quintessence of prayer?

CONCLUSION

It is hoped and prayed we all have been blessed by the many principles imparted, mysteries revealed and blessings provided unto us by God through this document. There have been so many tidbits given that we all should come away with something that will bless our prayers and our living. We have truly been increased this day; thus, we all should thank God for His allowing us to get a little closer to Him. There was a time in Biblical days when His children attempted to build structures in order to reach the Heavens; only to be thwarted by God confusing their languages *(Genesis 11:1-9)*. So, again I say, we should all be very thankful that God permitted and directed this document.

To the unspirited I say, God remains as the ultimate authority who knows our hearts and intents, and He has the power to bless your prayers or curse your prayers, just the same. This document is not some magical formula that will turn all things gold. On the contrary, it has been given unto us that we may get closer to He who is our formula for golden living.

To all, I say, do not become arrogant as spiritual growth comes by leaps and bounds. Count all the growth as joy unto the Lord, for He alone grants us the ability and the blessing of being His children, set apart for battle and increase. There will even be others who will despise the lack of arrogance and claim it as a different form of arrogance or as a weakness. These are merely wicked attempts to discourage the power of Christ within. Just remember the Bible verse wherein Paul declares, "... that the power of Christ may rest upon me .... for when I am weak, then am I strong" *(II Corinthians 12:9-10)*.

Power comes with learning strong prayer, and with that power vested by Christ Jesus comes a responsibility of Kingdom building and of glorifying God the Father. Embrace this power and responsibility with boldness so to increase the spirit to levels unheard and unseen. It is that time! Be ye empowered and be blessed. Let this document also serve as a warning to the devil and all his imps.

As a short summary, 100,000 strong prayer warriors shall come forth by instituting the *8 Elements of Prayer Progression*™ in their lives and in their prayers. Let us all remember to first *acknowledge* the Lord in prayer, so to get His attention, give Him honour and establish submission in our spirits. Second, give the Lord *praise and adoration* so to set the plate of grace and to gain deeper access into His presence. Third, *thank* the Lord for all He's previously done and for who He is; for why should anyone, including the Lord, be compelled to grant blessings unto someone who is unthankful for the things done for them in the past? Fourth, make a *request* known unto the Lord. Cry unto the Lord with the things that are on the heart and spirit, but remember a request is not to be in the fashion of a demand. Fifth, ask the Lord for *discernment* and wisdom to further know His will and directions for us and for the things we requested. A great part of being blessed is knowing what to do with or without the requested blessings. Sixth, ask the Lord for a *Sign* or confirmation so to ensure we are in His will and not moving upon our own desires. Seventh, give the Lord *pre-praise thanksgiving* in expectation of His blessing our prayer requests. Eighth, listen for the Lord's voice in answer to all that's occurred in prayer. *Meditation* is the solidifying portion of prayer which culminates the very reason we venture to pray in the first place: to hear from Heaven. We shall be blessed if we act upon these precepts in prayer, for the Lord is a prayer answering God. To some it may initially appear as many steps, but they become ordinary practice after a short while of them being instituted.

Do not hesitate to read and study this document a second, third, or fourth time. After thoroughly digesting these principles, visit the web site at www.powerfulprayerprogression.com and send an email stating how you have become a powerful prayer warrior. This document is not designed to gift you with a title, but is to motivate and encourage you to go to this next level in communion with God. I am excited for each of you who successfully becomes one of the 100,000 prayer warriors; readied for battle and armed with victory.

I am emphatic about prayer and I am excited for you and your renewed prayer life. Send a letter or an email to me to express your excitement once you have received a spiritual increase and/or once you have finished reading this document for the first time. At the end of your letter say, "I am a prayer warrior ready for battle." Take time to send an email to me at RevATyCook@powerfulprayerprogression.com. Also take a moment to testify how you are now a Progressive Prayer Warrior by sending an email to 8prayerelements@comcast.net or mail a letter to A. Ty Cook, P.O. Box 22484, Baltimore, Maryland 21203. I do look forward to hearing from you.

KEYS

The following is a compilation of keys from throughout the chapters within this document. These keys are of great importance to our prayer development and power. They are not the only importance in this document, yet some are fundamental to the strength of certain points, while others are explanatory of mysteries of God and His word. At each key take time to ruminate and digest the Spirit's wisdom bestowed so your prayer life may go to the next level.

INTRODUCTION
1- *Progression through Elements 1, 2 and 3 prepares our spirits 13*
2- *To Hear from Heaven — Solitude and Thirst 15*

FORWARD MESSAGE ABOUT PRAYER KEYS
3- *A Foundation Built upon our Need to be Intimate with the Lord 22*
4- *Be Honest, Respectful and Truthful unto the Lord 26*
5- *Pray in His Spirit in order to Discern of What to Pray 33*
6- *Our Minds and Spirits are Changed; Not God's 34*
7- *Believe in Victory Even When All Seems Impossible 43*
8- *Realize our Lives are Not our own; Submit unto God's Control 47*
9- *Believe in the Spirit of Truth in order to Submit unto God 47*
10 -*Pray for the Lord's Covering in the Meanwhile of the Blessing 51*
11- *Make the Lord our First Job Instead of our Part-Time Job 66*
12- *We Must be Willing to Receive the Principles God Sets Forth 68*
13- *Be Mindful of the Way We Request 68*

ACKNOWLEDGMENT KEYS
14- *Not Calling God out of His Name 84*
15- *God is the Greatest Blessing 92*

ADORATION KEYS
16- *Commune with Him in Accord with Who He is 105*
17- *Focus on God More Than on Our Own Needs 107*
18- *A Heart Set on Praising God 113*
19- *A Positive spirit's Condition 114*

THANKSGIVING KEYS
20- *Show Appreciation for the Giver 128*
21- *Change Your spirit's Condition 133*

REQUEST KEYS
22- *Have a Willingness to Pray According to God's Will 157*
23- *Making an Appeal using God's Promises 167*
24- *That God's Word Shall Come Forth as Truth 169*
25- *That the Lord's Name will be Glorified 171*

REQUEST KEYS *(continued)*
26- That Others will come to a Saving Knowledge of the Lord   174
27- Be Willing Overflow Vessels   175
28- Pray in the Spirit of Christ   178
29- Believing in the Lord's Abilities   180
30- Right Living   185
31- Pray for His Judgment — Be Convicted Beforehand   189

DISCERNMENT KEYS
32- Mature Previous to Receiving   210
33- Mature vs Duplicate   212
34- Put Prayers into Action   214
35- God is No Bank Machine   218

SIGN KEYS
36- Success is Not Always Receiving   228
37- Jesus is Prosperity   229
38- What God Desires. Not What's Easy   229
39- Live in Reverence Not Disbelief   232
40- Discern the Source: Validate the Sign   234
41- Be Aware and Be Sensitized   235
42- Things Eternal   237
43- Look for Signs, not Indications   240
44- Stay the Course   242
45- Get Closer to Hear the Faint   245
46- Do Not be Ashamed   247
47- Hearing From God is Fruitfulness   248
48- Have Faith to Move with Assurance   248
49- Connect with God's Answers to Prayers   250
50- Heed and Move   252
51- An Ultimate Goal in Prayer is to Receive the Lord   253

PRE-PRAISE THANKSGIVING KEYS
52- Withheld Blessings due to our Reluctance to Praise Him   262
53- Must be Sold-Out no Matter how the Lord Answers   264
54- Be Empowered by the True Context of God's Word   267
55- Remember God's Promises and that He is a Promise Keeper   272
56- Our Change and Deliverance Begins with our Change in Belief   274
57- Some Things may be OK, but Just not What is Meant for Us   276
58- God Provides in His Own Ways and Timing   276
59- Be Mindful of What is Asked Outside of God   277
60- Demonstrate Faith by Giving the Lord Pre-Praise   283

MEDITATION KEYS
61- Listen to the Spirit in Order to get into the Spirit   290
62- Do Not be Eager to Speak During Meditation   295
63- Do Not be So Excited that Answers cannot be Heard or Received   29

MEDITATION KEYS *(continued)*

64- We Must Actively Listen for the Lord's Voice 296

65- Block Out Noise in Order to Hear 299

66- Meditation is a Key, in Itself, to our Success 300

67- Carve-Out Time and Create the Atmosphere 302

68- Drop our Pre-Suppositions so to Freely Receive Answers 305

69- He Already Knows a Thing, so We Should Rather Listen 306

70- Show the Lord Respect by Constantly Seeking His Voice 308

71- Increase our Level of Thirst for the Voice of God 311

72- Respectfully Expect God to Answer; not Just Hear 311

73- Pray for Prosperity in Jesus 314

74- Claim the Victory Before Entering Prayer 319

75- Do Not Use Meditation as a Substitute for Prayer 322

ATTRIBUTES, CHARACTER AND NATURE OF GOD KEYS

76- We Must Know the Essence (Character) of Who We Pray Unto 328

77- The Attributes, Character and Nature of God are Key as a Whole 329

78- Praying Without God's Attributes can Render Prayers Fruitless 330

79- Make God Number One in Our Prayers and in Our Living 339

80- God Has Real Power as He is All-Powerful 342

81- Have Faith that God can Bless Everyone, Everywhere, and at Once 344

82- Pray in Accord with God's Attributes to Align with His Will 345

83- Pray in Accord with God's Faithfulness unto His Promises 347

84- Be Faithful to Our Own Request 349

85- Successful Prayer Parameters are Set by God's Attributes 352

86- Allow Mercy to Reduce/Eliminate Selfishness 357

87- Believe God to be Limitless to have Boundless spirit & Faith 369

88- Accept and Submit to God's being Incomprehensible 372

SHORT LIST OF BIBLICAL PRAYERS

♦ Abraham's prayer for a son — Genesis 15:1-3

♦ Joshua's prayer for leadership and direction — Joshua 7:7-9

♦ Gideon prayed for a sign — Judges 6:36-40

♦ Hannah's covenant and prayer for a son — I Samuel 1:9-15

♦ Solomon prayed for wisdom — I Kings 3:6-15

♦ Solomon's illustration of prayer and praise — I Kings 8:56-60

♦ Prayer of Jabez — I Chronicles 4:10

♦ David's prayer to build Temple, and God's "no" answer
I Chronicles 17:16-20; 22:7-10

♦ Jonah prayed while in the belly of the large fish — Jonah 2:1-10

♦ Jesus teaches Model Prayer — Matthew 6:9-13 and Luke 11:2-4

♦ Jesus prayed for deliverance — Matthew 26:36-42

♦ Jesus' intercessory prayer — John 17:9-26

ANSWERS TO CHAPTER QUESTIONS

Acquire the Instructor's Guide for the answers to the questions in each of this Document's Chapters. Answers to the Workbook questions are included, as well.

It is additionally encouraged that you acquire Workbooks for your study group. It is truly a blessed increase to the power of this Series on prayer.

SELECTED BIBLIOGRAPHY

The Holy Bible
    King James Version
    Thomas Nelson Bibles, a Division of Thomas Nelson, Inc.
    1977, 1984, 2001
    (Scripture references and quotations unless otherwise indicated)

Life Application Study Bible
    New International Version
    Tyndale House Publishers, Inc., Wheaton, IL 60189
    and Zondervan, Grand Rapids, MI 49530, USA 1988, 1989, 1990, 1991
    (Names of God)

Strongs Exhaustive Concordance of the Bible
    King James Version
    James Strong 1822 - 1894
    and Abingdon Press, 1962, 1972, 1980, 1986
    (Hebrew and Greek definitions)

Merriam-Webster's Collegiate Dictionary, Eleventh Edition
    Merriam-Webster Incorporated 2003, 2004
    (General definitions)

The New National Baptist Hymnal
    National Baptist Publishing Board, Nashville, Tennessee
    Triad Publications 1977
    (Hymn and Articles of Faith references)